FIFTY YEARS OF HURT

www.**transworldbooks**.co.uk

FIFTY YEARS
OF HURT

Henry Winter

Matt,

loving working
with you at last,

Henry

BANTAM PRESS

LONDON • TORONTO • SYDNEY • AUCKLAND • JOHANNESBURG

TRANSWORLD PUBLISHERS
61–63 Uxbridge Road, London W5 5SA
www.transworldbooks.co.uk

Transworld is part of the Penguin Random House group of companies
whose addresses can be found at global.penguinrandomhouse.com

First published in Great Britain in 2016 by Bantam Press
an imprint of Transworld Publishers

A CIP catalogue record for this book
is available from the British Library.

ISBNs 9780593077122 (cased)
9780593077139 (tpb)

Typeset in 11.5/14.5pt Minion by Falcon Oast Graphic Art Ltd.
Printed and bound by Clays Ltd, Bungay, Suffolk.

Penguin Random House is committed to a sustainable
future for our business, our readers and our planet. This book
is made from Forest Stewardship Council® certified paper.

1 3 5 7 9 10 8 6 4 2

For Toby and Electra

Contents

Introduction

'ARE YOU SEEKING redemption?' This weighty, rather personal question from a local evangelist is a familiar sound to England supporters emerging from Wembley Park Tube. The main question on this occasion, the final home qualifier for Euro 2016, is: can the gifted Evertonian Ross Barkley impress against Estonia on his first competitive start? An answer in the affirmative would stir some optimism for the finals in France. I stop briefly to admire the view, mingling with fans taking photos of the famous stadium in the distance, before descending the steps to the underpass and hurrying up Wembley Way. Amid the noise of the faithful converging excitedly on the iconic arch can be heard this strident voice. 'Are you seeking redemption?' demands the preacher man of the congregation flocking towards the church of St George. He's usually there, standing on a raised walkway to the left, leaning over the railings, clutching a microphone in his right hand and portable speaker in his left. He asks the same question again and again. 'Are you seeking redemption?' We're just seeking three points, really. A decent performance free of fear. Some magic from Barkley. A good night out, even a hint of hope for the future, please.

Mr Missionary does have a point. Salvation is sought by the river of humanity flowing past him on 9 October 2015, heading towards the statue of Bobby Moore. England's finest captain and centre-half still guards Wembley after all these years; 538 games have passed since Moore lifted the World Cup. The years of hurt that David Baddiel, Frank Skinner and the Lightning Seeds sang so eloquently about keep lengthening. Thirty years of hurt was reached at Euro 96. Another score of years, and painful scorelines, elapse. The fiftieth anniversary of England's finest sporting achievement is a landmark to be cherished, and the participants royally feted, but it is also a time for sober reflection, and anger. In twelve World Cups since '66, England fail to qualify three times and make the semi-finals only once. In the twelve European Championships over the same period, England do not qualify four times, and progress to the semi-finals only twice. For a country obsessed with football, England's tournament record is a national disgrace. Wembley stands as part-shrine to 1966 and part-monument to catastrophe.

Growing up in London, I'd dash out of Wembley Park, turn left and play matches on the London Transport pitches behind the station. I'd see the old Twin Towers of Wembley from afar. At my senior school, Westminster, pupils were quietly made aware of the history of football, the school's role in shaping the game, including laws encouraging forward passing, and those six boys who went on to represent England back in the Victorian era. Respect deepens for those like Barkley with the ability and application to pull on the Three Lions shirt. But frustration swells at the country's failures. This is England, the country that not only invents football but codifies it, helps spread its joys to all four corner-flags of the globe and then conquers the world in 1966. Humiliatingly, this is the country that forgets how to play the greatest game of all. England take their eye off a ball they arrogantly thought they owned, allowing other nations to run off with it. As the country loudly celebrates fifty years of Hurst, Wembley should really be cordoned off as an accident scene requiring urgent forensic examination.

For half a century, England bemoan wretched misfortune, blaming a dodgy beer here, an infamous cheat there, even metatarsals and meteorology and the iniquity of penalties for the inability to repeat that special summer when Bobby Moore, Geoff Hurst and the Charltons ruled the world. It's all nonsense. It's not Lady Luck being perfidious towards battered Albion. It's self-inflicted damage. England's arteries are blocked by addled thinking. Fault lies all around.

It's the fear stalking the Wembley dressing-room, and conflicting agendas between Football Association and Premier League with two-thirds of players in the elite division ineligible for England. How can the tide be turned? The tide rolling in from overseas.

It's the 'too much too young' culture pervading some Academies, where teenagers trouser £20,000 a week even before figuring prominently in first-team plans, killing their hunger. It's the kids getting boot deals at 12. It's irresponsible parents being in thrall to agents or screaming 'Get stuck in!' on the touchlines, inhibiting kids.

It's the time-bomb of obesity, the fast-food and fizzy-drink addiction afflicting the conditioning of Academy recruits, and yet football happily takes the sponsorship money of these sugar baddies. It's societal changes extending the years of hurt: many parents won't let kids stay out late, or go off down the park to play. What's the solution? Politicians think too short-term when long-term reform is required in the health and sporting opportunities of the younger generation, our future.

So many questions. So much culpability. It's some England managers also deserving of their place in the public stocks. It's the distracting sexual foibles of Sven-Göran Eriksson, court cases blemishing Terry Venables' reign, Glenn Hoddle's views on reincarnation, the tactical shortcomings of Graham Taylor, Kevin Keegan and Steve McClaren, and not forgetting Fabio Capello's poor grasp of the English psyche and language. But is it the man or the job itself? Does it send capable people insane? How can they be helped? Wembley's preacher poses only one question. Wembley registers hundreds.

It's the serial fiasco of penalties. It's the media obsession with personality over philosophy, newspapers railing against such nemeses as Diego Maradona in 1986, Cristiano Ronaldo in 2004 and 2006 and Luis Suárez in 2014 while ignoring the need to breed such maestros ourselves. England are a noisy orchestra packed with drums but no conductor. Where are the playmakers, responsibility-takers and game-changers? Dele Alli lifts spirits with his dash and daring in the stunning 3-2 friendly victory over Germany in Berlin on 26 March, but England need more of such verve, and in tournaments.

Rare creative creatures like Stan Bowles, John Barnes, Chris Waddle, Paul Gascoigne and Paul Scholes at times have resembled an endangered species. They are never used properly, given the platform enough. Will Barkley be granted a licence to thrill as he can? Will Dele Alli? It's the institutionalized suspicion of flair in this country. It's about England players being inspired, not scared, by pictures near the Wembley dressing-room of Hurst completing his hat-trick in '66. Capello always called it 'The Fear'.

It's FA insistence on reviews when a revolution's required. But how? It's the £757m wasted on Wembley when grass-roots need urgent tending. It's the need to play football in the summer. It's the malfunction in the FA system and the paucity of rigorous post-tournament quizzing of players, and gleaning lessons from departing managers. An enraged media wants a debagging of the manager when a proper debriefing is more beneficial for England. No US-style President's Book exists, in which outgoing leaders leave messages for successors, passing on wisdom acquired in office, often painfully. Wembley needs a tome of gathered intelligence in the archives. If it's good enough for the White House, it's good enough for the home of the White Horse.

Some help is at hand. Fans remain remarkably loyal. Wembley gates are frequently the highest in Europe even for low-key visitors, even for friendlies. More than 6,000 fans travel to Kiev for the Euro 2012 quarter-final against Italy while 23m watch on TV. The passion for England endures despite the pain.

The FA strives increasingly hard to end the years of hurt. Its gleaming £120m National Football Centre at Burton upon Trent is certainly testament to the governors' sound intentions. Mounted on the wall of the England coaches' room at St George's Park is a clock counting down to the World Cup final of 18 December 2022. It's needed changing once already because shady old Fifa realized it might be too hot in summer in Qatar and switched the tournament to winter. Too hot? Who knew? What isn't altered is the FA's conviction that England can win the World Cup in 2022. One has to admire FA ambition.

But is it possible? Craving information, insight and advice on how the years of hurt can end, I embark on a six-month journey from

London to LA, Lithuania to Liverpool (and those are just the Ls) via Wembley Way, maintaining a personal run of reporting on 250 consecutive England games. I talk to members of each tournament team from 1966 to 2014. One of the most enthusing conversations comes with Gary Neville, who eloquently describes England's lasting importance. This must be remembered. England still mean so much to so many, player, supporter and reporter. Neville tells me about the adrenalin chamber that was the home quarters inside Wembley at Euro 96. 'I was in the dressing-room, sitting close to David Seaman, number 1, then me number 2, Stuart Pearce number 3, Paul Ince number 4, Tony Adams number 5,' he says. 'Everyone might think it was this loud dressing-room at Manchester United, but we had the television on half an hour before kick-off. We were so relaxed. We watched football, the news, whatever was on up until we went out for the warm-up. Come back in, television would go off. You might get the odd "come on, boys", but you'd never get anyone screaming or shouting. With England, I remember Stuart Pearce standing up next to me and shouting: "THIS IS OUR FUCKING TURF! NO ONE COMES TO OUR TURF!" He had this passionate drive. Then Adams would stand up and shout similar and be smashing the ball against the wall. I'm thinking: "Shit, I played with Robson, Cantona, Hughes, Keane and Ince at club level and never seen any of them do this." I'm sitting there, putting my shin-pads on, thinking: "Woooah! What's going on? Shit, these guys are up for it." They genuinely loved playing for their country. From that moment, I never, ever believed that thing of "players don't care".'

They do care. Just listen to Alan Shearer. 'I sacrificed so much, moved away from home at 15, left school early, then I realized all the hard work has probably come true when I got the England call,' recalls the tough, prolific Geordie striker who made the first of his 63 appearances against France in 1992. 'Straight away after my debut I realized that's where the hard work begins. Some people get 1, 3 or 5 caps. Others go on to achieve 50 or 100 caps, and that tells you what they are made of.' England caps constitute a powerful currency.

'I look at the England squad now and I'm jealous, jealous,' says

Jermaine Jenas, whose last contact with the shirt came in 2009 against Brazil in Doha. 'They're really lucky. It's when you stop representing your country that you realize how lucky you were to play for England. I'm proud of my 21 caps and all the squads I've been involved in. I miss it a lot. I remember going to the training ground at Newcastle and Woody [Jonathan Woodgate] and Kieron Dyer said: "You're going to get picked." "No," I said. I didn't think anything of it.' Then the phone-call comes from Eriksson summoning him for the friendly with Australia at Upton Park in 2003. 'I was in the squad and there was Becks, Lampard and Rio! I stepped on the pitch realizing the whole nation is watching me. I absolutely loved it. The shirt didn't weigh me down. When you're stood in the line and hear the fans singing it's intense; away games were almost more intense. Seeing one section of the stadium with those England fans singing that National Anthem gave me tingles in my body. I'd walk out every Saturday for a Premier League game and, yes, I was pumped up, ready and excited, but England was something different.

'It's complete bollocks that players don't care. I was in the squad at 19 and didn't come out until 2009 at 26. I wasn't as involved as I'd have liked and there were frustrating periods. I was getting dragged to all different parts of the world and then put in the stands for the game.' Jenas spectates from Vienna to Geneva, Barcelona to Zagreb and for all the 2006 World Cup in Germany. 'I'd sit there and my mates would be texting me from Dubai with family and friends, relaxing, coming back refreshed, and I've been sat there in a hotel and in the stands, nothing to do, and it starts to grind on you a little bit. That's where the perception of players not being bothered came from. But the reality is, when it's taken away, and I wasn't in the squad any more, it hit me hard. I'm a fan. We've all been through that phase of not enjoying watching England playing at certain stages but you'd always watch. Oh God, I'll always watch the match.'

The passion remains. Few withdrawals disrupt Roy Hodgson's squads. The 75,427 marching on Wembley for the Estonia tie know about Barkley's obsession with representing England, dating back to when he was 7, sitting at home on the couch, watching David

Beckham's free-kick against Greece, a picture of which adorns a pillar near the Wembley dressing-room. Barkley, Dele Alli and Harry Kane, among others, hold the England shirt in reverence. There is hope.

England matter for so many reasons. Players fall in love with football partly through England. When Paul Ince becomes the first black captain of his country against the US in Foxboro, Massachusetts, in 1993, he receives nearly five hundred letters lauding him as a pioneer and role model. Ince replies to all of them, mentioning the graft he's put in to achieve the honour. It's a lesson for some of the new generation.

'To play for your country is the biggest honour,' says Mark Wright, the cultured centre-back who won 45 caps between 1984 and 1996. 'Playing for your club is fantastic but to say you're the best in the country in that position is an honour in itself. Then to go and play for all the supporters, and to have that passion and drive, that's what I love. Every now and again I get a little bit sentimental and go "let's refresh the memory," and look back at DVDs of me playing. I still haven't watched the semi-final of the World Cup [in 1990]. I don't know if I'm being a coward not watching it. I don't want to keep seeing how close we were.'

Players care for differing reasons. 'Getting the shirt was special,' says John Barnes, the winger of touch and pace who participated at Mexico 86 and Italia 90. 'But for me it was more to do with the fact that I loved the World Cup. When I talked about playing for England, what I was thinking about was playing in a World Cup. For me that is the pinnacle of football – more than the Champions League final in terms of prestige and importance, yes, but not in terms of quality.'

Barnes is one of the most clear-eyed observers of the England scene, a purveyor of some mesmerizing moments during his 79 internationals between 1983 and 1995. He peers into the history books to explain England's demise. 'We're very good at inventing things but we don't actually carry it on,' he says. 'We rest on our laurels. We don't grow, don't evolve. While everyone else was looking at the technical aspects of football, we weren't. It was all "let's get stuck in", the good old British mentality. So although we invented the game, I remember [watching footage of] a game against Hungary in 1954 with Nándor Hidegkuti and Ferenc Puskás and they showed us how to play the game, as Brazil did in 1970.

'I remember when we played Tunisia [1-1 before Italia 90], they had more possession than us, were technically better than us, but we'd live with them because we were good in the air – and aggressive. The laws of the game allowed us to do that. The laws have now changed. The old up-and-at-'em spirit where you kicked shit out of people doesn't work. Over the past ten years we are espousing this technical style, trying to develop technical players, but other countries have been doing that for the last thirty years. We've lost time. We've fallen behind.'

Calmly and cerebrally, Barnes even places England's World Cup peaks into perspective. 'I look at it very objectively. In 1990, Cameroon should have beaten us [in the quarters] and Belgium should have beaten us [in the round of 16]. We forget that. In 1966, we would not have won had it not been in England.' He quickly emphasizes: 'I know that '66 team was a great team and they won the World Cup, and at Euro 96 they did very well to get where they got to [the semi-final at Wembley].' His inference is clear: home fires burn strongest.

'Pressure comes from unrealistic expectations,' continues the two-time Footballer of the Year. 'Players aren't obsessed with history but the expectation coming from the press and the fans is "you should be winning it". I never felt we were the best team in the world. England qualified for Euro 2016 in style but anything past the group stages is a bonus. In the last World Cup, if we'd gone through the group it would have been a bonus. I'll tell you about the England team back in 1986 and 1990 – there was a humility about the team, not necessarily from the press or the fans but we players never felt like we were the best. When you don't feel you are the best, you actually aspire to give 100 per cent, maximize the potential you have, which means if you get to the quarter-finals against Argentina, semi-finals against West Germany, you appreciate that because we were never the best team.'

The best are the Germans, current world champions who reacted to perceived under-achievement in the early 2000s by rebooting their player-development system. They have the highest standards: their strong mentality and tournament nous still got them to the final of the 2002 World Cup. England need to learn more from abroad, and to benefit from a properly coordinated FA and Premier League approach. Germany educates twenty thousand school teachers to coach pupils, builds training centres for the 11–17 age-group, works with government to get 3- to 6-year-olds fitter. Solutions include rivalling Dutch dedication: an 8-year-old Robin van Persie reacted to taunts of 'your shot with your left foot is rubbish' by practising and practising from nine a.m. until late at night in the cage near his Rotterdam home.

It's about remembering that kids develop at different speeds, like Jamie Vardy. Rejected as a teenager by Sheffield Wednesday, he joins non-League Stocksbridge Park Steels, toils in a factory and works his way up to a Premier League consecutive goalscoring record and England recognition. It's about paying youth-team coaches properly, tightening work-permit regulations, and introducing a January winter break. There are so many steps on the road to redemption. It's about the FA taking a more broadminded view of coaching qualifications: some ex-pros won't do the courses as they are daunted by the theory sections because they suffer from dyslexia or poor writing skills.

It's about not exhausting players. 'England have to stop running the players so hard post-season before a tournament,' says one Olympian who knows some of the players. 'They don't need it.' It's about the right tempo to training, though, certain senior players feeling that Hodgson's drill sessions in Rio in 2014 lacked urgency. It's about taking inspiration from all quarters, even from a referee. 'It can change your life,' remarks Howard Webb, the referee from Rotherham who earned plenty of sympathy for attempting to curb Dutch aggression against the stylish Spanish in the 2010 World Cup final in Johannesburg. Webb should have sent off Nigel de Jong for stencilling his studs on to Xabi Alonso's chest but otherwise lived up to the 'Can't Play But Can Ref' motto on the St George's flag held by his father at Soccer City. 'Looking back, I'm surprised I was able to be as composed as I was. It's such a momentous occasion. The eyes of the world are on it for 90 minutes. It's the sport I love, I've worked in for so long and watched for so long. I was aware of the history. That was put in the front of my mind when I met Jack Taylor the night before.' Webb and Taylor, the 1974 final referee who sadly passed away in 2012, talked of the honour, and the prize at stake for the two teams. 'I was stood in the tunnel, looking down towards the pitch, waiting for the teams to join me that night in Johannesburg,' continues Webb. 'I could see the World Cup trophy on the podium which Fabio Cannavaro put there a few moments earlier. I remember thinking to myself: "This is it. This is what we're playing for tonight."

'A few England players mentioned the final to me subsequently. I got loads of messages, particularly from managers and coaches, from Alex McLeish and Roberto Martínez, saying "well done". They recognized the significance of the game, they recognized the achievement to get there. Don't get me wrong, you need a bloody big slice of luck to get there. Some high-profile guys who would have been in with a real shout of the final were involved in some controversy that ruled them out.' Roberto Rosetti's failure to expunge Carlos Tevez's goal for offside against Mexico at Soccer City counted against the Italian. 'That kind of thing meant I was able to do the final,' adds Webb. But this was no serendipity; Webb's consistency of performance and decision-making was simply superior. It's a lesson for the players on the road to redemption.

Can Barkley be the beacon, lighting the way? Leaving the preacher behind, I hurry into Wembley, keen to watch the youngster, a maverick talent getting a rare starting chance. He's tall, quick, muscular and skilful, an athlete with an artist's temperament. England expects. We always do. Estonia seem inviting opposition for Barkley, given a largely free role in midfield anchored by James Milner. Wembley looks on and hopes.

Here we go. As late-comers scurry in, Barkley tries an ambitious pass and gives the ball away cheaply to Sergei Zenjov. Here we go again. Here's the negative side to Barkley's game that vexed Hodgson in the warm-up games at the home of Miami Dolphins before the 2014 World Cup. Up in the BBC Radio 5 Live booth, Chris Waddle and Danny Mills debate Barkley's need 'to look after the ball more'. Better sides will punish his lax pass. Will he be inhibited? Play it safe? That's not Barkley's style. He gets on the ball again, and goes for it again. He sprints through and has his heels clipped by Ken Kallaste. Barkley's technique shines through in the confident way he sweeps the ball with his right instep first time at keeper Mihkel Aksalu.

Barkley is fearless, sliding in to contest a loose ball and receiving a clattering from Karol Mets, his tracker for the night. His final ball continues to perturb Hodgson so Barkley keeps it simple for a while, laying the ball off to Raheem Sterling, Theo Walcott and Adam Lallana. He slips a pass through to Harry Kane. This is the disciplined Barkley but England also need the risk-taker. One England fan tweets mid-match about Hodgson destroying Barkley's confidence, making him a shadow of the vibrant force he is with Everton.

Seconds from the break, the 21-year-old makes Wembley fall in love: closed down by Mets and Aleksandr Dmitrijev, Barkley calmly threads the ball through to Walcott, releasing the ball at the perfect time to ensure the attacker is onside. Walcott scores. Joy erupts. In the second half, Barkley embarks on a 50-yard run, driving through the middle until falling under a challenge from Dmitrijev. 'Gazza-esque,' remarks the man from the *Express*. Barkley's truly emboldened, taking on four Estonians in one shimmying run. Maybe there is a glimmer of hope for England. Maybe Wembley can dream again.

And so it should. We have to believe. England excel in other sports, like cricket. Why not football? But ending the years of hurt remains a monumental challenge. The willpower of that 1966 side was immense, and embodied in players like Jack Charlton. It's time to hit the A1, an unlikely road to redemption, to meet one of England's all-time greats.

1

The Greatest Day

JACK CHARLTON HOLDS the famous photograph in his right hand and runs the fingers of his left gently over the surface, tracing familiar faces immortalized in sepia print and sporting legend. He gazes at the picture, remembering the supreme team, filling again with quiet pride in the greatest day he shaped and shared. On the left as he looks, there's Jack himself, the gap-toothed Nobby Stiles and then Gordon Banks, almost hidden among those celebrating on the Wembley pitch after defeating West Germany to win the World Cup on 30 July 1966. There's Alan Ball, Martin Peters, and a glimpse of Roger Hunt. As he studies the scene intently, Jack sees 'Our Kid', his distinguished brother Bobby, so totally drained by two hours of duelling with Franz Beckenbauer that he almost needs propping up by George Cohen. Dominating the tableau is the celebrated centre-piece of Geoff Hurst and Ray Wilson chairing the golden-haired captain, Bobby Moore, who raises the Jules Rimet trophy to the heavens almost as an offering. 'Happy days,' Jack smiles.

Along with his team-mates, England's gangly, indomitable centre-half does not appreciate fully what he's just done. 'It was the World Cup, OK, fine, but at the time it was just another game of football to us,' Jack recalls, his eyes not moving from the picture. 'Look at Geoff. He's happy. Martin's fine. Nobby's happy. Bally's happy. Ray Wilson's happy. George is happy. Banksy was at the back. Our Kid is in tears. Afterwards, yes, I knew it was the greatest day of my life. Whenever I went anywhere, and I used to do a lot of speaking at dinners, people introduced me by saying: "There's plenty to talk about – he's won the World Cup!" It was just another game to us at the time but, aye, I'm proud of it. I'd like to see England produce another team that can win the World Cup. I'd really like to see that. It was such a long time ago.'

Fifty years.

It's late morning and Jack, a native of Northumberland, is sitting in the tranquil Copthorne Hotel in Newcastle, watching the Tyne flow past, reflecting on time's passage too. He is an English footballing icon for what he did at Wembley, for his 6 goals in 35 internationals as well as formidable work at Leeds United, scoring 95 times in 762 appearances and winning the League, FA Cup, League Cup and Fairs Cup twice. He subsequently immersed himself successfully in management, most famously with the Republic of Ireland. Yet modesty defines the man as he speaks, not trumpeting his many feats, just calmly recounting historic events, his memory helped by the photographs. As he reminisces, Jack confirms the strong bond between players in Alf Ramsey's squad, making the collective so much more than the sum of the parts. That camaraderie kept them going through adversity, notably at Wembley when the Germans fought back. His words underscore the importance of leadership, especially in the inspiring figures of Moore and Ramsey. 'Bob was a smashing lad,' Jack says of Moore. 'I've seen his statue at Wembley. I liked Bob. He used to pick me up and take me to a pub in London when I was with Leeds, playing in London somewhere.

'Before the World Cup, we were in the hotel [Hendon Hall] and Bobby and a few of the other lads went out for a walk to a pub. What Bobby did, we did. Alf had a room overlooking where we went out. We all waved at him. Alf looked at us, waved, and then went back to his bedroom! We went across the road, up the hill to a pub. We just sat in the pub. I had a pint and then went back to the hotel. We were OK. We weren't doing anything silly.' They never felt they were challenging Ramsey's authority. They had too much respect for the manager, mixed with a touch of fear. 'He threatened you: "do this", "do that", "don't do this", "don't do that". Alf was a good manager.'

Ramsey exudes the aura of a manager, and a team, on a mission. Everything is devoted to the realization of one aim: lifting the World Cup. He demands and receives dedication to the cause. If Jack and the players are watching television late in the evening, Ramsey will simply say, 'Goodnight, gentlemen.' They'll know it is time to turn off and turn in. Ramsey drills them hard in June at the FA's Shropshire hideaway at Lilleshall, employing the tough trainer Les Cocker to build stamina for the extensive summer examination they eventually pass so gloriously. Ramsey proves adept at providing diversions, filling in the down-time monotony and easing the tension that so trouble the modern generation. Fifty years on, photographs still trade on the internet of Ramsey's players at their southern base, Roehampton, indulging in some impromptu cricket after training. Ball keeps wicket; Stiles lurks at first slip as Bobby Charlton fends off a ball rearing up off a length. On 12 July, Ramsey takes his squad to Pinewood Studios. It's the day after the disappointing stalemate with Uruguay, the opening match provoking inevitable criticism from the press, which notes England's failure to score at Wembley for the first time since 1938. In the *Daily Telegraph*, the esteemed correspondent Donald Saunders delivers a typically balanced report, pointing out that Uruguay came to stifle, but he still concludes: 'When one remembers that there are better defences than this lying in wait for Mr Ramsey's men in the later stages of the competition, one's hopes tend to sag.' The sidebar-quotes piece by Roger Malone trumpets 'Ramsey Still Thinks His Side Can Win'. Scepticism rolls along Fleet Street. But as Jack points out, 'We had some very difficult games before the World Cup final but there was only one that we drew, against Uruguay.' They believe.

The trip to Pinewood offers a welcome distraction. Photographers are allowed in to record the moment when Ramsey's players meet a succession of movie stars. One picture captures Sean Connery, who is filming the latest Bond film *You Only Live Twice*, looking respectfully at Bobby Moore – 007 and No. 6 in the same frame. All the players are smartly attired, Jimmy Greaves with a white handkerchief peeping from his breast pocket, clutching a half of bitter, chatting to Connery. Another snap shows Yul Brynner, sporting a ski cagoule while making

The Double Man, talking to Ramsey's squad. When the gathering is joined by the British actress Viviane Ventura, pausing from her work with Cliff Richard on *Finders Keepers*, she is immediately placed next to a beaming Banks. Ventura stands on the steps of the Pinewood pavilion. Jack Charlton still towers over her. The players relax, the sniping headlines after Uruguay forgotten.

This is the clever Ramsey way, working the players hard, but knowing they need to unwind. He keeps the pressure off them, and they respond by beating Mexico 2-0 on 16 July with one of those trademark Bobby Charlton rockets and Roger Hunt pouncing. Momentum builds. Then come France on the 20th. 'I remember heading a ball and it hit the inside of the post, went across and Roger knocked it in,' says Jack of his part in England's first goal. In an encounter lacking in entente cordiale, Hunt strikes again with France remonstrating that the string-pulling Jacques Simon is hors de combat following a filthy challenge from Stiles. 'And that is Simon, Simon of France, number 20, the man rolling in agony,' observes the BBC commentator, Kenneth Wolstenholme, in his inimitable tones. After the move climaxes with Hunt heading in, Wolstenholme adds: 'And the French don't like that because they say, "We had a man injured." The referee is quite right.' The Peruvian referee, Arturo Yamasaki Maldonado, has given the goal, ignoring Stiles' offence, although England's combative No. 4 is given a retrospective yellow card by Fifa for 'rough play'.

Under pressure from Fifa to take further action over Stiles, the FA effectively demands that Ramsey omit his main ball-winner from the ensuing quarter-final against Argentina. Their subsequent oft-quoted exchange in training provides a reminder of Ramsey's loyalty and pragmatism; he needs Stiles against Argentina. 'Did you mean it?' Ramsey asks Stiles of the Simon tackle. 'Of course not,' Stiles replies. 'That's good enough for me,' concludes Ramsey, before standing up to 'those people' at the FA, amateurs he holds almost in contempt. Ramsey indicates he will resign if they interfere. The FA backs down. Stiles starts. Before kick-off, as Stiles is putting in his contact lenses, the trainer Harold Shepherdson points out in no uncertain terms how unequivocally Ramsey backed him. 'Don't let Alf down,'

Shepherdson tells him – another comment that has gone down in English folklore. He doesn't. Ramsey's loyalty is rewarded.

'Nobby was a good tackler,' smiles Charlton. 'He was only little but he got in there.' Barring the odd over-zealous intervention early on, Stiles responds with a disciplined performance in the snarling face of some sickening Argentinian behaviour at Wembley on 23 July. Watching the tape fifty years on evokes sadness as well as shock. Argentina field some elegant players, not least Antonio Rattín, their captain, who ludicrously loses all composure and is ordered off. The men he lets down succumb to a goal forged on the West Ham training ground. 'Martin Peters was on the left-hand side,' recalls Jack, 'and he crossed the ball to Geoff.' Heading in, Hurst takes his chance well in every sense. It is embedded in the English memory bank that Hurst is now playing in place of Greaves, the prolific Spurs forward incapacitated by a bad gash to the leg sustained in a challenge with France's Joseph Bonnel. Ramsey is fortunate to have talent to call upon, and his tactical switch, removing Ian Callaghan and stiffening midfield with Ball, also works. Never one to fret over public opinion, Ramsey upsets many with his tasteless 'animals' jibe about Argentina. For a man sensitive about enunciation, he seems to worry less about his words.

England march on, leaving behind the controversy. After their 2-1 semi-final win over Portugal on 26 July, growing praise for England can be found in the Fifa vaults, in the verdict of its technical staff, including Ramsey's predecessor Walter Winterbottom. 'Passes went to the advanced forwards as quickly as possible and unselfish overlap running by players including defenders put increasing pressure on the Portuguese defence,' reads the report. 'In this game, R. Charlton's support play was outstanding, and Stiles effectively shielded the attacks of Eusébio. The physical condition demanded of this fast tactical interchange between attack and defence was typified by the play of Alan Ball, who one moment was defending and the next initiating attack or unselfishly running to provide opening for other attackers.' Jack Charlton concedes a penalty late on, allowing Eusébio the chance to score from the spot, but his brother's earlier brace proves sufficient. England are in the World Cup final.

A myth has taken hold in certain quarters that England bore their way to glory in '66, that Stiles is a simple destroyer and width is non-existent, whereas Moore is elegance personified and voted player of the World Cup by the foreign press, the roaming Charlton is vibrant and soon becomes European Footballer of the Year, and Cohen raids down the right. Ball never stops driving upfield and Stiles can also contribute creatively, as one of his surging runs into the box to help create England's first against France shows. England are no work of intoxicating beauty, agreed, but they create some special moments and are united by a ferocious will to win. Ramsey proves a master at evolving the team tactically, fostering this sense of mission while keeping the players relaxed. The night before the final, the squad troop off into Hendon to watch *Those Magnificent Men in their Flying Machines.*

Ramsey's tactical fine-tuning, clipping the wings, relying on the full-backs for width, works, as does his decision to employ Hurst. But Greaves is now fit, his wound healed, and everyone awaits Ramsey's decision. 'None of us knew the team we'd play in the final,' says Jack. His heavy cold briefly casts doubt over his involvement; Ramsey even puts Ron Flowers, of Wolves, on standby to replace him. Jack, of course, declares himself fit. It was only when Alf said: "When we have lunch I will tell you the team," that we knew. We all went down to lunch before we went to Wembley. Alf had his sheet in front of him and said: "This is the team that will start." Banksy in goal. Ray Wilson left full-back, George Cohen right full-back.' Fifty years on, Charlton reels off the names as if reading from Ramsey's sheet.

He grasps another photograph, this one portraying Cohen. 'George was quick, very quick. If he had to race somebody to the ball, he'd always get there first. I could pick up a position where he could see where I was and, when he got there first, he'd knock the ball back to me and I'd give it back to the goalkeeper. George would get forward on occasion. George used to be very good at overlapping, very quick, down the line. His worst part was where he had to cross the ball into the box. Ray Wilson was more of a defender. He'd make his runs and come back. Ray was always there at left-back. Ray virtually never crossed the ball with his left foot. The back-four was always the same. I was right centre-half, Bobby Moore was left centre-half. We knew we'd play.'

Charlton returns to the original picture, the one with all the players, and admires the scene again. 'The two smallest players on the field were Nobby Stiles and Alan Ball. Nobby never stopped running. Our Kid played in midfield with Nobby. Bobby was the one who was making runs, running with the ball, but Nobby was always the one who went and got the ball and gave it to Bobby. He would then cover across behind. Alan never stopped running. He could find somewhere he wasn't marked, you could knock the ball to him, he'd turn on the ball, and run and pass. He'd knock balls to the full-backs for them to cross. In midfield, Martin Peters was a left-sided player but right-footed; he was a good player, he would get running, getting the ball to Geoff and Roger.' And what of Greaves? 'I was surprised Jim wasn't involved. When we went into the World Cup, Jim was the outstanding player. It was quite a decision not to play him. If somebody was going to score goals, it's going to be him, but he never got in. Geoff had the hat-trick.'

Before those celebrated goals flow, the squad head to Wembley and the footage shows the coach pulling up outside the stadium, Stiles with his teeth in, grinning at the reception committee of a London policeman. After clearing the dressing-room of interlopers, Moore addresses the players before leading them into that famous old tunnel, sloping upwards, towards the light. 'I was the last one,' says Jack. 'I was always the last player at Leeds, so I was always going to be the last player with England.' The noise of the 96,924 fans intensifies as the players stride towards their destiny, driven by myriad reasons in pursuit of victory. This medley of motivations is something current Academies, the FA and England managers must learn to understand fully. The best players and teams are stirred by a cause, whether a desire to settle a score, a passion for representing their country, simple love of the game, camaraderie or a realization of life's likely mundanity without this special profession. All this fosters a carpe diem spirit in Ramsey's players. Ball's hungry running is partly rooted in his struggles to find a club when younger, when he's considered too small. His heart isn't. His lungs aren't. Hurst needs to show he's worth Ramsey's vote ahead of Greaves.

Alternative employment hardly offers similar attractions. The Charltons' father, Bob, grafts on a shift underground during the World Cup semi-final until the *Daily Mirror* contacts Ashington Colliery to get him up to the surface in time for kick-off. Jack himself briefly spends time in the mines, crawling along small tunnels to reach the coalface, shuddering as the explosions go off, revealing more of the seam. The Charltons' brother Gordon is away in the Far East with the Merchant Navy and spends the two hours of the final toiling in the engine room. Jack and Bobby know that playing football for a living is a privilege. They seize their chance.

In seeking to understand what forces shape a dressing-room mindset it can be dangerous or naive to attribute historical factors, but there can be little doubt that the identity of the opposition, the Germans, gives the 1966 final an added edge. The war remains in the forefront of many minds. Peters' wife was named Kathleen Doris Winifred after the three sisters her father lost when a Luftwaffe bomb hit the East End of London. Jack, though, prefers to emphasize the sheer sporting nature of the challenge. 'To get the Germans in the final was terrific. Good team, good players. I looked at them and thought "Franz Beckenbauer", but really the only one that we talked about before the game was the goalkeeper, Hans Tilkowski. We didn't think he was a great goalkeeper.'

Yet footage of the final immediately shows Tilkowski making a smart save from Peters, and it is Banks of England yielding first. Helmut Haller accepts a gift from Wilson, misjudging a clearance, and shoots low. Caught out, Jack Charlton and Banks allow the ball to continue without a hint of apology into the net. 1-0 West Germany. The pair stare at Wilson. Jack signals his displeasure, although it needs restating that communication is poor between centre-back and keeper – a rare occurrence. 'I always knew where he was,' Jack explains. 'If I was chasing a ball backwards, I knew whether Banksy was coming or staying. More often than not, he would get to the ball first. Banksy was a very good goalkeeper, very good at making saves. He used to catch balls all the time, run out, jump up, catch it, fall on the ground with it, get up and throw it out to somebody.'

On the final goes, ebbing and flowing, absorbing all within Wembley, including thousands of Germans adding to the intensity, noise and spectacle. England rebuild, hunting the equalizer, Jack assiduously covering for Moore when the Rolls-Royce of defenders glides forward. 'Bob would suddenly go into midfield, make a good tackle, win the ball, get up and have a look, and then he'd run,' says Jack, staring into the distance, as if watching Moore motor off again. 'I very rarely ran with the ball. If Bob used to run I'd come across, so if anything happened when he went away running with the ball, I'd be central. He'd see me come across. We were OK, comfortable.' And soon level. When Wolfgang Overath fouls Moore, England's quick-thinking captain lifts the free-kick in for Hurst to material- ize seemingly from nowhere and head past a stunned Tilkowski. 1-1. Game on. The 'West Ham won the World Cup' legend begins to grow. Similarly enhanced is Moore's reputation for relishing the grand occasion. Calm, precise, in control.

England are full of purpose, and Bobby Charlton eludes Beckenbauer, but the pair are close together, almost dancing partners rather than duelling rivals. 'He probably had less space in that World Cup final than in the other games,' recalls Jack. 'In the other games Our Kid was a great runner, a great striker of the ball, and scored some great goals, but in the final, well, he had to mark Beckenbauer. He did, which is probably why he hadn't got involved in the game so much. They didn't let him play as he was capable of. Beckenbauer didn't either. He was marking Bobby. The pair of them cancelled each other out.' Bobby's style is still seen in some driving runs, signalling England's ambition.

Otherwise, well-matched opponents block each other out for a time, the final all attrition and athleticism. England need all their team-work, their one-for-all mentality. 'Roger and Geoff came back into midfield quite a lot of times,' says Jack. 'There would always be one upfront and one would come back into midfield. If the Germans pushed, Nobby would drop back.' Communication is key, tracking incoming danger. 'I talked a lot. I'd say to Bobby [Moore] "come in here", "get this side" of somebody or "get the other side" if the ball was coming into the 18-yard box. I can always remember Bob listening to me. Bobby Moore didn't shout at anybody. He may point something out, tell somebody to "pick him up", but he didn't yell at people. I did. I yelled at a few: "Get back in here!" I used to shout at Our Kid to "get back here . . . get in near Ray" and "close him down". I just yelled and shouted. The rest of them liked that.' Jack's constant cajoling galvanizes, keeping everyone fighting. 'They understood what their job was but I kept reminding them. I'd say to Nobby "get across", "pick him up", "fill in", leaving me to go in there behind him. Nobby was a great ball-winner, good tackler; him and Bally, there was no size to the two of them.' Five feet six inches of defiance, each of them. 'Bally never stopped running,' Jack almost whistles in admiration.

Even now, fifty years later, the tale of the videotape is of Ball's remorseless dynamism. He powers everywhere like a human tornado, winning a corner after 78 minutes, lifting it into the German box. England scent a goal. Hurst turns the ball back across and it seems the moment is lost, that the full-back Horst-Dieter Höttges must clear. As fans lean forward in expectation, drawn towards this penalty-area drama, Höttges succeeds only in slicing his clearance into the air. It looks to be falling across for Jack. 'I used to go up for the odd header, corner-kick or free-kick, and the ball was coming back to me,' says Jack, his body tensing as if ready to meet the ball again, half a century on, 'and then Martin came running in and knocked it in the back of the net.' 2-1 England. 77 minutes. Peters has surely won the World Cup for England.

'But the Germans kept coming at us,' says Jack, resuming the epic story, remembering the response of Helmut Schoen's gutsy competitors. 'When the Germans are knocking the ball into the 18-yard box I had to get them.' Unfortunately, in his determination to clear after 89 minutes, Charlton falls foul of the Swiss referee, Gottfried

Dienst, who believes, harshly to English eyes, that the defender is fouling Uwe Seeler. Frustrated, England man the barricades, hoping to repel what is surely West Germany's last assault. In it comes, Lothar Emmerich's free-kick, causing chaos, a blur of bodies stretching for the ball. Wolfgang Weber slides in. 2-2. Nightmare. The rosettes adorning many an England fan shed some of their satiny sheen. The crowd responds, seeking to inspire the team with exhortations, but Jack's oblivious, consumed in this furious fight. 'The fans never entered my head. I was focusing on what I had to do.'

Dienst blows for the end of normal time. Ramsey gathers his players around. 'We all stood there and listened to him,' says Jack of his manager, his leader now going to work on tired minds and bodies, banishing exhaustion, replenishing belief. Ramsey chooses his words shrewdly, effectively, rousingly, but simply. 'He didn't mention me, Bobby Moore or anybody,' says Jack. 'Alf just said: "You've won the Cup once – now go and win it again."' Oft-repeated down the decades, such renowned rhetoric never loses its lustre. Unleashing the sort of powerful sentiments to lift any flagging heart, Ramsey seizes the moment, espousing his utter faith in his players. In return, they look at him, hear his words and know they're not alone; their manager fights with them. These are the seismic seconds when reputations are defined, when the image of a monarch conferring a knighthood takes shape, and when a lesson is bequeathed to all those craving long-term residency in the England dug-out. Ramsey delivers. Those seduced by the modern-era hype who believe mind games begin with José Mourinho need educating in Ramsey's response. In that long corridor of classrooms at the National Football Centre nestling in St George's Park, FA educators draw attention to Ramsey's actions, as well as words. By insisting England's players stay on their feet with extra time awaiting, Ramsey flaunts their fitness at the Germans, some of whom lie slumped on the floor, requiring the urgent attention of trainers. 'They're finished,' Ramsey stresses to his players, looking over at the opposition 20 yards away. 'Stand up. Don't let those Germans think you're tired.' England are a unit, together, on their feet. All that pain on the training fields at Lilleshall, that sweat shed on Shropshire soil, is now worth it. England reach for the gleaming Jules Rimet trophy.

They go for gold. Ball embodies their winning edge, their spirit of indefatigability, a battle-hardened fighter in a 21-year-old's body. Fifa's technical boffins record their admiration of his contribution to extra time 'when again the stamina and individual attacking ability of Ball was a notable feature'. Notable? Principal. Ball races on to Stiles' pass down the right and crosses to Hurst. What happens next will always be debated when followers of England and Germany cross paths and swords. Three points of impact are endlessly analysed. First impact: the swivelling Hurst makes powerful contact with the ball which rises up past Tilkowski. Second impact: the ball strikes the wooden crossbar now hanging close to the corporate corners of Wembley, outside the Bobby Moore Room. After attending the last competitive match at Wembley before Euro 2016, the 2-0 win over Estonia, I stand underneath the crossbar as the suited hordes stride past, most of them oblivious to such an important relic of English sporting history. It hangs in the air, much like the legitimacy of Hurst's goal. Third impact: the ball bounces down and lands on or over the line depending on your nationality. The English perspective is simple: they think it's all over the line. A Sky Sports investigation in 2016 confirms this. Other viewings contradict this. Academics in the Ruhr and Bavaria, clearly with too much time on their hands, prove it isn't a goal by analysing angles using the latest Teutonic technology. Computer says no. Lino says yes. A slightly bohemian character from Azerbaijan, then part of the USSR, enters English legend. Tofik Bakhramov signals a goal. As Wembley holds its breath, Dienst consults Bakhramov and concurs. Goal given. 3-2. England jubilant. No wonder the FA is so keen to lay a floral tribute to Bakhramov at the stadium bearing his name when England visit Baku in October 2004, a fixture so wind-afflicted some of us file our reports on a Michael Owen-inspired victory from underneath our desks.

Back at Wembley in '66, the Germans pour forward, with Siggi Held magnificent as the clock challenges them with every ticking second. England can pick them off. 'The Germans were trying to go over the top of us, through us, and we broke out, particularly Geoff,' continues Jack. Up in the TV gantry, Wolstenholme memorably informs his rapt audience that some people are on the pitch. But Hurst hasn't finished. He soon has. 'Bobby Moore knocked him a helluva long ball,' smiles Jack. 'The Germans had already pushed up and Geoff took the ball, had room and time to stop, look up and just whack it in the back of the net. We knew then we'd won it. 4-2!' An august campaigner pauses, loving all these joyous recollections. 'Geoff scored three goals! Martin scored!'

When Dienst blows to confirm the most historic moment in English sport, Jack tries to catch up with Hurst and Peters celebrating near the centre-circle. He rushes upfield, closing on them, nearer and nearer, getting to within 20 yards before emotion and exhaustion overwhelm him. Jack falls to his knees near the centre-spot and holds his face. It means so much. He's given so much. 'I was sat on the ground, with my head in my hands. Our Kid was sat on the ground too. I don't know whether I went to him or he went to me but we did have a hug. I can remember our Bob saying to me: "What else is there left to play for?"' Two boys from Ashington scale the heights. Bobby does, of course, go on to become a champion of Europe with Manchester United in 1968, a formidable achievement lent even greater poignancy by the Munich disaster a decade earlier. Jack's excellence with Leeds sees him voted Footballer of the Year in 1967. But nothing can match the events of 30 July 1966 at Wembley.

Noise reverberates from all quarters. Delirious home fans sing 'England's won the Cup, England's won the Cup, ee-aye-addio, England's won the Cup!' Chants of 'Ramsey, Ramsey!' ensue, saluting the coaching catalyst who greets Dienst's final whistle by just sitting there on the bench, in control of his emotions, even now. Ramsey's stillness contrasts with the activity all around. Jimmy Armfield, a revered former captain and current squad member resplendent in his red jersey as if representing a particularly stylish Blackpool golf club, leans forward to congratulate Ramsey. The England manager's vanquished counterpart, the noble Schoen, holds his left hand to his forehead in dismay. Greaves, his lean, fit-again frame slipped into a suit, peers around the back of trainer Harold Shepherdson before stepping on to the pitch to salute Ramsey's chosen ones. Heaven knows the conflicting state of his emotions: so near to nirvana and yet so impossibly far. One ill-timed injury changes his life with all the force of a wrecking ball.

Moore climbs the thirty-nine steps to collect the Jules Rimet trophy from Her Majesty the Queen, descends from the heights, and the jubilation spreads across that fabled patch of grass. Jack waves down a camera lens, the players congregate around Moore, and a legendary assembly is captured for eternity by the photographers. 'We're all smiling except our Robert,' marvels Jack, reaching for the picture again. 'Our Bob was stood there, tears running down his face. I was just waving at a few people who told me where they would be.' His and Bobby's parents were there. 'My wife was pregnant so she couldn't come to the match,' he adds. Charlton's gaze meanders across the photograph, stopping at a distinctive face. 'Nobby without his teeth!' he laughs. Stiles is soon doing his jig with the cup. The party's really starting. Jack, though, gets delayed as he's dragged off for a urine test. How inconvenient – that is really taking the piss. But he's soon on the bus, heading back into town, towards Kensington and the Royal Garden Hotel for the victors' post-match banquet. On its own fiftieth anniversary in 2015, the Royal Garden calculates it has opened 175,000 bottles of champagne in its history, six times the height of Everest, many of them consumed on just one night in 1966. Some bottles are already on ice as England hove into view.

Slowly, inching its way through the human throng, the team bus reaches the Royal Garden, fans rushing behind, waving, shouting, some taking pictures with unwieldy cameras. The country's traditional stiff upper lip is loosened by bliss and a beer or two. Police try to keep them back, but people break through, standing underneath the balcony, calling for their idols like Romeos with rosettes. It almost resembles VE Day. Jack and the players emerge and throw flowers down to the merry mass. Even his parents, arriving hot-foot from Wembley, join in. 'We had a meal there,' Jack recalls. 'All the wives came and joined us. Mine wasn't there, but the rest were.' They then disperse. Peters retires to his room with his wife and one of those bottles of champagne. Bobby Charlton is so shattered he has an early night with his wife Norma. Others have late nights, early mornings, very late mornings in Jack's case. 'We went out,' he explains. 'The lads went different places.' Jack bumps into Jim Mossop, a distinguished football reporter noted for his genial company as well as the quality of his copy, and embarks on what proves a lengthy, very enjoyable excursion through London. 'We went to a club where there was a long table,' Jack says, the details still sketchy. 'We then went out to somebody's house and went in for a drink. We stayed there for a while.' Quite a long while. Jack ends up asleep on a sofa at this flat in Leytonstone, east London. 'We then went back to the hotel.' He's mildly reprimanded by his mother on his return to the Royal Garden, but he's just won the World Cup. Any chiding is cursory.

The carousing continues. A fortnight after the final, Jack and Bobby parade through the streets of Ashington in an open-top Rolls-Royce. People spill off the pavements, reaching into the car to shake hands with local heroes. It doesn't get much better than this homecoming.

Jack goes on to feature briefly in the 1970 World Cup finals, against Czechoslovakia in Guadalajara, but the 35-year-old has lost his place to Everton's Brian Labone. 'We won the World Cup at home. If we'd done it away from home . . . ' Jack's voice tails off, leaving it unsaid what a herculean achievement that would have been in Mexico.

He stops reminiscing for a few moments, admiring the Tyne again. On the table at the Copthorne lies a copy of the *Evening Chronicle* detailing a 6-1 defeat for his beloved team Newcastle United, and noting a line-up boasting no Geordies. 'I used to come to this hotel when Bob was manager, to see him,' he recalls of Sir Bobby Robson. 'I was good friends with Bob. I used to enjoy playing against Fulham [for whom Robson played]. Bob was always smiling.' Jack's smiling too, remembering his old friend. He's always diligent in his duties helping out the Sir Bobby Robson Foundation. Now 80, he's been driven to our meeting at the Copthorne by Helen and Will Logan, the kindly owners of Northumberland Tea, who make donations to Robson's charity for every box sold. Helen's parents both passed away from lung cancer. 'The Freeman Hospital looked after my dad and I know the care and support that the Sir Bobby Robson Cancer Trials Research Centre unit gives,' Helen says. A theme rapidly evident during six months' travelling around interviewing people for this book is the huge support for the Sir Bobby Robson Foundation. Jack's always raising funds. A photograph of him, resplendent in flat cap, adorns the tea boxes that generate tens of thousands of pounds for the charity. 'The best cup since '66' runs the slogan next to a beaming, cuppa-holding Charlton.

One of the many privileges of being a football reporter is the occasional opportunity to meet the Boys of '66, including Moore and Ball before they were so cruelly snatched away. I've done speaking events with Banks and Hurst, the hat-trick man who briefly managed the England press team, an assignment that really does constitute 'the Impossible Job'. Not only is it humbling being in the presence of modest souls who gave the country its proudest sporting moment, it is uplifting to see their continuing effect on people. England matter. The pursuit of international glory matters, even in a club-fixated era. As Jack sits in the Copthorne, residents spot him, nod and smile. He's a reminder of 1966, a time when the Three Lions evoke respect and fear, and every passing year and tournament deepens admiration for their achievement. Health permitting, the remaining members of the squad meet annually. Charlton holds another photograph, a more recent one, outside a club-house. Hurst clutches his golf shoes. Jack stands at the back. Banks is at the front, shoulder to shoulder with Hunt. Joining them are reserves like Ron Flowers, Jimmy Armfield, Ian Callaghan, George Eastham, Peter Bonetti and Norman Hunter. 'George Eastham and other lads who hadn't got into the England team always turned up for the reunions,' says Jack. 'We always played golf once a year, in the south, north or Midlands. Some of them didn't play golf but they still came. Some of them who played golf couldn't play golf! I can hit the ball but I need to be in a wagon to get round now!'

He wishes his involvement with England had continued. In 1977, Jack wrote to the FA to apply for the job after Don Revie resigned. 'I qualified for all the badges at Lilleshall,' he recalls. He knows players, understands them, can get the best out of them. He was voted English Manager of the Year in 1974 because of his acclaimed work getting Middlesbrough promoted. The FA, an organization riddled with snobbery in those days, never even had the courtesy to acknowledge the letter of an England great. The suspicion is that he was always too associated with Revie. 'Don was great at Leeds,' Jack says now, 'but I don't know what happened with him and England.

'I had plenty to do with Sheffield Wednesday, Middlesbrough [where he returned briefly as caretaker] and Newcastle. All the clubs I went to, all been successful.' Frustratingly for him, especially given his childhood allegiances, Jack endured a torrid end to his time at St James' Park when some of the fans turned on him after a transfer target, Eric Gates, chose Sunderland instead. His eyes fill with pain as he recalls those events in 1985. 'A section of the crowd in the corner were yelling, "Charlton out, Charlton out, Charlton out." I looked at the crowd in the corner, and thought: "Listen to them!" I was very upset with the crowd. I'm not having that. I told the directors: "I'm finished. If the fans want somebody else, let them have somebody else." Then I went to Ireland.'

His anger at the FA never responding intensified on learning of an apparent exchange between a Lancaster Gate official and a counterpart at the Football Association of Ireland. The FA man was reported to have told the FAI it had 'made a mistake' in appointing Charlton manager of the Republic in 1986. Mistake? He qualifies them for two World Cups, defeats England in Stuttgart at Euro 88, draws with them in Cagliari at Italia 90, and is still revered there. 'I was always very popular when I was in Ireland, and they weren't very happy when I said I was leaving. But I'd done things for them. I was there for ten years.' They will always share the memory of Ireland defeating Italy at Giants Stadium during USA 94.

Jack returned to Dublin on 7 June 2015 as guest of honour before the Republic's friendly with England at the Aviva Stadium. 'They just told me to go down on the pitch before the game, and I had to walk on to the pitch, and there was an unbelievable reaction from the fans. I just waved at them, and the crowd all cheered. I was crying. It's true. I've got my eyes running, my nose running and there's nothing I can do about it!' He turns and waves to all four sides of the ground, and then settles back to inspect the latest heirs to his noble tradition, getting a close-up of England. 'I always watch them on the television. I'd like them to win the World Cup again. We were the last team. It's so many years ago.'

1966 is unique, so special, yet the mood at the time among many England followers was that this was the start of a golden age, especially with the infusion of new talent like Alan Mullery.

2

Mullery and Mexico 70

WALK INTO WHITE Hart Lane, climb one flight of stairs, and step into a room that takes away the breath of those entering for the first time. Inside lies a treasure trove of memories, a wealth of footballing experience. It is where Tottenham Hotspur legends gather and relax before heading out to assorted lounges and suites to entertain the club's many corporate guests. Privileged visitors advance under the lilywhite lintel and immediately stop, looking around in admiration. Even those with no affiliation to this north London institution are overwhelmed. It is like shaking a football sticker album vigorously, watching all the stars fall out and then marvelling as they come to life. Seated at one table before the game with Crystal Palace on 20 September 2015 is Martin Chivers, deep in conversation with Pat Jennings and Darren Anderton. Ray Clemence strolls past, beaming, swapping a bon mot or two. And now here is Alan Mullery MBE, England's pre-eminent player at the 1970 World Cup, walking over, extending a hand in greeting before finding a quiet place to reminisce about Bobby Moore, Gordon Banks and Sir Alf Ramsey.

Articulate, chirpy company with just a trace of mournfulness, the Londoner expresses deep pride at representing his country while also voicing fears for the current standard-bearers. An understanding of the qualities that propel Mullery through his England career from 1964 to 1971, traits such as patience and perseverance as well as talent, would serve any aspiring international well. Mullery's story should be required reading for members of the modern generation hoping to end the years of hurt.

Having re-located to the adjacent West Stand Box Holders' Lounge awash with Ledley King and Jermain Defoe memorabilia, Mullery politely asks bar-staff to turn down the music. He talks cogently, mixing anecdote with analysis, demonstrating why he is so in demand on the after-dinner circuit. Setting up the meeting was enlightening in itself: one call to Spurs and they arrange everything with 'Mullers'. Tottenham cherish their England connections, a tradition their intelligent manager Mauricio Pochettino maintains by backing native talent. Later on, Mullery joins the 35,723 spectators to delight in the performance of the 19-year-old Dele Alli, a sinewy, silky embodiment of hope for England's future. Alli shows his stamina from box to box against Palace, making a couple of interceptions late on to preserve their lead, and earning a laudatory tweet from a Spurs and England legend, Gary Lineker: 'Tell you what, England has some real talent finally coming through. Very excited by Dele Alli.' Everyone is: Alli looks the part.

The rangy midfielder is beginning to break through, building on his 88 appearances for MK Dons. Mullery empathizes with his progress, having found England recognition at the Lane after nearly 200 games for Fulham.

Mullery will never forget the moment in 1964 when he was informed he'd been called up by Ramsey. He is out with his wife June, shopping in Worcester Park, a suburb in south-west London. 'This bloke came up and said: "Congratulations, you're in the England squad." I thought he was taking the mickey. I said: "OK. I'll believe it when I get home." When I got home, the letter from the FA was there.' Lancaster Gate provides details of where the midfielder is to report for the friendly with Holland in Amsterdam on 9 December. 'I still thought somebody's taking the mickey. So I phone a reporter, Vic Railton, who wrote for the *Evening News*, and said: "I don't know if somebody is taking the piss out of me, mate, but they sent me a letter to say I'm in the squad." "Oh yeah," he said, "I've just heard it on the radio." I felt extremely proud that a snotty-nosed kid from Notting

Hill had achieved what every kid I played football with in the streets and the parks dreamed of: to become an England footballer. It was really special. I don't think my family really believed it. My father didn't pat me on the back. In those days, mums and dads didn't. It was post-war. You couldn't hug your son in those days. Every time I see my son I hug and kiss him. The first England cap didn't really mean anything to my dad. He didn't come and watch me [in Amsterdam]. He came to Wembley on the odd occasion, but he was more interested in a glass of beer than he was watching me play football.'

At 23, Mullery's not a character lacking in confidence yet he feels a shiver of trepidation as he reports for international duty. 'I was quite frightened turning up with Alf.' Mullery at least knows George Cohen from Fulham and Jimmy Greaves from Spurs but it's still daunting. Bobby Charlton of Manchester United strides into training. Ron Flowers of Wolves is there. Peter Thompson of Liverpool. Terry Venables of Chelsea. Big names. 'That first day, I was apprehensive around these fellas. I was quite shy about that even though you wouldn't think so now! Only Alf, Harold Shepherdson and Les Cocker came up and said: "Congratulations."' Listening to Mullery all these years on, and seeking clues to solving the years of hurt, the thought takes hold that a process of introduction needs to be instigated by the FA. Club-mates can be guides. It should send a mentor, an ex-pro, to a club to prepare a player called up for the first time. The usual process of having a quiet word with a trusted senior pro ebbs as dressing-rooms become more fluid places, especially in the age of the foreign invasion. 'I learned from it,' Mullery resumes, drawing on his experience as manager of Brighton & Hove Albion from 1976 to 1981. 'I signed Gary Stevens as a 15-year-old from Ipswich and he got a call-up.' Although he has left Brighton, Mullery still gives words of advice to Stevens. 'I said: "Hey, don't do what I did and stand away from it. Mix in with the players, get to know them, get to understand them and really learn as much as you can from talking to people."'

Mullery himself learns how to deal with frustration when overlooked by Ramsey for the 1966 World Cup – he does not even make Ramsey's forty-strong provisional list, a reflection of the quality around. His response to this should be sent with all the training schedules and match-day tactics to the iPads of every England player. 'I was disappointed I never got in the squad but then there were players like Nobby Stiles, who was fantastic, and Gordon Milne, who was in the same position I was.' Even Milne gets cut from the squad on 18 June as Ramsey trims his squad to the final 22. At 24, the same age as Stiles, Mullery feels he should have been there, at Wembley, challenging West Germany. 'To be honest, I was pissed off watching the final because every time I saw Nobby get the ball, I thought: "That should have been me." But Alf picked him and they won the trophy. It gave me more impetus to want to be a better player.' Rather than sulk, he fights back.

Mullery enters a personal golden period from 1967 until 1972, winning the FA Cup, League Cup and Uefa Cup with Spurs and slowly establishing himself with England. 'We beat Chelsea in the FA Cup final [in '67] and on the Wednesday we were playing Spain at Wembley, when I got my second cap. Me and Johnny Hollins were the two midfielders. Johnny got his one and only cap that night. To play for England at Wembley was really special.' He gradually replaces Stiles in Ramsey's starting plans. He laughs when I relay the description of him by Clive Leatherdale in his 2002 book *England's Quest for the World Cup* as 'more creative, less savage' than Stiles. 'I like that! I like it very much! I wouldn't say that to Nobby! I've been compared to quite a few people but that's the best one I've heard. When I missed out in '66, and got into the side for the Spanish game, for the next five years Nobby only played a few times (eight) and one of those was when I got sent off and he played the following game.'

Ah, the infamous sending-off of 1968, an incident of permanent embarrassment for Mullery but an event providing perpetual testimony to Ramsey's genius. Great managers are loyal, particularly to those offering residual value. 'I don't think I've ever met a manager or been under a manager who felt so strongly about his players as Alf Ramsey,' continues Mullery. 'He would have nothing said against his players. If he had a pop at you it was in private. He looked after players.' He certainly looks after Mullery after a vicious night in

Florence. One of the most cultured cities on the planet is the setting for one of the most unedifying encounters. Locked in a 5 June semi-final duel in the 1968 European Championship, Yugoslavia and England launch into each other. Typically, Norman Hunter, the Leeds United hard man, does not hold back, and soon the playmaking Ivica Osim is hobbling. But the worst offender in Stadio Comunale is Dobrivoje Trivić, Yugoslavia's midfield enforcer, who attempts to neutralize Bobby Charlton and Alan Ball early on. Yugoslavia provide the most sophisticated moment of the night, the graceful left-winger Dragan Džajić exploiting rare errant positioning by Moore to chest a cross down and beat Gordon Banks, but the game's unwanted record-making nature is confirmed when Mullery becomes the first Englishman ever dismissed, following retaliation in the final minute. Even the grainy footage of Trivić's last-minute assault on Mullery cannot obscure the malevolence of the act, the arrival at speed and the raking of the Englishman's right calf. Blood flows and boils. Mullery turns and kicks Trivić in the groin. He rolls on the ground, holding his arms, pleading for succour and retribution. As the Spanish referee, José María Ortiz de Mendíbil, points Mullery towards the dressing-room, Trivić leaps up, his mission accomplished. When Alan Ball marches over to remonstrate, Trivić runs away. Coward.

Buttons bursting off blazers, the FA is apoplectic at Mullery's ignominy, chuntering away, imposing a fine. Ramsey knows he'll need Mullery in the World Cup, sees his potential in replacing Stiles, and stands firm. 'I was in the communal bath at the end of the game when Ramsey came in. I went under the water and he picked me up by my hair. He said: "I'm ever so glad that somebody kicked those bastards like they've been kicking us all the game." And, bump, he let me drop back into the water. I got fined £50, a lot of money in those days. When I got this letter through from the FA, Alf phoned me up and said: "Look, I'll pay that." Alf paid my fine out of his own pocket. The players were his chickens, his rabbits, his dogs, his cats. He looked after us. He treated you press lot sometimes like shit, to be honest. When we were at Roehampton, he'd walk out and read the team out for a Wednesday night at Wembley, and that's all he'd do! He'd turn round and walk away. He was so engrossed in the group of people he had over the years. I don't think there will ever be anybody like him again.'

Nor Bobby Moore. 'For Bobby to not have a knighthood as he should have had for all the things he gave to football was a scandal. Putting up the statue for Bobby at Wembley was wonderful but when you see the sort of people getting knighthoods, well, he deserved a knighthood. Bobby would be in the top three greatest sportsmen we ever produced. If you travel round the world now, and you're in a certain country, and they don't speak your language and you mention Bobby Moore, they know who you're talking about. Throughout the world. When I was a manager, I'd go and look at players. If I'd have looked at Bob, I'd have said: "No, can't head a ball, can't jump, slow, wouldn't buy him." But I played with him. I saw all the qualities he had, how he grew from a midfield player to a central defender. I saw all the timing he had, the reading of the game. I knew how special he was.' To laud the man even more, Mullery draws on his club familiarity with two of the greats of English football, Johnny Haynes of Fulham and Jimmy Greaves of Spurs. 'They could all see things in advance. Johnny Haynes knew if a ball came to him, the outside-left would be far left on the touchline and he'd hit a 60-yard pass straight to his feet. Didn't have to look up. He had this picture framed. Before scoring, Greavsie knew where the ball was going to go and would knock it in the back of the net. Like them, Bobby read everything so quickly.'

Hailed as the master of timing, the king of the stealthy tackle, Moore executes one of the most fabled interceptions in the history of the game at the 1970 World Cup. As that streak of Brazilian lightning called Jairzinho sweeps rapidly and menacingly down the right in Guadalajara on 7 June, Moore runs back, waiting his moment, eyes on the ball, staying balanced and poised before calmly stretching out his right boot to rob the winger, with all the ease of a man collecting a piece of paper in a hurricane. 'It was absolutely brilliant, but it wasn't a one-off,' smiles Mullery. 'He did that time and time again. The only other player I'd seen read the game like that was Mark

Lawrenson, who I signed for Brighton as a 19-year-old from Preston.'

Mullery also sees at close hand how Moore deals with pressure when the England captain is accused of stealing a gold-and-emerald bracelet from the Green Fire jewellery store in the Tequendama Hotel in Bogotá, Colombia, where England are playing a World Cup warm-up. The story is so well known, and the case against Moore so clearly contrived, that it seems almost laughable now, but it dominates headlines across the globe in 1970. Only a man of Moore's mettle could withstand the stress, the days detained, the attempted smearing of his reputation, and the difficulties in preparing for World Cup combat when separated from the squad. 'Colombia's quite a frightening place, in those days anyway,' recalls Mullery. 'We had bodyguards with guns.' While watching the James Stewart classic *Shenandoah* in the hotel, Moore is quietly arrested by plain-clothes police. Those players aware of what's happening are outraged. Mullery still is. 'The British ambassador said to us: "Look, he won't be allowed to leave until this is all sorted out." So we just had to leave for Guadalajara.' Minus their captain, England travel on to their World Cup base.

Justice eventually prevails, the evidence is discredited and Moore is released. It still takes until 1975 for the case to be officially closed. 'He looked like death warmed up,' recalls Mullery, who was waiting for his friend at the Hilton Hotel in Guadalajara. 'I was outside the lift on the fourteenth floor, guards everywhere, absolutely noisy outside with all these bands going on, and Bobby walks out of the lift. I gave him a great big hug. He'd lost almost a stone because he couldn't eat, he was worried about what was going to happen.' Whatever the inner angst, Moore stays outwardly composed and dignified. 'I phoned Alf and said: "Bobby's here! He's arrived." "Right, order some champagne," Alf said.' Ramsey has already been to the airport to greet his captain and is in the mood to celebrate. 'Up comes the champagne, and the four of us just sat there, Alex Stepney, myself, Alf and Bobby, knocking it back. Bobby took his tracksuit off, and just threw it out the window. When we looked down, there were three hundred people fighting to get this tracksuit top and bottom! He was probably the only person who could have survived that. He was probably one of the players of the World Cup – and that just shows you what a strong person he is.

'The only time I saw Bob flummoxed was when he came to Fulham [in 1974]. I said to him: "If you come over from West Ham, for the next two or three years you'll have fun. We're not going to win anything." Yet we got to an FA Cup final [in 1975] which was great for him. His first game for Fulham was against Middlesbrough when Big Jack Charlton was manager, and we were 4-0 down at the Cottage. Bob's picking the ball out of the net, and we were walking back towards the halfway line. "Can I ask you a question?" he said. "Yes, what's that?" "Does the goalkeeper [Peter Mellor] ever use his hands?" "Sometimes." "Well, he's supposed to use them all the time."' Otherwise, little fazes the peerless Moore.

Not even 1970, Bogotá and life in Guadalajara. 'We brought our own food, but some of that [mainly the steaks] got stolen after they wouldn't let it through customs,' continues Mullery. 'We lived on fish-fingers and chips for two weeks, and then got invited to the British Embassy and had meals there. There were English people who lived in Mexico at the time who invited us down to the cricket club. We played the press at football one day – we did win. It was good fun. The camaraderie was fantastic. I was 28 then, and that's the best time you're playing football. I'd had so much experience. I just felt one of the party now.'

Having missed the Wembley party, Mullery is doubly determined to grasp his chance in Mexico. England hardly endear themselves to the Mexicans with some more of Ramsey's undiplomatic comments, the perceived arrogance in bringing their own food, plus the contro-versy over Moore and the sight of Jeff Astle unsteady on his feet after imbibing to soothe his nerves on the flight to Guadalajara. 'England – A Team of Drunks and Thieves' is the infamous verdict of the Mexican daily *Esto*. Grudging respect is gradually paid to the world champions after they withstand some robust challenges from Romania to win their opening game through Geoff Hurst's shot. Next up are Jairzinho and Rivelino, Tostão and Pelé. Mullery knows what to expect, having played in a tour match at Maracanã a year earlier, tracking Pelé. He's long followed the Brazilian maestro. 'I remember watching on a black-and-white television this 17-year-old kid in Sweden at the 1958 World Cup, scoring twice in the final when Brazil beat Sweden, and never, ever thinking that one day I'd have to play against him. You could see he was special as a 17-year-old: he took control of that final. In Mexico, Alf said to me: "When Brazil have the ball, you have to mark Pelé. When we have the ball, you can go and play." The lovely thing I always remember Alf saying was, "If we can stop Pelé playing, and stop you playing, then we'll win the game." Thanks Alf, thanks a lot! I had to cut Pelé out. At the time he was easily the best player in the world and I'd still say now the best player I've ever seen. Pelé had everything: fantastic skill, fantastic touch and an ability to score goals like you'd never seen before. Now we have Messi and Ronaldo, and Greavsie in his time, but Pelé was just something special. He was quick and like a brick wall if you hit him. He was psychologically and physically strong. You could kick Pelé and he'd come back for more, like Bestie. I kicked Pelé a few times.

'I saw him in London six months ago at a big do. I hadn't seen him for forty-odd years. As I came through the crowd, Pelé was there with a very, very pretty young lady at one of the tables. He pointed to this young lady and pointed his finger at me and went: "Alan Mullery." I thought: "Bloody hell, how can he remember me? I've got grey hair now." Pelé didn't look any different at all. Blimey! He got up and gave me a great big hug. I said: "Can I have a look at the scars you've still got on the legs?" He burst out laughing.

'I told him I swapped shirts with him in Maracanã in 1969 but when we moved house, somebody stole it. The guy who looked after Pelé, who used to be a director here [Paul Kemsley], said: "We'll get you a new one." A month later, a package came through the post and it was a Pelé shirt saying "To Alan, from your friend Pelé". That was fantastic. That's hanging in the house. It will stay there until the day I die and I'm sure my son will then look after it all the time.'

Mullery versus Pelé is one of many sub-plots of this Guadalajara drama between the tournament favourites. Local antagonism towards England has still not dissipated. The choir outside the Hilton chants 'Bra-sil, Bra-sil!' Fifa even notes this nocturnal crooning in its official report on Mexico 70: 'barn-storming of hotels by chanting mobs of supporters provided an unexpected disturbance when players were required to sleep'. Ramsey and his players could be forgiven for raising a wry eyebrow about the complaint registered in the 1966 Fifa Technical Study that 'Mexico were worried about noise from the street' when selecting their hotel in England. Even with sleep disturbed, and confronting 98°F temperatures, Ramsey's side settle against Brazil. The current generation of players, so troubled by heat at tournaments, could do worse than devote 90 minutes to watching the Guadalajara tape. It is a joy to see England playing with intelligence and belief, taking care of the ball, and to admire that remarkable Gordon Banks save from Pelé in the 10th minute following a quick Brazilian break. 'Jairzinho got down the right-hand side with pace, clipped it, and we all moved across,' remembers Mullery. 'Tommy Wright was marking Pelé, as I'd moved across, Mooro had moved across, Brian Labone moved across as well. You know how Bobby used to get in front of everybody and pick up those runs, but Jairzinho chipped everybody. Pelé just glided in. As he headed it, he shouted "goal". Pelé did shout "goal"! Banksy, bless him, gets across and in mid-air, horizontal, gets the smallest of fingers on it, and flicks it on to the crossbar, and over the top. It was absolutely fantastic. And then me, walking up to him as Banksy was lying on the floor, patting him on the head and saying: "Why didn't you catch it?" You can guess what words Banksy said back. Swear words!'

Banks continues to perform marvels, denying Paulo Cézar, Jairzinho and Rivelino. Banks' prowess, that shot-stopping agility, is enhanced by an indomitable character. 'He absolutely commanded the box, and would give a running commentary as the game was on,' says Mullery. He then relates a poignant story. As an ambassador for Brighton & Hove Albion, Mullery goes with the club's keeper, David Stockdale, to offer condolences to the parents of the two local Worthing United footballers, Matthew Grimstone and Jacob Schilt, who tragically perished in the Shoreham plane crash on 22 August

2015. 'We spent some time together after going to see the mums and dads of those lads killed in Shoreham. I spoke to David about Banksy. David's a big man, six foot four, built like a modern goalkeeper, like Thibaut Courtois at Chelsea, and I said to him: "I played with some of the greatest goalkeepers, Jennings, Banksy, and they would always say the penalty box is their house, and anybody who tried to get in their house is a burglar. It's your house, you command everybody, you should be giving a running commentary to every defender because you're facing everything. That's what Gordon and Pat did." Jennings came out and caught me on the chin once. They commanded their area. David took it all in.'

Banks is finally beaten. Tostão slips the ball through Moore's legs and Pelé shepherds it across to Jairzinho, who scores. There is still time for that wretched miss by Jeff Astle from close range, and for the magnificent Ball to hit the bar, but England lose a high-class game hailed as 'a match for adults' by the Brazilian coach, Mário Zagallo. England are never outclassed or out-thought by a side that goes on to win the World Cup, devastating Italy in the Azteca final, and widely believed to be the greatest international team of all time. Barring one moment, England match Brazil despite the gruelling conditions. 'I was taking sodium tablets,' remembers Mullery. 'In those days we weren't getting bottles of drinks off the sidelines, it wasn't allowed.' At the final whistle, Mullery is selected for doping control. 'We couldn't go anywhere until they gave us permission to leave after they'd taken the drugs test but I couldn't pee. I was drinking water and Coca-Cola. After all that drink, I decided to go again, but it was a minute amount of urine, so I put a tap on and put water from the tap. I just didn't want to stay any more hours. And it passed! I thought with the Mexican water, which you don't drink or you kill yourself . . . but I just took that chance. I'm so sick and tired of it, we've lost to Brazil and been waiting here hours, and I just wanted to go back to the hotel. The game kicked off at noon and it was getting on for eight p.m. before I got back to the hotel. The doctor called me in to weigh me. I started the game at 12st 12lb and finished at 11st 12lb. I was aching from top to bottom.'

Indefatigable competitors like Mullery show a zeal for England, a willingness to take the pain and suffering and weight loss, a stoicism he fears is disappearing. 'When I was playing as a kid, the only thing I wanted to do was play for England. The only thing Bobby Moore and Jimmy Greaves wanted to do was play for England. Ahead of the club. Playing for England was the pinnacle of what I wanted to achieve in football. I became an international footballer never even thinking I would get 35 caps. People say to me, "Bloody hell, that was a lot in those days." It was. Blimey, I must have been half decent.

'Kids don't have the hunger now. It's too easy now for kids. Everything's done for them. The Academies are magnificent. If you go to Brighton's Academy, it's one of the best in the world. It's absolutely superb. The schooling's done. They have an Under-21 League which is iffy and butty. I learned a lot at 15, playing in Fulham's reserves, by 16 I was captaining the side, by 18 I was the vice-captain of Fulham behind Johnny Haynes, and when John didn't play, I was captain. I don't see leaders now I'm afraid. Steven Gerrard was the one leader we had. Name me a character – English – now in the Premier League.' John Terry? 'He's not playing for England any more. He was a leader for all the time, and still is when he plays. We had leaders everywhere. At this club [Spurs], you go back to Blanchflower, Mackay, Mullery, Peters, Perryman – leaders. I don't see leaders in football today. I see players when they concede a goal walk back with their heads down. I don't see somebody going out and patting them on the back and saying, "Hey, we've got to do this." If we were losing 4-0 at this football club, Mackay would think we can win 5-4. And if you didn't, you'd get a kick up the backside from him.'

Reflecting on the 2014 World Cup, Mullery praises a German side full of responsibility-takers like Manuel Neuer, Philipp Lahm, Bastian Schweinsteiger and Thomas Müller. 'Absolutely brilliant. That's what it's all about. Roy Hodgson's a very good friend of mine but the World Cup we had in Brazil was a disaster. I'm afraid the kids aren't coming through here. We had a nightmare at the last Under-21s. I feel sad about it. We have some wonderful foreign players in this country but there are too many. It's a big problem. I'm very patriotic. I played in a golden era when England were the bees' knees for seven years. I don't think that golden era will come back in the next ten, twenty or thirty years. Sixty-six is so long ago. To think we've won the World Cup once.'

England strive hard to cling on to it in Mexico. Allan Clarke's penalty brings victory over Czechoslovakia and a reunion with West Germany on 14 June in León. England are traditionally bedevilled by off-field glitches at tournaments, yet 1970 is particularly draining. Not only is there Moore's wrongful Bogotá incarceration, and the moonlight sonatas outside the Hilton, but now Montezuma's revenge pays a painful visit. A few of Ramsey's squad are afflicted by the stomach bug but none as bad as Banks. Conspiracy theories circulating since include the outlandish claim that the CIA wanted to bring harmony to the region by ensuring a Latin winner, so nobbling Banks and England going out would help (although the Germans would benefit). 'Whether Banksy had been turned over or not, I don't know, but nobody else in the squad had anything like that,' says Mullery. It's fanciful. Banks may well have just picked up a nasty germ swigging from an unwashed bottle. Peter Bonetti, aka The Cat, is told to prepare himself in case Banks doesn't recover in time. 'We got on the bus to go to the game and were all sitting on there. I used to sit in the front because I'm a terrible traveller on coaches. Alf was sitting behind the driver. He says to Harold Shepherdson: "Harold, have a count up, who's on." Harold has a count up. "One's missing." "Who the bloody hell is that?" "It's Banksy." "Go and get him." So Harold goes to his room, comes back, and I'm sitting there, listening to this. "He can't get off the toilet. He's got Montezuma's revenge." "What can we do about it?" "We can't do anything about it. If he gets up, he'll mess himself. He's really ill." Alf looked up the aisle to Bonetti and said: "Catty, you're playing." Catty went: "What?" "You're in goal today." Catty was like, "Bloody hell, I'm playing." But he was looking forward to it.'

León proves to be Mullery's finest game for England. Shortly after the half-hour mark, Mullery takes the ball from Terry Cooper, exchanges passes with Franny Lee, looks up and picks out Keith Newton on the right. As the full-back advances, Mullery hurtles through the middle, arrowing towards the near-post, meeting the return with a merciless finish past Sepp Maier. Summoning up another accurate delivery after 50 minutes, Newton crosses to Peters, it's 2-0 England and the semi-finals beckon. England, surely, are kings of León; but now the years of hurt really begin. England have yet to recover from what unfolds in the punishing heat. The bare facts have been ably chronicled. Bonetti is not an adequate understudy for Banks. Helmut Schoen's substitutions work, Ramsey's don't. Jürgen Grabowski replaces Reinhard Libuda after 55 minutes, begins troubling Cooper, and West Germany sense some momentum. England try to play keep-ball, conserving their energy, but a pass goes astray. Franz Beckenbauer makes it 2-1 with a shot Bonetti dives over. Banks would have saved it. Colin Bell comes on for Bobby Charlton, Ramsey seemingly protecting him for the semi-finals. Free from his Charlton-tracking duties, Beckenbauer has even more room to roam upfield. Cooper is fading, surely needing replacement, but it is Martin Peters giving way, to Norman Hunter. Brian Labone's weak clearance gives the Germans hope; Uwe Seeler beats Mullery and loops a header over Bonetti. 2-2 with ten minutes to go. At 90 minutes, Ramsey delivers another rallying call with "we beat them in '66, we'll do it again", but Gerd Müller's volley settles it. The world champions are out. The inquest begins. It's never stopped.

'I think we'd have won with Banksy in goal,' says Mullery. 'With the first goal, Beckenbauer just drops his shoulder, hits his shot and it's a bobbler. It bobbled just in front of Catty, straight underneath his body and – boom – into the back of the net. The second one, I'm marking Seeler on the edge of the box and all he did was flick the ball on. He wasn't looking at the goal. Perhaps I could have got a bit higher to head the ball. Catty was two yards off his line and – woof – it went over the top of him. I wasn't close enough to Seeler. I blame myself for that. Catty probably lost a bit of confidence letting the ball under his body.'

Ramsey's substitutions come in for much unfavourable examin-ation. Still do. 'Whenever I do Q&As at functions, it's always a question: why did Alf take Bobby Charlton off? Bobby was the oldest player in the team, 32, and against Brazil he substituted him after an hour [63 minutes, for Bell], with all the heat and the altitude, with the game against Czechoslovakia after an hour [65 minutes, for Alan Ball] to save his energy.' Mullery insists the players were not psychologically affected by Ramsey withdrawing Charlton in León. 'No, because he'd done it before. Then again, he was probably one of the fittest players. But Colin Bell could run for ever and had great skill as well.' The main effect is on West Germany. Beckenbauer has already scored but Charlton's exit lifts them further. 'I'd have thought so. Beckenbauer's job was to mark Bob, to do a similar job that I did on Pelé. He stopped Bobby playing. When Bob went off, Beckenbauer became the natural, creative footballer that he is. When Bobby went off, they changed completely, to give us a match.

'We just accepted it afterwards. We were so down after losing to West Germany after playing so well and going 2-0 up. Some of us were not able to really believe what had happened. This was the team that won the World Cup in '66 and now they've given it away. I can remember sitting down after the game and Alf ordered a dozen bottles of champagne. We were sitting round the pool, and he started giving a little speech. "What I've got to say, gentlemen, to all of you is that the group of players I had in '70 was better than in '66." It was a very, very fair point. The versatility of the team in '70 was far more than in '66. But playing on your own turf . . . ' He pauses, not wishing to be considered disrespectful. 'But it was a great achievement and probably in the rest of my life I doubt whether we'll see England win a World Cup again. That's the sad part.'

Mullery's also saddened by the behaviour of certain individuals at the FA, especially during his last contact with England at Wembley in 1972. 'There were some old fogeys there at the time. I was on the bench against West Germany at Wembley when they beat us 3-1. Just as the whistle goes, I run round the track because I was freezing, feet cold. I was starting to get changed and felt a touch on my shoulder. I turned round and it was Bert Millichip, the old chairman of the FA [an FA Council member at the time], not with us any more, and he said: "That's the best game I've seen you play for England,

Mullery." I looked at him. "Are you taking the piss?" "What?" "I was on the substitutes' bench." "Oh, oh, all right." And he walked out of the dressing-room. You could see what the Football Association was like. It can't be anything like that now. It's far better now.'

With that, Mullery heads off to entertain the punters, to regale them with stories of his past. He leaves with one final thought: 'I felt really proud to be in the England side at the 1970 World Cup.' Sadly, that tournament marks the true beginning of England's years of hurt.

3

Hard Times

PETER SHILTON JUST cannot bring himself to watch. England's goal-keeper sits on his haunches at the edge of his 6-yard box, back to the action, head bowed, right hand touching the ground for balance, left hand nervously scratching his face. Down the other end, Poland's end, Allan Clarke places the ball on the penalty spot. To a nation's consternation, England trail at Wembley to Jan Domarski's strike in this decisive qualifier for the 1974 World Cup. Clarke, the goal 'Sniffer' of Leeds United legend, makes contact firmly, side-footing the ball confidently into the roof of the net. Poland's heroic Jan Tomaszewski, a keeper unwisely dubbed a 'clown' by Brian Clough in the pre-match television discussions, is finally beaten. Wembley's roar of relief releases Shilton from his stasis. He leaps up, exhaling and celebrating. His joy is short-lived. Tomaszewski resumes his unorthodox defi-ance, the second goal England require never comes, Sir Alf Ramsey manages his last competitive international and England enter the seventies shadowlands. 'Soccer Shocker' and 'The End of the World' screams the following day's *Sun* front page, also claiming that irate fans threw beer cans at Ramsey.

Events of 17 October 1973 are scarred into England's psyche. 'It was devastating,' recalls Shilton. For all the pillorying England and Ramsey receive, it's a freak of a result. Even when reviewed nearly forty-three years on, the contrast between footage and eventual scoreline is astonishing. England have thirty-six attempts on goal to Poland's two, twenty-six corners, four efforts cleared off the line, are denied by the woodwork twice and by Tomaszewski at least seven times. Modern-day statisticians would run out of graphics. 1973 has become a byword for English embarrassment, for the start of their woes. Seven years after ruling the world, England are also-rans. Some collapse. The hysterical reaction merely accentuates the anxiety. A more cerebral nation would analyse the stats, inspect the performance against Poland, and coldly put it down to experience, not trigger panic stations and scramble the life-rafts. This is a serial fault of the English, this tendency of players, managers, administrators and reporters to respond with emotion rather than thought, lashing out rather than working things out. So much for the Stiff Upper Lip. England have plenty of ability on show at Wembley, starting with Shilton in goal behind a back-four of Paul Madeley, Roy McFarland, Norman Hunter and Emlyn Hughes, all capable defenders. Midfield comprises Colin Bell, Tony Currie and the captain Martin Peters, complementing an attack of Mick Channon, Martin Chivers and Clarke – again, more talent. England's bench brims with class: Ray Clemence, Peter Storey, Bobby Moore and Kevin Keegan, while Derby County striker Kevin Hector comes on for Chivers. Yet already the English club system stymies the national team; Ramsey is not helped by an intransigent Football League refusing to contemplate postponing the previous Saturday's games to give England more time to prepare for the key tie. 'If England do lose, the game is not going to die,' harrumphs Alan Hardaker, the League secretary. 'It will be a terrible thing for six weeks and then everybody will forget about it.' Hardaker's attitude pervades football today: players are often tired when reporting for England duty, while the manager of the national team has little time to train them. Same old, same old. Same old blinkered.

To understand the calamitous events of 1973 it first needs remembering what a good Polish side this is, blessed with such stars as Grzegorz Lato, Kazimierz Deyna and Jan Domarski (and missing Włodzimierz Lubański), a group gifted enough to finish third in the World Cup in West Germany the following year. Poland could even have reached the final but for a sapping, rain-soaked pitch against the Germans in Frankfurt.

Poland's ambition at Wembley is accentuated by the final words of their coach, Kazimierz Górski, before they answer the bell summoning them to the tunnel. Górski first fills his players' minds. His tactical instructions are to slow the game down, frustrate England and the 90,587 crowd. Górski then appeals to their hearts. 'Win against a weak team and there is no joy,' he tells them in a speech now embedded in Polish folklore. 'You can play for twenty years and in a thousand games and nobody will remember you. But tonight, in one game, against a team like England and at a place like this, you have the chance to put your names in the history books.' Even now, with the national team struggling, England should never underestimate what a prized scalp they are and how opponents raise themselves, seizing the chance to go down in history.

And so Tomaszewski becomes the bogey-man of English football. Early on, he saves at Clarke's feet, whose right boot breaks the metacarpals in Tomaszewski's left wrist. Poland's eccentric but effective keeper pulls his glove off and hops around in pain as Wembley decries what it perceives as early time-wasting. Chivers walks past and looks witheringly at the Pole. Adrenalin kicks in, masking the pain, and Tomaszewski resumes his mission of frustrating famous England. He blocks a shot from Chivers, pushes away Bell's 18-yarder with his right hand, tips over Channon's header and repels a shot from Currie. He's no clown. He's a fearless acrobat in yellow jersey and red shorts, throwing himself around to intercept the ball. He puts his name in the history books and into the dark recesses of English minds.

The siege lifts long enough for Poland to break out and claim the lead after 57 minutes. Lato dribbles in from the left, exploiting a disastrous attempt at controlling the ball by Hunter, Domarski is too quick for Hughes, and his shot goes under Shilton embarrassingly. 'A tragedy,' proclaims the ITV commentator Hugh Johns. 'It was a strange old game,' recalls Shilton. 'It was one of those games, and I've had two or three in my career, when no matter what I did, I knew I wouldn't get the right result. They had one chance, and it wasn't a great goal. Norman Hunter missed a tackle he would not normally have done, and I let the ball through. I didn't know whether to stop the ball with my legs or my hands and the pace beat me. It did me good in a way. I changed my style after that. I basically got a little more loose with my body, got my shoulders a bit more forward, bent my knees a bit more as I thought I was a bit upright for the shot. It really did help me. A fella called Len Hepple wrote to me and helped me.' A ballroom dancer from the north-east, Hepple has connections in football through his son-in-law 'Pop' Robson, the Newcastle United and West Ham striker. Hepple encourages Shilton to rotate from the hips more, giving him a split-second extra when dealing with an incoming ball. 'It helped me for the rest of my career,' adds Shilton.

For an England legend who boasts his country's appearance record of 125, became the first player to reach 1,000 English League games and won the European Cup twice with Nottingham Forest, Shilton is quite low-key. He's been appointed to the Order of the British Empire but lives quietly with his jazz-singing fiancée in Colchester, Essex. He's done a bit of *Strictly*, is busy on the after-dinner circuit, and does some media. He's popular with his old team-mates. When Mark Wright bumps into Shilton at the Soccerex convention in Manchester in 2015, he shouts 'GOALIE!' and gives his Italia 90 comrade a hug. But for somebody who has acquired a wealth of experience playing under Alf Ramsey, Don Revie, Ron Greenwood, Sir Bobby Robson and Brian Clough, Shilton is rarely called on by the FA.

Shilton's endured financial issues, partly through gambling and divorce, and I find him in Manchester promoting an American technique-enhancing ball-delivery system called Sidekick which he's convinced will help England. Bayern Munich already use it, Shilton points out. 'It's great for coaches,' he explains over coffee. 'It's a great aide. It won't replace a coach. A lot of coaches are ex-players, not getting any younger and probably carrying a few old injuries, and it's very difficult to keep hitting footballs five days a week at goalkeepers and getting the quality of service, getting the power and the pace. The Sidekick machine does that. It can do it at random, it can do different speeds, it can bend it, dip balls. If I want to practise a particular cross, whipped in to the near-post, I can set it to that speed and get that consistent service, so I can practise.'

Practice has always been a prominent word in Shilton's vocabulary. He worked hard as a schoolboy at Leicester City, gradually displacing the mighty Gordon Banks for club and country. Shilton will never forget being summoned by Ramsey for the first time to face East Germany at Wembley on 25 November 1970. 'Oh yes, it was incredible. I was so proud to be called up. I was at Leicester City, my home-town club, and I'd played for England schoolboys, which was my first big ambition, at Wembley in front of 90,000 against Scotland when I was 15. I'd played for the England youth team, got to the world final in Turkey, where we unfortunately lost 1-0 to Russia. I played for the Under-23s, which is now the Under-21s, so I'd got the full set. I went to the World Cup in 1970. I was over there for a month, although I didn't make the final 22.' A week before the tournament starts in Mexico, Shilton flies home (imagine if Ramsey had kept him instead of Bonetti). Ramsey chooses him for the first game after the World Cup. 'We played against the old East Germans at Wembley.' He's just 21. 'It was quite a funny game. I kicked the ball, the old leather ball, three-quarters of the length down the pitch. Allan Clarke flicked the ball on and Francis Lee ran through and scored. I thought the first thing I'd done on my England debut was to make a goal! The game went well.' In winning 3-1, Shilton feels particularly calmed on his debut by the presence of an eminent figure. 'I played behind the great Bobby Moore. He was great because he had that aura. He was one of the boys but you knew he was a leader, and he was special. And he was a great player.'

Fast forward three years and Moore's on the Wembley bench against Poland, having been caught out by Lubański in Chorzów. Hunter starts. It's a controversial call by Ramsey to omit his most celebrated defender, his World Cup-winning captain, for such a tense game. After Hunter's error and Domarski's goal, England hunt the equalizer. Within six minutes they have it. Peters cuts in from the right, taking a tumble under Adam Musiał's challenge and obtaining a soft penalty. Clarke converts. Shilton leaps up in jubilation. The home fans expect the onslaught to resume. It does. All expect Tomaszewski to yield again. He doesn't. He's like a wall, a wobbly one at times, but somehow keeping England at bay, keeping Poland on course for West Germany. He makes an astonishing save from Clarke, who is already turning away in celebration before realizing the ball has not made reacquaintance with the net. Ramsey is later criticized for being too slow to sharpen his attack, for never getting to grips with the idea of changing the game with substitutes. Confusion briefly reigns on the bench with Ramsey's delayed decision to bring on Kevin Hector, a scorer of 19 goals in 49 appearances for Derby that season. Initially there's a scramble to get Kevin Keegan prepared. Hector finally replaces Chivers but for only two minutes. Hector goes close. So does Bell. It's agonizing for England. The Belgian referee Vital Loraux blows the final whistle, which signals the final curtain falling on England's 1974 World Cup dream. 'It's over,' intones Hugh Johns. 'For England, one of the blackest days they've ever had. Sir Alf Ramsey must be a very disheartened man.' The Fifa president, Sir Stanley Rous, looks on. How humiliating that his own country will not be at the Fifa festival of football in West Germany the following year.

Poland will. Their players rush to embrace their keeper. The name of Jan Tomaszewski will now always feature in England's nightmares. Such is his reputation that when Rob Shepherd, then of the *Daily Express* and a buccaneering centre-forward for the press team, manages to score against Tomaszewski in a media match in Katowice, all the English present are stunned. Barring Shep, who leaps into Tomaszewski's arms and kisses him on the cheek.

But that night in 1973 ends with England players sloping from the field, the likes of Hunter with their heads down, scorn building around Ramsey. A fin-de-siècle feel ripples through Wembley. England fans are unnerved, confused, aggrieved at being denied entry to the world party. What happened to our VIP membership card? Ripped up. No longer valid. The shock is enormous. The sixties has bequeathed a sense of entitlement to England. The elation stirred by '66, and also '70 from afar, is so intense that sudden exile is baffling, heart-rending and painful, a stiletto to the heart of the nation. After the 'Swinging Sixties', the 'Dark Ages' headlines capture the seventies of power cuts, industrial disputes and hooliganism, 'Red Robbo' replacing red shirts in the mind's eye and the land of The Beatles now getting off to Slade. I remember heading into school in the dark with the street lights off and warnings ringing in my ears about the need for vigilance as the IRA are targeting central London. Even my satchel gets searched. The seventies prove a largely charmless decade. And yet English clubs are in the ascendant, enjoying a golden era with Liverpool, particularly, Nottingham Forest and Aston Villa dominating the European Cup. We have the best clubs and the worst national team. To be a fan in that era is to suffer a bipolar existence. Spring brings joy with English clubs – admittedly extensively helped by Scots like Kenny Dalglish and Graeme Souness – but when summer comes, anguish deepens as World Cups fall to old foes West Germany and Argentina.

It will be nine years until England grace another World Cup. 'At the time it was devastating,' adds Shilton. 'I could have been playing in five World Cups. '74 in Germany would have been brilliant, we would have got through that. Alf Ramsey would have been manager and I'd still have been England's goalie and Don Revie wouldn't have been the manager of England. Alf Ramsey was the best England manager I played under. Don Revie was good defensively. He had that sterner image. I quite liked Ron Greenwood. A lot of people said he was complicated, but I thought he worked well with Don Howe. Ron liked to play the game the right way. I loved Bobby Robson but Bobby was like a coach-manager. Sir Alf didn't use words lightly and had tremendous respect off the players, a bit like Cloughie. He knew players' strengths and weaknesses, and didn't complicate the game.'

England's World Cup keeper at '82, '86 and '90 hopes the team will prosper at Euro 2016 but has reservations. 'We've got a lot of skilful players but they've got to prove they've got the other qualities to win big games in tournaments,' says Shilton. 'I'd like to see us stronger defensively. Sometimes we do give goals away too easily.'

Before returning to his promotional duties, Shilton has a message for the current England generation. 'I'd tell the young players putting on the shirt now: "Don't miss the moment. It's what you've worked for as a player to play for your country, and certainly in major tournaments, so go the extra mile. Don't just do enough. Don't wait for things to happen, make it happen. Do whatever it takes to get the result, mentally and physically. If you know you've done everything mentally and physically, and you've fought for every ball, and tried to make things happen, then you've got no regrets."'

After Sir Alf Ramsey is bundled away by a graceless FA, England enter the strange era of Don Revie. The mastermind behind the prominence of Leeds United seems a logical appointment, but by the end of his three years in charge, Revie's relationship with the FA will be in the hands of the lawyers. It is one of the most unedifying episodes in English football history, on and off the field. Twenty-two years later the FA, showing not one scintilla of class, sends no flowers, no letter of condolence, no representative to Revie's funeral. It's as if Don Revie OBE, one of English football's foremost managers, never existed for the rulers in their ivory tower at Lancaster Gate. It's as if he's been airbrushed from history. FA wrath over his sudden resignation as England manager in 1977, and the subsequent legal skirmishing, has still not abated when mourners gather at Warriston Crematorium, Edinburgh, on 30 May 1989. Cursed by motor neurone disease, Revie has withered away, dying in exile in Scotland at the tragically early age of 61. The spite in FA hearts and minds is not shared by the England dressing-room. Kevin Keegan, Revie's captain on seven occasions, travels from Spain to pay his last respects. Before entering the chapel, Keegan speaks emotionally to television reporters about Revie. 'He was a father figure to me,' he says. 'He was a great manager, who was just very unfortunate that we didn't have many good players. If the players had been good enough he would have been as good as Alf Ramsey.' Keegan is given to flights of fancy but many respected observers at the time acclaim Revie's exceptional faculties.

The perplexing and sad story of Revie's three-year tenure is one of several mysterious periods that riddle the fifty years of hurt. The accepted version is that Revie is a man obsessed with money who chases United Arab Emirates petro-dollars when England labour.

The situation is more nuanced. Here's one of the most pioneering managers of all time, a title-winning organizer who builds strong teams, most famously at Leeds United. In the ashes of the Ramsey era, a spark is found. Revie, surely, will rekindle England's dream, leading them back on to the road to redemption after losing their way to the 1974 World Cup finals.

So, is Keegan right? Is the playing stock really that diminished? Revie's first selection, against Czechoslovakia on 30 October 1974, is endowed with such talent as the redoubtable keeper Ray Clemence (an able understudy for Shilton), the majestic Colin Bell, the exuberant Mick Channon, Keegan himself and mavericks like Frank Worthington. Launching the Revie era in style, England triumph 3-0. Boos are heard during Revie's second game, a stalemate with Portugal at Wembley. But in the next international, in March 1975, Colin Todd, Malcolm Macdonald and Alan Hudson are involved as West Germany are defeated 2-0. On the eve of his shock departure in July 1977, nine of the Liverpool side that win the European Cup that year are eligible for selection by Revie. The cupboard's not that bare.

Yet Revie feels misgivings about the squad early on, according to his son Duncan. 'The first inkling I had there was a problem was our first match when we beat Czechoslovakia at Wembley in the [qualifiers for the] European Championships,' recalls Duncan, an affable character talking in Manchester at the Soccerex convention he masterminds. 'We played really well. Colin Bell played in midfield. We went back to the suite next door, where all the press were, having drinks, and he looked miserable. I said: "Dad, come and sit down. You don't look happy." There was all this "Revie Messiah" going on, all this "we're going to win the European Championships". "We haven't got the players," he said. The first match! Then he lost Colin Bell. Alan Ball ran out of legs. He lost Gerry Francis as well. The whole midfield went. He had this thing that Bremner, Giles and Gray could be reproduced in an England team, and their attitude and professionalism, but he really struggled with the players.'

On accepting the England role, Revie leaves behind a footballing family at Elland Road and finds it difficult to embrace or create another one. He plans to rebuild England in Leeds' image, international white shirt for club white shirt, when many of his Leeds stalwarts are Scottish or Irish. He introduces dietary restrictions and the quirky custom of free-time activities like carpet bowls, not always appreciated by players of rival clubs. Leeds obsess Revie. 'As kids, my sister Kim and I were booted out of bed at 7.30, dropped off at school at eight, an hour before anybody else, kicking our heels in the playground because Dad wanted to get to the ground to open it,' remembers Duncan. 'He had a key, opened the big padlock in the door at Elland Road, spent two hours with the groundsman and washing ladies, everyone in the ground, before the stars started to come in the ground at ten.' Revie relishes this day-to-day involvement, this opportunity to spend time drilling the players in his tactical ways – a luxury simply not afforded an England manager who must treat the team like a mistress, grabbing hungrily every second of the few hours spent together.

Much hoopla is generated by the 'dossiers' Revie presents to players at Leeds, a version continuing with England. 'It was completely ridiculous,' says Duncan. 'This dossier thing never existed. What he did do was send scouts out to look at the opposition centre-half, and tell Allan Clarke: "If you go past him on his left, he's stronger than if you go past him on his right." It's common-sense stuff. People didn't do it in those days. They got translated into these "dossiers". They weren't dossiers at all.' Digital dossiers are de rigueur now. FA staff send short analyses of opponents to England players' iPads. Revie's a revolutionary.

If his Leeds fixation complicates his England attitude, this much-maligned manager deserves some sympathy. Revie has to contend with the rise of some fine teams on the Continent, not least the Czechs who recover from their Wembley setback to qualify ahead of England for Uefa 76 and win it with Antonín Panenka's serene 'falling leaf' penalty in the final against West Germany in Belgrade. Losing 2-0 to Italy in Rome on 17 November 1976 deeply damages England's World Cup qualifying hopes but is hardly a humiliation given the quality of opponent, such able Azzurri as Dino Zoff, Claudio Gentile, Marco Tardelli, Giacinto Facchetti, Franco Causio, Fabio Capello,

Francesco Graziani, Giancarlo Antognoni and Roberto Bettega. Italy finish fourth at Argentina 78.

Revie enjoys decent playing resources to construct a capable team but is ambushed in qualifying and never seems comfortable with England. Playing the underdog card works at Elland Road, a collective assailed as 'Dirty Leeds', but not with the national team, supposedly a breed of top dogs, the best in show in the country. 'I was sitting on the patio in Spain with him after he'd retired,' continues Duncan. 'When Dad looked back, he talked more about Leeds but he was not afraid to talk about England. He talked about England with passion. A lot of people forget he was a good player.' During his time at Manchester City, Revie scores four times in six England internationals. As a player, he's ahead of his time. 'He played the "Hidegkuti" role, the deep-lying centre-forward,' adds Duncan.

As a manager with England, Revie misses his beloved Leeds and despises the FA. 'The regret with England was that he hated not being involved day to day. He hated the politics. He hated the fact that decisions couldn't be made fairly quickly by fairly sensible individuals.' Old enmities from his time at Elland Road also conspire against him. The only thing that Revie and FA chairman Sir Harold Thompson, an Oxford Blue and distinguished chemist, share in common is a mutual loathing. Thompson's condescension towards the working-class Revie is vintage FA. 'He and Thompson hated each other from first sight,' says Duncan. 'That didn't help. Professor Sir Harold Thompson was very much "these people are serfs, they work for me, bowing and scraping, and tugging the forelock". Dad didn't like that. He almost gave up on getting decisions made quickly.' At one point, Revie goes to see Alan Hardaker, appealing for him to move those Football League games before an England game. No chance. 'There didn't seem to be any help. Even in those days the international team seemed to be secondary where the Football League is all-powerful.'

The authorities must bear some culpability for the manager's growing frustration. So must Revie. For a man whose mantra is 'keep fighting', Revie folds too easily. He begins feeling in the dark for the exit door. In June 1977, on the pretext of preparing for the

Italy qualifier at Wembley on 16 November, Revie misses a friendly against Brazil and makes contact with the UAE. 'He was told by good sources that he was about to be sacked after the Italy game,' explains Duncan. 'They [the FA] were talking to Bobby Robson.' Revie has one significant, honourable supporter in the corridors of power: the former FA president George Lascelles, 7th Earl of Harewood. Leeds United's president, a man of grace and conscience motivated only by doing what is right for the game, becomes aware of plotting against his friend and former manager. 'Lord Harewood said he'd heard exactly the same thing,' adds Duncan. 'It was fairly turbulent.'

By now a frustrated figure, Revie leaves for the UAE, announcing his defection in an exclusive with Jeff Powell of the *Daily Mail*. 'Revie Quits Over Aggro' shouts the headline over Powell's story. 'I know people will accuse me of running away . . .' Revie tells Powell. And they do. Piqued by the *Mail*'s agenda-setting exclusive, rival newspapers pour scorn on Revie from a great height. 'My mum's family were coalminers in Scotland and Dad was a very, very tough person, so we were a fairly resilient family,' recalls Duncan. 'It was very upsetting to see him vilified but it goes with the territory. The big mistake, looking back, was doing the exclusive with Jeff Powell. All the other press lads were killed because their editors were saying: "You were supposed to be big friends with Don Revie so how come you didn't get the story?" So he got doubly castigated.

'He never was "in disguise" when he went to the Middle East. There were no "hoods and scarves". It was a load of rubbish. However he'd left the England job he would have still been castigated because it's not something you were supposed to do. He had this image of being greedy. He wasn't greedy. He was from a working-class background. He was always careful with money, but generous to a fault. It's a really strange dichotomy.' The press nicknames him 'Don Readies'. Duncan winces. 'It does annoy me. The people who knew him knew the real Dad, and knew he was quite the polar opposite of that. That's not just a son looking through rose-tinted spectacles. Anybody who knew him even half well, from the cleaning lady at Elland Road right through to the biggest stars, knew he wasn't driven by money.'

Telling the Blazers at Lancaster Gate to go to blazes comes at a cost. A humiliated FA clicks into full vengeful mode. Thompson wants Revie in Purdah, not in Dubai. A ten-year suspension on managing any English side is imposed for bringing the game into disrepute. Outraged, Revie inevitably fights this punitive sentence, taking the case to the High Court. He wins, but at further cost to his reputation. Endorsing public revulsion of Revie's flit to the Gulf, the judge Sir Joseph Cantley accuses him of 'a sensational and notorious example of disloyalty, breach of duty, discourtesy and selfishness'. The enlightened Harewood apart, the establishment detests the former apprentice bricklayer. His son believes Cantley to be in awe of Thompson. 'I don't think I've met anybody who didn't have problems with Thompson apart from the judge who did Dad's case. The judge was very much "Professor Sir Harold Thompson, Corinthian-Casuals" and carried a lot more weight than the bricklayer from Middlesbrough, who played at the very highest level. Kevin Keegan was European Footballer of the Year at that stage and the judge had to ask, "Who is Kevin Keegan?" and get his name spelled – and he was judging the case. So we didn't get a good press from him. Even though we won, Dad had gone back to Dubai so I was in court taking the verdict and then I was mobbed on the outside steps. The press said: "What are you going to do?" "First of all, I'm not going to say anything. Secondly, I'm now going to phone my dad in Dubai and tell him we won." But if you looked at the press the next day we could have lost. It was unbelievable! Although we knew it was a completely 100 per cent watertight case. It was Thompson who forced it through. It was totally illegal. It was total vindictiveness. You're not supposed to resign? Alf Ramsey heard about his sacking on the television, famously, and he is still the most successful manager of all time.'

Harewood frequently observed that Revie was the most under-rated manager in the history of football. 'There was a top ten of all time and he got in at eighth or ninth,' smiles Duncan. 'I don't think within football circles that he's under-rated at all. People around at the time of the bad publicity got a jaundiced impression of him. Now he's come back, funnily enough, from that Clough–Revie film [*The*

Damned United]. Even so long after his death he's still in newspapers. Leeds fans still hero-worship him.'

Duncan Revie is larger-than-life, a successful businessman with his Soccerex conferences, but he shrinks when speaking about watching his much-loved father succumb to motor neurone disease. 'I can almost not talk about it. It was horrendous. Being him, he didn't give in to it. He fought it. He went from my size, 16 stone, to 6.5 stone. He could only speak through blinking, once for "yes" and twice for "no". He lost everything. But his brain was as sharp as it had ever been. It is a horrible, horrible death. It took the best part of two years and it was the worst time of my life. He and I both knew it was completely terminal. I have to say the Sheikhs in Dubai were sensational, not just in backing him with the FA case, but they flew him behind the Iron Curtain to try and get the best medical assistance. They thought they had some sort of breakthrough on motor neurone disease and they were absolutely wonderful. They flew him to Moscow to get specialist treatment. It was Cold War time but they weren't part of it.

'The Clough–Revie film was interesting, not a bad watch, but they got it so wrong at the end, that Dad went off to some desert hide-away. Mum and Dad had six of the best years of their life out there. It was wonderful. The people out there were wonderful.' In his latter years, Revie moves to Kinross to honour a long-standing promise to his wife Elsie, who hails from Scotland. 'My last conversation with Dad was in an Edinburgh hospital [the Murrayfield], and it was three days before he died. He knew he had gone in there and wasn't going to come out. I knew from previous times that, almost as if he'd been able to articulate it, "Son, this is enough now." On the last day I spoke with him – well, communicated with him – he was still able to half smile. That was the last time. I miss him every day. He was magnetic – unlike the image portrayed by the press.

'The name Revie is still an inspiration right now. People do react in the strangest places. Some people are so young that I can't believe they'd know who Dad was. Then there's a certain vintage who knew exactly who Dad was, and I do get that "no relation?" He was a hugely warm father. It was a wonderful upbringing. My sister and I are going to put up a plaque on the statue at Elland Road this year because there are little spaces for plaques, saying, "He was a great manager but an even greater father." And he was. He did come and see me play at Repton, a great football school. I came off and said: "What do you think?" "Well, you're not bad in the air, got a good right foot, and you can see a pass but, frankly, son, I could turn a double-decker bus quicker. Stick to the studies."' Duncan laughs at the memory.

He glowers at the memory of the FA's callousness after his father passes away. 'The FA didn't send flowers or a representative to his funeral. There was no minute's silence at any of the games. Nothing. It's outrageous. It's so petty-minded and it summed up the FA then. It's different now. The new chief executive Martin Glenn seems a proper chap. I've got great hopes that he will move the FA even more forward. It couldn't get worse than Thompson.'

It's an age of FA arrogance and, even more damagingly, a suspicion of creativity.

4

Fear of Flair

WITH THE BALL at his feet, Glenn Hoddle has the world at his feet. Aged 15, and turning out one day for his father's amateur side in Harlow, Essex, in the early 1970s, Hoddle begins running with the ball at the opposition. He beats five players with his quick feet before stroking the ball into the net. Four decades on, Hoddle's eyes sparkle at the memory. 'One fella on the other team came up to me, shook my hand, ruffled my hair, and said: "That's unbelievable! UNBELIEVABLE!" Another came right up to me and said: "You do that again, I'll fucking BREAK YOUR LEG." I smiled. I thought he was messing about. "I fucking mean it," he said.' While recalling the incident, Hoddle grins as well as grimaces. 'There were 20 minutes of the game left and he was flying in, furious, trying to break my leg. I was one touch, two touch.' Safety first. The teenager doesn't dare risk another dribble with such a nihilist stalking him.

Listening to the story evokes only sadness. How many skilful kids become fearful and alienated, even lost to English football, because of such Neanderthals? Swathes of the game in that era are locked in 4-4-2, roughhouse tactics and balls launched into the mixer. The anti-flair brigade terrorize football for too long, given a licence to kill creativity by parents screaming 'Get stuck in!', supine referees, macho coaches and an FA misguidedly committed to robust, direct football as promoted by its director of coaching, Charles Hughes, dubbed by the newspapers 'Doctor Death of the Beautiful Game'. His approach is slightly more nuanced than perceived but hardly establishes a platform for virtuosos.

Hoddle's grace in possession is appreciated at Tottenham Hotspur and then Monaco but one of the rarest natural talents ever produced in England, a beacon during the dark ages, is never properly used by his country. What a waste. England ignore the message in Spurs' DNA and in Hoddle's soul: 'To Dare Is To Do'. Hoddle dares. England dither.

As a creative player and forward-thinking coach, Hoddle's frustrating experiences go to the heart of English travails and the lengthening years of hurt. There's always been a sense that the King of White Hart Lane is a monarch misunderstood by the rest of the land. In other countries, Hoddle would be running the technical department of the national association. Instead, we meet in a restaurant in cold but scenic Vilnius hours before Hoddle goes on ITV to dissect the performance of Roy Hodgson's side against Lithuania in their final Euro 2016 qualifier on 12 October 2015. Beyond an instructive column in the *Mail on Sunday*, Hoddle can be wary of the press, following the painful, controversial denouement to his time as England manager for making offensive comments about the disabled. Deeply distressing and disgusting as such personal views were, Hoddle remains one of the most perceptive thinkers about the game and it is sad that the FA is still cautious about drawing deeply on his profound knowledge. His story has many lessons for the FA and modern England.

He reflects sanguinely on that teenaged brush with the brutes, accentuating the positives, believing it prepared him for the rigours to come in the professional game. 'That taught me such a lesson,' Hoddle says. 'That helped me, because in the real game it was so physical. I didn't need to be told again. I just knew they'd snap me in two if they had the chance. I learned about the physical side from a young age. As a schoolboy at Tottenham, we'd sit right near the pitch at White Hart Lane, with the linesmen running just in front of us and with people standing behind us. I was only 13, 14. I actually felt in the game. My God! The smell of the liniment! The physicality of it! I watched Mike England and Peter Osgood, and heard the sound of the studs clashing. Mike England puts his elbow straight into Osgood. Nothing's said. Next minute, Osgood's done him. Claret everywhere. You could get away with it then. Mike England would stick his elbow in Osgood, and the ref would go: "Tut, tut, tut! Don't do that!" Then maybe in the second half, he might have to book him. It was outrageous! Phil Beal once came sliding in, took Osgood out and came flying into us. The verbals! Joe Kinnear! Playing in front of us for one half. "Fucking useless cunt," Kinnear would say. I learned a lot sitting on those little benches. I thought: "Hang on a minute, Glenn, you're not going to just get the ball and do what you want to do." I went home and said: "Dad, I can't believe how physical it is. They're kicking lumps out of each other!" In France, Spain and Germany it would still be tough but creative players could play. In England it was so physical.'

Not Hoddle. He's the arts scholar expressing himself in the school of hard knocks, the antithesis of the clattering classes. His nickname of 'Glenda', a pejorative perspective from tribal terraces, hints at English unease with footballing sophisticates. A more progressive view came from Brian Clough, who states 'it takes moral courage to play the way Hoddle does'. Hoddle plays with courage and imagination, sweeping passes around, scoring majestic goals – 110 in 490 appearances for Spurs – and always loyal to the club creed that 'the game is about glory'. Dead ball or moving, dribbling or first time, Hoddle takes the ball on a magical journey in an era of many journeymen. There's the Cruyff turn on Watford's Jan Lohman and chip over Steve Sherwood in 1983, a balletic volley past Manchester United's Gary Bailey and glide through Oxford United's defence in 1987, the ball scarcely touched, the opponents bypassed with a flick of the hips before Hoddle rolls the ball into the net. Glorious. Hoddle's legacy at the Lane is immortalized in being the bench-mark and lyrical material for dazzling arrivals. 'He's just as good as Hoddle, he's better than Chris Waddle, his missus is a model, it's Rafa van der Vaart' sing Spurs fans in honour of their stylish Dutchman for a couple of seasons.

Hoddle is raised on the ingenuity of Frank Worthington, Stan Bowles, Alan Hudson, Rodney Marsh, Peter Osgood and Tony Currie, mavericks never fully trusted by a nation preferring the clenched fist to the velvet touch, muscle over adventure. It's no country for bold men. 'It's the British Bulldog way, isn't it?' continues Hoddle.

'Loads of people – professionals, fans, even my family – have told me: "You should have been born French." As soon as I go to France I get appreciated totally differently. I was lucky I played for Tottenham, a purist team, and we had to play with the traditions of the club, but with the way the game was played it was hard. To be a creative footballer, you were fighting against the tide with the way we played in England. As a kid growing up in the seventies when England did nothing, I was watching Worthington, Bowles, Hudson, Marsh, Osgood, Currie. There were some lovely players around then. Wasn't it ironic that we did absolutely nothing when we had all those creative players? We didn't qualify for the World Cup for ten years. Everyone's thoughts in England were 4-4-2. It was a long-ball game, the ball was in the air more than ever.

'It made me smile when I did the Palace–West Brom game recently and it was going back to the old days when goalies weren't throwing the ball out, back-fours were squeezing up and it was aerial battles all the time, and I was thinking: "I had to play in that." So did Peter Beardsley. So did loads of really skilful players, and it was tough. I was in the wrong country at the wrong time. 4-4-2! I was a technician with two feet. That's what Platini and Zidane were – natural foot-ballers. We distrusted the natural footballer, i.e., the maverick. I was thinking: "I'm a technician, where am I going to fit into this?"

'People still come up to me and talk about how I played, giving memories of different goals, not just one. If I'd wanted to be a maverick, I could have been the biggest maverick of them all. I could have abused the game with the talent I had, with what I could do with a ball, left foot, right foot. I could have dropped the ball on my toe, flicked it over someone, really taking the piss, being flash, just to be a maverick. I could have done so many more things on the pitch that weren't right for the team but were right for me. I never was like that. I had the talent to do it but I wasn't flamboyant or big-headed. I was very much the other way, because of the upbringing my parents gave me. I used to do some outrageous things in training but on a pitch it had to be done with an end product. If I was going to bring the ball on my chest and volley it was because it was going to get a player in.' Inventiveness dedicated to the team effort.

Fittingly, given the fog of doubt that follows Hoddle's international career, bad weather delays by twenty-four hours his England debut against Bulgaria on 22 November 1979. 'That was ironic! I waited as a schoolboy, dreaming of playing for my country. Ron Greenwood told me three days before actually naming the team. I tried to settle down and sleep, but was visualizing how I'd play. Then on the coach, I saw the fog and was thinking: "Surely not?" As we got closer to Wembley with the lights, I thought: "Hang on a minute, this is getting a bit serious." I went on the pitch, stood on the halfway line, couldn't see the goalposts and [was] thinking: "This could be off."' It soon is. Hoddle's phlegmatic. 'I might have had a nightmare that day. The next day I played really well, scored a really good goal, made the other goal and had a great game. So it was a blessing in disguise.

'I was so excited. Representing my country was something I'd always dreamed I'd do and then when it happens, walking up the tunnel, there's no feeling like it, walking up quite a steep slope and you suddenly start to see the opposite end of Wembley. The fog had gone! You first see the fans high up, standing in those days, the fans right at the top of the stands. As you walk up, the vista gets bigger, and you see more fans. Then suddenly you enter, and it's all the fans, all the noise. It was a magnificent way to enter an arena. I wish they'd kept that tunnel somehow in the new stadium. That walk was unbelievable, unique, and they've taken that away which is a great shame for players. It was just wonderful, and to score a goal was something dreams are made of.' Trevor Francis lays the ball across and Hoddle guides it adroitly home from 20 yards.

'Making my debut, I thought: "OK, here we go, set sail." But I played that Bulgaria game and then didn't play for three games which was really frustrating.' Despite this well-received debut, Hoddle is overlooked against the Republic of Ireland, Spain and Argentina before returning against Wales on 17 May 1980. 'I always enjoyed playing for my country but it was frustrating. I played mostly on the right wing which really did frustrate me.' Typical England: fielding creative players out of position (see Paul Scholes at Euro 2004). 'Stevie Coppell was a better winger than me. He should have played in that position. I probably played two games in the right position in a role that suited me, the number 10 role.' Hoddle does earn plaudits when partnering Peter Reid in an orthodox English midfield at Mexico 86, following the injury to Bryan Robson and suspension of Ray Wilkins. 'No, that was just 4-4-2,' he replies. 'I'm on about Hungary away when I played just behind the front two, [Paul] Mariner and [Luther] Blissett.' The date is 12 October 1983, at the old playground of Ferenc Puskás, the Nep Stadium in beautiful Budapest. 'I scored one and made one for Mariner,' recalls Hoddle of that game when he stars in a diamond formation. 'There was another game at Wembley against Wales when I played behind Peter Withe but that was like a British game, the ball was in the air.'

He uses his head, not really for heading, more for analysing possibilities in games. 'Even as a youngster I used to think about the game, and I had a lot of say at Tottenham, even at 20, 21. I was always saying what I felt because I'd see the game with a different eye. I used to think: "Why do we keep playing 4-4-2?" I remember playing against Spain, I scored [a fabulous volley], we lost 2-1 at Wembley.' It's 25 March 1981. Spain play one up in Jesús Satrústegui, and flood midfield. 'We've got Terry Butcher and Dave Watson, two big centre-halves who on a Saturday were going to go and head it, and that's where the manager would judge his centre-backs, but we were being run ragged. It was so rigid. There wasn't enough thought on how the opposition were going to play. It's a hangover from the 1966 World Cup. We got held in a vacuum where the rest of football went on, and we stayed rigid in 4-4-2. If George Best had been English in '66, I don't think he would have been a given with Alf Ramsey. If Alf wanted to take away the wingers, George Best might have been a question-mark whether he played. Bobby Charlton was a world-class player, a beautiful player. Alf Ramsey did what he did at the time when it was right and it worked. We stopped still for twenty years. We didn't advance the coaching system.

'The Spanish back then, they played a different way, making

different shapes on the pitch, but we kept playing the same way. We became too predictable. That was the FA, Charles Hughes, English football in general. That's why in those days we had to go long all the time. It used to drive me mad. At Tottenham they used to pass through the pitch. A lot of teams played long balls. Centre-halves were going, "I don't want to give it to him there [short], because he might give it to me back," so they were going boom, boom, boom.' The percussive sound of long balls and English oblivion. Some of Hoddle's best football comes when he has a midfield minder at Spurs in Steve Perryman.

Support for Hoddle comes from two of the most adept ball-users of that era. 'I remember even after training, Glenn would just be juggling the ball, doing incredible things with the ball,' says his old England colleague John Barnes. 'I could see he had this technical ability far better than anyone else. Left foot, right foot. Glenn would have had 100 caps in any other country because Glenn was a particular type of player, not a British type of player.' Chris Waddle concurs. 'We didn't use Glenn properly,' says his former Spurs, England and *Top of the Pops* collaborator. 'To get the best out of Glenn you'd need two lads sitting in front grafting to get the ball to him. You'd need two wingers who can move, get on the ball, make runs, and a striker who's quick. Ideally, Gary Lineker. I felt for Glenn. Everyone was obsessed with 4-4-2. If people questioned anything about Glenn it would have been work-rate, but he did his fair share. OK, he wasn't the best tackler in the world. I remember talking to Manuel Amoros who played with Glenn at Monaco and he went, "Wow, what a player." Arsène Wenger knew how to play Glenn: "Let him go and play."' Waddle pleads for platforms for virtuoso performers. 'Barcelona know how to get the best out of Messi, Suárez, Neymar – the side is built around talent. Yes, they close people down in areas, but once that ball's been transferred, they think, "Find space, and we'll get the ball to you." At Marseille that was all I got taught all the time. Why in England do you have to be running back all the time, getting on top of the full-back? I couldn't work it out. Managers in Marseille said to me: "Stop coming back, stay up there. I pay [Didier] Deschamps and others fortunes to get the ball back and give it to you." Why can't we play like that? At times, you have to run back and fill in, you do chase certain things and go deep, but they want you in their half ready to go.'

Further endorsement of Hoddle's talent comes from Peter Shilton. 'Glenn was in the side for a reason – to provide quality,' says Shilton. 'Glenn was a great player.' Yet his country largely wastes his unique capabilities. On becoming national coach in 1996, Hoddle is determined to avoid mistakes that held back his international career. At Euro 96, Terry Venables liberates England, encouraging more creativity after the stale Graham Taylor years, and Hoddle builds on that. 'My number one criteria was the fact that I played for England and I chased the ball, even against Yugoslavia and Romania,' resumes Hoddle. 'Technically they were better than us overall, and they had a system where they would try and pass through the pitch. We'd get outnumbered. So as soon as I got the England job, I looked at the players and said: "We can do this." That's why I played five in midfield and three at the back in possession. We needed extra bodies in midfield to win the ball back and it kept the two up – that's an England tradition. I thought: "I'm not going to go away from that." I had great strikers to choose from. I wanted to keep my two up which then forces the other team into a back-four and makes their full-backs defend rather than attack. The system took some time to bed in. It took some time for the players to go from club level to this – Sol Campbell and Tony Adams, for instance. Sol coming into the left-back position to get the ball was a fish out of water for the first couple of games. In the end he loved it, because he was getting the ball, and closing it up when we lost it.'

Hoddle's England management is no homage to gung-ho. Pragmatism colours his thinking too. He discards Matt Le Tissier when one of the most gifted technical players of the era does not deliver. Hoddle certainly brings the best out of a young Paul Scholes, using the Manchester United midfielder as the creative fulcrum of his 3-5-2 system. 'Scholesy was ideal for that,' says Hoddle. 'I loved Paul Scholes. You only had to tell him something once. He was really important for the system. There were times when he had to be really intelligent, and defensively had to pick up a different position. If a team were playing against us with two up, Scholesy would be fine. "OK, you can play in behind defensively and with the ball." I used to say: "Right, now you've got to play a little bit left side when we haven't got the ball." He was switched on, right away.'

The misuse of Scholes by Sven-Göran Eriksson in particular stands as one of the most grievous missed opportunities of the half-century of hurt. Here is a player hailed in his prime by Pep Guardiola as the 'best midfielder of his generation' and by Xavi as 'in the last fifteen to twenty years [. . .] the best central midfielder I have seen'. That Spanish pair should know about intelligent, classy central midfielders. Other prominent members of the Scholes fan club include Zinedine Zidane, Marcello Lippi and Edgar Davids. Although Scholes later argues that Eriksson's positioning of him on the left 'was never a problem', it is a clogged midfield at Euro 2004 with Steven Gerrard and Frank Lampard. Just listen to Hoddle. 'There were times when I looked at Scholesy and thought: "Yeah, I know how you feel. You should be in there, running the show, but you're out there on the left."'

Positioned in a string-pulling central role, Scholes flourishes under Hoddle at France 98 when the coach's tactical qualities are seen best in adversity. Shortly into the second half against Argentina in St-Etienne on 30 June, Hoddle faces his toughest challenge as a manager, re-jigging a depleted team. Falling into an Argentine trap and kicking out at the sly Diego Simeone, David Beckham's naivety costs England; he leaves behind ten men as he slopes away, dismissed and disgraced. 'Everyone looked at me,' recalls Hoddle. 'That's where you get tested as a manager. It's the biggest game of my life as a manager, and the biggest game of most of their lives on the pitch. It's a titanic battle.'

Although eventually sunk, Hoddle's calm, clever response adds to the reputation nurtured in that qualifying draw against Italy in Stadio Olimpico on 11 October 1997. 'Rome was the best performance. Argentina was the most courageous as well as good football, to go for an hour and ten, that length of time, against a good side. Most people would have thought: "Well, he'll take one of the strikers off."' Wrong. Hoddle stays strong. He could sacrifice Michael Owen, leaving Alan Shearer as the sole striker. 'I'm going to keep them both on,' he tells his trusted assistant John Gorman, organizing the resistance, ordering Shearer and Owen to take it in turns to play on the left. 'We'll do it in spells,' Hoddle advises Gorman. 'Then the centre-halves one minute have got somebody with pace, and then somebody strong. They're not getting used to the same person. I know Alan will see it off when he comes over on the left-hand side but if Michael can't deal with it, if he lets the full-back go, and we're struggling, and Graeme [Le Saux] has got too much overload, we are just going to have to take him off.'

'Are you sure?' asks Gorman, wondering about the wisdom of keeping two forwards on.

'Yes, I think we need a goal threat,' Hoddle replies.

Shearer and Owen take selflessly to their emergency duties. 'I did it on the left-hand side so we could coach them. I was playing the game for them, constantly screaming at them: "over your shoulder", "deeper, deeper, Michael". Michael showed unbelievable maturity for an 18-year-old to run with the full-back defensively. He had the pace to deal with it, then I'd give him a breather, shout "Michael, swap over", release him from the pressure and Alan had to do it. I wanted to go on and win the game because it was Golden Goal. One of them could score at any given moment. So why take one off? It wasn't a case of let's hang on for penalties.' The possibility of a Golden Goal in St-Etienne still inhabits Hoddle's thoughts. He's convinced Kim Milton Nielsen is about to award England a spot-kick for a hand-ball by Roberto Ayala during extra time. England could have won it with a Golden Goal penalty, especially with the nerveless Shearer on the field. 'That's why he didn't give the hand-ball: the referee goes like that with his whistle [he motions to his lips], and then waves play on. Ray Clemence and me reacted. I saw Alan react. He was in the area. He went like that [a hand-ball gesture], but I didn't see a reaction from the other players.' Penalties do eventually prove decisive, England going out in the shoot-out in the usual fashion.

Waving ruefully to the crowd on disembarking from Concorde at Luton, Hoddle still returns home with status enhanced. Coaches of the calibre of Rinus Michels and Gérard Houllier note in Fifa's Technical Studies Group appraisal that 'England confirmed the progress they have made under Glenn Hoddle, with their excellent organization, strong individual players and a good mixture of experience and young talent (Owen). But a lack of control at decisive moments (Beckham's red card) and bad luck in the penalty battle against Argentina saw them eliminated earlier than they deserved. Hoddle is to be congratulated for his courage in using all these young players in the World Cup.' Scholes embodies Hoddle's daring. 'At the tender age of 24, he is another player regarded as a future rocket in the English regiment. This is a team with a future; they will be a force to reckon with in the next major international competitions.' England seem in good hands.

'Glenn has a footballing knowledge and intelligence that was way ahead of his time,' says Barnes. 'If Glenn had been a coach in the eighties he'd have brought English football up to speed with the rest of the world. He implemented his ideas in '98, and should have continued. Glenn should still be the England manager now.'

The circumstances of Hoddle's departure form one of the darker chapters of England's history, and can be distilled into a moral for those who wish to do – and keep – the job one day. The lesson is to beware the proliferation of seemingly surmountable smaller issues building into a perfect storm when results turn disappointing. If results are good, the same problems blow over rather than coalesce into a hurricane. The start to Euro 2000 qualifying is disastrous, England losing to Sweden with Paul Ince sent off followed by a badly received draw with Bulgaria at Wembley. Hoddle becomes vulnerable.

Criticism already courses his way following the publication of *Glenn Hoddle: My 1998 World Cup Story*, a book of revelations he now regrets. It's ill-advised, ill-timed, and inevitably perceived as profiting from dressing-room secrets. A strain of hypocrisy still stains the outcry. Bobby Robson penned something similar to little rebuke. Hoddle's book sparks a furious reaction inside Lancaster Gate yet it is approved in advance by the FA; its director of communications David Davies even ghosts it. Along with the book, Hoddle's promotion of the faith healer Eileen Drewery, pint-puller, agony aunt and figure of fun/miracle-worker, embarrasses the FA and annoys some players, amuses others and helps a few. In the press we have a field day with the Drewery story before France 98: she's dubbed 'Voodoo Woman', with England flying out to the World Cup on a 'mumbo-jumbo jet'. Adding to media merriment is Ray Parlour's fabled 'short back and sides, please' quip when Drewery lays her 'healing hands' on Ginger-locks' head. The memory of Rome and his tactical prowess in St-Etienne fades. Hoddle is now a target. Questions surface about Hoddle's man-management, dating back to before France when Teddy Sheringham is angered by the manager's command that he read a statement to the press apologizing for being pictured smoking in a bar in Portugal at six a.m. Over at the Irish hotel, Jack Charlton and his players, including Sheringham's close friend Tony Cascarino, watch stunned as the England forward is made to say sorry to the cameras.

Tension simmers. Partly to improve media relations, Hoddle gives a phone interview to *The Times*' Matt Dickinson, one of the most respected journalists in this country. There's no question of Hoddle being misquoted, or 'twirled' in Fleet Street parlance. During the interview, Hoddle foolishly comments that the disabled are paying the price for sins in a previous life. 'You and I have been physically given two hands and two legs and half-decent brains,' Hoddle tells Dickinson. 'Some people have not been born like that for a reason. The karma is working from another lifetime. It is not only people with disabilities. What you sow, you have to reap.' The concept of karma, and its place in religious tracts, is an odd thing to mention in a football interview. Alarm bells should ring in Hoddle's head. Don't go there. He is naive even to stray down that line of enquiry. England managers are given media training but some don't listen. Similar nonsense spilled from Hoddle's lips in a previous radio interview but the results are worse now, the mood less forgiving. The fact that the interview is run in *The Times* and the byline belongs to Dickinson increases the gravity of the situation. Prime Minister Tony Blair gets involved, as headline-chasing politicians are wont to do given football's profile. When he tells the chat-show hosts Richard Madeley and Judy Finnigan that Hoddle should go, the coach is history. Under extreme pressure, the FA, an organization rarely steadfast in the line of fire, makes four demands of Hoddle: release a proper apology, hold a mea culpa press conference, stick to football comments in future interviews, and get rid of Drewery. Hoddle refuses. The FA sack him the next day, 2 February 1999. Presented with such raw material, Shakespeare would have feasted on the tragedy of a footballing king brought low by character flaws. A final indignity awaits the departing manager, a valedictory press conference in a west London hotel gate-crashed by the father of a disabled son. He calls Hoddle an 'absolute disgrace' as he ploughs through rows of chairs and startled reporters towards the podium. It's an excruciating end to a reign that promised so much.

Still only 40 during the World Cup, Hoddle really needs a mentor, an experienced, older manager to provide advice without agenda. He needs a gnarled guide to urge care and caution when stepping through the media minefield. He requires somebody to warn of the particular perils of giving phone interviews: the interviewee cannot see the inquisitor's reaction to certain questions, a raised eyebrow or stare that might prompt a re-think about an answer.

During our conversation in Vilnius, and not relating to the circumstances of his own demise, Hoddle floats the idea of senior statesmen assisting the next generation. 'When I was a young manager, Bobby Robson or Terry Venables helped. Why not have a consultancy in football helping a young manager? Go in and say "that's good", "change that", "what about if you did this?". Learn off my experience. I'd forewarn them. Football's missing that experience and knowledge. I've always thought out of the box just as I played out of the box. I play golf with a lot of people, corporate stuff, and talk to people, ask them what they do, and they say: "I've had twenty-five years in the oil business, retired, but I go to America to do a bit of consultancy." I smile. Why doesn't football do consultancy like the oil business?

Other businesses keep people who've been in the business a long time and use them in different ways.'

Maybe a wise owl would have steered Hoddle away from the rocks of hubris and sanctimony. His fall, albeit self-inflicted, is a calamity for England. He's a visionary as a coach, a manager who gets England players performing with belief, skill and tactical intelligence, building on Venables' work. Hoddle uses Scholes properly. He wants to build on the strides made at France 98, instilling more fluidity. He watches aghast ensuing events at Euro 2000 under his hapless successor, Kevin Keegan. 'I'm so frustrated with what happened at the Euros,' reflects Hoddle, his voice full of regret. 'I had a young Rio Ferdinand, who I had massive plans for. I played him in my last game, against the Czech Republic at Wembley, and he was magnificent: he came through into midfield, on the ball. He was 20. I took him at 19 to the World Cup for experience. I had this exciting way of playing that I knew Rio would have elevated even more. I had Incey's experience to just fill in. I had Scholes and Beckham who were going to progress even more, get to their peak in the next couple of years, and then Michael Owen, who set the world alight with his goal against Argentina, as well as having the likes of Seaman, Shearer, Adams, Neville, that nucleus of experience. I had that magic formula every manager looks for of experience and really good young players. That's what frustrated me about not getting the chance through the next two years. What we could have done with that group of players.' But Keegan, all heart but not enough head, takes over. 'It was back to 4-4-2 and I laughed. It was frustrating as an Englishman to know where I could have taken that team with those players. It would have been really exciting; because we had extra pace at the top with Owen, we could stretch the pitch even more, to bring in people like Scholes even more.'

Post-karma, Hoddle's star wanes. All along, though, devotees convene, willing this footballing philosopher to contribute to the national debate. Truly world-class in terms of natural gifts, as shown when dovetailing with Diego Maradona during Ossie Ardiles' testimonial in 1986, Hoddle would have loved to be cherished properly by his country, to be more central to England's plans. He delivers some painful home truths to Greg Dyke when the FA chairman stages his 2014 Commission into England's woes. A coffee and a couple of hours with Dyke later, Hoddle is ready to give evidence to the Commission.

'What's the one ingredient a World Cup-winning team always had?' he asks the Commission. 'A world-class player. Bobby Charlton was world-class. Some teams had two. So why are we not actually grooming youngsters who've got talent? Instead of making the creative player feel an outsider, you've got to embrace him early. You've got to choose the right couple of youngsters. Normally a world-class player would hit you in the eye. Rooney would have been an example at 17. Say, one day he's injured for Everton, and he's learning. So the England manager says: "Right, he's done his rehab, can I take him with me to a game?" We're making him a special case, this kid. OK, mentally, we've got to keep him on track, working hard, but he comes with the manager to a game, sits next to you, and you'd teach him so much. I'd say things like: "Look how he's made that run, he's gone too early, the ball's not ready to come; now he's going, that's better." You teach him. Then you take him on to the training ground, and you're talking to the kid like you're talking to the captain. All this will make this kid hit his peak at 23, rather than wait and hope that he might do it at 28.'

It's a powerful argument, a sign of Hoddle's imaginative thinking. 'But the Commission wouldn't do it,' he sighs in Vilnius. 'I knew it would fall on deaf ears. It was frustrating. If we're not going to get loads of English players coming through, we have to do something different. If we had a mini-Zidane or mini-Messi, you've got to embrace him, give him sun and water. Not have a situation where Ross Barkley thinks: "Fuck me, will he play me again if I give the ball away?"'

The Commission's refusal to listen to Hoddle seems even more curious when set against the 'England DNA' defined by its technical director, Dan Ashworth. 'Future England players have the opportunity to redefine stereotypes,' declares this blueprint for the new England international. 'As a football nation, we have long been characterized by our passion, fighting spirit and effort. Although there are aspects of these characteristics we wish to retain, we do not wish to be solely defined by them. English football history includes many examples of creative and technically excellent players and teams as well as innovative coaches. It is these aspects of our history we want to emphasize and develop.' More Glenn Hoddle, less Carlton Palmer, basically. So why not co-opt some of the ideas of Hoddle, a 'technically excellent' player as well as 'innovative' coach?

Hoddle enjoys a more sympathetic hearing when talking to the Commission about the dangers facing home-grown players because of the hordes of foreigners filling up the Premier League. 'The future's a bit scary for the English player,' he says in Vilnius. 'We're in a position where the owners are foreign, so they're going to trust foreign managers more, and they trust foreign players more. There's a lack of English players going to get opportunities. If they change the rules, it could easily be done, but the Premier League won't change. That's why you've got to admire the Germans. They hit a lull, so they change how they run clubs and everything was mostly German coaches, German players, and they bought top players in [from abroad] to get them to become better players. There's nothing wrong with that, English players learning off the pitch. I don't see how this cycle's going to be broken because the money's astronomical and it's the money bringing the foreigners here. At the moment we have a pot of players who are OK, but if that starts to dwindle, in ten years' time are we really going to be picking from the Championship? It could happen.

'We've too many foreign players, too many foreign owners and too many foreign coaches, but the good thing about them is that they've brought a completely different technical side to the game and outlook. Back then, everyone was a British manager, and everyone was thinking too much the same way. It got staid, bogged down, played in a 40-by-60 box, normally on crap pitches by the time October came.'

He looks forward to Euro 2016 with interest. 'I am hoping personally for the tournament that Roy goes with Kane and Rooney; that will give us more box threat, and then stiffen it up behind those two.' He understands the difficulty in starting Rooney and Barkley, both of whom exult in the creative possibilities of the No. 10 role. 'Not really, not unless you're putting Ross out wide and let him come inside. But Barkley has got to go. Tactically we have to get it spot on. We have a lot of pace in certain areas of the pitch and we have to use that to our advantage. We are not going to have more possession than other teams in the Euros. It would be silly to do it. We need to suck them on to us, protect our back-four and hit them on the counter with our pace. If we don't become a counter-attacking team we'll be in trouble. When you think about Welbeck coming back, with his pace, Sturridge, Walcott, Oxlade-Chamberlain, Sterling – it's hitting you right between the eyes.' The need for speed. Jamie Vardy adds to the sprint squad.

If England are to defy the odds and flourish, Hoddle believes they need a quick course in the dark arts of tournament survival. 'Our players have to become streetwise. Friendly matches, before the tournament, have to be used for that.' Play trickier teams, learn how to counter stunts and machinations. Hoddle nods at Rooney's remark at the 2014 World Cup about England needing to be more 'streetwise', specifically in pressurizing officials to get an opponent banished. With Uruguay's captain Diego Godín already on a booking, England fail to lobby for further sanction when the defender fouls Daniel Sturridge. 'Godín should have been sent off,' says Hoddle. 'There's nothing wrong with players reminding the referee of what he's just done: he's been booked, and he should be booked again. That's professionalism. That's part of the game.' England's players should surround the referee, complaining about Godín.

'Don't the English pride themselves on fair play?' I ask Hoddle.

'It's not us being unfair,' he replies. 'Godín's the culprit, not us. He's the one who's done wrong, not our guys. He's gone outside the rules of football, and we're calling ourselves the bad man by reminding the referee that he's broken the rules?'

Hoddle has seen it close hand. When Simeone preyed on Beckham's petulance in St-Etienne, four other Argentines worked the referee. 'You know that's going to happen when you play against South American teams. How many times do we see in the Premier League people pretending they've been hit? That's what I think is cheating, that's what I hate. There's been a bit of contact here, in the chest, and they go down on the ground, rolling over, holding their face as if they've been elbowed or punched. That's cheating. The referee should be able to reverse the free-kick. That would stop it.' Hoddle still sees nothing wrong in England players campaigning for Godín's expulsion.

Hoddle's views on gamesmanship would make a lively seminar on the Pro Licence course at St George's Park. 'South American footballers and coaches don't think it's crossing the line – that's natural and normal to them. We do. But there comes a time when why should they have a hundred free-kicks, and we get twenty, because they are diving? I'd never tell a player to dive but if he gets touched in the box, if he gets fouled, then make sure you go down.' Michael Owen's knack of running across defenders, drawing fouls, earning penalties, is believed to have been taught by Hoddle. He laughs at the thought. 'You teach that to a 12-year-old in an Academy! If you're last man, and you've got through and you know he's quicker than you, go across his line. He's got to get out of the way and you're through. That's not cheating. That's shrewd play. If you've got Michael's pace you don't have to do it because Michael's too quick. Now the defender's got a problem. Michael's thinking: "If he tries to tackle me, and brings me down, it's a penalty."'

Hoddle loves talking about the game he played so stylishly. In 2014 he's invited to help out Harry Redknapp at QPR. Visiting their windswept Harlington training ground under the Heathrow flight-path one day, I spot Hoddle working one-on-one with a younger player, pointing out the correct body shape for some pattern-of-play move. The youngster listens spellbound to his enthusiastic coach. It seems such a waste of a talent that Hoddle is still not used in some coaching capacity by the FA, even if just imparting his wisdom on Pro Licence courses. Surely he misses the adrenalin of nights like Rome and St-Etienne? 'No, I don't miss it actually. It's a different job now. Professional players' attitudes are different. They're earning a lot of money. I'm not sure the hunger's there. I'm not sure the respect's there for the managers and the coaches working with them. You're never going to get on with everyone in a group of twenty-five players, and management, but you have to respect each other, work together, and that's fragmented in most clubs now. That's what scares me about the future of the game. I don't know if they're really pushing themselves to the very limit to become better players – mentally, physically or technically.'

Hoddle sighs. He's experienced so much. His playing days include the humiliating World Cup qualifying defeat in Oslo in 1981 that prompts the epic 'your boys took a helluva beating' outpouring from Norwegian commentator Bjørge Lillelien. England still reach Spain 82 under Ron Greenwood, start strongly against France and concede only one goal in their five games. Unfortunately, Kevin Keegan and Trevor Brooking return too late from injury, are never sharp enough and miss good chances when coming on in the second round Group B game against Spain. England are out. Hoddle's thoughts slowly turn to the next World Cup, to Mexico, where England encounter the tricks and trickery of Diego Armando Maradona.

5

The Merchant of Menace

SHORTLY BEFORE NOON on 22 June 1986, a distinctive, stocky figure struts into the centre-circle of the Azteca Stadium, commands the ball's presence and commences juggling. Many among the sweltering 114,580 crowd gaze in awe. Even members of the England squad preparing for this World Cup quarter-final in Mexico City cannot keep their eyes off Diego Maradona. 'It was incredible,' recalls John Barnes. 'He just kept the ball up and up.' Argentina's cocksure captain is so technically blessed that such elegant keepie-up comes as naturally as breathing. This show of sublime expertise has another purpose, though. 'It was designed to bring fear,' says Barnes. England have no antidote, no answer. 'Gazza would have gone over and pulled Maradona's shorts down,' smiles Barnes of how Paul Gascoigne would respond to this one-man festival of flair. Sadly, the fearless Geordie, only 19, is still more than two years away from his introduction to the national team.

Any analysis of the fifty years of hurt must pay due homage to the merchants of menace who wreck English ambitions. Cristiano Ronaldo, Andrea Pirlo and Luis Suárez have outwitted England in recent times. But over the half-century, Maradona is the most spectacular nemesis, punishing England through fair means and foul. Maradona, Ronaldo, Pirlo and Suárez provide a painful reminder to English football of an obligation to breed world-class performers who spread sustained distress among opponents, not just intermittent concern but 90 minutes or two hours of high anxiety.

England's inability to deal with that special quartet also underscores the importance of adopting a more sophisticated game-plan to stifle them. Debagging Diego is not enough. More thought is required. But how do you subdue a magician with a wand of a left foot, a burst of pace to turn even fleet-footed shadows into statues, and the balance, determination and robustness to withstand even the most bruising attention? Seeing Maradona in the flesh is an unforgettable privilege. The memory remains vivid of being in the Stadio delle Alpi at Italia 90, marvelling at Maradona as he powers through the middle of the Brazilian ranks, eluding Alemão, Dunga and Ricardo Rocha before, off-balance and with his right foot, threading the ball through for Claudio Caniggia to round Cláudio Taffarel and score.

How do you solve a problem like Maradona? Earlier at Italia 90, Cameroon tried straightforward assault. After shaking hands with Stephen Tataw at San Siro, Maradona stamps down on the stationary ball with his left foot, flicks it up, hoists it three metres in the air and then juggles it four times with his left shoulder. Very aware of his threat, Cameroon treat Maradona like a punchbag. It's brutal. Benjamin Massing goes through the back of him, then brings him down, before Victor N'Dip joins the wrecking crew by going in with a boot lifted so high it leaves a stud-mark above the captain's armband on Maradona's left arm. As the medics piece him back together, Maradona just shakes his head. Cameroon win but there are surely more subtle, and legal, means of halting this genius. Disciplined man-marking can work. In Gary Neville, England employ an inquisitive and bold coach who could host a seminar for the players, debating the Maradona conundrum, and asking whether they would man-mark him or go zonal. Set them thinking, get them ready for when they next encounter such precocity. Maradona has become such a bogey-man for English football that the FA's coaching hub at the National Football Centre needs to study this remarkable talent. Maybe invite Maradona to St George's Park to give the talk himself.

It is typically redolent of the English game's Corinthian roots that man-marking is frowned upon as too unsporting. Ridiculous. The art of closing down an opponent legally, restricting his influence, needs teaching even more extensively in Academies, so that more agile, intelligent limpets are available to the national coach and they are educated enough in the role to avoid bookings. This is no rigid manifesto for man-marking, more a plea for tighter monitoring of opponents, whether it's midfielders tracking runners, or defenders becoming more dutiful and dogged in sticking to a forward. It's basic stuff that England do not fully grasp. Ashley Cole, quick, tenacious, and knowing when to back off and when to dive in, does well against Ronaldo, but nobody gets close to Pirlo in 2012 and 2014 and Suárez exploits poor marking to score against England in São Paulo in 2014.

In Mexico, Bobby Robson's side take an ad hoc approach to dealing with Maradona, partly based on communication, passing him on, ensuring responsibility is spread around. 'Bobby just said: "Look, whoever is closest to Maradona, take him and stand up to him,"' says Peter Reid, the whole-hearted Evertonian frequently in Maradona's vicinity in the Azteca. 'But we didn't put anybody on him man-to-man. It would have been negative. We didn't want to resort to that. I don't think it's the England way. We didn't man-for-man for him. Belgium did in the semi-final with one of the best markers at that time, Eric Gerets, and Maradona went through them. He had everything. The first time I came across Maradona was when he played Scotland at 18, and I watched on TV as he went past "Jocky" Hansen like you wouldn't believe.' Maradona scores Argentina's third in that 3-1 friendly win at Hampden Park on 2 June 1979.

The following year, the prodigy from the shanty-town mean streets of Buenos Aires illuminates Wembley. 'He went past Kenny Sansom, and just put it past the post,' remembers Barnes. 'England won 3-1 but Maradona was great.'

His talent blossoms in Mexico. Sitting with Barnes, Chris Waddle watches events from the Azteca bench for 66 minutes. 'I didn't think we had a player in that squad who could man-mark Maradona, somebody you could just go and glue to him,' says Waddle. 'Terry Fenwick wasn't quick enough. Butch [Terry Butcher] wasn't that type of player. We could have done with somebody like Paul Parker, quick, strong, and [he] probably would have enjoyed the challenge.' Parker, like Gascoigne, would prove his worth four years on from Maradona's mayhem in Mexico. But where are the adhesive Parkers of today? Italian clubs like Juventus take defending seriously, drilling youngsters in the knack of blocking off an opponent's run to the ball. England don't.

England are hardly angels in the Azteca. What becomes particularly apparent on re-examining the tape of that blockbuster quarter-final is that Fenwick should not have lasted until half-time, let alone full-time. It's worth noting given ensuing and legitimate grievances about the referee Ali Bennaceur. England's approach to Maradona is crude rather than stealthy. Scarcely has the image faded of that mesmerizing juggling act than Maradona is back in possession, chesting the ball down, gliding inside Sansom. Hurtling in from the right is Fenwick, late and unforgiving, scything down the Argentine danger-man. Bennaceur races up with all the smug zest of a traffic warden espying a parked car a minute over the meter. He administers appropriate sanction, raising the card in his left hand. Maradona climbs to his feet and gives Fenwick a look that should freeze blood. Undeterred, Fenwick continues his occasional hacking.

'Games and rules have changed,' observes Waddle, reflecting on the general approach to Maradona, not just Fenwick's. 'The thing with Maradona is that he got kicked pillar to post. I'd love to see Messi and Ronaldo when they pick the ball up expecting somebody to thump them. And I mean thump. They still would be very, very good players but it's a different way of receiving the ball when you're getting the ball and you can feel it coming. You think "here we go", and you know they're going to do it, and you know they'll get a warning rather than a yellow, whereas today it could be straight red. Back then it was "give him one early to see what he's like". Would Ronaldo and Messi be able to play in that? Crikey, the tackles that George Best got. He was a genius.'

So is Maradona. In unforgiving heat, England sweat hard to contain him. Butcher and Trevor Steven close him down. Steve Hodge, then Reid, nick the ball from the man with the powerful frame of a young bull and the creative touch of a master artist. This is smarter defending, pressing and intercepting where possible, picking pockets like footballing Fagins. Watching the game back brings a reminder of what an under-rated player Reid is, what a determined character, playing on with an ankle problem and surviving a filthy challenge from José Luis Brown. Although wary of over-committing forward with Maradona lurking, England are hardly sterile. Peter Beardsley's snake-hipped shimmy steers the ball away from Nery Pumpido. Another change of direction brings a glimpse of goal and a firm strike almost brings reward. Butcher strides 20 yards into enemy territory. Gary Stevens and especially Sansom push down the flanks. Robust men inhabit this squad of Robson's, a group containing far more leaders than the current crop. Maradona still dominates English minds. As Steven gives chase, this human bundle of vim and virtuosity looks inside, fooling his pursuer, before playing the ball down the line to Jorge Valdano.

The BBC commentary drifts into a prescient debate about the wisdom of Fifa 'using inexperienced refs from emerging countries in vital games', according to Jimmy Hill. The appointment of Bennaceur 'is a little surprising', adds Barry Davies. It is a topic the whole nation soon turns to with a vengeance, and still does thirty years on.

On Maradona goes, setting the tempo, exchanging passes with Jorge Burruchaga, being pushed over by Reid and knocked over by Hodge but carrying on. He's irrepressible. He curls one free-kick just wide and another into the wall as a Mexican wave staggers around the sticky Azteca. Maradona appears on the left, deceiving Stevens and lifting in a cross a split-second before tumbling over the dead-ball line. Peter Shilton catches. Maradona runs back, builds another attack, a wave of relentlessness. He darts through the middle, feeds the ball right, and encounters Fenwick. Maradona gestures an elbowing motion to the Englishman. On he goes, back-heeling to Sergio Batista, sent sprawling by a legitimate challenge from Reid before Bennaceur grants Robson's side fifteen minutes' respite.

The contest resumes with the surreal sight of a white dove flying past – no harbinger of peace though. Five minutes into the second half Butcher's clearance to Hodge is cut out and Argentina respond, initially confidently, ultimately controversially. It's all a blur, Maradona at his incisive best, cutting through midfield and defence, left foot, left foot, left foot, covering the ground quickly, then right foot past Glenn Hoddle. He glides away too easily from Hoddle, Reid arrives too late, Butcher and Fenwick move out, but Maradona is too good, flicking the ball with his right foot towards Valdano. Hodge intervenes, hooking the ball back towards the penalty spot.

Everyone knows what happens next, a moment recorded for eternity in the history of infamy, let alone the annals of the game. Maradona, 5ft 4in, continues his run and leaps, reaching up and steering the ball over the six-foot Shilton with 'an instinctive flick of his hand', in the tournament summing-up of the Fifa Technical Committee. Sepp Blatter's opinion is long greeted with derision but it is still alarming that the then general secretary of Fifa should treat almost blithely an incident that shames the whole game. Writing in Fifa's technical report about refereeing standards, Blatter concludes that, 'The decisive games were without problems. The controversial goal in the Argentina–England game was an exception. Such cases will always exist.' Nonsense. Why should they? Immediate steps should have been taken to prevent such miscarriages of justice, notably in improving the standard of refereeing. Only now, thirty years on, and with Blatter in exile, does Fifa stop resisting video technology. Blatter's arrogance spills off the page. Fortunately, his gnarled, stained hand is now prised from the Fifa tiller.

In the Azteca, the blame game is underway, focusing on the underhand Hand of God and the officials. As the shameless Maradona runs off celebrating, all eyes turn to the officials. Bennaceur moves towards the centre-circle while looking at his linesman, the Bulgarian Bogdan Dotchev, who initially remains still. Much of the subsequent criticism is aimed at Bennaceur, who never referees for Fifa again. In mitigation, the Tunisian's view of Maradona's misdemeanour is obscured by Fenwick. The Hodge–Valdano duel which could impede Dotchev's sight-line, being on his side of the pitch, is not an issue as Maradona runs through the traffic, into space. Dotchev has a clear view 40 yards to where Maradona's fist is raised. Tuned into the ways and wiles of the game, having played professionally in Bulgaria, Dotchev should really be more alive to the possibility of duplicity. He's experienced, having officiated at the 1982 World Cup, even running the line for England's encounter with Czechoslovakia in Bilbao. Dotchev is most culpable. 'Everyone saw it as clear as day, everyone went, "Hand-ball!"' says Barnes. Waddle adds: 'Ray Wilkins ran down the dug-out and said, "He handled that."' As the subs look on, England's players speed towards Bennaceur. Fenwick's in his face, complaining. Beardsley spreads his arms out, half appealing, half offering evidence. Hoddle hits his hand in frustration, and to indicate Maradona's misdemeanour. Shilton remonstrates.

Three decades later, Shilton's anger has yet to subside. 'Cheating's not part of the game whether it is a goalkeeper who pulls the ball back from behind the line, players feigning in the box to go down for a penalty when they know they've never been touched, or hand-ball,' he says. 'It's all gamesmanship, it's all cheating. It shouldn't be part of the game but it is unfortunately. In the professional game, people will do anything to win. Normally the referee and linesman are there to stop that sort of thing, and if they don't see it, normally the people who do it, like Thierry Henry against Ireland [for France, in 2009], admit to it after the game: "I got away with it, I shouldn't have done, and I apologize."' For Shilton, it is not simply the crime itself, but the absence of contrition that leaves Argentina's No. 10 most condemned. 'The thing with Maradona is that it was the referee and linesman's fault but he never really admitted to it. He celebrated as though it was a legitimate goal. He never really apologized. Those are the reasons why people in this country, and the England players, lost some respect for him.'

Reid expands the argument. 'From an Englishman's point of view, that goal was something I'll never forget. Is Maradona tarnished? Is Thierry Henry tarnished? If you don't walk at cricket are you tarnished? Was Mike Atherton out when Allan Donald got him?' A keen cricket fan, Reid's referring to the incident at Trent Bridge in 1998 when the England batsman refused to walk after the South

African bowler whipped in a delivery that brushed Atherton's glove and was caught. 'You can tell I love my cricket!' laughs Reid, who once faced an over from Muttiah Muralitharan in the nets and didn't get near any of the Sri Lankan's bamboozling deliveries. Maradona certainly has Reid in a spin. 'I had a couple of scrapes with Maradona. On the pitch, I tried to nail him once or twice and I might have caught him. We had banter. He understood what I said to him because it's an Anglo-Saxon word. I've met him since, had a chat with him in Doha when he was there working.' That 2011 meeting was captured by Abu Dhabi Sports TV for its *The Beautiful Game Show* and features Reid kissing Maradona's guilty left hand. Maradona, almost looking sheepish, stares into the camera and says "excuse me" in English. 'I like to see your face because in Mexico I only saw your back,' smiles Reid. Maradona, who has put on a few kilos since his svelte prime, hugs Reid and laughs "now you can catch me" in Spanish. The Hand of God story rumbles on. At the 2014 World Cup in Brazil, Lineker is invited on to Maradona's live TV show, grasps his host's right hand and asks, '*Cómo está la mano?*' Showing a surprising attention to detail, Maradona pushes his left hand forward, laughing.

In 2015, the Hand of God continues to make headlines. Shooting a Coca-Cola commercial in Tunisia, Maradona pops in for an 'emotional reunion' with Bennaceur. 'I gave him an Argentina shirt and he gave me the picture of that game that hangs in his home. My dedication: "For Ali, my eternal friend",' Maradona tells his millions of Facebook followers. Meanwhile, back in Manchester at the Soccerex convention an Argentinian film-crew waits outside the VIP lounge, hoping to ask the visiting Shilton about Maradona. The Hand of God is always news.

The debate reverberates, partly in examining whether the moralizing English would do any different. 'If Gary Lineker had done it the other end he would have got a lot of criticism from the world media, but everyone would have shrugged,' argues Waddle. 'Maradona did it well. Whether the officials were up to that level of football, I don't know. I was surprised. For big games, you need big refs.'

Like Waddle, Barnes is one of the most thoughtful voices on the game. 'People said he was an inexperienced referee but I'm an inexperienced referee and I saw the hand-ball,' he observes. 'You don't have to be experienced. He was conned. I didn't have a problem with it. Of course you in the media will. Terry Butcher and Peter Shilton will say he was a cheat. But if we'd done it, would we have said, "Let's replay it?" I don't think so.' Playing for Manchester United, Paul Scholes blatantly punches a Wes Brown cross into the top corner of the Zenit St Petersburg net in 2008 and departs for a second yellow. 'It's not win at all costs but I'm sure if Paul Scholes dived in and hand-balled it, and if the goal had been given, he would have said "goal", and maybe there's a press reaction,' continues Barnes. 'Would we ban him for life? No we wouldn't. We like to be holier than thou at times. I have nothing against Maradona or Argentina. Paul Scholes has done it. Everyone's tried it on. That's when you look at the referee and say: "You have to see it, make the right decision."'

For all the iniquity of Maradona's infamous hand-ball, and the incompetence of Bennaceur and Dotchev, it would be a travesty had England prevailed in the Azteca. English fixation with the Hand of God masks the truth that Argentina were superior, a fact confirmed by Maradona's second goal four minutes later, starting by spinning away from Reid and Beardsley. Reid and Barnes, good friends chatting over coffee in Manchester, recall the moment. 'You know those recurring dreams you have when the wind's blowing against you and you can't move? I have that when I think of Maradona,' begins Reid. 'I just couldn't get to him. People say, "Why didn't you bring him down?" Honestly, if I could've just got there, I would've done, but I couldn't. I do have the odd dream about that goal . . .' Barnes interrupts, laughing: 'He tackles him in the dream, though, and scores a hat-trick!' 'I fucking don't!' replies Reid. 'He turned me and Beardsley on the halfway line.'

Phenomenal technique and acceleration account for Butcher, pace burns off Fenwick, and a little touch commits Shilton. The position of keeper and ball suits a right-footed finish but Maradona addresses the ball with his left, giving Butcher a slight chance of recovery.

Maybe against a lesser mortal. No chance against Maradona. The Argentinian's faith in his weapon of choice is total. Keeping his balance, he strokes the ball left-footed past Shilton as Butcher arrives in vain, like a fireman long after the blaze has taken hold. Gary Stevens, the Everton full-back, covers back but the ball flies in. 'You have to say that is magnificent. There is no debate about that goal, that was pure football genius,' intones the great Barry Davies on the BBC.

'Maradona made it look so easy,' says Barnes. 'You've got Terry Butcher and Terry Fenwick there, Gary Stevens is so quick, but Maradona made it look effortless. I felt like applauding the second goal as he was going through. You've got to appreciate things like that – unless you're Terry Butcher or Peter Shilton. They still want to kill him.'

Barring anger over the lack of penitence, Shilton is actually sanguine. 'Maradona was the greatest player I played against. It was a great goal, the second one, but we were a bit down, still thinking about the first goal, weren't really concentrating, weren't really up for it. But take nothing away, it was a great goal, great finish at the end.' Reid concurs. 'Maradona's touch is so good. The pitch is bobbly but the ball doesn't move from his foot. To go through, deep into the box, and roll it in, left peg, in difficult conditions makes it one of the best goals ever. I get asked about it every day.' The Evertonian smiles. 'By the way, I won League championships, an FA Cup, a European trophy [the Cup-Winners' Cup], and I get asked about Maradona more than anything. I keep seeing on Twitter: "Who is the best? Messi or Maradona?" But you can't compare. Both of them at the time have been the best player in the world. Pelé was the best when he was about. Maradona's ability was fantastic, allied to a physical strength and great balance. The great players had that. I always knew he was going left but it's like Gareth Bale now, how do you stop it? I actually think Maradona was quicker running with the ball than without it.'

As Maradona weaves through, admiration flows from the England bench, including Waddle. 'I was watching it, thinking: "No, he's not going to go all the way, is he?" Then I was thinking: "He's going to go all the way!" Then I thought: "No, something's going to happen." Then I saw the ball in the back of the net. Me and John Barnes looked at each other and went: "Wow!" His second goal was worth two goals. We didn't applaud it but sometimes you've got to put your hand up and say: "That is just sheer quality." Maradona carried Argentina. They had good players but with Maradona it was like they had twelve players.'

The technical report on Mexico 86 criticizes Robson's side for being 'too cautious' and emerging from their 'passivity to have a crack' only after Maradona's second. England respond with a Sansom shot. Beardsley goes close. Robson acts, sending on Waddle for Reid, then Barnes for Steven, giving England wings. Suddenly the fans' flags, celebrating allegiance to Swindon Town and Pompey, Oxford United and Hartlepool United, flutter more breezily. Reddening, sweating supporters in their Union Jack singlets bellow defiance. Maradona even tries to run the clock down. Pumpido pushes away Hoddle's free-kick. England finally find some momentum, the substitutes, especially Barnes, energizing the team. With 10 minutes remaining, Sansom and Hodge combine and Barnes is released, evading Héctor Enrique and Ricardo Giusti and speeding towards the bye-line. The cross comes in, dropping perfectly for Lineker to score with a downward header. The debate now among England fans is: why didn't Barnes start? This is his first experience of the finals. 'If I'd got on for only two minutes and fallen over the ball five times I'd have been delighted,' replies Barnes. 'Just to get on was fantastic, to be on the same pitch as Maradona, the greatest player ever. Viv Anderson [went to] two World Cups ['82 and '86] and didn't play, so how do you feel part of it? You want to be part of the history of being in the World Cup, so to be involved in the quarter-final against Maradona was spectacular.'

Maradona immediately shows why he is so venerated by Barnes, spinning and delivering a ball to Carlos Tapia. England are fortunate the midfielder's shot strikes an upright. Maradona mixes defence-splitting passes with time-wasting, his close control holding off Hodge and Sansom down by the corner-flag, close to Dotchev.

Fenwick's coarse streak surfaces again, flattening Valdano. As medics rush out with what resembles a foldaway sun-lounger masquerading as a stretcher, Bennaceur somehow decides not to dismiss Fenwick.

England offer one last foray. Hoddle's fine pass finds Sansom, and Barnes is off and running again, beating Enrique again, delivering another cross surely destined for Lineker. Only a refined piece of defending denies the England striker: his marker, Julio Olarticoechea, manages to get the back of his head to the ball, flicking it to safety. Great defending, of a type England still need to learn. 'People talk about the cross that I put in and Gary missed an opportunity,' Barnes says, 'but if we'd scored we would have got Maradona angry and he would have scored another goal. That World Cup was Maradona's.'

Looking on as Maradona marches on, shaking his head in dignified disappointment, is Bobby Robson, the manager who goes closest to ending the years of hurt.

6

Sir Bobby Robson

GENTLE AND ELEGANT, Lady Elsie Robson perches on the edge of a sofa outside Rockliffe Hall, a calm, friendly golf club not far from the River Tees, and enthuses about how much her late husband, the great Sir Bobby, cared for his players. She remembers his final visit to St James' Park, on 26 July 2009, for a game between England and Germany raising funds for his charity. Sir Bobby's very ill, weakened by his fifth skirmish with cancer, this time terminal, but he wants to see his boys, Shilts and Gazza, Platty and Barnesy. 'He wanted that last farewell,' recalls Lady Elsie. 'He wasn't well enough to be there but he was determined he was going to be there, absolutely determined, so we got a car to the door which we could put his wheelchair into. You know what he asked my son Mark when he got back into the cab after the game? "How did Gazza play?" Mark said: "He did well, Dad." "That's OK." It was very quick after that when he died.' Five days later, Sir Bobby passes away, aged 76, and a nation mourns a lion of a man and manager.

A common lamentation of the modern age is that England require a deeper talent pool of managers as well as players. Aspiring coaches at St George's Park are encouraged to read at length about Robson, understanding the traits and experiences that made him so revered by players and public. As they study for their Pro Licences, and walk past the Sir Bobby Robson ballroom at St George's, they may also consider investigating why the FA refused to offer a manager adored by his dressing-room, if derided by sections of the media, a new contract on the eve of Italia 90. 'It wasn't the greatest of kindnesses,' says Lady Elsie understatedly, recalling the time when the FA, and particularly its then chairman Sir Bert Millichip, turned its back on her husband. Patience is a virtue if clear-sighted employers see the substance of a man.

Back in 1990, Robson demonstrates on Italian soil many qualities the FA forsook. He's more than the inspirational leader who guides England to their most exciting moment since 1966, that unforgettable run to the semi-finals of the 1990 World Cup. It is also the values Robson espouses that endear him to all, that steadfastness in adversity, that integrity, compassion, respect, eternal optimism and supreme pride in his work and his country. A hunger for life. A love of football that manifested itself in one of his final utterances before his breath left him, asking how Gazza played. Robson's *libero* at Italia 90, Mark Wright, played behind Gascoigne in that fundraiser at St James' Park and remembers the occasion with emotion in his voice. 'Sir Bobby was very poorly, and he had us all in tears,' says Wright when we meet in Manchester. 'Sir Bobby, God rest his soul, was like a dad to all of us. He did so many things for us. His kind heart, and all the goodness he pushed into us, stand us in good stead. I remember when I was managing at Chester and I had to play all the 16-year-old kids because all the players were being sold. The phone went.

' "Mark? Sir Bobby." He was very poorly at the time.

' "How are you, Gaffer?"

' "Well, you know, son, I'm not so good. But enough about me, how can I help you?"

'That sums up Bobby Robson for me.' Caring, looking out for his old boys, wanting to pass on his expertise.

'He'd be thinking about Mark Wright, thinking: "Well, maybe he needs a bit of moral support," ' responds Lady Elsie when I relay the story to her.

'I loved every part of what Bobby Robson was about,' continues Wright. 'He was a fantastic coach. Him and Don Howe together left no stone unturned in preparing a team. I loved playing for England and for those [two] more than anybody else. They were an absolutely fantastic pairing. But the Gaffer would stand for no trouble. If you were talking out of turn, or doing something wrong, he'd make sure you put it right. He made England a family and we've stayed a family. I was talking to Terry [Butcher] last year and he said no one will ever realize the bond that the 1990 World Cup side had for each other, and still have to this day, put together by Sir Bobby.'

All of Robson's teams feel like families. 'I looked on him as a father figure,' says Jermaine Jenas, whom Robson brings to Newcastle United from Nottingham Forest in 2002. I meet Jenas in San Marino where the former midfielder continues to win admirers on BBC Radio 5 Live with his thoughtful and eloquent evaluations of England games. He laughs at the reminder of his introductory press conference at St James' Park. Robson sits there, bubbling with enthusiasm, next to the composed and mature £5m teenager. Robson is excited by Jenas's potential, quickly throwing him in against local rivals Sunderland, of all people, and always watching over him. 'There was one time that me, Kieron Dyer and Bellers [Craig Bellamy] bombed down the motorway to an Usher concert in Manchester on the Thursday when we weren't really supposed to go,' says Jenas. 'In Newcastle at the time people were calling us "the Brat Pack" when we were just young lads, playing really good football, and enjoying ourselves. We didn't drink at the concert, just bombed down, bombed back up and got back to training. When we finished training, everyone went in and Bobby called me over. "Listen," he said, "I know you went to this concert. You shouldn't have gone. You know club rules. I love Bellers and Kieron to bits as players, they're absolutely amazing players, but I wouldn't invite them to my barbecue. But I'd invite you." I just started laughing. "I get what you're saying."' Robson cared for his welfare and development.

Anyone wanting to be England manager, indeed to take on any demanding managerial role, has to study Robson's remarkable career and numerous inspiring traits. The FA should host courses in Robson at St George's Park, not just name rooms after him. A special man, stoical to his core, Robson would deal graciously with a frequently brutal media, shaking hands with those whose pens once dripped poison about him during the fiercest moments of the newspaper circulation war. He was invariably courteous, especially when asked to reflect on England. Sir Bobby was a manager that a journalist would instinctively don a tie and jacket to interview. Talking to him was a privilege and an education.

Before interviewing him once at Newcastle, I'm politely advised by the club's press officer that 'Sir Bobby only has twenty minutes'. Forty minutes later, Robson is still immersed in a marvellous monologue about one night in Turin. Listening in and smiling at his manager's articulacy and tardy time-keeping is his driver for the day, Gary Speed. When Robson finally gets up to catch his lift home from training, having put the world and the World Cup to rights, I apologize to Speed for delaying his distinguished passenger. Speed, a much-missed friend of football, laughs. 'Typical Bobby,' he says. Everyone knows Robson can talk for England, especially on England.

'That's what Bob was like,' smiles Lady Elsie, back on the terrace of Rockliffe Hall, on hearing the tale. 'He was always generous with his time.'

As manager of England, Robson brings dignity and energy to the most demanding position in English sport. Nodding respectfully to Terry Venables for his deeds at Euro 96 and Glenn Hoddle for his tactical nous, Robson is England's last great manager, second only to Sir Alf Ramsey. Robson undeniably enjoys the good fortune of being assisted by fine coaches, including Don Howe, ensuring the tactical and training-ground work is right, but he sets the mood, he bonds the team and makes players believe in themselves and in each other. Robson shows loyalty to them, taking the furious flak from the press when results and performances are poor, protecting his dressing-room, appreciating that professionals are human beings. 'He was interested in the whole man, not just the skills on the football pitch, and that's where his strengths came from in man-management,' adds Lady Elsie.

She believes England players are as committed as ever to the cause her late husband served with such distinction. 'I don't think the modern boy is any different. It's the wage structure that has made things change. I do watch the England games. I watch far more football than I ever did when Bob was alive. I used to find it monopolized the timetable. I'd go and read a book, or cook a cake, but now it's been part of my life for so long, and I'm interested in it. I know what's going on. Bob would be just amazed.'

He would also be amazed at the monumental success of the Sir Bobby Robson Foundation. As Lady Elsie speaks, Alan Shearer is disappearing into the distance, striking his golf-ball with the same power with which he used to smite a football past petrified keepers. It is the annual Foundation celebrity golf-day and Shearer is among a number of north-eastern sporting titans helping raise money to fight cancer. The fund is now pushing past the £9m mark. 'Wow, is that what it is?' Shearer gasps on being told the figure. 'Sir Bobby wanted to leave something special behind and, boy, has he! That's him all over. He was down to earth, humble and hungry.'

Back on the terrace, Steve Harmison whizzes past on a Segway, offering to lend it to Lady Elsie if she needs to tour the course, inspecting the competitors. 'You can go round on this,' the cricketer laughs. She politely declines. Another Ashes-winning cricketer, Graeme Swann, dishes out one-liners. Michael Gray, the former Sunderland and England left-back, is smiling and gliding round the course, close to Steve Harper and Steve Howey. It seems every Steve in the north-east is involved. Steve McClaren turns up later for the dinner, backing the Foundation. Middlesbrough's owner Steve Gibson contributes much, not least access to Rockliffe Hall. One of his Boro players, Rhys Williams, comes over to help out after training. Lady Elsie delights in the enduring love for her late husband. 'I did feel I was sharing him with the country!' she says of her fifty-four-year marriage. 'I miss him every day. I do. I do. I do. He's a big miss.'

She talks warmly of Bobby's formative years in Langley Park, County Durham, shaping the man who became an icon for English managers. 'Bob came from loving parents with a large family, five sons, in a mining community. It was a very, very regimented upbringing. It was controlled by the mine, which never closed; there were three eight-hour shifts to keep the mine going, so the men's work revolved around that. Bob's father might be at home asleep for the day because he's been on that shift through the night, so the children are taught to be quiet. Discipline was important. It wasn't a bible-punching family, but they were taught Christian values. The children were brought up to respect their parents, to do as they were told, and value the people around them. That shaped Bob. Your values are always the same. Mine are. Bob's were. We tried to pass that on to our children. Values were different in those days. It has all changed so much. They were extraordinary times. That was our childhood. There was the war.' Aged 7, Robson would stand outside his house, looking to the north as the Luftwaffe spewed parachute mines and incendiary bombs down on to Tyneside, targeting the Swan Hunter shipyard and munitions factories. In 1941, one bomb killed 103 people sheltering in the Wilkinson's lemonade factory in South Shields.

The war features in Robson's team-talk before the Italia 90 semi-final against West Germany. 'Sir Bobby endeared you to the idea of Englishness, of representing your country with pride and passion, from the old Empire days of how great we were,' says John Barnes. 'If you know the history of England, you know we fought everybody. We'd think how could a war against this particular country pertain to this particular game? In his team-talks, he talked about the Germans, the war, the Battle of Waterloo, about Winston Churchill, about being English. Sir Bobby was fiercely proud to be English and that is what his team-talks were all about. Yes, they were about tactics and organiz-ation, but it was more to do with the passion and pride of wearing the shirt for England. That's why Bobby was special.'

After the war, St James' Park becomes a place of pilgrimage for Robson, swelling the congregation worshipping the prolific centre-forward Jackie Milburn. 'His father took him there every fortnight,' resumes Lady Elsie. 'He stood in the queue to get into the ground. His father was a tremendous fan both of football and of Bob. He would tell you about a player. If he saw an 8-year-old he could spot their potential, because in those mining villages they watched the children play their sport, they knew the families, they knew if the child had talent. Of course that's where the Charlton boys came from. They weren't born far from us – Ashington, only twenty-five miles away, same sort of background.'

At 15, Robson follows his father down Langley Park mine, spending eighteen months as an apprentice electrician, braving life at the coalface. 'You didn't necessarily have to come from a pit village to appreciate what you had in life later on, but it did help,' continues Lady Elsie. 'Bob did have great enthusiasm for and loyalty towards the England job. Bob was very patriotic. He loved the Proms, the National Anthem, it meant a lot to him.' An inside-forward, he represents England with distinction, scoring four times in 20 internationals.

Younger managers striving to impose themselves on a mercurial occupation in the high-stakes modern epoch will never succeed without one of the attributes defining Robson's career. From being a miner at Langley Park to player with Fulham and West Brom and then manager with Ipswich, England, PSV Eindhoven, Porto, Barcelona and Newcastle, Robson is sustained by a prodigious capacity for hard work. Lady Elsie looks back on her late husband's start in management, the problems at Craven Cottage and then the move in 1969 to Portman Road where the charismatic Cobbold brewing family ran a happy, slightly laissez-faire operation. 'The Cobbolds said to us: "You can come and work for us but we can't give you a contract, we'll just see how you do,"' recalls Lady Elsie. 'I don't think managers work like that any longer! We were pretty desperate because we'd been fired twice before that [from Vancouver Royals and Fulham], and we had three little boys and a mortgage. Bob was looking for a job, looking to prove himself, so every day he travelled from where we lived in Weybridge in Surrey, took the train into Waterloo, across London to Liverpool Street [and] up to Ipswich. He did that for six months. He was determined to do it. Then the board said: "Look, Bob, you can't go on like this. You've got to bring your family up here, get settled up here, and we'll give you a year's contract."'

During the ensuing thirteen years, an enchanted epoch for Ipswich, Robson wins the FA Cup, the Uefa Cup and the eternal gratitude of Suffolk. Robson's desire to lead his country in succession to Ron Greenwood in 1982 is seen in his acceptance of a £7,000 pay-cut from his £72,000 annual salary at Ipswich. He sets about the role with his usual enthusiasm, seeming to enjoy what is widely hailed as a benign draw for Euro 84 qualification. 'England On Easy Street' trumpets the *Daily Express* when Robson's men are pitted against Hungary, Greece, Denmark and Luxembourg. Unfortunately, Denmark's dashing princes rip up the odds. Preben Elkjær, Michael Laudrup, Allan Simonsen and Jesper Olsen prove too strong, pipping England by a point to qualify, and the ritual evisceration of an England manager resumes. When a side containing Peter Shilton, Bryan Robson, John Barnes and Trevor Francis lose 2-0 to USSR in a Wembley friendly on 2 June 1984 chants are heard of 'Robson out' and 'what a load of rubbish'. Only 38,125 attend. A World Cup quarter-final before 114,580 seems a distant dream.

Yet England possess good players who believe in their manager, and they reach Mexico 86. At the hotel in Monterrey, Robson goes round players like Waddle, Reid and Barnes proffering folksy little maxims as tactical aide-memoires. 'A lot of the sayings he got wrong: "Keep your high balls low and your low balls high,"' recalls Waddle. 'I was by the pool one day and Sir Bobby said my saying was "don't admire hustling, join in",' laughs Reid. 'I don't think Sir Bobby fucking fancied me with the ball!' Barnes adds: 'We'd be lying by the pool, and Bobby would come to us with a saying and sometimes he couldn't remember it either.' He grins. 'He'd say: "When in position, be in possession." It was the other way round! "When in possession, be in position."' This was a familiar Robson instruction to wingers to stop them wandering, to keep the shape. 'Now that's a good saying,' Reid observes to Barnes during our conversation in Manchester, 'but if you'd gone off your line when we had possession, Bobby would be going "get wide". It's a contradiction. You were on the left but because of your talent, without pissing up your back, I thought you could play in the hole.'

Initially the players feel a tactical rigidity cramping them in Mexico. 'Tactically we were far behind the other teams,' adds Reid. England struggle early on in the Tecnológico Stadium in Monterrey, losing to Portugal 1-0 on 3 June and three days later labouring against

Morocco. As in 1982 with Kevin Keegan, England once again travel to a tournament with a wounded talisman, this time Bryan Robson, one of the warriors of England history but stricken with shoulder problems. 'Bryan was fearless,' says Barnes. 'They called him Captain Marvel, and he was. He didn't fear any pain, he was just 100 per cent, very positive, definitely a leader. Commitment, desire, passion – basically everything that Bobby preached, Bryan had it all. He was brave, could get in the box, could score goals, compete, pass, box-to-box. He was an ideal player for the way England played: we weren't a slow-ball team, who got it out of the back and kept the ball for twenty passes, we were up 'n' at 'em. We did play basically a 4-4-2, so you had to have an engine in that midfield. If we'd played 4-5-1, 4-3-3 or three at the back, you could easily have accommodated a flair player in the middle of the park, but we didn't really play like that. He needed an engine.' Bryan Robson was that engine for Bobby Robson.

Once again, club-versus-country tensions count against the national team. Robson's manager at Manchester United, Ron Atkinson, insists that any operation on his captain's shoulder not interfere with his involvement during the 1985/86 season. Tugged back by a Moroccan, Robson's shoulder pops out again. Seared into a generation's consciousness is the sad image of England's No. 7 being helped away by the physio Fred Street. Robson's sweat-soaked head is down, his damaged right arm held against his chest while the striped armband clings to his left arm. Steve Hodge replaces Robson, and when Ray Wilkins is dismissed for throwing the ball at the referee, England are relieved to hold on for a draw.

The debrief is lively. With Robson a doubt and Wilkins banned, England have to decide who partners Glenn Hoddle in the centre. Robson gathers his squad in a monastery up in the hills, a more tranquil location away from the heat and bustle of Monterrey. The ecclesiastical hush is soon broken. Reid, sitting alongside Barnes, remembers it well. 'When we had the team meeting in the monastery, fucking three hours in the team meeting, I said to Sir Bobby that he played Robbo, Ray and Glenn and there was no balance. It was like Sir Alf – because of the balance he put Nobby Stiles in there. It was lopsided when either you [Barnes] or Waddle were playing because he wanted the three in there. Not because I was a midfield player, but I said to Sir Bobby: "Play Robbo at the back." Franz Beckenbauer played there. The way international football is when you need to come out with the ball – and that's no disrespect to the central defenders – Robbo would have been ideal to do that, to bring the ball out, getting the balance.'

Aspiring managers need the decisiveness Robson now shows. Robson the player is insistent he can soldier on for the final Group F game against Poland at the Universitario Stadium in Monterrey on 11 June, but Robson the manager acts strongly. Captain Marvel is out. With a midfield understudy also required for Wilkins, the manager turns to a Hoddle–Reid central axis; Hodge tucks in, giving England better balance than the Hoddle–Wilkins–Robson unit which saw Hoddle forced into infertile pastures out wide. Robson also takes the decision to break up the traditional target-man/poacher attack and omits Mark Hateley for Peter Beardsley, who offers more subtlety to the attack in support of Gary Lineker. 'We never thought of playing one up, one off,' argues Barnes. 'Peter Beardsley came in, and he was a striker, he helped out Lineker, but realistically it was a 4-4-2.' With no Hateley to service with crosses, Waddle is left out for Trevor Steven.

Triggered by circumstance, and also a plea from Fenwick, England's reboot sparks them into life. A theme of Robson's life shaping England's fortunes from the dug-out is taking important decisions when the stakes are highest. England vanquish Poland 3-0 and Hoddle enjoys the stage, allowing him 'to make use of his brilliant skill in the middle' according to Fifa's technical report on Mexico 86. Beardsley flits about like a firefly on a mission while Lineker scores a hat-trick, delighting the manager. 'Bobby was the most enthusiastic bloke I've ever worked with, not just about football, about everything,' observes Lineker, the poacher-turned-presenter, talking at his art-filled members' club in south-west London. 'If Bobby were here now, he'd go up to this picture and say: "I wonder if he did that in the studio?" I remember doing the final documentary on him. He took me round St James' Park and he was exuding enthusiasm about it, the quality of the wood in the boardroom. He was the kind of manager you really wanted to play for. Tactically? Average.' Isn't that where Howe stepped in? 'No, Bobby ran it,' continues Lineker. 'But tactically he was basic. He had a brilliant understanding of footballers in terms of what they needed mentally and he would stick by you. He was massively loyal. He'd know if he'd got a world-class player and he'd never be influenced by the media, who as soon as you go three games without a goal say "he's gone, he's no more, get him out". Robson stuck with the players he knew he could trust.'

Thanks to Robson's changes and Lineker's goals, the momentum picks up. 'We started terribly in the first two games,' remembers Shilton. 'The Poland game was the springboard, then we beat a poor Paraguay side.' England brush aside the Albirroja 3-0 in the second round in the Azteca on 18 June, leading to the date with Argentina and Diego Maradona. 'Bob didn't believe it,' Lady Elsie says of the Hand of God. 'If you look at that clip, he turns to Don Howe and says: "Don, I think he's used his hand." It had been so cleverly done, and so quick.'

Without Maradona parading the fraud and the beauty in his game, England might have gone on to become champions of the world. 'I know,' Lady Elsie sighs. 'What if they had . . . what if they had . . . yes . . . yes. He did talk about him [Maradona] to his colleagues and friends, and family members, the men, but I wasn't really clued in very much to what was going on. I was busy in those years, being a primary school teacher, and those thirty kids took up all my time.' Her husband has only twenty-two to look after in Mexico. 'Yes! They were great years. He was a great man. The fact that he had a stable upbringing, a stable home life and a family who were always there waiting for him – those things are important to men. It gives them that . . . ' Bedrock? 'Yes, that's a good word.'

Robson needs that family bedrock amid a turbulent period. Support is also strong from his second family, the England squad. 'He was a nice guy,' says Waddle, who like all the players warmed to their manager's occasional eccentricities. 'His team-talks were legendary. He got names wrong. I remember in Turkey [in 1987] when he said:

"Turkey have some good players now, they've improved a lot and play with two wingers who are Vicky and Verky." He kept moving his hands about to show how they played. He went on for five minutes about Vicky and Verky. One player put his hand up and said: "Gaffer, which one's Vicky and which one's Verky?" He meant the wingers were "tricky". I remember sitting in another meeting when he kept going on about "Tony pulling off to the far-post, Tony do this, Tony do that". Everybody was looking around, thinking "there's no Tony in the room". He kept looking at one player. "Do you understand, Tony?" "If you call us Mark I'll understand." It was Mark Hateley, not Tony Hateley.'

Including Hateley (Mark) and Waddle, Euro 88 proves grim with the commanding figure of Terry Butcher absent with a broken leg, Lineker weakened by hepatitis B, Packie Bonner proving unbeatable in Stuttgart and Tony Adams terrorized by Marco van Basten in Düsseldorf. England's tournament musical offering, 'Going All The Way', proves over-ambitious in sound and sentiment. At least it comes with a hilarious video featuring Adams steering a racing car and a mass appearance on *Wogan* that has Bobby Robson, flanked by Lineker and Neil Webb, lip-synching. The change in musical quality two years later to New Order's seminal 'World In Motion' is politely described as seismic.

Before reaching Italia 90, Robson endures an assault course of vicious criticism personally and professionally. Painful accusations surface briefly about his private life. A quizzical stance on his management is, though, more permissible. England fail to qualify for Euro 84, are whacked by the Hand of God in '86 and subside swiftly at Euro 88. The jury's out. So are the knives. Unconvincing performances in the build-up against Uruguay and Tunisia darken the storm clouds chasing England to their World Cup base in Sardinia. 'The media were on his case, saying, "Why have you left certain players out, what system are you playing?"' recalls Waddle. 'It's a stressful job. You could see at times it got to him. He was very loyal. It would have been very easy for him to bow and get rid of a lot of players after '88 when we didn't perform in the Euros. He went on to '90 with a lot of the players who were slagged off, told they were not good enough by fans and the press. He got unbelievable stick. We drew with Tunisia, and it was "don't bother going on to Italy, come straight home, you're a disgrace".

Millichip of the FA is particularly harsh, wanting him gone, and with indications that the FA is sounding out Graham Taylor, Robson negotiates post-tournament employment at PSV Eindhoven. Who can blame him? Employers move against him. Headlines spit venom at him. 'PSV Off Bungler Bobby' screams one. 'That was a very tough time,' recalls Lady Elsie. 'They were vindictive, spiteful, unkind, but he came out on top of it all.' She still shudders at the treatment meted out to her husband by the press and also by the FA. 'They'd already said to him: "You can go, we want you to go." That was said to him a couple of months before the tournament. It might have been the policy in those years. It was a very hard role for anyone else to fill – as time proved. But these things happen, that's life, and it's best to try and get on with it. Bob was very stoical. It came from that background. It's not to say he wouldn't be feeling angry. He could let off steam at home but he did control it. He wouldn't be normal if he didn't let off steam.'

The siege merely strengthens squad support for their embattled leader. 'Yes, I think it did,' agrees Waddle. 'The team spirit was fantastic in Italy.' Steve McMahon rips up one newspaper in front of the cameras as the squad look on, approvingly, backing their manager. 'Bobby was desperate to do well,' adds Waddle. 'He was so patriotic. I remember somebody at the World Cup saying: "We are away six, seven weeks." Bobby said: "Yes, but people were away six years in the war." I said: "Yes, but they didn't have to play 4-4-2!" The atmosphere was great under Bobby. He wasn't a particularly great coach; he was a motivator. He'd pull you one-on-one and say: "I need more from you. I've got people writing you off, saying you're not good enough. I think you are. You have the ability. Go and show it, give 100 per cent." He made it us against them. "I'm getting stick, you're getting stick," he'd say. The criticism did get to him. But after getting to the semis at 1990 he could walk on water. He could walk away thinking: "I can stick two fingers up to anybody who doubted me, and doubted these lads." He was very loyal to that group of players. I'd have been very happy for him to stay on.'

As in Mexico, England begin the 1990 World Cup slowly, drawing with Ireland in Cagliari on 11 June, and then, five days on, there's the famous tactical tweak against Holland involving Mark Wright as sweeper. Ever since that pivotal game, dispute rages over whose idea it was to go to a back-three – managerial foresight or player power? Some players certainly press for it. 'We were all talking about it,' says Waddle. 'Me and Barnesy were banging the drum for three at the back. Not just against Holland. I'd sampled it at Marseille and we played it really well. Barnesy picked up on it. In training, we used to preach it, saying: "Imagine that: Wright at the back, coming out, into midfield, linking with upfront." I talked to Don Howe, who always had a good ear. I said to him that the Germans were playing three at the back. We were as good as the Germans player-wise: me, Barnes, Lineker and Gascoigne, Wrighty's good on the ball, Des [Walker] is a good defender, Butch, Paul Parker is a good man-to-man marker. Trevor [Steven] goes to wing-back.

'We talked to Butch and Shilts. "Come on, come on, tell him," we said to them. I heard the players pestered Bobby. I don't know whether they did persuade him or he had it in his mind but they did go and talk to Bobby about it because one day he came on the training ground and said: "Right, three at the back." "What! What's happened here?" If we'd gone into those games 4-4-2 we might have come home early. Maybe Bobby thought we had something.'

The man at the centre of the change, Mark Wright, is categorical about what occurred in Sardinia before the Holland game. 'I've heard so many stories about this and I need to put this to bed,' he says. 'It was nothing to do with the players. Of course the boys would have talked about it but the player-power bit is a myth.' Wright explains that he was alerted by Robson to the sweeper plan at England's training camp at Burnham Beeches in May. 'Bobby came to me two or three weeks before that tournament started and talked to me about that. I had a little tweaky [thigh] injury and I had to get over that before he could put me in the squad for the World Cup. He said: "Listen, son, I want you in the squad but we need you fit. The reason is we'll be changing to three at the back and I want you to play in the middle because you read it better, you can dictate to them. You've got a big, loud voice. Your understanding and reading of the game is what I want. We're going to use that after the first game." ' When Wright recovers, Robson cuts Tony Adams from the squad on 21 May and then puts into operation his plan to nullify the Dutch. 'In '88 we got murdered by Holland,' recollects Wright. 'When we go to the 1990 World Cup, we owe them one. We changed the system and they couldn't handle it. We were by far the better side, and that was down to Bobby and Don.'

The rest is history: swamping the Dutch, negating Van Basten and Ruud Gullit; then the Wright header against Egypt, the David Platt volley to defeat Belgium, Gary Lineker's penalties to edge out a superior but indisciplined Cameroon before reaching Turin. Strong characters drive them towards the Stadio delle Alpi. 'There were captains all over the field in that '90 team,' says Wright. 'There was Shilton, Pearcey, I was a captain, Terry Butcher was a captain, Bryan Robson [who damaged his Achilles against Holland and returned home], David Platt. Gazza wasn't a strong person but he was an inspiration. There was Barnesy and Gary Lineker – major international players. Every one of them was a character.'

Characters off the field too. One evening in Sardinia, Butcher, Waddle and Chris Woods decide to make a special sartorial effort for dinner. 'We all wore collar and tie and jacket – and just had jock-straps on underneath,' remembers Waddle. 'Bobby came in and said: "Right, lads, start your meals, and by the way the chairman's coming." We didn't know that night Bert Millichip and all the International Committee were coming. We gulped. We pulled the tablecloth over us. Bobby was saying to Millichip, "Look how those lads are dressed, how smart." At the end, we all got up to go out and Butch touched his toes. I don't think it went down too well at the FA. We did daft things every night.'

Every day, excitement and expectation levels rise back home. 'I kept saying to Bob on the telephone, "The crowds here are so enthusiastic, the atmosphere's great", reminisces Lady Elsie. 'You see, they were in camp and weren't always aware of that. I went out to some of the games. The FA didn't expect us to go through and through but we did. Then they had to try and book hotels for us and we were taken around on these coaches, down country lanes – good fun! There was quite a crowd of us, wives, daughters, sons, parents, getting on this coach to go to this hotel. We didn't know where we were going! I was in Turin. Paul was with me, Mark, some of Bob's brothers came as well, his father was there.' All witness the shoot-out agony against West Germany. 'That was shattering, really.'

'I always think about Italia 90 whenever I hear "Nessun Dorma",' says Shilton. 'It does bring a tear to my eye because it was so special. I didn't realize how special it was until I came home. The whole country was talking about it. Incredible. We were so close. I played against Germany a lot of times in my career but that final period of extra time in Turin, the Germans settled for a penalty shoot-out. We were the team pressing and Chris Waddle hit the post. I felt for the first time if we could have just stuck one in then, someone did a bit of magic, we'd have taken them, but the rest is history.'

One of the players in front of Shilton, Mark Wright, has an interesting take on Turin. 'With the way we played, and the camaraderie and strength of people in that side, we'd have won that semi-final if Bryan Robson had been fit – guaranteed,' says Wright. 'We were the better team, and we'd have won it with Pop. He was the best midfield player I played with – ahead of Glenn Hoddle. Pop could score goals, defend, was brave. He could head, play with either foot, put a tackle in. Pop had the all-round game that was better than anyone. I had so much admiration for him. Even if he'd been out [for a drink the night before], he'd train like a trooper. When you see your captain leading from the front like that, that's what it's about. Most players in that side would say if Pop were fit, we'd have gone on to win it.' Instead the Germans win a wretched final against Argentina. After the meaningless third-place loss to Italy, the squad fly home, Robson following on with the Fair Play Award. 'He got a shock when he returned to the euphoria,' says Lady Elsie. 'The whole country! It lifted the whole country!'

They soon leave the country, off on their travels, with Eindhoven the first stop. Robson's subsequent success abroad, notably in winning the Dutch and Portuguese titles at PSV and Porto respectively and the European Cup-Winners' Cup with Barcelona in 1997, highlight what England are missing, especially after Graham Taylor flounders at Euro 92 and fails to qualify for USA 94. In the long litany of FA mistakes, few errors can match the decision not to wait until after Italia 90 to decide Robson's future. Lineker disagrees. 'He'd probably done enough. He also went at a good time, a time when a lot of our best players, Shilton, Butcher, Robson, Waddle, myself – not all went at the same time but [they were] right at the end of their international careers.'

Tragically, it is shortly after Italia 90 that tests begin to reveal cancer's onslaught on Robson's body, into his bowel, face, brain and lungs. Robson fights hard the enemy within. 'He was physically very, very strong, mentally very strong, and he valued everything he had worked for in life, and he had worked very, very hard for all those years,' remembers Lady Elsie. 'It was very important for him, every single morning of his life, to get up, get going and go to his work. The morning that stopped he was a different person. It was very, very hard for him to accept that. It was so very hard for him to give up. It was a body blow, I would say.'

And so came that last journey, sporting a black fedora, to St James' Park for a repeat of the fixture that defined his career, England against the Germans. At least the FA then has the good grace to organize, superbly, a service of thanksgiving for Robson's life at Durham Cathedral, on 21 September 2009. Lineker delivers a typically articulate eulogy, mentioning how Robson so cared for his players that he chased Gascoigne around a golf course to ensure he donned a top in the boiling sun. Gascoigne, a gaunt figure sitting next to Terry Venables, brushes a tear from his eye. 'He loved Gazza and Gazza loved him,' recalls Lady Elsie. 'He's a very nice boy, a lovely boy, he's got a big heart, a heart of gold, he's too kind for himself.

He made some good friends in the team who have stuck by him.'

Sir Alex Ferguson, speaking without notes but with trademark expressiveness in Durham Cathedral, talks of the class shown by his friend in September 1981 when Uefa Cup holders Ipswich are beaten by Ferguson's Aberdeen. Robson goes into the Scots' dressing-room to congratulate them, hiding his disappointment at going out of the competition in the first round. David Moyes speaks for many managers when he reminisces about the handwritten letter he receives from Robson at Barcelona, inviting him to come and watch training. Barcelona are there in force: Joan Laporta, Txiki Begiristain and Pep Guardiola. 'They came because Bob was very respected at Barcelona,' says Lady Elsie. 'He had great success. In Porto they always used to call him "Mister" and that carried through to Barcelona. Very respectful.'

Those who follow him in the England job, Graham Taylor, Sven-Göran Eriksson and Fabio Capello, sit in one pew. Steve McClaren and Venables are close by. All leaf through the Order of Service, lingering on one page in particular with a photograph of Robson laughing, and six words: 'Thoughtful Leadership, Passionate Commitment, Inspirational Friendship'. Katherine Jenkins sings a haunting rendition of 'Pie Jesu' and Tenors Unlimited roll back the years to Italia 90 with 'Nessun Dorma'. After interviewing Newcastle players when they trained at nearby Maiden Castle I'd always try to catch evensong in the cathedral – a moving experience – before catching the train south. Jenkins and Tenors Unlimited do the old church proud, using its acoustics beautifully. I look around. England internationals are everywhere: Terry Butcher, Bryan Robson, Jack Charlton, Terry McDermott, Sir Bobby Charlton, Malcolm Macdonald and Jermaine Jenas. 'His wife Elsie invited me,' says Jenas. 'That was special for me. She didn't invite everybody. It was an amazing opportunity for me to go and see him off. He always spoke very kindly of me and we were very close.'

The congregation stands for 'Praise, My Soul, The King Of Heaven' and 'Abide With Me'. The organist plays 'Local Hero'. 'It was extremely moving,' remembers Lady Elsie. 'It was heart-rending, really. He would have been astonished. Bob was proud of what he'd done in football but really he was a very modest person.'

Heading south from Durham on the train, I alight at Peterborough with two passionate Norwich City supporters, Delia Smith and her husband Michael Wynn-Jones, the club's guiding forces now heading back into East Anglia. When Norwich are relegated from the Premier League in 2005, Robson sends a message of support to Delia, wishing the club a speedy return to the top flight. 'Remember,' he tells Delia, 'fortune favours the brave.'

Classy Bobby. Boldness personified. Three years after that emotional day at Durham Cathedral I receive first-hand evidence of the power of the Robson factor. On tweeting a degree of scepticism in October 2012 that Mike Ashley will ever back his manager Alan Pardew long-term, and blithely boasting I'll swim the Tyne if he does, I'm immediately inundated with gloating responses from the Gallowgate when Newcastle's owner awards his manager an eight-year contract. Everyone's an instant expert on Twitter and quasi-marine biologists rush to offer advice. Some urge against venturing into the Tyne in a dark wetsuit as it's 'the seal-mating season'. Apparently it isn't, although I am advised to beware horny sea otters. A promise being a promise, I take the plunge, deciding to do it for the Sir Bobby Robson Foundation. Mere mention of his name cuts through a swathe of red tape, ensuring instant support from the Port of Tyne, Newcastle City Marina, HMS *Calliope*, local sea cadets, the dredger *Sir Bobby Robson* and my guide through the murky depths, Tony Greener, an upbeat, experienced local swimmer whose only expression of disappointment comes early on when I mention I'm swimming the Tyne widthways, not lengthways.

Newcastle being Toon-mad, and keenly backing any event raising money for the Sir Bobby Robson Foundation, a considerable public and media presence has formed on the Quayside when I arrive on a sunny Sunday for the eleven a.m. splash-off. Sky Sport's Geoff Shreeves kindly helps me into the Tyne with the encouraging words, 'We've never had a drowning live in HD before.' Anyway, a few grand is raised, not least from Pardew and Ashley themselves, as well as many fans lobbing change into buckets. That's the Robson factor at work.

His Foundation continues to grow and grow, helping the Freeman Hospital in Newcastle. 'It is just going to go on, from strength to strength, with beautiful days like this,' says his widow, looking out at the sun-dappled fairways of Rockliffe Hall. 'He would just be proud that this is what he's achieved, this is his legacy; everyone who has come today they've come because of him. It's a wonderful legacy, isn't it? Saving lives.' And making a nation dream for one glorious summer, as Bobby Robson did at Italia 90.

7

Gascoigne v. Gazza

IT's TURIN, THE eve of the World Cup semi-final against West Germany, and Bobby Robson is holding his key team meeting. England's manager outlines to his players how he wants them to line up when the opposition have possession. Chris Waddle takes up the story. 'Bobby said: "Right, three in midfield." That was me, David Platt and Gazza playing against Olaf Thon, Lothar Matthäus and a tricky little winger, Thomas Hässler. "In an ideal world," Bobby said, "when we lose the ball, Chris, you pick Hässler up, Platty, you pick Thon up, and Gazza, if you can latch on to Matthäus as much as possible, it'll be a good battle." They dutifully absorb the manager's words. 'Yes, yes, yes, yes, all right, yes,' is Gascoigne's response, according to Waddle. As the meeting breaks up, Gascoigne looks at Waddle and asks: 'Who the fuck is Matthäus?'

As the players vacate the room, Robson calls Gascoigne over. 'I need a word with you,' the manager says. Here we go, thinks the 22-year-old, I'm about to be dropped. The night before, Robson caught his hyperactive midfielder playing tennis when he should have been rest-ing up. 'The tennis last night . . . forget about that,' Robson begins. He has a more urgent message to impart, expanding on his team-talk. His gifted, scatty, endearing No. 19 is about to step into the drain-ing domain of Matthäus. 'Tonight,' explains Robson, 'you're playing against the best midfielder in the world.'

'No,' replies Gascoigne, 'he is.'

Awareness of opponents' capacities should always be encouraged but so should bloody-mindedness towards imminent acquaintance. No fear please. England need the audacity and love of the game that Gascoigne embodies to pervade the modern generation. When Ross Barkley or Dele Alli start moving upfield with the ball for Roy Hodgson's team, comparisons are made with him. Forget the technical affinity; the more flattering echoes are temperamental. Be bold. Express yourself. 'Gazza was as good as anybody in that World Cup, if not better,' says Waddle. Arrogance never suffuses Gascoigne the player, solely self-belief. The shirt with the Three Lions never burdens him as it has so many of the 1,200 to wear it since 1872. 'He had no fear,' continues Waddle. 'He didn't know anybody. If I said "Gullit" before the game with Holland, Gazza would go: "Heard of him." But it wouldn't be: "Oooh, I'm playing against Gullit and Rijkaard." He would be: "Who? I'm better than them." That's how he was. He had this streak of, "I don't look at anybody else. They might be great players but I'm not bothered, I'm not interested in them." He just said to me: "Point out Matthäus for us when we're on the pitch because I don't know who he is."' Strolling from the dressing-room into the tunnel at Stadio delle Alpi on 4 July, Gascoigne glances across at the Germans, Matthäus included, and smiles to himself. 'I knew Germany were a strong team but I was enjoying it. I thought I was at the boys' club when I was younger. I feared no one.'

Gascoigne's story is part inspirational lesson, part morality tale that needs to be heeded by all members of the latest feted fraternity of England starlets. It's encouraging to hear Jack Wilshere become one of the first to acquire a copy of the documentary *Gascoigne*, in 2015. He even watches the bio-pic of Gascoigne's life on the flight to Ljubljana, crediting it with helping inspire his two elegant goals in the Euro qualifier against Slovenia. Some English footballers are frequently too lazy, or averse, to analyse the faults and strengths of those of yesteryear. They don't seek education. Arriving in the England set-up is just the beginning, demanding even more work, even more understanding of the game's stresses and responsibilities. Scrutinizing events in Gascoigne's life, on and off the field, provides information to improve them as players and people. None of them has seen what

Gascoigne has, a World Cup semi-final and a scary world outside that continues to haunt him. A sensitive, scarred Geordie is hounded, hacked, sectioned, belittled and always, always cherished.

Making a TV commercial for the *Telegraph* about the 'Meaning of Life' (as you do in the media village) twenty years ago, I state that it's 'Gascoigne not Gazza'. It's pure footballing talent, not the hyped stereotype and off-field chaos, that should quicken the public pulse. Gascoigne's a man of two halves, insecure and inspirational: there's Mad Gazza, the tabloid clown telling Norway to fuck off and wearing plastic boobs, and there's also Majestic Gascoigne, the national icon taking the game to Matthäus. No fear and Lothar. Injuries and that deep lack of self-esteem away from the pitch cost Gascoigne. During Euro 96, he speaks so intelligently about the game's ills, and especially the need to light the fire of creativity in youngsters, that I ask him if he fancies becoming technical director as there is a situation vacant at the FA. Sitting in a bay window at Bisham Abbey, he ponders the question. Only briefly. Faced with a serious situation, Gascoigne typically grabs for the Gazza guise, and responds with a joke about training just involving dribbling and shooting from now on. He's back being daft as a brush again, to borrow Bobby Robson's phrase. We all laugh obediently, sadly keeping Gascoigne pigeonholed as Gazza. Pity. Gascoigne has much to offer the FA off the pitch as well as England on it.

'I made him aware that after '90 he was my hero,' says Michael Owen of his admiration for Gascoigne, giving an insight into an eccentric, lovable individual who fears loneliness. In 2000, when Owen is playing for Liverpool, he receives a call from Everton. 'You're Gazza's daughter's favourite player and it's her birthday,' explains the official from Goodison. 'So is it all right if he comes round to your house just to say hello as a surprise for her?'

'Yes, all right then, fine,' says Owen, hiding his bemusement.

He takes up the story. 'A few hours later there's a knock on the door and there's Gazza with his daughter, surprising her with meeting me. I said: "Hi, happy birthday, have a photo."' Owen thinks that'll be it. 'Then Gazza invites himself in. Eight hours later we've played snooker, table tennis, darts, I've taken them out to the local restaurant, my family are all round, and Gazza's just entertaining everyone. Gazza was brilliant company. I relaxed in his company within minutes, because he's naturally nice, naturally loves people. I could imagine him being really lonely if he was in his own company.'

A dark side lurks within Gascoigne, and it spills out occasionally and damagingly, but he remains hugely popular with the public. They appreciate characters as well as intrepid footballers. In the past quarter-century, we seem to have forgotten the spirit of Gascoigne, certainly in Academies where character is discouraged. The public haven't forgotten. As players become more distant from their roots, the flawed, very human Gascoigne becomes even more appreciated. He embodies a trait always loved: the impudent becoming imperious in exacting sporting circumstances. Gascoigne plays the game every kid dreams of: dribbling, daring, chasing goals and glory. Gascoigne is football unplugged, the sport stripped to its elemental joys, one-on-one, going for goal. As the years pass, his approach becomes even more cherished. When the *Gascoigne* film is launched at the Ritzy cinema, Brixton, south London, on a sunny summer eve in 2015, the pavement teems with besotted supporters of all ages, some in Italia 90 shirts, others in Hummel tops of Gazza Spurs vintage. Twenty photographers jostle for prime position, beseeching the star to stare down their lenses. Dressed in a dark blue suit, hair slicked back and with a goatee beard, Gascoigne resembles an art director ready to pitch for an ad agency. Inside the Ritzy, fans excitedly take their seats, awaiting the film of Gascoigne's life, enjoying the anecdotes, the footage of him at Italia 90 when a nation dares to dream. Distributors later reveal they handle the UK rights to the *Twilight* series and not even the photogenic vampires generate as many press column inches as *Gascoigne*.

That night, the film is simulcast to hundreds of screens across the country, as is the ensuing Q&A. Gascoigne appearances are relatively infrequent, partly because of his anger over his phone being hacked by the *Mirror* which eventually brings £180,250 in damages, and also issues with his health as he continues to combat alcoholism.

But Gascoigne is here at the glitzy Ritzy, walking towards the stage moments after the credits roll on his film. Having covered much of Gascoigne's career, I'm asked to host the Q&A, an honour but also a potential hospital pass depending on the mood of a mercurial man. But he's wonderful, mainly Gascoigne but with occasional Gazza blips. For half an hour, and emboldened by the enlightening presence and contributions of Stuart Pearce and Pete Davies, the acclaimed author of the Italia 90 book *All Played Out*, Gascoigne transfixes the audience in the Ritzy and across the country.

The obvious place to start is Turin, asking him about the moment in the tunnel, when he looks over at the Germans and feels he can take them on. Does he feel fearless? 'Definitely – I felt that when I was three, mate,' Gascoigne replies. He glances to his left, to Pearce, a fellow warrior from Italia 90. 'When you've got guys like this in the dressing-room, you dare not be scared. When you hear them roar: "This is fucking England!" Terry Butcher: "This is my house!" Stuart ready to get wired in. I had so much confidence in these guys behind me. These guys would say: "Go on, express yourself. If you lose the ball don't worry, we'll win it back for you and give it you again." We had a strong team, an unbelievable team. What a team we had! Psycho was fearless. Butcher, Wrighty, Shilts, Chris Waddle, all world-class players coming into their prime.' I ask him who of the current England team would make the Italia 90 XI. 'I'd like to think nobody.' Rooney? 'Wayne, yes. Maybe put him right-back! Brilliant! Sorry, Paul Parker!' The comment sparks a brief furore on Twitter but also a more reflective discussion on England's current playing resources. 'Shallow' is the conclusion. The emergence of Alli, Kane, Stones and Barkley provide some measure of riposte.

Games provide a refuge for Gascoigne, an individual troubled by the childhood trauma of seeing a young boy he's looking after on a trip to the shops run out into the road and being hit by a car. As the film painfully reveals, Gascoigne blames himself. 'That's maybe where some of the problems stemmed from,' he tells me in the Q&A afterwards. 'And football was a release for me. I knew I didn't have any of these problems for 90 minutes.' Italy seems almost a sanctuary.

Even in the stodgy opening game against the Republic of Ireland in Cagliari on 11 June, Gascoigne is busy, striving to impose his talent. Against the Dutch five days later he is now in his element, showing no respect to illustrious reputation, knocking over Gullit, leaning over the renowned striker, at one point tugging his dreadlocks, and then doing a Cruyff turn on Ronald Koeman, playing the Dutch at their own game. He drives through the middle, wrong-footing Koeman, his passage to goal halted only by Adri van Tiggelen's foul. 'He could inspire a team,' recalls another of the heroes of Italia 90, John Barnes, when we meet up. 'When we played against teams and people said they were better than us, Gazza would do something stupid to them and that made us feel that we were as good as them. No matter who you were playing against, who he met, he'd be unfazed. If Gazza met the Queen or Nelson Mandela, he'd go, "Hi, Queen" or "Hi, Nelson." '

Five days on from the Dutch draw, Gascoigne's free-kick to Mark Wright brings the winner against Egypt. 'Gazza was brilliant,' says Wright. 'You couldn't coach him anything because he just had it. If you did try to coach him and put things into his head, he wouldn't have got it or gone, "Just leave me, just give me the ball and I'll get on with it." He was like Bobby Charlton.'

Wright recalls a tale from his days under Alan Ball at Southampton. 'Alan told me a story about the day Sir Alf pulled him and Nobby Stiles over.

' "Lads, do you have dogs?"

' "Yes, we do, Gaffer. Why are you asking?"

' "Do you take them for a walk?"

' "Yes, we do." I was wondering what Bally was telling me.

' "Do you take a stick or a ball with you to throw for the dog?"

' "Just a stick, you see them everywhere."

' "When you get that stick, do you throw it – for the dog?"

' "Yes, of course."

' "Does that dog bring it back to you? Nobby? Alan?"

' "Yes!"

' "Well, that's exactly what I want you to do for Bobby Charlton. Just get it, and give it back to him. Because he'll score goals." That was brilliant. That was like us. We had to get the ball and give it to Gazza. No one in the opposition could read what Gazza was going to do. Give it to him, and let him go.'

Responding to the lyric of New Order's evocative World Cup song that flies to No. 1, Gascoigne sets England's world in motion. In the first knock-out round, against Belgium in Bologna on 26 June, Gascoigne's effervescence brings reward. Never one to stand still on ceremony, he sticks his tongue out at the cameras. He creates England's goal: his run draws fouls from Eric Gerets and Stéphane Demol and his free-kick draws a sublime, athletic response from David Platt. Caught up in the excitement, he lunges in on Enzo Scifo and is rightly booked. It does not seem that significant at the time. England are too busy celebrating reaching the quarter-finals against Cameroon to focus too much attention on Gascoigne's caution. With the score 2-2 in extra time in Naples on 1 July, Gascoigne shimmies through the middle before passing towards Lineker, who is tripped by Thomas N'Kono. Lineker's penalty sweeps England into the last four.

At full-time, Gascoigne is enveloped in a hug by Robson. Back in the Ritzy, Pete Davies recalls the Robson–Gascoigne dynamic. 'There was an absolute father–son relationship,' says Davies, an author so trusted by England's manager and players that he became almost embedded in the squad at Italia 90. 'There was an absolute belief in his talent. As the tournament approached, it was clear that Bobby desperately wanted to take Paul to Italy, but that he had that fear about responsibility at the highest international level, and is someone he called "daft as a brush" going to make that mistake that's going to cost you? The love of the talent and belief in the talent far outweighed that fear. He let Paul go and do what only Paul can do. Who was the player of the tournament? Diego Maradona might have dragged Argentina to the final on sheer, mad willpower, but the joy of playing football, what we all dream football can be, makes the player of the tournament the one sat there.' The Ritzy murmurs its approval.

Gascoigne smiles and fidgets as Davies' praise continues, focusing on his livewire presence off the pitch in Italy as well as on. Gascoigne is a study in insecurity and genius. 'He's Zebedee, he's Tigger, he never stops until he goes: "You know what? I'm tired." And gone. Then he gets up and is bouncing around again. Everyone else runs out of energy, and he's got no one left to play table tennis with, so he played against himself. He hit the ball and ran round the other end. The rallies weren't very long but the energy was just phenomenal. That translated through the squad and on to the pitch. That character and personality lifted them when they were down, gave them a sense that anything was possible. Gascoigne lifted twenty-one million people at home who watched that game and it transformed football in this country.'

He is unique. His team-mates know it. 'In England, we love Gazza,' says Barnes of a complicated joker off the pitch and a magician on it. 'Gazza was a great player, just a bit bonkers off the pitch, a bit annoying sometimes,' recalls Peter Shilton. 'But give him a football, let him on a pitch, and that was where Gazza was at his best. Anywhere else he could be a nightmare!' Back in the Ritzy, Pearce enthuses: 'I'd liken Gazza to Messi nowadays. I was fortunate. The majority of the games I played with England we played together so I had a genius in my team. He could win a game on his own. England have never had a genius of his type since Bobby Charlton when we actually won the World Cup. [Gascoigne] played 57 times for England, and been on the losing side four times if you discount penalties, and that tells you everything about the fella.' Pearce's words are almost lost in the wave of applause flowing across the Ritzy floor.

While managing the Under-21s and (for one game) the seniors, Pearce works with the country's best youngsters, and with many of the more established talents in recent years, but 'I've not seen the genius that I saw with Paul'. He adds: 'The modern game is so sanitized, and so exposed to the media, that it gets dumbed down, that it almost suppresses personality, which is sad. The one thing Paul has, for good and bad, is personality, and he expresses that in everyday life and on the pitch.' Personality. A fear frequently expressed during my journey through English football is that the youth development system can suppress character.

Experts at prising possession from a gifted opponent vouch for

England's World Cup win in 1966 was forged off the pitch as well as on it. Sir Alf Ramsey made sure the players were kept entertained, whether by games of cricket, such as this one at Roehampton (*above*) or at Pinewood Studios (*below*), where Jimmy Greaves and Bobby Moore met Sean Connery and Yul Brynner.

Nobby Stiles gets stuck in against France. Following his 'rough play', the FA demanded that the midfielder was omitted from the next game, against Argentina, but Ramsey stood by his man.

A version of one of the most iconic images in England football history, and one that brought out the emotion in Jack Charlton when we met for this book.

Never let it be forgotten that the players gave every ounce of their energy, as you can see etched particularly on the face of Bobby Charlton, here with Stiles, Moore and Ray Wilson.

Jules Rimet still gleaming. This was at a reception at the television studios in Elstree on Sunday 31 July, the day after the final, with Gordon Banks and George Cohen, alongside Jack Charlton, Ramsey and Moore, pictured in awe of the famous trophy.

It's sometimes forgotten that England reached the semi-finals of the European Championship in 1968. Alan Mullery's red card in the 1-0 defeat by Yugoslavia — England's first sending-off — is notorious, but Ramsey again looked after his man, even paying the fine imposed on Mullery by the FA.

Mullery did all he could to stop Pelé (*below*) in Guadalajara in 1970 — it was one of England's greatest ever matches — but heartbreak would follow against West Germany in León, where Sir Bobby Charlton played his 106th and final international (*bottom*).

Jan Tomaszewski, aka 'the clown', the morning after England's exit from World Cup qualifying at the hands of Poland in 1973.

Neither Don Revie (below with Kevin Keegan, Brian Greenhoff and Stan Bowles) nor Ron Greenwood (*bottom*) could arrest England's slump in the seventies, despite the quality of players like (*left to right*) Viv Anderson, Ray Kennedy, Phil Neal, Phil Thompson, Mick Mills, Peter Barnes and Glenn Hoddle.

Hoddle would make his debut in a European Championship qualifier against Bulgaria in 1979, but was always used too sparingly, or out of position. At Euro 1980, he was left on the bench as a draw with Belgium and loss to hosts Italy saw England crash out at the group stage.

After Hoddle, more exceptionally talented players like Paul Gascoigne, Chris Waddle and John Barnes were treated with distrust. England must conquer this fear of flair.

Gazza in his prime, running rings around Holland at Italia '90, with Ronald Koeman left on the deck.

Gary Lineker's attention to detail in both preparing for and then taking penalties was exemplary, twice outwitting Cameroon goalkeeper Thomas N'Kono and the spy who watched England training the previous day in Naples.

Sir Bobby Robson came closest to leading England to a second World Cup victory, but to Franz Beckenbauer's West Germany went the glory.

He is never forgotten, but Sir Bobby's successors (*below*), here at his memorial service, failed to come anywhere close.

His widow Lady Elsie (*bottom*) continues to work tirelessly for the Sir Bobby Robson Foundation, helped by devoted supporters of the charity like Alan Shearer.

Gascoigne's technique and personality. 'I remember at Everton we were great at squeezing, shutting down – they call it "pressing the ball" now,' says Peter Reid. 'I was playing against Gazza in front of the Gallowgate End. Newcastle got a throw-in and I'm half a yard off Gazza with his little belly and I'm thinking: "Go and give it to him." So they give it to him on the 18-yard box. I went to tackle him, and he's given me the old drag-back and gone the other way. I couldn't believe that. That was his talent. He believed he was still in the schoolyard.'

English football has lost much of the 'schoolyard' culture, partly because Academy prospects are discouraged from playing with fellow pupils at school. Technical players are produced but not with the brio of Gascoigne, running at opponents as he did in Italy, his arms out to fend off would-be tacklers, weaving and forcing his way through like a determined bargain-hunter at the MetroCentre sales. 'He was an entertainer and a lovely, lovely human being,' continues Reid. 'I remember winning a tackle against Gazza at Man City as player-manager. I'm getting up and he said, "Good tackle." You can imagine what I said back! Five minutes later, he did the same. "Good tackle." I'm thinking: "Is he taking the piss?" That was Gazza.' In total love with the game. Reid detects a vulnerability. 'Gazza had a raw talent which was breathtaking but if you're asking me, "Did he have it all?" there was something missing; whether [it was] the winning mentality, I don't know. He was a genius. George Best had the genius, he finished too early, but he did it all.'

Gascoigne tries. His personality, blemished and beautiful, shines through in Turin. And so to the infamous tennis match. On the day before the semi-final, Gascoigne can be found limbering up in the hotel grounds. 'Gazza's in a pair of shorts turned up, pair of trainers on, nothing else, dripping with sweat,' recalls Waddle of the impromptu Turin Open. 'Bobby Robson saw him and said: "Gazza, what are you doing?"

'"I'm just bored. I'm having this game of tennis with this Italian bloke."

'"We've got a bloody semi-final tomorrow."

'"I know."

'"Make that your last game and get in."
'"All right."
'"What's the score anyway?"
'"Six-five in the fifth set."'

Waddle laughs at the memory. 'That's Gazza! He had energy, he was hyperactive. He never slept a lot. Every light had to be on. Telly had to be on. Lucky enough, I can fall asleep easily. But a lot of times I'd wake up at two in the morning and think "What?!" Every light was on, lamps, lights, telly going buzzzzzzz. It was like sleeping in the Blackpool Illuminations. I had to go round turning everything off. Gazza would wake at six a.m., open the patio doors, run out and I'd hear a splash. He'd dive in the pool and do thirty lengths. He was obsessed with his fitness at the World Cup. He has always been obsessed with his weight. That was the fittest he ever was at that World Cup. He never got back to that World Cup weight ever. He did eat but he was a picker. He was super-fit in that World Cup; whether playing tennis, swimming for an hour, he had energy to burn. We had to keep him calmed down. I had to look after him 24/7. It was like the key in the back was wound so much he was ready to go. He came out of the blocks quick at the World Cup, he had so much confidence and momentum.'

Lining up between Waddle and Pearce in the Turin tunnel, Gascoigne stares briefly across at the Germans. Captured by the television cameras, footage shows a player undaunted by vaunted opponents, simply impatient for the signal to leave the tunnel, and then the whistle to commence hostilities. 'In that tunnel, I thought what I'd been through, dreaming of that moment, playing for your country, being 90 minutes away from the final,' he tells that enraptured audience in the Ritzy.

He pours heart and soul into the semi. A snap shot from the edge of the area forces Bodo Illgner into an athletic, sprawling save. Andreas Brehme and Lineker swap goals. 1-1 – extra time. Gascoigne's renowned exuberance then proves expensive. Over-running the ball, he clatters Thomas Berthold. It's not malicious, anything but. The Englishman, who's having a fine game, immediately holds his hands up in contrition as Berthold puts in an extra roll. Streetwise. Behaving with all the sternness of a judge passing down a stiff sentence, the Brazilian official José Ramiz Wright reaches for his card. Always expressive, Gascoigne's face registers the significance. His second booking of the World Cup: he's suspended for the final should England progress. No matter how many times the scene is reviewed it never loses its impact on an England fan. The heart bleeds for Gascoigne. He's bereft. He knows. He cares. He's in bits, tearful, the picture of distress. Lineker immediately conveys the delicacy of Gascoigne's state of mind to Robson. 'Have a word,' he mouths to his manager. Sensing their hero's anguish, the England fans on the terraces of the Delle Alpi begin chanting, 'We love you, Gazza'. For the young heirs to Gascoigne's tradition, the incident stands as a reminder of the need for discipline, to be mindful of the price that can be paid for excess. But also caring so much it hurts.

As the 120-minute mark passes, Gascoigne falls to his knees before the shoot-out. He knows he's down to take a penalty but decides against. Too emotional to focus. Doc Crane wipes down Gascoigne's face, removing the sweat and tears. Robson, typically, says a few kind words. 'You've done your country proud,' he tells Gascoigne. Yards away, others prepare to take their penalties. 'Unfortunately Stuart missed his penalty but at least he was brave enough to take his penalty,' reflects Gascoigne in the Ritzy. At the denouement, as England's brutal relationship with penalties begins, Gascoigne's in tears again, kissing the hem of his shirt, highlighting the power the England top holds over him.

He returns a hero on 8 July. 'We flew back to Luton because that's where Chris Waddle's penalty ended up, just to get the ball back!' he laughs at the Ritzy. As they prepare to disembark, Lineker whispers to Gascoigne: 'Be careful.' This sage of strikers senses how Gascoigne's world is about to change beyond recognition, much as his had after his Golden Ball at the previous World Cup. Lineker, however, has always possessed the sangfroid and support system to handle fame. Gascoigne struggles. 'We want Gazza, we want Gazza!' chant the 250,000 fans as he emerges from the Britannia flight, giving a thumbs-up. 'When I got off that plane, and witnessed that, I didn't realize the impact,' says Gascoigne, back in the Ritzy.

For a sunlit period, Gascoigne surfs the wave of success, enjoying the lucrative endorsements gushing his way. In a discussion on the relative merits of Gascoigne and Bryan Robson, Barnes makes the point that in 1990 Gascoigne catches the zeitgeist of a nation increasingly in thrall to the cult of the celebrity. He's a sporting icon with a lovable, human side, action man with tear-ducts, and the public adore him. Personality rules. His *Spitting Image* puppet, complete with tear-launching eyes, is on display at the National Football Museum in Manchester. 'Gazza was a great footballer but Bryan Robson was better than Gazza,' says Barnes. 'Robbo was incredible. As great as he was in 1982, Robbo was never a celebrity footballer. In the nineties, football started to change. This whole celebrity footballing culture came and Gazza was ideal for that particular time. When people needed a hero to step forward, Gazza was the one. In terms of prestige, the perception of him was far greater than other footballers. He was a fantastic player but there were players who were equally as good as Gazza.'

After the tournament, Gascoigne travels north to Dunston Park, his old Gateshead stamping ground. He stands and looks at the field of his childhood dreams. 'I couldn't believe I used to play there as a young kid, and my dream came true,' he says, surveying the crowd at the Ritzy. 'To any young kids, it can come true.'

Dreams can turn into nightmares. Injuries nudge Gascoigne down a dangerous road, removing him from the realm he loves most, and where he feels safest; they damage him as a player, and harm him as a person. Waddle rues the bad breaks that befall his friend, preventing him climbing higher in the game. 'People forget that for all Gazza's attributes, running with the ball, dribbling and beating people, he was a box-to-box midfielder,' says Waddle. 'I just wished he'd had a ten-year run where he didn't get injured, and got six hundred games, probably scored two hundred goals.' Gascoigne still records 98 goals in 462 matches for Newcastle, Spurs, Lazio, Rangers, Middlesbrough, Everton, Burnley and Boston United, plus 10 goals in his 57 England internationals, and not forgetting 2 goals in 4 appearances for Gansu Tianma in China. Waddle's right, though; Gascoigne's career can almost be split into before and after the 1991 FA Cup final between Spurs and Nottingham Forest.

On the eve of that game, Gascoigne's excitement is off the scale when meeting the Boys of '66 at the Royal Lancaster Hotel where they're celebrating the twenty-fifth anniversary of lifting the World Cup. The following day he is too hyped up, apparently needing Valium in the build-up, and should really be cautioned, ordered to calm down, or even dismissed by Roger Milford after a filthy studs-up assault into the chest of Garry Parker. Fired up, Gascoigne flies into a reckless challenge on Gary Charles, tearing cruciate ligaments in his right knee. 'From the World Cup, doing his knee within a year, and then that's when all the things started, on the field, off the field,' observes Waddle, surveying the pitch at Wembley where Gascoigne fell. 'His knee wasn't right, he had pulled thigh strains, hamstrings, calves, so we never really got to see what the next level would have been for Gazza. The level he was at was very high, don't get me wrong, but he could have gone on to another level. He would have added more to his game. I used to say to him: "Don't tackle all the time." He said: "I love to tackle." "Don't, you're needed on the ball; you can compete, we know that." He had this thing where he wanted to be a presence, like a Bryan Robson, launch in, win the ball, and everyone go "wow". It cost him all the time. He did his ankle, his knee. When he used to have a fifty-fifty, nine times out of ten he would limp away. It wouldn't be the other guy.'

Moments of wizardry still surface: a powerful header from a Beppe Signori free-kick in the Rome derby, his first for Lazio, and juggling the ball over Colin Hendry's head at Euro 96, flicking it up with his left foot and finishing with his right. His celebration of that goal against Scotland is glorious, mocking press criticism of his Dentist's Chair drinking antics during a raucous refuelling stop on England's tour to the Far East, lying back as Teddy Sheringham sprays water in his mouth. This is the joy of Gascoigne the footballer: he makes people laugh as well as gasp in admiration at his technical prowess.

'I wish English players would show emotion like Gazza did when he pulled on the England strip,' one fan posts online about the *Gascoigne* documentary. 'There is not one England player who is fit to clean Paul's boots playing at the moment.'

Those players could learn from his off-field travails, understanding how to avoid them. Gascoigne and controversy are frequent neighbours. When England players are derided for those Dentist's Chair antics on the eve of Euro 96, 86 per cent of *Daily Mirror* readers polled want Gascoigne banned from the tournament. Fortunately for Gascoigne, Terry Venables stands firm, and he contributes to some of the majesty of that semi-final summer.

After the *Mirror* reveals pictures of Gascoigne's bruised wife Sheryl on 17 October, England are forced to stage a toe-curling press conference before the World Cup qualifier with Georgia. Gascoigne and Glenn Hoddle walk into a room with a febrile atmosphere. Headlines howl abuse at the new manager. 'How Can a Christian Select a Wife-beater for England?' reads one. Once again, England are lost in the moral maze. Gascoigne should never be picked for the tie. It transmits a poor message seeing him associated with the honour of representing his country. Hoddle tries to defend his decision, using biblical imagery in explaining that 'if we can make him into a role model, that is more positive than casting him out'. Gascoigne then appears at the press conference to voice his 'regret', saying that he doesn't 'blame the likes of women's rights' for campaigning against him. The FA's then chairman, Keith Wiseman, a likeable man but a weak leader, and the chief executive Graham Kelly discuss the situation with Hoddle, who says he wants Gascoigne to see a counsellor. The FA agrees to his plan. 'Rock Bottom, Gazza's In' concludes the *Evening Standard*.

Even Hoddle has soon had enough of Gascoigne. Having spotted his midfielder drunk in the bar at La Manga, England's training base in Spain, on the eve of France 98, Hoddle knows he can't take such a troubled soul to the World Cup. Michael Owen tempers that refuelling argument with a tactical angle. 'Glenn was going with Scholesy as his playmaker, and he probably thought if Gazza is not in the starting eleven, what's he going to be like? Yes, he can come on and turn a game. Yes, if Scholesy gets injured. But on balance if he's not starting he'd not be a great player to have there for so long. It was a huge shock to everyone.'

Owen is afforded his first real experience of the sights and sounds of the long-running Three Lions circus with events in the Royal Suite at La Manga. It's in that room that Hoddle excises Gascoigne from his World Cup squad to the background noise of saxophonist Kenny G and the shattering of a bedside lamp. 'It was horrible in a way,' recalls Owen. 'We all expected Gazza to get in the squad. The news spread straight away that Gazza was not in the squad. Then the word was out that "he's supposed to have flipped and smashed the room". Walking into Glenn's room, I was so nervous about my slot but also wanting to look around to see what damage he'd done. To be honest, I couldn't see much at all. I expected the beds turned over.'

Gascoigne's career drifts, and his life certainly darkens as he deals with demons of his own and others' manufacture. But is he aware how much the country still loves him? Gascoigne looks again at the adoring audience inside the Ritzy. 'That means so much to me, seeing people come here to see me.' Outrage then tumbles from his lips at becoming a plaything for newspapers to throw around without considering the consequences, at the way his addictions, his domestic life and strife, and his mobile phone are deemed fair game by sections of the media. 'There's only so much a man can take,' he says. 'I've got no escape route. I did with these guys [like Pearce] in the dressing-room. I don't mind being followed 24/7, it's when they write lies, and it's constant. I got hacked for six years, then sectioned for eleven days, and it hurt. I got hacked again. I don't look for perfection, I look for progress. It's difficult when I wake up in the morning and read more lies about us. Being famous is not all glory. I just wanted a decent life and to enjoy football. I didn't become a professional footballer so I could get to be hounded to bits for the rest of my life, and I've not played for twelve years. What have I done to deserve this? I ended up an alcoholic. Just leave us alone. But they are constantly there. Keep getting knocked down, keep getting picked up. One day they are going to crucify someone who's weaker than me.' He looks lost yet loved. The Ritzy stands to salute him; to support him.

A few days later, I contact Gary Lineker for his view of a gifted footballer but troubled soul. 'Gazza cared,' he tells me. 'He was a law unto himself. He was great fun. In his prime he was very sharp, witty, fun, but mad as a box of frogs.'

8

The Specialist One

SURROUNDED BY QUICK-thinking Scottish friends in the most fervent home section of Hampden Park, I feel firm hands on my shoulders when England score, pre-empting the instinctive joyous, upward response. It's 26 May 1984, eight minutes from half-time, and Tony Woodcock equalizes Mark McGhee's opener. It's a poignant occasion, closing the Home Internationals after a century of internecine combat. A day for mourning the passing of a grand tradition also provides a glimpse of the future with a 23-year-old Leicester lad called Gary Lineker sprinting on for his England debut.

Viewed through visitors' eyes, there's plenty to admire, including the four-prong attack of Mark Chamberlain, Luther Blissett, Woodcock and John Barnes, Bryan Robson's surges from midfield, Peter Shilton's saves and the unexpected bonus of Lineker replacing Woodcock in the second half, launching one of the finest international careers that brings 48 goals and 80 caps. Scooping up a discarded 'Remember Bannockburn' flag, a souvenir that prompts a very English relative to remark, 'But darling, didn't we lose?', I also take home the memory of Lineker inflicting his intelligent movement on opposing defences. He is revered for rescuing his country at moments when all hope seems lost, for the sporting manner in which he plays the game, and the eloquent way he represents his teams and his profession. Millions now tune in to watch a national treasure perform on BBC's *Match of the Day* and BT's Champions League coverage, appreciating how he skilfully coaxes opinions from studio guests, yet he has even more to offer. If he wasn't such a calm, capable presenter, Lineker would be on the front row of the pundits' grid with Gary Neville and Graeme Souness. When in December 2015 Neville makes his first foray into management with Valencia, analysis levels dip.

That is why an hour in Lineker's thoughtful company, at his stylish but understated London members' club, is an education. He arrives absolutely spot on time, reflecting his approach towards the 6-yard box and also underlining a general theme of this voyage of discovery into England's travails: many of those with experience of elite sport acquire a respect for time-keeping not discarded in retirement. Assiduous in his preparation, Lineker's opinions are well-informed. He talks to players, and has insight into the Academy system attended by one of his four sons, Tobias at Chelsea. He's upbeat about the future, tweeting regularly about Dele Alli's promise and voicing optimism over the technical qualities of the prospects emerging from the Academy system. He frequently name-checks John Stones. But there's a caveat, a polite plea for the new breed to work harder at their craft. As usual, Lineker's right. Too many of the Gold Card Generation disappear from the training ground after lunch having completed what their club manager requires that day, not what their career demands long-term. Too few seek the advice of experts, ex-pros like Lineker. Too few take a sufficiently scientific approach to their calling, analysing opponents or themselves. During his playing days, Lineker challenges himself every day, improving, listening and learning. If a powerful assault is to be mounted on the World Cup again, England need more like Lineker, the Golden Boot winner at Mexico 86 and serial saviour at Italia 90.

He possesses an instinct for goals enhanced by intellect. 'If I knew a team were playing a high line, I'd go and be deliberately offside,' he reveals. 'I'd let them catch me two or three times in the first ten to fifteen minutes. I did that loads of times, especially against Arsenal. The defenders then get a bit cocky because they're catching you every time, and they'd give it "offside" and maybe you're a little bit offside, but the linesman has put his flag up three times already, the crowd start getting on to him, so subconsciously he's thinking about the crowd, and you go through.

'I always used to think about the game from a fairly early age but I wasn't like Rooney or Owen, a young superstar. I didn't get in the England team until I was 23. I was a slow developer, with very late maturity in terms of growth. I was tiny. Eventually I shot up at 18. What helped me was I had the freakish chance to be coached as a schoolboy at Leicester by George Dewis, a prolific goalscorer, and all he ever did in training was finishing. Brilliant for goalkeepers, and wonderful for strikers, but pretty damn useless for defenders! That's all I did for years. There isn't any coincidence that my finishing ability was massively enhanced as he took the first two years of when I was an apprentice, so I had that until 18. I was so quick that you could hoof it over the top and I used to run, and get four one-on-ones, and I was always good at one-on-ones.'

Goals pay the rent, as David Coleman wisely commented, in which case Lineker would make the ideal house-mate. He's a specialist in the art of plundering goals, 192 in 340 League games, preparing for those killer moments through constant practice. 'I never quite under-stood football training. Everyone does the same thing. "Right, today we're doing defending." You're standing around doing some shadow things for the defenders. Why would you want to be doing defensive training if you're a forward? Just standing there like a cone. You could stick a dummy out there. It used to drive me mad. I had a reputation for not liking training but I didn't like training because I never felt I was getting anything out of it. Ninety per cent of the time I felt it was completely pointless. I'd sooner rather do really hard physical training for my fitness than stand there doing tactical stuff for defences. Then: "Right, let's do some finishing." Everyone does. There are twenty-two of you in the squad and you wait about five minutes for a shot – it's pointless. I used to say to Terry Venables at Spurs: "Can I just go off and do it on my own? Give me some balls, give me a coach, give me two goalkeepers." By the end of my career I could do that, because I had enough status – I know what I'm doing here. We didn't practise frequently enough the skills I'd use in the game.' Lineker does, though, but only after the session has expired.

His old England team-mate Peter Shilton smiles when I mention

Lineker and training. 'Gary didn't like training! But great managers know that certain players like to train hard and others don't. But if you did a bit of shooting practice at the end of training, Gary would be there. That's what strikers are about, putting it in the net, and Gary loved that. Running around, and dribbling, wasn't Gary. But he was the greatest striker I played with for England.'

A common complaint heard from former internationals is the apparent reluctance of current contenders to contact illustrious forebears for assistance and instruction. 'Players have never done that,' replies Lineker. 'They should be doing that at their own clubs. They are quite shy these kids and some of them probably think they know it all already. We'd all happily help them at any stage. It seems sensible to bring in specialist coaches.' As they build towards Euro 2016, England belatedly consider this, reaching out for experts, dividing the squad up more into units, almost becoming like American football in the proliferation of individual coaches. As much as we covet the concept of the total footballer, a team is a variety show. Specific roles and abilities need constant rehearsing. A model of meticulousness, Lineker has always learned his lines, a professionalism extending into his television work with hours spent scripting. 'He knew where he wanted to go,' recalls Chris Waddle. 'He used to practise on me and Gazza. He said: "Can I do some interviews with you?" We used to call him "Junior Des". He's good at it. He's got a good sense of humour, comes across well. Nice guy.'

Mr Nice Guy prepares. Take penalties – and few took them better than Lineker in crunch moments for England. 'I practised penalties always. I didn't really take them at Leicester because Steve Lynex was a really good penalty-taker and he took them. I didn't take penalties at Everton because Trevor Steven took them. I was penalty-taker for England in '86, took over before the World Cup, but we didn't have one until '90. I became penalty-taker at Barcelona and Tottenham. What I did every week after training was take some balls and practise penalties. No goalkeepers because I didn't want anyone saving them. I'd decide which penalty I'd take in the match and then I'd hit thirty or forty – bosh – into that corner, into that corner, into that corner. That was my technique.' Practice makes perfect.

The day before England face Cameroon at Italia 90, Lineker works on his spot-kicks at Stadio San Paolo in Naples. 'Bobby Robson knew I used to practise the same penalty. At training, he said to me: "I've heard Cameroon have got a spy in the stadium, so you might want to think about your penalty-taking." "Oh, all right." That day after training, I hit ten penalties, bottom left, bottom left, bottom left.'

Fast forward twenty-four hours. With England trailing 2-1 in the 81st minute, Lineker takes Mark Wright's pass in his stride, heads for goal and is felled by a threshing machine called Benjamin Massing. 'He hits me, penalty – shit, I've got to take this. All I could think was, "Do what you do in training – just hit the same penalty." I put the ball down, went back.' Lineker looks at the referee, nods, and wipes a bead of sweat from his face with his right forearm. He addresses the ball just as in training, but opens his foot slightly, skewing it right rather than left. 'As soon as I hit it I knew I'd flushed it.' It still flies in untroubled. Thomas N'Kono dives towards the corner Lineker targeted in training. A spy must have lurked in the stadium shadows. 'As I hit it I saw him going bottom left. Now I don't know if there was anything going on, but at 90 minutes Bobby Robson walks up, hits me on the leg and says: "Told you!"'

'The problem is then extra time, and we get another penalty. Shit!' The chance arises because life is beginning to drain from Paul Gascoigne's legs. He's just sauntered through the middle and seen Lineker make his run. Again, this is shrewd from Lineker. He knows Gascoigne's tiring, and is unlikely to want the ball back as he usually demands. 'Gazza would generally only pass it to you for two reasons: he was knackered or he knew you'd have to give it straight back. We had a few rows about that! Gazza was perfectly capable of threading the balls through but it wasn't part of his game he'd look to do unless circumstances [dictated].' Exhausted, Gascoigne releases the ball through the middle. 'Gazza was that good that he just looked up and found me.' For such an experienced goalkeeper, N'Kono rashly sprints out, hurtling towards Lineker, and catches the striker's feet. Penalty. 'So I thought: "Right, what do I do here?" I thought the one thing he did do for the first penalty was dive early. So I thought: "Hit it hard and down the middle." Thankfully he dived out of the way.' N'Kono goes the same way as Lineker's first penalty and is beaten.

Changing routine reveals Lineker's ability to think coolly in the heat of sporting battle. He applies a cold, almost calculating methodology to his match-day work, pushing the boundaries of acceptable sporting conduct without crossing the line into the cynical and the unforgivable. He notes the tacky behaviour of Gabriel Batistuta and Cristiano Ronaldo in pressuring officials, shamelessly contributing to the World Cup dismissals of David Beckham and Wayne Rooney respectively. 'I can't ever condone surrounding referees. It's one of the things I hate about football. It should be an automatic yellow card the moment you stick your face in front of the referee.' Lineker's approach to influencing officials is far more subtle, echoing his more cerebral style. 'In the tunnel before games, I'd go up to the ref and say: "Listen, we're playing Arsenal. [Tony] Adams or [Steve] Bould, first minute, are going to kick me up in the air." Which they always did. "If you don't do anything about it then they'll do it all day." It's streetwise.' Do they do it now? 'The intelligent ones might! John Stones is a smart footballer.'

He acknowledges Rooney's own theorizing at the 2014 World Cup that England must become more 'streetwise' – a regular debating point of the years of hurt, especially when an opponent is on a yellow. 'Yes. It's a tricky one. Do you condone cheating or be more streetwise?' Lineker preyed on defenders on bookings. 'We've all done that. When I played, cards weren't dished out as frequently as they are now, but all sorts of things went on.'

On the emotive issue of diving, Lineker argues English players have been at it for a while. 'We've had our moments when players have gone down easily enough. We all play the game now. Over the years I don't think you can say, "Actually we British players don't do that kind of thing." That changed a long time ago. I'd play to get fouled. I'd never, ever deliberately dive over somebody's legs in my life but if I could see a goalkeeper coming, I'd fractionally slow down so I could time my run so I could hit it past him, he'd come flying out and I'd make no attempt to jump over his hands. That's using a goalkeeper's naivety and stupidity to your advantage. It's a different thing to knocking it and then flinging yourself in the air. You have to make sure you're hit. But the game has progressed where players go over easily and it's ridiculous. Our players do it just the same. There was a period when we didn't. I watch them all the time now. We don't necessarily make a meal of things that some might do.'

It seems an opportune moment to ask about Diego Maradona. Did he curse his Argentine nemesis in the 1986 quarter-final? Wasn't the Hand of God despicable, a flicked two fingers to those who feel football should not be win-at-all-costs? 'He got away with it,' shrugs Lineker. All professionals say that, I reply. It's such a cop-out, this concept that there's no crime because there's no punishment. 'I wouldn't do it,' replies the two-time Footballer of the Year. 'You have to understand culturally that in that part of the world that's seen as clever. I've had the conversation with Diego about it. He goes: "Well . . . " It's trickery. To them, that's not seen necessarily as cheating like we would see it. We wouldn't do it.' There would be a critical reaction. 'It would be a mixed reaction. If it was against Argentina, I'd think it would be OK. But as it is the Euros next summer, I think the chances of that are remote! If it was just a little hand-ball or something, we'd probably accept it, but if he punched it into the net like Diego . . . ' We do obsess about morals. 'We do. And we do like to be outraged. By anything. Sometimes I do think we like something to be outraged about. That's why Twitter is more popular in this country than anywhere else. We can be outraged! I like the way Lionel Messi doesn't do any of that and he's from the same country as Diego. Sergio Agüero is honest, straight, although he throws himself down a bit. Messi doesn't. He doesn't dive. He stays on his feet and gets whacked. He doesn't go ranting and raving to referees. He behaves in a perfectly decent manner even when he's been kicked. We don't want to drift down that route of, "We're really good and holier than thou and the rest of the world are a bunch of cheats." I don't think it's quite like that. Over the years we've drifted more the other way towards, not necessarily cheating, but using every possible avenue to let ourselves win. It's always a fine line. We go round trying to win free-kicks all the time; if they get nudged they go down intentionally. They all do it.

'But Diego's second goal was the best goal I've ever seen, the closest I've ever come to applauding. The pitch was so bad it was like a potato field; every time you put your foot on it, the whole pitch slid, so to do what he did, all that way, was just astounding. I remember thinking: "Oh my God, what a fucking goal that is!" Poor old Peter Reid. Still chasing him now. In '86 we were a little bit short. Decent try, but it wasn't a side likely to win a World Cup. Defensively we weren't as strong.'

He still departs Mexico with the Golden Boot, and a couple of battered Adidas boots. Even this quirky story provides invaluable insight into what makes a leading World Cup player tick, reminding students of the game to appreciate human traits among even the toughest competitors. At the time, Lineker owns these lucky boots, a pair serving him brilliantly for Everton in the season leading up to Mexico. 'I used to be ridiculously superstitious. Someone forgot to put my boots in the skip for one game.' Oxford United away, 30 April. 'I'd scored a goal a game with them from Christmas [7 December], twenty in twenty, and they hadn't put them in the boots skip. I had to borrow somebody's boots which were a size too big. I missed a few chances, we lost [1-0], and it cost us the League title. So I got them back for the last two games [against Southampton and West Ham] and scored five.' Five days later, after the League concludes, Lineker finishes with his right in the FA Cup final defeat to Liverpool after Bruce Grobbelaar parries his left-footed shot. Packing for Mexico, he realizes the shocking state of his boots. 'They were that knackered, holes in them, so Adidas repaired them for me. I got them back for the World Cup, played three or four games and then they went again, so somebody came over and repaired them again. And I ended up getting the Golden Boot. They are now in the Adidas museum for some bizarre reason. They are a bit of mess.' He should get them back. At least one. 'The right one!'

He returns home with reputation soaring and is soon off to Maradona's old playground, Barcelona – the footballing equivalent of going from school to university. 'Lineker's movement was great and improved even more when he went to Barcelona,' says Chris Waddle. Lineker developed his skill-set, exploiting his innate astuteness of penalty-box life. 'People say footballers are stupid,' reflects Lineker. 'They're not. They might be uneducated but the players who get right to the top are intelligent. It's cunning, nous and incredible spatial awareness that ordinary people have no understanding of. You know everything around you.' Barcelona again flit through his mind. 'Lionel Messi's not a particularly articulate person, probably not very educated at all, but he has the phenomenal ability to know everything around him, to do the right thing 99 per cent of the time. How does Messi know he's got to hit the ball through that gap? It's easy to see from above but on the pitch it's not that easy. You can learn, and people will help you, tell you to see everything around you, but you're born with it to a degree. It's the same with goalscoring. I keep thinking to myself: "How can you not score twenty League goals a season?" All it's about is movement and gambling on a space. To me it seems obvious: you just go before they are about to cross it.' He attacks areas, the 6-yard area, his timing and burst of pace taking him ahead of his marker to reach the cross, frequently sliding in to turn the ball home. How does he keep managing to lose his centre-half? 'That's an uncanny natural knack,' he replies. It's more. Lineker scrutinizes the defender, noting strengths and weaknesses, assessing how well he anticipates danger. He revises for an examination that lasts 90 minutes, occasionally 120. Science is added to the 'uncanny natural knack' Lineker's blessed with.

Do current players polish their gifts with the same assiduousness? A successor in the Spurs front-line, Harry Kane, seems to have learned that 'knack' of coping with centre-backs. 'It doesn't necessarily mean he's learned it,' argues Lineker. 'It could be other things coming together: his growth, his pace, lost a bit of weight. What's Harry now, 22? That's about like me. I made my England debut at 23. Different people mature at different stages.' Kane, though, is definitely one of the modern generation who strives diligently to accentuate abilities. England boast more skilful individuals, such as Daniel Sturridge, but few rival Kane's passion for self-improvement.

They should all seek to emulate Lineker's attention to detail. He thinks deeply about the game, looking back over the generations and looking forward, convinced that a new group will emerge, following a belated refocusing of the youth development system towards flair as well as athleticism. 'We will get pockets of time where we produce enough players to be competitive. Obviously way back in '66, but more recently in '86 we were OK, if a bit short technically. In '90 we were better and we had that fluidity of system. We always trapped ourselves in 4-4-2, regimented, easy to play against, but suddenly in Italia 90 Bobby changed to three at the back and we were free, with more movement, and massive natural talents like Barnes, Waddle and Gascoigne. You are always going to get one or two talents through regardless of the system but we certainly didn't have many technically gifted players.' Especially defensively. 'While Des Walker was an absolutely brilliant defender he couldn't pass it from me to you.' And I'm sitting a yard away. 'Paul Parker was quick, a good competitor, but couldn't really pass it. Terry Butcher was OK. Mark Wright was actually quite a decent footballer. Always one or two but not enough of them. And we always seem to get one of our big players injured and are overly reliant on the few. If Spain lost a gifted midfield player, there are about fifteen to twenty of them who could come in.

'We've been inferior technically, with exceptions that arise in spite of our youth policy, but we've never had the biggest numbers so we're over-reliant on a few, rather like Spain were until they changed things. They transformed their whole process of teaching youngsters, with La Masia [youth academy] in Barcelona, the Johan Cruyff approach, and it rolled into producing loads of technically proficient footballers with tactical nous. We're only just coming to that now. We've finally discovered the way football has been taught. It was only recently we got rid of big pitches for 8-year-olds. Absurd. Big pitch and big goals for little kids means they hoof the ball so we never learned playing out from the back. The limited success we've had has been in spite of an old-fashioned and poor development process which ultimately has now changed. Academies still have faults but kids are being taught about passing. We are starting to see some real talent coming through: Ross Barkley, Alex Oxlade-Chamberlain and Raheem Sterling. Defenders as well: Stones, Luke Shaw, Nathaniel Clyne, Calum Chambers possibly. They are not just defenders. They can play. Look at Stones: what a delightful, lovely footballer. I still hear people go: "Yeah, but he makes the odd mistake, he shouldn't be messing about with the ball." No, let him; he'll learn when's right and when's wrong. Stones is a good footballer, quick, confident. He looks a leader to me. I never want to put this on people because it's not fair, but given a fair run and no injuries, I'd be very surprised if he's not captain of England. We've got some lovely midfield players, comfortable, [can] keep the ball. If you look at some of our Under-19s, 18s, 17s in recent tournaments, it's so much better, and playing the same kind of football that Spain, Brazil and France play. It's time. It's not just four or five, it's twelve or fourteen. If we don't exhaust those players, as we often do, we have half a chance. The one that might prove the best of the lot is Dele Alli, a delightful footballer. There are high hopes for him.'

Alli is given his chance at Spurs by the enlightened Mauricio Pochettino but many youngsters find pathways blocked. 'We've definitely got an issue of that batch between 18 and breaking into first-team football in the Premier League, mainly because there's so much money in the Premier League they just buy people in,' Lineker continues. 'That's an issue that needs resolving. If you've got enough good players coming through that will gradually decrease. It's only now that we are just starting to get the benefits of teaching kids how to play properly. I don't think this will be such a problem in ten years because we're producing enough home-grown talents. There won't be this necessity to go out and get Joe Average from Borussia Mönchengladbach.'

Along with cost, one of the attractions of these imports is professionalism. The most pointed barb launched at home-growners is they can fall into the 'too much too young' culture on acquiring their first contract at 17. Buying a new Range Rover for your brother becomes more important than employing a specialist coach to work on technical flaws in private. 'Many ingredients make a footballer,' Lineker says. 'The key one is hunger. Some of them will not have that hunger within them. If you're earning a few quid, some are distracted, whether it's too much to drink, party life, or they can't handle it mentally. You have to have hunger. We all start playing football because we love football and want to be really good at it. Some kids will lose their way. We have a lager-lout culture in this country which is a little bit different to elsewhere – they don't do that in Spain.' Familiar with modern mores in Academies following Tobias's experience, Lineker appreciates that hopefuls starting off at 8 are constantly reminded of the need for total dedication if they are going to be the one in two hundred who makes it. 'It's much better here now. They know it's so competitive, so hard, that you've got to have hunger, mental strength and natural ability. If you're a little bit short on any one of those you're not going to make it as a top player.'

A frequent criticism of the system is that it envelops pupils in luxury, preaching hunger yet sating it with five-star attention. England cry out for leaders, responsibility-takers, officer material. Lineker urges perspective. 'Producing leaders goes in cycles, which we've seen at various times throughout England's history. At other times, like now, we are going through a huge transitional phase.' The Gerrard–Lampard–Beckham–Owen epoch melts into history, being replaced by the Sterling–Stones–Barkley–Kane–Wilshere–Alli age, with Wayne Rooney straddling both eras. 'At this present moment, the so-called Golden Generation have gone, with the exception of Rooney, and it's a load of kids who've not yet reached their prime. So we are going through that transitional period, as we saw in the last World Cup. While it was quite promising in some ways, we started to keep the ball better than we're used to because [the players are] better technically but there wasn't that maturity or strength you need. We've gone from the Golden Generation period where perhaps if they'd been a little bit mentally stronger . . .' Lineker trails off. He expects more from a gifted dressing-room. 'While a lot were wonderful footballers, I'm not sure there was among them that kind of personality that you need. John Terry obviously, Rio Ferdinand as well – big personalities, big performances in big tournaments. Have some of them produced well enough in these big tournaments? Have they been able to handle the pressure enough?' Clearly not. 'But then you go to other eras ... you wouldn't have that amount of talent but teams perform pretty well because of that real gritty character, like Terry Butcher, Peter Shilton and Bryan Robson, people who can handle pressure and perform at their best.'

Few FA courses provide the insight offered by Lineker, a prodigious performer in tournaments and an authority on dressing-room dynamics. 'You can't get to the very top in football without being mentally very strong,' says England's most prolific player in World Cup tournaments with 10 goals. 'I never thought I was one of the best, but I did have that strength that however big the game was, the more relaxed I felt, the more I cherished it rather than feared it. That's how I was made.' An ambitious competitor at two World Cups, Lineker never felt the weight of '66. 'No. No. That should inspire you, not hinder you. That Bobby Moore statue shows you it is possible for us to do it. Yes, it was in our own country, and football is a much more worldwide competitive game than it was then, but it's still a great achievement. That should inspire the current players. There's more media nowadays and they're being constantly reminded of '66. The more distance there is from that day the more the motivation should be. Sometimes I can see there are too many nerves. The thing about "the players don't care" is complete nonsense. The probability is they care too much, the pressure is too much. Everybody I ever played with cared about England. They were playing for their country, that's the most important thing, and still is. All the players turn up, all want to be there, despite the fact that most of the time they get pilloried.'

No England team has begun a tournament under more sustained acerbic attack from the media than those heading into Italia 90 and Euro 96. Any analysis of the years of hurt swiftly exposes the presence of a psychological frailty, particularly in those teams post '90 or '96. To prosper at Euro 2016 and beyond, England crave that confluence of courage and talent, well organized by a manager, to outwit the best. In '66, England's toughness of character was laced by individual class in Gordon Banks, Bobby Moore and Bobby Charlton and a driven manager in Ramsey. The years since have been a search for that holy trinity of spirit, virtuosity and tactical organization. They almost had it in Italy with Lineker in attack. That first sighting of Lineker in an England shirt back at Hampden Park in '84 proves instructive. Even now, thirty-two years on, Lineker serves his country well with his exhortations for players to enhance their potential with dedication and specialist attention. As he leaves his club, leaping down the stairs and on to the pavement, his innate optimism bursts forth. 'I'm quite confident for England's future,' he says.

9

When in Rome . . . Do the Wright Thing

FALLING TO HIS knees and bowing his head, Ian Wright clasps his hands in prayer. Tears chase beads of sweat down his face. Wright's speechless, a rarity for the usually voluble Londoner. He's momentarily silent as he absorbs what he's just achieved. It's shortly after 10.30 p.m. in Rome on 11 October 1997, and Wright's selfless, tactically disciplined display of lone-forward play has helped England qualify for the World Cup finals in France. As a striker, Wright is perceived as a creature of instinct, a passion player, yet he demonstrates in the Eternal City that he can play with his head as well as his heart. The DVD makes required viewing for those Englishmen wanting to acquire the acumen to deliver against the best.

Dazed and dismayed, Italy depart for the play-offs, and a tough trip to icy Moscow. To Russia with gloves, I follow to the Dynamo Stadium to discover a member of the mafia occupying my press seat because it offers shelter from the snow. He won't move, stewards and soldiers refuse to shift him, so I file the story of what could have been England's fate from the terraces, dodging snowballs and wolfing down a strange-tasting half-time hamburger. 'Horse,' explains a helpful local. England have been saved from the myriad challenges of Moscow by Wright in Rome. It's little wonder the 33-year-old's shattered at full-time in the Stadio Olimpico. He spends the full 90 minutes closing down Azzurri defenders, holding the ball up and haring down channels. This is one of those too-infrequent occasions when English footballers, even such intuitive players as Wright, reveal they can perform with concentration and streetwise savvy when prepared properly by a smart manager like Glenn Hoddle.

Robbie Fowler runs over and tries to lift Wright up. 'What the fuck are you doing?' Fowler laughs. Seven photographers rush to capture the scene, crouching down in front of the pair, snapping away, recording Wright's exhaustion. Other pictures eventually adorn the back pages, celebrating the prodigious work of a bandaged Paul Ince and the mastermind Hoddle, but Wright's slumped figure embodies how much England gave and how much it means. It means the World Cup.

Representing his country means everything to Wright. 'I cried the first time I took the England number 9 shirt,' he recalls. His emotional response to his international debut contrasts with events elsewhere on 6 February 1991 inside Wembley, where Cameroon's Roger Milla declines to grace the friendly after a disagreement over his appearance fee. 'I went to the toilet in the dressing-room to put the shirt on and had a moment just looking at it,' Wright continues. He hangs it on the back of the cubicle door. He looks at the white shirt with the navy blue collar and the little button, the long sleeves with the blue cuffs, the Three Lions crest over the left breast and the red number on the back. Wright pulls the shirt on, almost reverentially. He's craved this moment, this dream that seemed impossible when failing a trial at Brighton & Hove Albion as a teenager. He plays non-League, making a living as a plasterer, even cleaning tunnels – back-breaking work, soul-destroying – before seizing the chance to prove himself at Crystal Palace aged 21. Even then, the competition to force his way into the England squad is ferocious. To be called up, and then handed that No. 9 shirt by Graham Taylor, is special. 'With the way I ended up getting into football, to get to play for England at Wembley, to play next to Lineker, Barnes and Gazza, was a very emotional moment for me. I didn't think: "Oh my God, I'm going to cry." It just happened. Looking at the Three Lions! Looking at the nice light blue in the shirt! What it brought home was that I was actually here. I'd watched all that through the seventies [and eighties], and I was now going to play for England. I was overcome by the moment.'

He has previous experience of Wembley, famously striking twice against Manchester United in the 1990 FA Cup final and coming on again in the replay. The historic stadium transfixes him. 'I never, ever thought I'd get to play at Wembley, let alone play at Wembley for England. I never, ever thought I'd get to hear the studs in the tunnel, that brilliant white tunnel which they should have kept. I was in the tunnel getting ready to play Cameroon. I walked up there and felt like I wanted to belong – be part of it. I was walking out with England greats, like Lineker, who I really did admire as a striker. I had a pretty decent game as well.'

Scrolling through the tape confirms the good impression made by Wright that February night. He creates the opportunity for Lineker's first goal, athletically heading back Trevor Steven's cross, inviting his attacking partner to run at goal. Brought down by Joseph-Antoine Bell, Lineker jumps up and converts the penalty, continuing a personal theme against Cameroon. When Stuart Pearce then whips in a corner, Mark Wright flicks on and the new boy stretches for the ball, but it's a familiar figure turning it in. 'Lineker and Wright went together and Lineker is the scorer,' runs the commentary from Barry Davies. As Lineker embraces Mark Wright, Ian gives him a quick congratulatory hug in passing. 'Lineker nicked my one that I'd have tapped in,' he sighs, remembering the questions thrown at him during his early England games without a goal. 'That is what helps with a striker, you need to score soon.' He takes a while with England – twenty-seven months.

He never stops scoring during his time at Palace (117 goals in all competitions, dovetailing brilliantly with Mark Bright) and then Arsenal (185), but he still cannot fully convince Taylor of his worth. It's bizarre when Wright is ripping up defences domestically that the England manager does not show more faith in him. Taylor ignores him for Euro 92, despite his claiming the Golden Boot after a thunderous season at Arsenal, pipping even Lineker. In his twenty-man squad for Sweden, Taylor takes Lineker, Nigel Clough, Wright's club-mate Alan Smith and Alan Shearer, the Southampton 21-year-old with a couple of caps. Taylor talks of needing the right blend of forwards, and Lineker and Wright can duplicate runs. Personality undoubtedly plays a part. Wright's exuberance, occasionally veering into excess, seems too much for Taylor. Too much instinct. Too much playing on the edge, frequently falling foul of officials and the FA. Having covered a few of his disciplinary scrapes with the beaks, I always feel Wright has almost his own parking space outside Lancaster Gate. He's a regular visitor. Having waited so long for his chance in the game, and been doubted so often, Wright tears into matches. He cares too much, the fuse burns and sparks fly. It's a far cry from the mature, controlled figure in Rome.

Although mellow now, Wright's still lively. We speak on three occasions in San Marino and Lithuania as Roy Hodgson's side cruise through qualifying for Euro 2016. At one point, disappearing for lunch with Hoddle, Wright asks me to look after his phone, charging in a Vilnius hotel lobby. Lithuanian locals wandering past are startled by the sound of a motorbike revving up. Wright's ringtone. He loves bikes. In his eyes, Harley and Davidson go together like Wright and Bright. Life's often noisy with Wright about. But there's a sound of hurt in his voice as he reflects on England. 'I missed out on Euro 92,' he continues. 'Graham Taylor didn't take me and I'd won the Golden Boot, beating Lineker, the year after going to Arsenal when people were saying, "He won't even make the Arsenal team." At the time I thought: "That's all right, I've got plenty of time to play for England in tournaments."'

He focused on helping out, when given the chance, in England's attempt to reach USA 94. Finally, on 29 May 1993 – his ninth appearance – he strikes his first England goal, timing his run to meet Tony Dorigo's cross, and finishing with a right-foot half-volley to rescue a point against Poland with six minutes left in Katowice. 'I saw a picture the other day when I was running off with my arms held out in Poland, and you can see in my face exactly how much it meant to me. I was just pleased in Poland to come off the bench, do something for my country. I don't know what a soldier must feel like but I feel that patriotism.' And he shushes those 'you'll never score for England' jibes.

A month later, he travels on England's tour to the US but remains unconvinced about Taylor. 'By then he'd lost it,' is his pithy verdict. Hopes of returning Stateside are shredded by the defeat to Holland in Rotterdam notorious for Ronald Koeman's luck and dead-ball brilliance and Taylor's 'do I not like that' rant. 'I missed out on '92 and didn't qualify for '94. My time under Taylor was a sad, sad time. People constantly ridiculed us if we didn't do well, like when we didn't qualify for '94.' Wright takes it personally.

Taylor's inevitable departure brings in Terry Venables, lifting Wright's spirits until he realizes that the new manager's preference for a Christmas tree formation effectively precludes him. Shearer, now the main man, is up top with Sheringham supporting. Venables' chosen four strikers for Euro 96 are Shearer, Sheringham, Les Ferdinand and Fowler. Wright is out in the cold again. 'That was heart-breaking. It would have been my tournament. It was in England. The Golden Goal was there. To hear somebody of Venables' stature eventually saying "I think I made a mistake not putting Ian Wright in that squad" gave me a little bit of "fine, he's admitted that", but it doesn't stop the fact that I wanted to be an England great. I wanted to do something that would be great for England, like score that Golden Goal to get us through that Germany game to the final against Czech Republic, who we'd have beaten. Euro 96 was a hard one to take. As great as we were, I just cannot get over the fact that I should've been playing to score the Golden Goal. You can't have regrets but that was my biggest regret. I was more than good enough to be in that squad. Yes, I think about it all the time.

'What I can't ever fathom properly was why someone of Venners' experience didn't take me there. Was it my personality? He didn't use Les. He didn't use Robbie Fowler. I could've had an impact off the bench. I've previous: FA Cup final, Poland. Was it something personal? I ask myself these questions all the time. The only regret I've got in football is not to play in Euro 96 and score the Golden Goal. Yes, Venables took us to the semis, but Glenn Hoddle is by far the best England coach we've had.'

Even with competition for places remaining fierce, Wright becomes entrenched in Hoddle's thinking. 'I was pleased I had to duke it out with Shearer, Fowler, Ferdinand, Cole, then Michael Owen came through. I had to do it week in, week out, just to keep my head there, so people say, "Yes, Wrighty's still doing it." Now, you can score four goals by fucking February and still get in the England squad. I'd never say I wish I was playing now, because when I played it was *the* time to play. It was fucking proper. It was a good time to play for England.'

Guided by Hoddle, Wright and the England team even win the Tournoi de France in the summer of 1997. 'I know people say it was only the Tournoi and people weren't really bothered but we played a French team that were up for it, a Brazil team that were up for it and an Italian team up for it. That proved to me that our team was more than good enough to have won something under Hoddle.' They open Le Tournoi on 4 June 1997 with a confident display against Italy in Nantes. Having learned from the 1-0 loss to a Gianfranco Zola-inspired Italy at Wembley in the World Cup qualifiers, Hoddle believes the best way to exploit an experienced Italian defence is via quick passes, using Wright's pace at the tip of a 3-5-1-1 system. Covering the game awakens hope in the possibilities of England under Hoddle. Even now the mind's eye can see Paul Scholes in Nantes sweeping a 60-yard pass through, Wright outpacing Ciro Ferrara and angling a left-foot shot past Angelo Peruzzi. A quick check of the goal on YouTube confirms an uplifting memory. Even the Italian commentator screams, '*Stupenda!*' Wright punches the air, then falls back on the ground, lying there, almost paying personal homage to Gunner Charlie George. Wright then returns the compliment, running on to another early pass, this time from Phil Neville, and turning the ball across for Scholes to score. 2-0 England. Emphatic. 'I remember Gianfranco Zola saying "wonderful football" as he came off the pitch, as if they were surprised we could play that way,' recalls Hoddle. 'With the system we played in Le Tournoi we beat them really well.'

Light training in La Baule the next day is peppered with howls of laughter as Hoddle's players try to copy the astonishing free-kick by Brazil's Roberto Carlos against France: his strike looks to be going well wide, even making a ball-boy duck in anticipation, before swerving into the goal. England's attempts at 'doing a Roberto Carlos' prove spectacularly wayward, almost a menace to nearby traffic.

Training highlights the strength of the camaraderie that accounts for France, and even defeat to Brazil cannot deny England the Tournoi trophy. It's silverware of sorts, better than nothing. More importantly, Nantes gives Hoddle his plan for Rome in October. 'We showed the players a tape of a lot of good bits of that game,' adds Hoddle. 'I felt really strong. We went early to Rome to drill the team in how we were going to play. We readjusted Teddy and Gazza. I said: "Look, Ted, I don't want you playing up there square with Wrighty."' Gascoigne is charged by Hoddle with filling in the 'pockets of space' close to Sheringham, who is behind Wright, but staying in touch with the two defensive midfielders, David Batty and Paul Ince. Wright has specific instructions. 'Glenn told me it would be a tough one, saying that I'm going to be up there on my own. He told me in training: "You've got to hold the ball, stop flicking the ball."' For one night only, Wright must curb his all-out attacking instincts.

Maybe Wright, at 33, senses time running out, especially with a teenaged striker called Michael Owen invited to train with the seniors at Bisham Abbey before England fly out. Maybe it is the sense of purpose, the feeling of being on a real and achievable mission, that Hoddle fosters. Chatting with Gareth Southgate on landing at Fiumicino, I ask him whether he will get a chance to see the city, even a stroll to the Trevi Fountain? Southgate sighs ruefully, saying he will return on holiday to see the sights, and smiling wanly on hearing the planned press itinerary of Colosseum/Sistine Chapel/Chianti. Southgate, Wright and the rest of the players are too 'in the zone'. They're hidden away from prying eyes, holing up in an isolated hotel, placed under lock-down by Hoddle.

England's game-plan is a master-class in preparation that should be high on the study list on the Pro Licence course at St George's Park. Hoddle gets all his major calls right in Rome, making Ince captain ahead of Tony Adams because he knows how much the Italians respect the former Inter Milan midfielder. He plays mind games around the fitness of David Beckham and Southgate, without revealing the reasons. Hoddle's kidology is only marginally undone when Roy Hodgson, translating for the Italian media, points to his thigh and smiles when discussing Southgate's mystery injury. Beckham and Southgate both start and play well. Hoddle ensures that when his players speak in their few brief meetings with the media they mention the need for the Dutch referee Mario van der Ende to watch Italian holding at corners. On the eve of hostilities, Sheringham delivers a mini-seminar on the sly nature of Italian defending, and the difficulties strikers face in getting a 'clean' run at the ball. The press nod and write it up, reminding Van der Ende of his duties. Hoddle's Operation Rome is underway. He also plays on Manchester United's excellent result against Juventus, a 3-2 win, in the Champions League ten days earlier. So the English can live with the Italians. He transmits belief, sending another strong message to the dressing-room of his faith in them. 'I remember walking off at Wembley having lost 1-0 to Italy [earlier that year, in February] and facing the press, and everyone was down,' Hoddle adds after his lunch with Wright. 'I remember being very bold that night, saying: "We will still win this group."' To do so, England need a point in a stadium where Italy have won their last fifteen World Cup games.

Tension rises on the Saturday because of the vicious behaviour of English hooligans the night before, rioting in Rome and certain surrounding towns. At midnight, I venture out with an FA official to inspect the damage and he confides that it's like a scene from ancient days, 'watching Rome burn'. On returning to England, I go on BBC Radio 5 Live's 606 phone-in with David Mellor, the verbose politician who argues that the Carabinieri have been heavy-handed. He hasn't just come back from Rome. He hasn't seen the carnage wrought by the English. Mellor is in full adversarial QC mode, very eloquent, very entertaining, but very wrong.

Entering the Stadio Olimpico that night is to cross lines of twitchy police whose negative perception of England's unruly camp followers deteriorates during Italia 90 and does not improve. The theme of the trip is the off-field indiscipline of the English, even extending to the misbehaving of some of the Under-21 players unwinding in Rieti, contrasting with the maturity and responsibility-taking of Wright and company on the pitch. The pre-match prediction of Italy's coach, Cesare Maldini, that the English can only 'play with their hearts' is too one-dimensional. Cleverly set-up tactically and temperamentally by Hoddle, Wright and the rest play with their heads. Passion still thuds through Wright, as always, driving him on, remembering those early years of rejection, but what happens is an exercise in control. England keep control of the tempo, their shape, their discipline and their destiny. When in Rome . . . play the locals at their own game.

From the moment Van der Ende signals the start, Wright shows for the ball, receives it and lays it off to Sheringham, keeping possession, frustrating Italy, then getting behind the defence. 'Hoddle recognized what I brought. The way I played suited his game. He needed somebody to run the channels. Hoddle was brilliant. Tactically, he was very good.' Obeying their master's orders, England are magnificent. Ince makes light of having his forehead opened by Demetrio Albertini's elbow and only partially closed by stitches, inserted quickly after a five-minute wait to find the dressing-room key. Gascoigne, once of Lazio, is an indefatigable gladiator on his return to his old sporting Colosseum. But throughout, the eye keeps being drawn to the man in the white No. 9 shirt. Wright runs himself into the ground for his country, hounding Italy's decorated defence of Alessandro Nesta, Alessandro Costacurta, Fabio Cannavaro and Paolo Maldini. No real fury can be detected in the Englishman's challenges, just a relentless, percussive attention paid to whichever Italian dares bring the ball out from the back. A serial pest, Wright stretches and distracts Italy's defence. Wright himself gets kicked frequently, winning free-kicks, running down the clock, earning cheers for his ceaseless commitment. He cares.

Talking in San Marino, Wright believes that players don't care as much about the national team nowadays. 'I don't think they do, and the reason is because they get so rewarded for so little so early. We used to have to get into the national team to get national recognition, and then you can go into the club and maybe get a rise because of your form. Now you play a couple of games in the Premier League, score a couple of goals, you're instantly lauded and go from £10,000 to £50,000 a week. It's ridiculous. You haven't got any drive. England is not the driver for you. The Premier League is so global, you're getting it there. You're getting the money, everything you need.' He excludes from the critique his son Shaun Wright-Phillips, who scored six times in his 36 internationals. 'Shaun was very relaxed about England. Of course, he was proud to play for England. It was great. He went to the World Cup in 2010 which I'm so proud of.' But others, Wright argues, are less passionate about the Three Lions. 'They think England's more pressure than it's worth. If some of these managers really let loose, they could do stories where they can actually explain about how certain players don't want to go to England. Of course I know there are players. When I was playing I don't remember too many players who threw one [a sicknote] in. The last ten to fifteen years, with the way it's gone, there are players who say: "I'm not going to turn up to England." I never dreamt of it. That's why I never took any kind of expenses or money from England to play. I thought it was a privilege and an honour to play. It was a different time. When I went to Palace I said to [manager] Steve Coppell: "I will play for England." That's what I wanted to do. I'm not sure how many now are saying, "I want to play for England." They say, "I want to play for Man United or Man City." My goal when I got to Palace was, "I want to be an England great."'

He earns endless approval in the Eternal City. Italian angst mounts. Angelo Di Livio flies in recklessly on Sol Campbell and is sent to the unlocked dressing-room by Van der Ende. Cesare Maldini consoles the miscreant as he slopes past – surprisingly, as the foolish Di Livio has let him down. Italy almost go a goal down as well. In the final minute, Wright races away from Cannavaro in pursuit of a long ball. He can head left, towards the corner-flag, killing off more seconds, but he senses a goal. Here's the real Ian Wright, rounding Peruzzi, keeping the ball in play with his left foot before curling it right-footed goalwards. Panic-stricken Italians rush back but are saved by the post. The ball bounces out and they spring a counter, one last rescue mission as the game melts into injury time. Has Wright erred in not going for the corner-flag? Alessandro Del Piero crosses from the left towards Christian Vieri. Time accompanies England defenders in standing still. Vieri leaps, meets the ball firmly, and the play-offs loom for England. But Vieri's header flies fractionally wide of David Seaman's right-hand upright. Seaman stays so calm, so convinced the header is missing, when 81,200 fans and both benches are having their emotions put through the wringer. Van der Ende finally ends the drama, the last action fittingly being Wright sliding in to close down another Italian before collapsing. On being helped to his feet, Wright is embraced by Gascoigne, then Ince, and the tears flow. He's soon standing in front of a Kidderminster Harriers flag, celebrating with the England fans, launching a shirt dripping with sweat into the jubilant throng.

'I look back on Rome as my finest 90 minutes in an England shirt,' Wright smiles. 'It wasn't my style to play that way but I did it. It was my greatest moment, the magnitude of it, how important it was for us, and playing Cannavaro, the only defender to win the Ballon d'Or [along with the versatile Franz Beckenbauer and Matthias Sammer]. People constantly say: "I remember you in that game in Rome." That's why it meant so much to me. People like Gary Neville said he didn't know what all the excitement was [about]. He has a different frame of mind being at Man United with Fergie, the winning mentality they had, having achieved everything. For people like me, that was the actual mountain top. More than the cup finals, simply because it was England. It meant something to the whole country.

'What it feels like to me is it's modern-day war. You're represent-ing your country against another country for the honour of your country. You win the game, and England are triumphant. The reason why I had that vibe in my head is wherever we went, England were big news. The whole country knew the England football team were there. Everybody wanted to beat us.' Italy can't. England collect the required point. 'It was terrific the way we played in Rome,' recalls Hoddle. 'Italy were a good side with Zola and Vieri. Maldini was at his peak.' Hoddle just makes England believe they can live with such stellar names.

Sadly for Wright, injury wrecks his hope of finally playing in a competitive tournament for his country. 'Hoddle told me I was going to France but I got injured against Morocco before the World Cup. I did my hamstring with ten minutes to go. But my time under Hoddle made me realize, yeah, I was good enough. I did warrant being there, and maybe I would have got more of a berth there if he'd [stayed] there.'

Hoddle is forced to relinquish the England reins on 2 February 1999, after making those insensitive comments about the disabled and karma, which followed some poor performances after France 98 and stories of man-management issues. Wright defends Hoddle on the latter charge. 'The reason why they had issues with him is because he would slaughter them and show them what he wanted them to do. And he could do it. That's what they didn't like. That's where the nicknames for him came about like "Chocolate". He could eat himself. 'The problem that a lot of the players had was because he was so good still as a technical player, if we didn't do the training right when he put the sessions on, keeping the ball up, knocking it back 25 yards, if we let it drop, he was very, very upset. "You're meant to be the best players in the country and you can't even do this fucking exercise."

'He really drove us to do well. He used to coach me about my touch, where to take the ball, how to beat a man, how to get the ball, face the man and then turn. Because I respected him so much as a player, I was in fear of him, and in awe of him. The press knew there was a man-management issue, and that fed them to fire him. Let's face it, he was pretty successful in the way we played – we were good. They found it with the Eileen Drewery thing, and the karma was his downfall. They found ways of getting in to try to penetrate him. That came from the dressing-room because they knew there were players in there who weren't happy with him. Of course, you'd do things differently. He was tucked up over the comments.' The comments were fairly reported, but the backlash is fierce. 'It's detrimental to the England team because we would have been a lot better with him at the helm. It's a shame. I still feel that way. Hoddle had unfinished business [after France 98]. He was able to motivate the youngsters

– Beckham, Scholes, Nevilles – brought them in. His coaching ability. Rio and Michael Owen coming through. He was somebody you respected, tactically. Now we're mates. It's quite a nice relationship.'

Before returning to an ITV team meeting with Hoddle in San Marino, Wright remembers his last international, against Czech Republic on 18 November 1998, having just turned 35. 'I set one up for Merse [Paul Merson], and might have set two up, but I knew it was over.' He dwells on the word 'over' and a look of sadness fills his eyes. Ian Wright cares.

10

Headhunting

Qualifying for Euro 2016 intensifies, and England's Auld Enemy, Scotland, are rattling into Germany at Hampden Park. The game is screened live at the architecturally dazzling, artefact-rich National Football Museum in Manchester and three hundred guests gather to watch. The interval allows the audience time to catch breath and stroll briefly around the magnificent museum. Hanging on one wall is a marvellous cartoon by Liverpool fan Mike Stokoe depicting an interview at the FA for the role of England manager. The applicant is advised by three FA Blazers: 'And if you lose one game on the trot you're sacked.' Such are the demands of the Impossible Job. Making the right choice itself frequently proves the impossible job.

New appointments often seem the antithesis of the outgoing manager, as the FA flip-flops. Since Italia 90, the sequence runs: solid FA man (Graham Taylor), popular non-FA man (Terry Venables), confident tactician (Glenn Hoddle), emotional patriot (Kevin Keegan), sophisticated foreigner (Sven-Göran Eriksson), a natural number two (Steve McClaren), disciplinarian foreigner (Fabio Capello) and avuncular Englishman (Roy Hodgson). The FA swings with the wind. Dan Ashworth, the current technical director, commendably tries to bring a more dispassionate, analytical eye to the vital recruitment process. A proper exit interview should be held with every departing England manager, not in the heat of the moment post-dismissal but a month or so later when anger ebbs and a more sanguine version of events, even advice, can be offered

to the FA. Insight into what the manager finds especially problem-
atic will assist in the hunt for the most suitable successor, whether
it's dealing with self-interested clubs, lack of a winter break, dearth
of world-class players, tricky media or how to fumigate the fear in
the dressing-room. It will also aid the FA in addressing broader flaws
bedevilling English football.

An ideal identikit England manager cannot exist but certain
traits, notably man-management skills, self-belief, a thick skin, an
ability to disseminate tactical ideas lucidly and not being in awe of
star names, are minimum requirements. Having offspring of school
age can occasionally be an issue with a press possessed of a cruel
streak. During his ill-fated spell in charge from 2006 to 2007, Steve
McClaren conducts some media briefings in a small, very sociable
Italian restaurant in Yarm near his home in the north-east. One
day a group of us newspaper reporters are sitting at a table waiting for McClaren to finish talking to TV. People come and go from
the table. Nobody pays too much attention to the young lad walking up quietly and perching on the end. Probably work experience.
The usual. The chatter continues about McClaren, some of it acerbic.
When McClaren eventually joins us, he looks at the end of the table
and says: "Hello, son, how was school?" The Impossible Job is made
even harsher by the pressures placed on the incumbent's family, when
headlines belittle a loved one.

McClaren tries to woo the press. Being media-friendly wins a
manager only a couple of defeats' grace before technical areas turn
into vegetable patches. A President's Book kept at St George's Park,
much like the old ledgers in the Boot Room at Anfield containing the
thoughts of esteemed managers and coaches, would hold knowledge
on this and other aspects of the job. One should have been opened
years ago, clarifying, for example, why the FA ignores Brian Clough.
If he's perceived as too much of an anti-establishment maverick –
'not an FA man' – then that critique needs challenging, at the very
least discussing properly internally. Does this bias linger? FA thinking
needs to be explained, as much for its own benefit. Bobby Robson's
successor, Graham Taylor, is seen as a safe pair of hands and he

oversees a disastrous period in England's history. A good club manager at Watford, and one of the most principled and conscientious men in a cynical profession, Taylor actually enjoys a twelve-game unbeaten start but tails off spectacularly in a haze of ranting at linesmen, outpourings in a damaging documentary and crazy substitutions. The most notorious of these moves involves taking off Gary Lineker in Stockholm at the 1992 European Championship with England needing to score against Sweden. Alan Smith of Arsenal comes on, but there is general bemusement. Why remove such a renowned predator? Taylor subsequently reveals he knows Lineker is retiring after the Euros and he wants to build for the future. Smith, a very capable centre-forward and an ideal foil for Lineker during their time at Leicester City, is 29. Hardly the future. Such key decisions need examining by the FA through conducting interviews and recording explanations, building up an understanding of a situation (in this case dealing with big-name players close to retirement) which might benefit a future practitioner of the Impossible Job – a phrase forever associated with Taylor because of that documentary also known as '*Do I Not Like That*'.

'Do you know,' says Lineker of Taylor's most contentious decision, 'the truth is he actually made a martyr of me – not deliberately, but I was playing in a team that weren't creating, struggling a little bit, and he brought me off. I always believed I'd score and I was obviously a bit miffed to come off. In hindsight the furore was all about him taking me off. If he'd kept me on, and I hadn't scored, I'd have been hammered with the rest of the team. He made me a hero! I should perhaps thank him for it! I never had any angst. I'd never got taken off, so it was more shock. "What?" I can't remember being taken off unless injured or shattered. It didn't wholly surprise me because there was always a little bit of scepticism about the old guard. He just genuinely thought, "I'll do something different."' And now for something completely different: remove your best scorer.

'I sympathized to a degree with Graham Taylor because he lost a lot of key players at the same time, rather like the end of the Golden Generation, and a lot of players coming in weren't good enough. But

Graham didn't help himself by also easing out Bryan Robson too soon, easing out Peter Beardsley too soon, Chris Waddle too soon, so all of a sudden we went from a really fluid team with more flair than the average England team by a mile to a very pedestrian, workman-like team, probably the worst bunch if you look at the squad in Euro 92. It was way short really of where we were two years prior.'

It worsens for Taylor. The thirteenth of October 1993 brings what is billed as his 'Rotterdammerung' in Holland. Fielding Carlton Palmer against Dennis Bergkamp at De Kuip is just one of his mistakes, although Taylor can point to the referee, Karl Assenmacher, infuriatingly not sending off Ronald Koeman for pulling back David Platt. He's through on goal, England could punish ten men, and the World Cup dream could be back on. A nation screams at the screen, at Koeman, Assenmacher and Taylor. After resigning the following month, Taylor subsequently proves a regular contributor to radio and print but is never allowed to forget failing to qualify for USA 94. He pens insightful articles in the *Daily Telegraph* but his arrival as a columnist sparks outrage in certain quarters. Dropping through my post-box one day comes a letter containing the front page of a recent *Telegraph* sports supplement trumpeting the fact that 'Taylor joins TelegraphSport . . . Graham Taylor writes the first of his exclusive columns, Sport 4&5' with the accompanying note: 'Sir, is your Sports Editor bonkers? Taylor is a cunt, always was a cunt, always will be a cunt. He is held in contempt pretty well universally throughout soccer. Who in God's name wants to read anything written by Taylor? Yours . . .' Leaving aside the feeling that debate is rendered defunct by use of the word 'soccer', the correspondent clearly will never forgive Taylor. Back on Civvy Street, an ex-England manager must prepare for a life of stares and enduring criticism for all the stigma attached to England failure. The shadow always follows. Only Robson and Venables have escaped it.

'In his club career Graham did exceptionally well, but there are different levels in football, from the top flight and then on to England, and it takes special people,' says Ian Wright. 'It didn't quite work out for Graham. My time under him was unhappy even though I was playing with Gazza, Incey, my best mates. It was just the way it went with Graham Taylor: whether he didn't fancy me, didn't like the way I was, he put me in his squad simply because of the form I had with Arsenal, and not really having any intention of playing me, which was always quite hard for me to deal with. I was always on the bench, or not in the squad, and I just feel that if it had been somebody like Glenn Hoddle, I would have had a better opportunity there.'

The question of whether the FA does due diligence on a manager is raised during the short, briefly promising reign of Terry Venables, Taylor's successor. Battle lines are drawn early. 'Over my dead body,' harrumphs the FA chairman Sir Bert Millichip at the possibility of his appointment – Venables' business activities arouse concern. Jimmy Armfield, the wise owl of the FA, consults and advises and eventually the FA unites in an uneasy truce behind Venables. Even such a seemingly straightforward event as Venables and Millichip meeting to sign the deal is accompanied by worrying noises off: sirens are heard outside as police scream up the Edgware Road in London to deal with a woman threatening to fling herself off a nearby ledge. (She doesn't.)

Venables endures frequent critical headlines. He has his head super-imposed in a noose on the back page of a tabloid before the friendly with Norway on 11 October 1995. His financial dealings over Spurs draw constant scrutiny. His legal wrangles with the club's owner, Alan Sugar, are lengthy. At times, covering Venables' period in high office, I feel more a financial reporter than a football correspondent. City news? Manchester or Mansion House? Press conferences become games of two halves: questions directed at Venables are about scouting reports one minute, DTI reports the next. After looking at Venables' connections with 'Scribes West, Edennote, Tottenham Hotspur and Tottenham Hotspur Football and Athletic Club', the DTI actually writes to the England manager saying it wants to disqualify him as a director. It's explosive, extraordinary, back-page gold. 'It appears to the Secretary of State that your conduct as a director of the above-named companies makes you unfit to be considered in the management of a company and that it is expedient in the public interest that a disqualification order should be made against you.' Just when we are about to ask him about the Christmas tree formation. This is no way to prepare for a tournament. A judge in one of the interminable legal cases observes that Venables' evidence is 'wanton' and 'not entirely reliable to put it at its most charitable'.

The Venables v. Sugar squabble has the FA squirming. The organization at the time possesses all the mores of a provincial golf club, with parochialism writ large. The FA hates the embarrassing headlines. Venables has many friends in the press, supporting him loudly, and some voluble enemies, denigrating when opportunity arises. Spurs seek to find some calm, even hosting a breakfast for a rancorous media at Simpson's-in-the-Strand where reporters debate the situation with Sugar. He's not for turning. Venables is too proud. It's an impasse, a mess, a shame for England. Venables' future is decided before the Euros. Influential figures at the FA like Noel White and Peter Swales want Venables to prove himself at the competition before they'll even consider giving him a new contract. Venables thinks them weak, uncooperative and wobbly. Armfield wants Venables to stay on as FA technical director, but his love is working with the players. So Armfield goes off to sound out Alex Ferguson as Venables' successor, but the William Wallace of management will never be interested (the proud Scot tells us one day he would consider the job 'only to get England relegated'). Eventually, the FA settles on Hoddle, who asks if he can watch training at Bisham Abbey and talk to the players before Euro 96. We smile knowingly as the FA confides it will put the idea to Venables. No chance, comes the predictable reply. Hoddle watches from afar.

Players are frustrated to hear of Venables' pending exit. 'I was gutted,' recalls Mark Wright, who features against Croatia in the build-up to Euro 96 but whose tournament ambitions end with injury after 12 minutes against Hungary on 18 May. 'When I got into the England side with Terry, the training was brilliant. Terry and Don Howe together was the hardest training I've ever done. Terry's coaching was fantastic. I was like a sponge, trying to improve. I'd have loved to train under Terry day in, day out. I'd have become a way better player. Terry is probably the best technical coach I played under.'

Whatever the niceties or otherwise of Venables' financial dealings, he elicits constant admiration for his stoicism. His strength of character keeps him and the squad sane through a build-up that courts controversy almost on a daily basis. Only in the madcap world of the Three Lions could England prepare for a tournament on home soil with a trip to the Far East. Venables' use of the Neville brothers, Gary and Phil, causes diplomatic mayhem in China, a land with a controversial 'one-child policy' to keep the population down (a rule rescinded in 2015). Only England could stumble into a debate about female infanticide: as parents want sons to look after them in retirement, baby girls are at risk of murder. It's horrific, and it's the emotional backdrop to the friendly in the Workers' Stadium on 23 May. The sight of two brothers lining up in opposition is viewed as taunting by the Chinese. Among the travelling circus, the young, approachable Nevilles win friends when they help a less-than-svelte photographer to get his camera equipment up the Great Wall.

Storms overshadow the tour. On reaching Hong Kong, England upset the locals by not using training facilities and then complaining about the length of grass at the Happy Valley Stadium for the game against a Hong Kong Golden Select XI notable mainly for the astonishing pink of their shirts, shorts and socks. Venables has a point about the pitch: it needs a machete, let alone a mower. We consult his coaching staff. Surely Ted Buxton's experience of fighting in the Malay jungle will come in handy here? Trouble rumbles on. The cunning plan to travel halfway round the world, keeping away from prying eyes, rather unravels when Gascoigne, Teddy Sheringham and Steve McManaman clamber into the Dentist's Chair at the China Jump Club. It's obviously quite a night. Later that evening I bump into one player whose shirt is so ripped I buy him a replacement top from behind the bar we're in.

It's Carry On Chaos. Even the video of the official song 'Three Lions' contains a car resplendent with an out-of-date tax disc. Such is the intensifying interest in England that the FA's media chief, David Davies, discreetly instructs designers to make the Three Lions' eyes more open. Can't have them appearing to doze off. Just to add to his extraordinary summer, Venables is almost wiped out on the tricky roundabout near Bisham on the eve of the tournament.

To the surprise of nobody in football, he proves an astute tactician and man-manager, getting the best out of the troubled Paul Gascoigne, who is outstanding against Scotland and Holland in the group stage. Venables also backs Alan Shearer from a year out to come good, even during the painful warm-ups. Game after game Shearer labours, but when it counts – against Switzerland in the first game, then against Scotland and Holland – the single-minded Geordie strikes. He converts a penalty as England squeeze past Spain in the quarter-finals and then scores in the 26 June semi-final against Germany, adding a penalty in that fateful shoot-out. Shearer vindicates Venables' judgement. Blessed with an exceptional collection of players and robust characters, Venables forges a good team, helped by the 'collective responsibility' response to criticism of the squad's alcohol-fuelled antics in Hong Kong. He is strongly supported by coaching staff like Bryan Robson, who tears into the press at Bisham Abbey after criticism of the opening draw with Switzerland. Venables' popularity among his peers is such that he receives a good-luck phone-call from Bobby Robson before the game with Scotland. So it is a frustrated Venables listening to Shearer, Adams and the rest of the players singing 'Football's Coming Home' in the Wembley dressing-room after the thrashing of Holland. He knows the adventure is coming to an end. He's going home. His World Cup dream will never be realized.

Hoddle is announced before Venables leaves, just as McClaren is revealed as Sven-Göran Eriksson's successor before the Swede concludes his reign at the 2006 World Cup finals. The FA confirms the start of the recruitment process on 24 January that year, and the accompanying music could at times be borrowed from the Keystone Cops. The FA forgets the primacy of moving stealthily, being mindful of candidates' sensitivities, initially returning to an old flame, an unrequited one – Fabio Capello, a coach it was briefly interested in after Kevin Keegan's meltdown in 2000. The FA wants Capello in 2006 because it feels the squad needs more 'discipline' after the

Eriksson years. Now at Juventus, Capello is wooed by the FA but club legend Roberto Bettega stops the English talking to him. So the FA looks elsewhere. Its pursuit of Guus Hiddink swiftly becomes public knowledge and the Dutchman reacts angrily. His agent, Cees van Nieuwenhuizen, tells 5 Live's *Sportsweek* programme on 9 April that Hiddink is not interested any more, and the decision to ask him for a discreet interview, for talks about talks, is 'an insult' to a coach with an impressive pedigree. A coach who has steered Holland and South Korea to World Cup semi-finals does not do auditions. 'They were interested in having a coffee or tea and finding out if he could be a potential candidate to be put on the shortlist,' says Van Nieuwenhuizen. 'We did not take it too seriously because you expect that if you are in the world of football then you know who Guus Hiddink is and what he has achieved [at] club level and on a national level.' The FA looks amateurish. Hiddink goes on to take Russia to the semi-finals of Euro 2008.

Events in 2006 highlight why the FA should leave the chase to one or two trusted individuals, operating quietly, consulting, building up a picture of the qualities required, which include handling difficult clubs; efficient man-management; easily absorbed, balanced tactics; few skeletons in the cupboard; mentally tough; good with the media but not matey; and ownership of a four-leaf clover, preferably a home-grown one. FA headhunters should identify the right candidate, sound him out and report back to the board. In 2006, the FA decides on a broad process, a beauty parade, inviting four of the five on the shortlist to interviews at Chippinghurst Manor, the Grade II-listed sixteenth-century Oxfordshire retreat of Sir Victor Blank, the chairman of Trinity Mirror. Usually the sporting guests are cricketers playing in Sir Victor's charity matches on his estate. In and out now are McClaren, Martin O'Neill and the Big brothers Sam Allardyce and Phil Scolari, all being whisked through the gates in people-carriers with tinted windows, to the Manor borne. The fifth man, Alan Curbishley, is absent as he's focusing on Charlton Athletic's imminent FA Cup tie against Middlesbrough. The FA doesn't want to interfere with its beloved Cup competition.

'I didn't see them [the other candidates] in the house,' smiles Allardyce, chatting in Salford after we'd done a BBC show. Facing a panel including Sir Trevor Brooking and members of the FA International Committee such as Geoff Thompson, Dave Richards and David Dein, each candidate is gently grilled over a couple of hours. 'I talked about preparation, about tournament level,' recalls Allardyce. 'I talked about speaking to my best mates who played for England, Reidy and Robbo [Peter Reid and Bryan Robson]. In their time, and still now, [a big issue] is dealing with the players' boredom. I talked about fatigue in the players, and that comes from still not having a winter break. I always voted for it. I took my [Bolton Wanderers] lads to Dubai for a week and wouldn't really train them. It was sun on the back, volleyball on the beach; some do their weights, keep their own regime. They'd come back fresher and you'd see a greater surge in the fitness. I talked about getting England stronger. We've not been able to kill a team off.' Allardyce pauses, leaving Chippinghurst reflections behind for a moment. 'We've never done what Germany did to Brazil [7-1 in the 2014 World Cup semi-final]. The mental toughness of Germany in that game was phenomenal, destroying one of the fancied teams on their own turf.'

Allardyce is a far deeper thinker than his slightly Mike Bassett public billing suggests. A passionate advocate of home-grown managers being given a chance, he relishes the opportunity to voice his ideas to the FA. 'I enjoyed the process. It was a bit difficult because it was in the middle of the season but it's the top job, isn't it? We were driven in. It was supposed to be a secret but all the press lads were outside anyway. I was in there a good two hours. I'd been told what they wanted me to present. I did a presentation. I spent enough time on it. Looking into the future about where technology was going, I explained that you don't have a huge amount of time with the players, so you need to get all the basics through to the players before they actually arrive. I would download software to them about travel arrangements, who we're playing, we're going to do these types of sessions, some video analysis on the game. I'd tell the players: "If you want anything on an individual player let us know and we'll have it ready for you when you come. You've got a lot of down-time when we're together, so if you want to sit with the analysis people, you can do. If you don't, it doesn't matter."'

The panel mention the weight of expectation from public and press. 'You have to live with that,' Allardyce shrugs. 'If you don't want it, don't go for it. If you do want it, you know what's coming your way. I spoke to Bobby Robson and Graham Taylor. They said: "It's the finest job to ever have, don't turn it down if you get the opportunity, you'll regret it for the rest of your life if you do." Even with all the troubles those two went through, Bobby and Graham still turned round and said: "Wow, it's a great position to have, the pinnacle of your career." It would have been the pinnacle of my career.'

Allardyce is driven out of Chippinghurst Manor at speed. 'It was a great ride coming out because all the press lads followed to try to find out who it was. They couldn't see because of the blacked-out windows. The driver did an unbelievable job, going through red lights, back streets, cutbacks; it took him forty minutes before he lost everybody. He was throwing me about in the back. I was hanging on. He took me back to Heathrow.'

As he boards his plane back to Manchester, Allardyce feels confident. He senses his presentation went well. He believes the FA is keen to appoint an Englishman after an expensive Swede. In keeping with the FA's colander nature, news leaks of its preferred candidate. 'The biggest disappointment was when they said they were going for Scolari. It was me, Steve, Martin or Alan and then all of a sudden it's Phil Scolari! I remember thinking: "What's going on here?" They said it would be home-grown. All of a sudden somebody had a brainwave to say, "Let's go for Phil Scolari."'

Dein is particularly keen on the Brazilian Scolari, England's nemesis at the 2002 World Cup with his country and at Euro 2004 with Portugal (and soon the 2006 World Cup). If you can't beat them, buy them. Flirting with the Brazilian ends up scarring the FA. The Portugal coach is chased by the media in London and Lisbon. His family is hounded. Portuguese media, public, players and federation officials understandably want to know Scolari's plans and he comes under sustained pressure. 'Phil decided when all the press landed on his door that he didn't want it, and the FA reverted back to us again.' Allardyce smiles, a touch ruefully, still smarting at the denied opportunity. 'I hit the crossbar. When you hit the crossbar you have to put it behind you, and get on with it. I wouldn't let it affect us.' By 'us', Allardyce means Bolton Wanderers: despite a brief wobble the club finish the 2006/07 season in seventh place and qualify for the Uefa Cup alongside Spurs and Everton.

Steve McClaren, the successful candidate, lasts eighteen matches, proving as unsuccessful as expected by those who see the difference between a coach and a manager. England plummet from fifth to twelfth in the Fifa world rankings. The influence of the International Committee subsides since the McClaren fiasco. Current members of the International Committee are hard-working dignitaries like Barry Taylor 'from Barnsley' and popular committee man Peter Barnes. Their ambassadorial work is much-needed by the FA. Taylor delivers the traditional 'thank you very much, we're delighted to be here' speech at the pre-match function in San Marino during qualifying for Euro 2016. Barnes is a frequent traveller, waving the flag, doing differing age-groups, representing the FA well.

Memories of McClaren's costly appointment should shape FA thinking when it seeks Roy Hodgson's successor. Technical director Dan Ashworth and chief executive Martin Glenn will effectively make the decision. When we meet in London, Ashworth prefaces our conversation about the next England manager with a caveat. 'We currently have an England coach who is very experienced,' he emphasizes. 'Roy is a top coach, a very experienced man-manager. People underestimate how good he is with the players. He's managed well over a thousand games. He's managed at international level four times in his career [with Switzerland, UAE, Finland and England]. He's managed across Europe, managed at big teams [like Inter Milan and Liverpool] and managed at small teams [like Swedish club Halmstads]. He knows the game inside out. We're in good hands.' In Paris before the Euro 2016 draw, Glenn even talks of the 68-year-old Hodgson staying on for the 2018 World Cup. His comments come days after Alan Pardew, the Crystal Palace manager who makes little secret of his desire to lead England, declares that the appointment should be performance-related tournament to tournament.

Before identifying Hodgson's replacement, the FA has first to establish whether he needs to be home-grown. Glenn says English will be good but he's 'not prepared to die in a ditch' for the principle. Yet if the FA's £120m coach development centre at St George's Park is not to be undermined, the England manager has to be English. The FA needs to make a statement, saying it believes in fostering home-grown coaches, that the England manager will be English, not Swedish or Italian, not Northern Irish like Brendan Rodgers or Spanish like Roberto Martínez – two coaches perceived within the FA as 'Anglos' because they learned their coaching skills at clubs embedded in the English leagues. International football should be the old tenet of 'our best against your best'.

'We do want home-grown coaches, but what is a home-grown coach?' asks Ashworth. The FA's policy is blurred because it includes 'Anglos', those like Rodgers who've spent the majority of their career in England. 'All right, Brendan's an interesting one,' says Ashworth. 'Brendan started his coaching career at Chelsea, in their youth team, did his qualifications, then did his development from Chelsea to Reading to Swansea to Liverpool. Roberto Martínez would not be too dissimilar. Came over here young as a player. What is the coaching pathway? If they've done their qualifications and their time in the trenches in this country, with this association, what's their development programme? If you look at it like a home-grown player rule, five years in any given country you have the right to be given a passport, so would you not apply that to coaching?' Rodgers considers himself Northern Irish. 'OK. [The American] Brad Friedel is on our Pro Licence course. He's done the A Licence and Pro Licence with the English FA. If Brad gets a job in the Premier League we'd be absolutely delighted as he's somebody who has come through our systems. Shouldn't they take any credit for his pathway through? I'm not saying Brad is English, but we are talking about the home-grown, the coach development programme.'

The Italians, Germans and Spanish appoint natives, so shouldn't the FA be looking at Pardew, Gary Neville or Eddie Howe? 'In an ideal world, probably yes,' says Ashworth. 'We want the best person for the job – and I firmly believe, by the way, that Roy Hodgson is the right man. Roy's in the post and it's a little bit disrespectful to talk about successors, but Roy is 68 years old and he's going to finish at some stage; whether that is 2016, 2018, 2020, who knows? We've got a really good Englishman who's the right man for the job at the moment. Going forward, I think we'd all agree in an ideal world it would be an English person but you don't want to cut your nose off to spite your face and rule certain people out who might actually be the best person for the job. If they were born in a different country would you really exclude them from the job? I don't know. I personally would need a little more convincing with somebody who doesn't speak English, or hasn't worked in the Premier League or England, and who has no affinity to it at all.

'You have three groups: English, those with an affinity to England, and foreign,' Ashworth concludes. 'Arsène Wenger has been here since '96. Has Arsène got a fantastic understanding of the Premier League, of English players, of the English media, of the expectations of England? Absolutely. So would you rule him out? Probably not. He might not want it.'

Wenger for England? That will spark a debate. One thing's for sure: whoever succeeds Hodgson will need to remember that Mike Stokoe cartoon in the National Football Museum. Don't lose.

11

Finishing School

THE SEARCH FOR answers to the years of hurt takes me deep into the Cheshire countryside, west from the manic M6, weaving between Crewe and Nantwich, reluctantly past the Cholmondeley Arms – the type of tavern you'd happily move into – before taking a sharp right turn down the long drive to Manor House Stables belonging to Michael Owen, fifth on the all-time list of England goalscorers. Questions forming in my mind on the journey include: why is he so inspired by wearing the Three Lions when others feel so cowed? What are the chief defects of the modern Academy system he still has contact with through his player agency? What was his thought process when slicing through Argentina's defence in 1998? Should the England manager be English? And, is it possible to win the tightest international matches without being streetwise, even devious? Again, some of the current crop of England players could do with seeking Owen's counsel, learning and improving. Raheem Sterling could certainly do with an hour in his company, undergoing instruction in the art of finishing.

The man who nets 40 goals in 89 internationals between 1998 and 2007 is waiting outside his expansive stables, clad in a British Champions Day Ascot 2013 fleece, tracksuit bottoms signalling past employment at Liverpool Football Club, and flip-flops revealing feet surprisingly unscarred by the breaks and bruises of his demanding profession. All around is the buzz of racing staff hard at work, the early-morning gallops completed, the horses fed and watered, but there's also sorrow in the crisp air. The yard's beloved Brown Panther, a Classic winner, died a fortnight earlier after snapping two bones in his right hind leg during the Irish St Leger at the Curragh. 'The saddest day of my life,' Owen tweets. Brown Panther was about to go to stud, the mares bought, the future good, and then this cruel blow. Owen shakes his head in sadness as condolences are passed on again.

We walk inside the main building, and head upstairs to a large room full of portraits of horses in full flight. A long-time devotee of racing, Owen occasionally looks out of the window, surveying those successors to Panther's rich tradition. The yard occupies much of Owen's time. He's a busy man. Later that morning he is flying down to London for more television work. He's invested in a company called M7 Aerials which rents drones to clubs like Everton to film training from above, giving forward-thinking managers like Roberto Martínez a different perspective of players' movements. Owen watches his son play football and his daughters ride in dressage events. He also has Michael Owen Management, tending the careers of promising youngsters, encouraging them to put away their substantial wages in three bank accounts: one for running costs, the second for more significant outlays like a car, and the third as a trust fund. It's about the long-term.

Owen's life rattles along at the quick, ambitious pace that defined his playing days, but such a driven individual misses the adrenalin rush of a career that brought a Ballon d'Or and glory in the Premier League, Uefa Cup, FA Cup and League Cup three times. He's always been competitive, whether boxing briefly as a teenager – winning a brace of three-round bouts on points – playing centre at rugby or, most eye-catchingly, when fastening on to a ball and speeding towards a frequently petrified keeper.

For England, his goals are scattered across the globe, everywhere from New York to Niigata, St James' Park to St-Etienne, the old and new Wembley, into Baku and beyond. He establishes an England record by scoring in four consecutive tournaments. A hamstring injury, the scourge of his career, ruins his hopes of competing in a fourth World Cup, South Africa in 2010.

Born into a sports-mad family – his father Terry served Everton as an attacker and mother Janette was a talented athlete at school – Owen has always enjoyed a great support network, giving him constant encouragement and the right advice. From an early age he's destined to play for England. Whispers about a bright new talent become shouts. A star pupil at the old FA National School at Lilleshall, where his year-group includes Wes Brown, Michael Ball, Kenny Lunt and Jon Harley, Owen is so prolific through the England age-groups that the statisticians almost don't count the number of goals, they just weigh them. For the record, he scores 37 times in 33 games for England Under-15s, 16s and 18s followed by 3 in 4 for the Under-20s. On 17 December 1997, Owen is given what amounts to an audition for the seniors with his sole Under-21 appearance in front of 14,114 spectators, including Glenn Hoddle, at Carrow Road. Those of us present on that freezing Norfolk evening are warmed by the sight of Owen shredding the Greek defence, scoring in a 4-2 win. The following day I phone Hoddle, requesting his verdict on Owen, the quotes then pooled among the other England correspondents. For an industry built on story-getting rivalry, there's plenty of cooperation between football writers. Only 17, Owen is already fascinating Fleet Street sports editors eager to find the man, even teenager, to end the years of hurt. Newspapers reflect a national desire for a messiah to lead the team out of the wilderness so prodigy status is bestowed swiftly. Owen is already a fixture in headlines because of his impact at Liverpool. Pundits and public demand he be a wild-card pick for the 1998 World Cup finals. The excitement in Hoddle's voice at the other end of the line tells its own story, complementing his positive appraisal. A supreme talent is racing towards the England fold. With the next game a friendly against Chile on 11 February, Hoddle is clearly considering fast-tracking the Liverpool flier.

'I was in a really good era of strikers – Alan Shearer, Teddy Sheringham, Les Ferdinand, Robbie Fowler, Andy Cole and Ian Wright – so to get an England cap was hard,' recalls Owen. 'I felt an incredible pride when I was told I was being called up for the first time. I was playing golf at Curzon Park in Chester. I was beating Dad easily, three up after five holes, and I got this call. We weren't allowed mobile phones on the course but I saw the number was Doug Livermore, assistant manager at Liverpool. I had to answer. I hid behind the trees so none of the members could see me. "Just letting you know, you've just been picked in the England squad," Doug told me. We continued playing but every spare minute I was on the phone to someone. I was so proud to be called up.' Even distracted, Owen still wins the golf.

As Owen passionately recounts the story, the power woven into the England shirt is reconfirmed. After scoring twice in a 3-2 loss to Southampton at Anfield on 7 February, Owen's itching to set off for Burnham Beeches, England's base in Berkshire. He resembles a sprinter, rocking in the starting-blocks, listening impatiently for the gun. 'I couldn't wait to get down there. I was so eager to impress.' Paul Ince, Steve McManaman and Robbie Fowler are also in the squad so the Liverpool quartet prepare to travel down together. 'Incey was taking his time in the bath after the game and then on the way someone said: "Shall we stop off for a pint? Shall we stop off at the services?" I was just wanting to get there. I don't want to turn up for England having drunk alcohol. We got there after midnight. Macca, Incey and Robbie showed me around the hotel, showing me where breakfast was. As we opened the door to the meeting room, there was my bloody hero Gazza playing a computer game and drinking a glass of wine. I thought: "Oh my God, I'm in the squad with Gazza! This is him!" Gazza, Gary Lineker and that 1990 World Cup team was when I first understood football. We went over to Gazza. I said, "Hi, I'm Michael," and stuck my hand out. He gave everyone a hug.'

On the Monday, Hoddle opens up training for fifteen minutes to an impatient media clamouring for a close-up glimpse of England's latest saviour. His England top too big for his small frame, the cuffs almost covering his hands, Owen immediately commands the focus of the photographers. Many capture the assured body language of a player feeling totally at home, his foot on the ball. He's been there twice before, having been invited to get a taste of training with another prospect, Rio Ferdinand. 'They used to bring one or two youngsters in to carry bibs but also training with them. That was good because I did feel a little bit more part of it. But it was still really, really daunting.' It is no surprise that those invited on work experience, Owen and Ferdinand, living with the lions and banishing butterflies, prove such long-term fixtures in the squad – something the FA should consider on a more formal basis with the junior age-groups. Currently it's an ad hoc arrangement: got a couple of injuries, let's borrow some kids from a nearby pitch at St George's Park.

Down at Burnham, Hoddle tells Owen 'you're going to start on Wednesday night' against Chile. 'My heart lifted. I couldn't believe it.' He's about to become England's youngest international that century, at 18 years and 59 days, breaking the record set in 1955 by the dynamic but tragically doomed Duncan Edwards. Wayne Rooney lowers the mark further in 2003. On the Tuesday, Owen's ushered in to talk to the press in the oak-panelled splendour of the Warwick Room at Bisham Abbey. It feels like awaiting royalty. The young prince considers each question thoughtfully before answering succinctly, always holding eye contact with inquisitors. Newcomers to the England scene often treat questions lobbed their way as if they're hand-grenades. Not Owen. He's polite and in control, 18 going on 28. Nowadays, too many young players emerge blinking into the media spotlight. They are so cocooned in Academies, so lauded by staff, that many are shocked when entering a room and facing questions. Some are excellent talkers like Jack Butland and Eric Dier but suspicion of the press grows in a website age where rolling news, and a click-bait culture, demands arresting headlines and any detail is seized upon, even tittle-tattle. Owen, though, is a natural in the press room, having dealt with proper interviews from a young age, not the 'you're wonderful, what's your favourite colour/band/boot/holiday resort' type.

Confident off the field, Owen shines on it. With kick-off delayed fifteen minutes because of turmoil on the Tube, Owen is finally presented to Sir Tom Finney – a gilded attacker from England's past meeting the future. Owen almost continues his run of always scoring on his England debuts but Chile's agile keeper, Nelson Tapia, somehow saves an early powerful shot. Owen impresses overall, going close with a header and creating chances for Sheringham and Ince while his pace proves a constant threat, but England are well beaten by Chile and the clinical Marcelo Salas. The brake's off the 'Owen for France 98' bandwagon. All aboard. Hoddle takes Owen to the pre-France training camp at La Manga, in Spain, and the teenager scores in the King Hassan II International Cup friendly against Morocco in Casablanca, a game so chaotically organized that I get in by flashing a Blockbuster Video card at the gate. Back in La Manga, Owen is viewed as a certainty to be among the final 22 Hoddle's about to name for France 98. The rising star even hit the mark in the shoot-out against Belgium to decide the tournament winners in Casablanca. The boy can take penalties too. Seems almost over-qualified for England. 'You're in, and you're not just coming along for the ride,' Hoddle tells Owen. 'You might not start but you will be playing a good part in this tournament.' Owen's off to the World Cup. 'I walked out feeling ten foot tall.'

The media almost convulses with ecstasy and conjecture. Polls, phone-ins and columns debate whether Owen should start, replacing Sheringham as Shearer's attacking partner. He's largely oblivious to the swirl of views. 'I was never going to be upset at being a sub at the World Cup in France. I felt I'd gone ahead of the likes of Robbie Fowler, Ian Wright, great players like that. I felt I was in third place and pushing.'

And pushing hard. With 5 minutes remaining of the 2-0 win over Tunisia in Marseille on 15 June, a bright day darkened by English hooligans and supine French policing, Hoddle looks to the future. Owen replaces Sheringham. A week later, against Romania in Toulouse, with 17 minutes left, England 1-0 down and almost 20,000 fans chanting for Owen, Hoddle repeats the switch. On ITV, Kevin Keegan provides the co-commentary alongside the even-handed Brian Moore. 'Well, that's fan-power for you,' remarks Keegan after Owen arrives, a view that belittles Hoddle's work and exasperates the England manager when he reviews the tape later. Hoddle's adamant that Owen has always been in his plans for when Sheringham runs out of impetus or ideas. Owen pounces on a rebound, just as his father always told him to do. After Dan Petrescu nets in the 90th minute to make it 2-1, the super-sub almost rescues England with a second goal in injury time but hits the post.

'Even when I came on and scored against Romania, I still wasn't sure whether I'd start against Colombia,' Owen recalls of the decisive Group G game in Lens on 26 June. 'I didn't know the whole circus going on back home and the wave of support that I was getting, people saying I should be playing. We were totally locked away in that tournament. If I'd been an older player I'd have felt "this is a long old World Cup", but I was new to it. There were no cliques, it was a good atmosphere.' Owen enjoys life in La Baule, England's base close to a magnificent beach and the old U-boat pens at Saint-Nazaire. Their hotel boasts a golf course once graced by Seve Ballesteros, a large pool and friendly staff. A group photograph of Hoddle and his squad still hangs in reception. 'Me and Rio were the youngsters, we hung out together, we spoke when we were spoken to at that stage. There was a Manchester United table because so many of them were in the squad, and naturally they were all mates. Every team will have groups. You're naturally more friendly with some people than others. There was an older scene, a cards table, with Shearer, Batty, Nigel Martyn, Tim Flowers, Seaman, Sheringham – that generation. Every team I've been in, there's always been a card-table, always a Nintendo table or whatever they play nowadays.'

Preparing for Colombia, Hoddle tries to work on a special set-piece routine he's devised. 'It was hilarious,' laughs Owen. 'Beckham and Scholes were doing this free-kick. Glenn wanted Scholes or Beckham to put one foot the other side of the ball. So when the other player comes and smacks the ball, it hits the top of their foot, gets a huge amount of top spin up and over the wall, goes massively quick and it comes down. "I want you to do this," Glenn said to them. Beckham tried it. Scholes tried it. It was going everywhere! Glenn couldn't understand it. Glenn walked up to Beckham and said: "I thought someone of your ability would be able to do it. Just take it direct then." The ironic thing is that in the game we get the free-kick, Beckham takes it and scores direct like he normally does!'

Hoddle's man-management skills are increasingly scrutinized, especially by Beckham's club manager, Alex Ferguson, in a scathing column in the *Sunday Times* about the way the England manager treats the sensitive midfielder. Ferguson's particularly aggrieved that Beckham is made to face the press knowing he's not starting against Tunisia. For those present at that briefing, Beckham handles the inquisition with his usual charm and dexterity. Even shredding this myth still cannot dispel the overall legitimacy of Ferguson's critique, questioning Hoddle's man-management. 'The general feeling among the team was that John Gorman did the man-management stuff because Glenn either didn't want to or wasn't good at it,' observes Owen. 'There were people who weren't in the team that didn't like him because he couldn't communicate. If you were playing in the team he didn't need to communicate to you. I thought Glenn was brilliant, the best England had for a long, long time, and I was sad when he went.

'People often say: "Do you have to be English to be England manager?" All my experience of foreign managers is that they're nothing different to what we've got. Not that I'm against having a foreign manager as England boss, I just haven't been overwhelmed by anyone.' During his international career, Owen plays under Sven-Göran Eriksson and Fabio Capello. 'No one has taught me anything where I thought: "Oh my word, that's a new invention." I never thought, "Wow, that's because he's foreign." In fact, Glenn Hoddle was probably the one person who taught us most about things off the pitch, like sports science. He was doing new things with us, real cutting edge.'

After that pre-Colombia session, Hoddle informs Owen he's starting the next day. 'I never had a problem with sleeping but before the Colombia game when I knew I was playing, I slept about two hours. I didn't really try to sleep. I was lying in bed thinking so much and wanting to prepare so much. I was getting up and stretching, doing weird things. I was so in the zone, so desperately wanting to do well.' He does. 'Beckham and Owen injected youth and optimism and urgency into a side that seemed to be stagnating,' thunders *The Times* after the 2-0 success settled by Darren Anderton and Beckham in the first half. 'I didn't score against Colombia, I played all right, so I didn't know whether he would bring Teddy back in,' recalls Owen.

His fears are unfounded. Hoddle keeps a winning team as England speed to St-Etienne on 30 June to face Argentina, a fixture riddled with recollection of past tensions, including the Hand of God. 'I was aware of the history but none of it mattered to me,' Owen shrugs. 'I didn't go into the game thinking "this is retribution for the Hand of God". It wasn't used as a motivation. The stakes are so high that we didn't need the manager to say anything. Jesus, on the bus to a World Cup game, you could cut the atmosphere with a knife. No one's saying a word. Everyone's so focused. Going to St-Etienne, God, it was more than focused, it was zoned all day. It's amazing; in a World Cup, it's different to anything else.'

The teenager is very keen to show his commitment. Sometimes the tension turns the competitor into a coiled spring, waiting to unwind and unleash on an opponent, as Owen proves in a rare detonation of his temper earlier that year, on 10 April. 'I remember playing at Old Trafford, and getting sent off for the only time in my career (apart from a perceived head butt for England Under-18s against Yugoslavia in 1977), I was that revved up, that focused.' It's United versus Liverpool, the deadliest of English club duels. 'I felt like I was ready to kill for a whole week. I went and tackled Peter Schmeichel and the ref said, "Be careful, you're going to get sent off here, steady."' Shown the yellow card by Graham Poll for that late lunge on United's keeper, Owen's fuse still burns. 'I'd go in for another tackle, then I'd go and break Ronny Johnsen's ankle.' Owen tears into the United defender, badly damaging the Norwegian's ligaments, and receives a second yellow for bloodthirsty intent which on its own merits red. 'I was a man possessed and I'm quite mellow, quite normal, quite calm. I'd been thinking about that bloody game for that long that [when] I was in the shower on my own, I almost felt like a switch going. God, you're almost back to normal. I took a deep breath and my whole body relaxed.'

Lining up in the tunnel opposite Gabriel Batistuta, Diego Simeone and Juan Sebastián Verón, Owen feels calm, ready, bold. 'Nothing fazed me, ever, right from a kid. I just think a little bit differently to the majority. It annoys my missus to death. I never think I had a bad game as a football player. Even if the papers said "Michael Owen missed three chances, so he's had a bad game", I'd be thinking how well did I do to get that chance? It was a brilliant run. Even though the ball went the other side of the post, I'd be thinking how well I'd done in committing the keeper. I could take any negative and turn it into a positive. As a kid, I never failed to get into a team. I was playing for my county Under-11s at 7, which is just stupid. Every time I did something it was successful or I perceived it to be successful. I just didn't think I could fail. I had this mindset.

'I knew we were playing Argentina, but I'd never even consider thinking who my opponent is in terms of a centre-half. I knew Gabriel Batistuta because he was a famous centre-forward but I didn't know their defenders. I didn't know their strengths and weaknesses, I never looked for one minute. At the end of my career, when I'm feeling I've not got the powers I did have, I was looking at people and thinking: "Oh sugar, I'm playing against him today, he's quicker than me, he's stronger than me, I'm going to have to play on the other one – oh, the other one's quick as well." You might as well pack it in.'

The only players contemplating retirement for much of that last day of June in 1998 are some harassed defenders. Before 30,600 rapt onlookers at Stade Geoffroy-Guichard, Argentina's back-line and the world are introduced properly to a creature of instinct and audacity. Owen's first impact is to engineer a 10th-minute penalty after the faintest of challenges from the centre-half Roberto Ayala. 'It probably wasn't a penalty,' admits Owen. But then nor is Argentina's after 6 minutes when David Seaman challenges Simeone and Batistuta converts. 'Exactly! Two wrongs do make a right!'

Pausing briefly, Owen offers an insight into the tricks of the penalty-box trade. 'I'm weighing up probability all the time, the probability if I pass it or shoot, which is the best chance of us scoring? Going away from goal, it's "one in ten I can score here" and it's about trying to entice someone. I'll manipulate this situation to get a penalty. I wouldn't keep my touch close to me.' Like a skilled angler setting a trap, Owen casts the ball far enough forward to invite the challenge. Ayala bites. 'He's running over quickly so I'm going to get a pen. I never dived without getting a touch in my life but I certainly went through a stage of if someone came and tackled me, and touched me, then I'd go down.' Feeling slight contact from Ayala, Owen presses the gravity button. 'I didn't get touched enough to go down, I could easily have stayed on my feet that day. It was a penalty in every English person's book. I was nudged, I was barged. Could I have avoided it? Yes. Could I have stayed on my feet? Yes. The ball was going out and I wasn't going to score; I was trying to get an advantage. Listen, the referee can always say "no, it wasn't enough". I didn't ask him to come and barge me.' The Danish referee, Kim Milton Nielsen, points to the spot. 'I don't know whether I'm proud of it, because it is bending the rules. There are not so many fouls in the box that totally wipe you off your feet. With 90 per cent of penalties people are looking for them, getting touched – yes – but not enough to bring them down. I never exaggerated them. I'm so torn because I'd like to think I've got principles. Honestly, I watch penalties and I think nine out of ten are easily avoidable if the centre-forward doesn't want to go down softly or look for the leg. I can see them coming. I did it.

'I'm jumping four years ahead here but early on in the game against Argentina in Sapporo, I was fouled outside the box,' Owen reflects of a tense 2002 World Cup Group F match refereed by Pierluigi Collina, the acclaimed Italian. 'I tried to stay on my feet, and lost the ball. I turned round and said: "Ref, it's a foul." He came up to me at the next break of play and said: "I can't give you a foul for that. Yes, if you go down, I'll give you a foul. You have to make my mind up." Ten minutes later, I went past Mauricio Pochettino and he actually nicked me, one of those little studs that iced me, that drew blood. It was only a scratch, I went down, and Collina gave me a penalty. This is the greatest referee of all time.' Pochettino actually tries to withdraw his leg but Owen's plunging towards the deck. 'That's why people getting touched do go down.' Opportunity.

Back in St-Etienne, six minutes after Shearer duly dispatches the penalty past Carlos Roa, comes the moment that changes Owen's life. 'This is Owen, taken it in his stride,' the BBC commentator Jon Champion tells 28m viewers back home, including Steven Gerrard leaping up and down on his parents' sofa in Huyton. 'Chamot is trying not to bring him down. It's still Michael Owen. He's scored a wonderful goal! Is there nothing beyond this 18-year-old?' Controlling Beckham's pass instantly with the outside of his right foot, steering it forward, outpacing José Chamot, Owen sprints towards the box, bemusing Ayala, another defensive sentry turned into a statue. Scholes is arriving fast, threatening to intercept the ball and shoot, but Owen's on a mission, lifting the ball back across Roa and in. He's in control throughout, employing almost a mathematician's knowledge of angles and velocity. This is the master-class that aspiring finishers like Sterling need to cram up on.

'My eyes were taking camera shots all the time, computing them to my brain, seeing the full picture,' Owen explains. 'When I took my first touch, my only intention was to take a touch away from him [Chamot], be direct, run towards goal. I take my touch, wriggle away from him and then look up, assess the picture, and that picture told me "keep running, don't pass". There's nothing on at the moment that's going to help the team more than me actually keeping running. With every touch, I'm constantly thinking: "What's the option? What's the option? What's the option?" And every stage it was, "Keep running, keep running, keep running."'

Owen lifts his head. Ayala comes into view. 'My eyes lit up. I thought: "There's one player there and he's stood still and I'm building up a head of steam." It's very exciting – very.' And familiar. Owen's been in this situation so often before, running through back-lines, plundering goals, including 97 in a single season for Deeside Primary Schools' Under-11s, rewriting Ian Rush's record. Questioning Academy culture as it does, Owen's theorizing on attacking principles needs absorbing by the FA as it strives to mould the next generation into internationals of real substance. 'It was ingrained into me, by repetition, by scoring five, ten goals in whatever game we played in. People now in Academies say, "You've got to play best against best, all the time, that's how you learn." You don't. You need to bully people.

You need to have ten chances in a game, because if I miss the first one, I know I'll be getting another in two minutes' time. If I'd been playing best against best all the time as a kid, all of a sudden I'd get one chance, miss it, and think: "Oh shit, I'm not going to get another chance." And if you do get another chance you play safe.'

The spirit of the playground in Hawarden, Flintshire blows through St-Etienne. Owen runs right past a frozen Ayala, confusing Roa even more. 'I never used to take the ball around the goalkeeper. My dad said, "Try doing this." I could do it but I'd learned at 10 that I'd get ten chances. I was refining how to prepare the ball, how to run at a defender, how I dictate where the keeper is. I could get a goalkeeper exactly where I wanted him from 40 yards away. I knew the angle I needed to run. When you get a chance in the World Cup, because you've done it so many times and you're confident of your finish, it's just a natural process. There's a lot to be said for playing in the school team, and being the stand-out player, winning 10-0 every week and scoring nine goals. I learned what my favourite finish was, I learned how to dink it.' He lifts the ball at speed over Roa from right to left. 'You don't just dink a keeper – that's the icing on the cake, that's the end. It's about how you get him to lie down before you, like how you get a horse to lie down and do whatever you want. It's about angle of approach, about your touch and wanting to tempt him to think "I can block his angle". If I keep my touch tight, tight, tight, he's never going to go down, he's going to think I'm going to go round him. If I made my touch a certain length, it entices him, before you dink him. I know I'm going to dink him from far out.' How many of Hodgson's youngsters, or those still learning in the Academies, appreciate that finishing is such a science?

Aware that his views run counter to the clubs' expensive Elite Player Performance Plan, Owen discusses them frequently with Liverpool's highly respected Academy director Alex Inglethorpe. 'I really like Alex. I think he's brilliant. We talk about this all the time. He's in effect saying the same thing – he wishes [there was still involvement for elite kids in] schools football and in the playground. You won't try something against good players when loads of people are watching for the sake of embarrassment. When you're playing in the play-ground, you learn how to beat players, even though they're crap, and you learn how to avoid clumsy tackles.'

Owen is lost in private thought for a few moments. Mention of avoiding injury prompts some anguish. He makes a detour in his narrative, reflecting on how his toughest opponent was always injury, especially on the excruciating occasion when he forgot his school-yard experience of riding challenges. Owen winces at the memory of damaging the fifth metatarsal in his right foot when playing for Newcastle against Spurs on New Year's Eve, 2005. 'The biggest mistake I ever made, and I knew I was going to hurt myself, was against Paul Robinson at White Hart Lane,' he recalls with a sense of self-admonishment. 'I knew going into that tackle "I'm going to break my ankle here, or do something". It was the timing, I could see it all happening. I knew I had no option. My foot was going to plant and that's the exact timing he's going to come. I should have just hurdled him, even though I got there first. I'll get another chance in ten minutes. I broke my foot, and that caused me to do my knee at the 2006 World Cup, and then I was finished.'

He shakes his head at that 'bad place' before resuming his France 98 recollections. The timing of Owen's approach to goal is faultless in St-Etienne as he plays Chamot, Ayala and Roa like puppets on a string before scoring one of the most astonishing goals in World Cup history. 'It's the best feeling in the world. You'll never, ever replicate the feeling of scoring a goal. Scoring any goal is just amazing, but scoring a big goal, FA Cup final ones, World Cup ones, the last-minute Manchester derby one, when it's an occasion when I have to score, is unbelievable. It's not a fun feeling; it's actually just a relief. I expected myself to be doing that. Every time I played football I was the best player basically, as a kid especially, so I always got my mates out of trouble, always won the game for them. I didn't ever lose that feeling. It was down to me. It's the adrenalin rush and the relief that you've done it. If you're winning 4-0 and score another one, that's a little bit of joy.'

The story behind his celebration, being mobbed by the team before looking up and scouring the St-Etienne stands, gives another insight into the seemingly small details that make Owen special, another reminder to Academies of the importance of a support network. 'I always knew where my mum and dad were. For my life, I've always needed my dad there. It's a comfort blanket, someone to impress; he's my best mate. Whenever I gave him a ticket, I knew where they sat at Anfield, Old Trafford, wherever. Whenever I used to give them a ticket in the away end, before putting it in the envelope I'd check what row it was, what seat it was. Now the seats I couldn't really fathom but I'd know which row it was. So in the warm-up, say West Brom away, I'd count twenty rows up and I'd know roughly they were on that level, so then I'd scan the whole stand and see them. I knew always where they were. When we played at St-Etienne, I didn't have a clue. The ticket was in French. It was a weird feeling. I ran over, everyone jumped on me, and as soon as everyone got off, you see me punch the air. I'm punching to the England fans and – I kid you not – I look in one direction and my dad and family are there. It wasn't a massive stadium but it's still a one-in-thirty-thousand chance. He's just there. It's freakish.'

England lead 2-1, but a lapse of concentration at a free-kick allows Verón to guide Javier Zanetti down the inside-right channel to equalize. England then get hit by another sucker-punch from the canny Argentinians. Just after the interval, Beckham falls into a trap laid by Simeone. England's young midfielder is known for his occasional petulance, as well as his ability on the ball. Simeone launches himself into the back of Beckham, seeking a reaction which duly arrives. Beckham flicks out his right leg which catches Simeone, who falls backwards, pointing to Beckham, signalling the offence. Matias Almeyda, Verón and Batistuta embellish the ambush, ensuring Beckham's rash response gains the attention of Kim Milton Nielsen. Shearer is so annoyed with Batistuta he tries to push him away. The damage is done. Milton Nielsen shows Simeone the yellow card and Beckham the red. England's depleted team manage to reach and then survive extra time but succumb on penalties. The inquest focuses on Beckham's dismissal. Newspaper presses roll on headlines like the *Daily Mirror*'s 'Ten Heroic Lions, One Stupid Boy'.

'It's hard,' replies Owen after being asked whether he feels let down by Beckham. 'It obviously harmed our chances of winning. I felt I had them, or we had them. Every time I got the ball I felt as though I was going to score, or run at them and win a penalty. Argentina were petrified. I scared them so much that they were camped out on the edge of their box. They were stretched as anything. That changed the game, as we went into defensive mode and tried to break. I was playing on the wing for ten minutes and then Alan would play there for ten minutes. We did really well to get to the shoot-out. Nobody disliked David. He was a nice lad. He smiled. It was early on in his career. Me and Rio were the pups in the group and David was in the next batch. We would have gone through if he hadn't done that. I have to say it was no one else's fault that he kicked out. It was his fault. Whether it was enough to witness all the stuff that went on afterwards, no. Does any human deserve anything like that, the burning of effigies? That's going to extremes. In the immediate aftermath I didn't think David had cost us the game. It's only as time went on that I think to myself that their streetwise nature won them the game.'

That word 'streetwise' again – it crops up in so many conversations during this journey through English football. Owen seconds Wayne Rooney's motion that England need to be more streetwise, and joins the wider debate, a staple of phone-ins, beyond the usual diving hullabaloo, that English players can be too honest. 'I think so,' says Owen. 'Is that a good or a bad thing? Do we want to win things? There's so much stuff that goes on that people can't see. I've played in five major tournaments, and two or three we've been knocked out because we're not streetwise.' Although not averse to milking contact in the area to obtain penalties, England tend not to react theatrically outside the box, in contrast to Simeone with Beckham. 'Who knows how far we'd have gone in '98? If Simeone had done that to Beckham, would David have reacted like Simeone? I don't think so. It wouldn't have been in his psyche.' But Owen can see the argument, and pushed the boundaries himself during his playing days. 'If you can get someone down to ten men, the advantage is massive. We are talking chess at the highest level. If you lose one of your pawns, you're dead. I've tried it.'

In justifying this admission, Owen doesn't quite drive a threshing machine through the moral maze but certainly cuts corners, willingly. Occasional subterfuge can be a striker's shield against the violence opponents seek to inflict. 'I've been kicked and fouled millions of times and not been hurt in the slightest. If I'd jumped straight back up he wouldn't have got a yellow card. I've not rolled, but stayed down for an extra one or two seconds, just to make the mind up of the referee. I'm playing against that centre-half, I need him on a yellow card, and now I've an advantage. They used to get a free volley at me. Martin Keown was horrible. Gary Neville wasn't that nice. Chris Morgan, the big captain at Sheffield United and Barnsley, was the one player [against whom] I feared for my safety on the pitch.

'People stamped down on my Achilles. When I came back from the World Cup we played Newcastle away [on 30 August] and Stuart Pearce was marking me. People think there's a lot of talk on the pitch but I was never a talker myself, apart from after some fouls when I'd tell somebody to fuck off. Stuart Pearce tried to intimidate me. As soon as we kicked off, I jogged up to my position. "You're playing against me today, son, you'd better watch it, I'll snap you." It was reasonably aggressive but it didn't completely intimidate me.' Clearly not. Owen departs St James' Park with the match-ball.

Dismay at England's demise in France is partially offset by people's ecstatic response to Owen's slalom strike. 'The biggest surprise to me was when I got off the pitch, and in the dressing-room, and the likes of Paul Merson were walking up to me and saying: "Oh my God, do you realize what you've just done?" What? I didn't even think I'd scored a great goal. I was either stupid or just expected it. I just knew I was going to do it. I was oblivious to scoring a great goal. I thought I'd played well, scored a good goal, but when I was getting in the showers I was more thinking: "Will we get criticized for being knocked out? Are we going to get praised for playing well? God knows."'

Vacating the dressing-room, Owen heads out into the car-park of the Stade Geoffroy-Guichard and encounters a briefly tense scene. 'All the Argentinian players were singing on the coach, parked up alongside us.' Spotting the crestfallen English, some of the triumphant

Argentinians aim chants at them. 'It was hard as some of the players had their kids there. I had my girlfriend at the time, my wife now. I was looking at the Argentinians and thinking "next time".'

England return to La Baule, then fly back to England on Concorde, a privilege offered by British Airways only slightly undermined when the company bills the FA for the extra fuel. Owen arrives at his parents' Hawarden home at 2.30 a.m. to find the front lawn filled with friends, neighbours, photographers and reporters. He's now public property. Fans of Southampton and Newcastle, Liverpool's first two away opponents in the 1998/99 season, applaud him. But after a stalemate with Poland in a September 1999 Euro qualifier, Owen's dustbin man harangues him over the shortcomings of the national team. England always expects. In its search for an antidote, the FA could do worse than make that drive deep into the Cheshire countryside, and draw on the expertise of Michael Owen. Too much knowledge lies untapped.

12

Golden State

STEVEN GERRARD'S SHIRT darkens with sweat as he trains with LA Galaxy. The Huyton lad's a long way from home, far from his treasured Liverpool Football Club and a decade embedded with the much-debated 'Golden Generation' of England players. The sun's piercing through now, burning off the cloud, broiling the urban landscape. California steamin'. Gerrard's working hard, hunting the ball with his usual intensity, releasing team-mates and taking the occasional long-ranger at goal. Deep into his thirties, Gerrard still prepares with his usual diligence for the Major League Soccer fixture against New York City FC and, fitness permitting, Frank Lampard, another distinguished member of the Golden Generation. Posters hanging nearby pit the pair head to head, boxer-style.

Galaxy's affable coach Bruce Arena signals the end of the session. Gerrard dashes from the field, flicking a stray ball towards Raul Vargas, the kit-man with the Frank Sinatra charisma. He conducts a brief interview with the assembled LA media on the touchline and then hops in a buggy, heading back towards the locker-room inside the StubHub Center. As the cart wheels left, Gerrard glances right and spots a knot of fans standing patiently and hopefully in the searing heat, some holding out Liverpool No. 8 shirts for him to sign. Others wear Galaxy tops. One, cheekily, sports Everton kit. 'How did he get in here?' laughs Gerrard, hopping from the buggy and running over to the group. He autographs shirts, accommodates selfie requests and then takes a short-cut into the stadium, quickly descending a flight of stairs, sliding his hands down the bannisters for balance as his studs click-clack on the concrete. As ever, a sense of purpose defines Gerrard's movement. England's captain on thirty-eight occasions, a player behind only Peter Shilton and David Beckham on the all-time appearance list, changes, grabs some lunch, and then appears in the LA Champions Lounge, clutching a bowl of fruit salad and ready to talk to me about England. Behind him hangs a photo of Beckham, Golden Balls himself and chief pin-up of the Golden Generation.

In his house in Formby, Gerrard's built a trophy room containing all manner of memorabilia from his Liverpool career, including Andrij Shevchenko's shirt from the 2005 Champions League final, medals and match-balls, but there's an empty area (even before much of the content is lent to the Liverpool museum for the duration of his stay in MLS). During an association with England lasting from 2000 to 2014, Gerrard acquires 114 caps and memories in abundance yet no medals, no finals, not even a semi-final. As honest as ever, he voices the emotions involved. 'It's a great time, a great feeling, a very proud feeling,' he begins. 'Even with all my happiness and feeling of pride at representing England, once that game starts you become very tense and very pressured because you have to deliver results.' He delivers in qualifiers, driving England to World Cups and Euros, but the championships themselves prove barren. 'In between tournaments a lot of the players in the team get a lot of praise, and rightly so if you win a match, but we all know what we want. Everyone in the country knows what we want and that's a successful tournament. Everyone's judged at the end of every two years.'

Liverpool's lion of Istanbul understands the glorious distraction of the Champions League for players. The technical and tactical spectacle of Europe's elite club competition rises inexorably; but Gerrard knows the eternal lure of international football, nation against nation, a whole country tuning in, hoping, fretting, supporting, just as he did when cheering deliriously from his sofa on the Bluebell Estate in Huyton as Michael Owen rearranges Argentina's defence at France 98. 'I don't think the Champions League has downgraded international football,' he says. 'When you're standing there in the tunnel, ready to go out for the big games, it's a phenomenal feeling to represent your country. I know the buzz back home in the major tournaments. For some players, tournaments are a once-in-a-lifetime experience. I was lucky to experience it six times. That's when I was judged.' Gerrard contests Euros in 2000, 2004 and 2012 and World Cups in 2006, 2010 and 2014. Let the record show that he gave everything. Let the record also show up the imbalance of the team and the naive tactics, inhibiting his impact. He fouls up on occasion, gifting an opportunity to France in 2004 with a bad back-pass (leading to Zinedine Zidane's penalty) and, a decade on, to Uruguay with a failed interception exploited by his friend Luis Suárez.

As well as the pride, Gerrard also feels the pressure. A good group of players, including Lampard, Beckham, Owen and Rio Ferdinand, are dubbed the 'Golden Generation' by Adam Crozier, the FA's chief executive at the time. Wayne Rooney soon enjoys fast-track membership. It creates expectation beyond reason. England reach three quarter-finals under Sven-Göran Eriksson but should really achieve more with the quality of individuals available. 'The Golden Generation tag was an annoyance,' says Gerrard. 'We didn't give ourselves it. Other people gave us it.' He feels they're now being accorded retrospective credit. 'The Golden Generation are getting a bit of respect because of how close we were getting to semi-finals. We were denied by two penalty shoot-outs to get to the last four of two big tournaments. What we would give now for this England team to get to a penalty shoot-out in the quarter-final of Euro 2016. England would take that at the moment. At Euro 2004 and the World Cup in 2006 everyone was expecting us to win it, so when we went out in the last eight on a penalty shoot-out it seems like a failure. But for me, we came finger-tips away from being in the last four in the world. I'm quite proud of that.'

The Golden State seems twinned with the Golden Generation this steamy day in August 2015. When Gerrard and Galaxy vacate the StubHub, Lampard and New York City stroll in. Lampard's not fully fit, training with strapping, but still showing the old touches, the passes round the corner, including one sublime flick to Andrea

Pirlo, keeping moves rolling, creating opportunities for David Villa. Back at NYC's base in Manhattan Beach, in a hotel hemmed in by a Hummus Factory and a Café Rio Mexican Grill, Lampard walks into a meeting room not required by Deloitte alumni that day. He shakes hands, swaps small-talk in that easy, smiling way of his, and addresses the enduring Golden Generation debate. 'The label did annoy us,' he says. 'It wasn't self-proclaimed. It was from the outside. The common argument was "you played great for your clubs but not so great for your country". People weren't not trying. It was just unfortunate that we didn't get to where we should have or where we wanted to. I knew how much all the lads of that period wanted it. They wanted it so much. It was a "Golden Generation" and it was a putdown in the end. It was a shame.'

Why are England less than the sum of their glittering individual parts? I ask Lampard. Do lucrative club contracts and the allure of European competition increasingly dominate the thoughts of many players? 'Club football has developed so much,' he acknowledges. 'Games like the Champions League final are on a par with inter-national football. I'm not going to lie. They are huge games.' Like Gerrard, Lampard lifts the European Cup. Like the Merseysider, the Essex boy always finds his pulse racing when stepping out cloaked in the white or red of his country. Lampard's a patriot. 'It's exhilarating playing for England at Wembley which, for me, is the number one stadium in the world. I know it's the new Wembley but it still has the magic of it. Being a young Englishman playing for your country is the most exciting, nervous thing you can do. I never lost that excite-ment at hearing the roar of the crowd, and that pride of playing for my country.'

Even such a confident character as Lampard, an awe-inspiring amasser of trophies with Chelsea, admits to suffering some anxiety with England, and notes how much the pressure constrains others. 'I had nerves. I had thoughts of: "This is such an intense cauldron that I have to play well because everyone's watching." There's a balance of nerves against the excitement. It never lost that feeling of being the most special thing you can do. The shirt will weigh heavily on different personalities. It's tough. I noticed that in the dressing-room, certainly. Some players are not built for it. That's not a criticism of them. I just think it's a huge pressure. There were periods in my career when I enjoyed it more than I did others when I was under pressure for my place or [because of] what people were saying. I was under pressure. I'm not stupid. I'm aware of that.'

Regrets are swept aside by a wave of emotion, of delight. 'The overall feeling at the end of my England career is that it was the most fantastic thing,' says Lampard of his 106 caps, before adding a poignant comment that every one of Roy Hodgson's current players should read, understand, discuss and remember. 'I wish I could go back and play one game now. It means that much. It's always a magnificent feeling to play for England so when I stopped doing it it was difficult. I know my career was long and I'm happy with it, but if I could go back and play again, just once, I'd do it because that feeling of pride is untouchable with the job that we do. There should be a patriotic element. I certainly had that always. As I got older, there was even more of a patriotic element. Being young, with the innocence of youth, I didn't always take that in so much. As I got older and had a family and realized how much it meant to my parents, that I was play-ing for my country, I understood it more. I appreciated and enjoyed it more. Singing the National Anthem should be drilled into the team. They should all sing it. You don't have to belt it out. We're probably all crap singers! But it shows you appreciate it. It shows you care. I don't think there should be any excuses. You sing the anthem when you play for your country – or don't play.

'The fans out at the World Cup or back home care. They sing the anthem. England's fans are phenomenal.' Lampard is thinking particularly of the unconditional, almost masochistic support follow-ing England during their brief sojourn in Brazil in 2014, including voicing an emotional tribute to him and Gerrard in Belo Horizonte as they bade farewell. 'The World Cup was special,' he says. 'There was a period with England, in Steve McClaren's days, when it wasn't so great. No bones about it. We travelled to Barcelona to play Andorra [in 2007] and it was a horrible night. The fans were aggressive. That was a bit of a one-off. There was a certain group of fans that day. But since then, the times I was in the squad after that, I've travelled to Macedonia and Montenegro and I remember fans singing from the minute we came out until after the game. There's a very good feeling with the England fans after the last few years. They are there for the right reasons – to support the lads. They were seeing this Golden Generation and going, "Come on then, win something for us." Now there's an understanding we are trying to do the right things; there are young boys there and they are playing for their country.'

The history of the Golden Generation carries lessons for England, the FA and managers. It begins forming under Kevin Keegan, who gives Lampard and Gerrard their debuts, joining Owen en route to Euro 2000. 'I like Keegan as a person but I didn't really like him as the England manager,' observes Owen when I visit his Cheshire stables. 'I didn't think he believed in me, strangely, although I'd had a bad injury when he took over and I probably wasn't at my best. I never thought I was a certainty in his team. I didn't really like his backroom staff either. I didn't feel as if I was really rated among them.' Derek Fazackerley, Keegan's assistant, in particular is deemed unsympathetic to the pressures on young players spending time away from home. Hidden in the dark forests of the Ardennes, England's Spa base feels like fertile soil for introspection. Gerrard confesses to homesickness. Gloom spreads. We travellers with laptops, billeted in a hotel across the road from England, so quickly run out of alternative entertainment in Spa that we take to mass early-morning lycra-clad lung-wreckers up and down a nearby hill called 'The Beast', a monster really only tamed by the BBC's determined dynamo Garth Crooks. Otherwise we spend the day debating with the FA how close England are to being kicked out of the Euros because of the supporters' success in redesigning Charleroi. The only real merriment is found in watching BBC types roaming the hotel corridors, Basil Fawlty-style, trying to discover from which room the brash new radio station talkSPORT is doing its unofficial live match broadcasts. I'm in the talkSPORT lair on the (whisper it) first floor during one game when the commentator, doing some Euro match 'off tube' – basically using the TV at the end of his bed – goes all sotto voce at a corner on hearing footsteps in the corridor. Auntie's on the prowl.

Otherwise Euro 2000 is a tournament filed under 'best forgotten' for the English, on and off the field. The decision to appoint Keegan post-Hoddle stands as another reminder of the need for the FA to do its homework and listen to informed opinion. Howard Wilkinson, the FA's technical director, privately questions Keegan's tactical qualities. The International Committee ponders his emotional volatility. A much-loved player, likeable man and flawed manager is now in charge. Cue the countdown to meltdown.

Having lost to Portugal in Eindhoven on 12 June, England appear to get their Euro 2000 campaign back on track five days later when they beat Germany in a Charleroi meeting spiced by Alan Shearer's flying header and a Gerrard wrecking-ball challenge on his club-mate Didi Hamann. The Germany midfielder should not 'squeal like a girl', Gerrard declares to a gaggle of reporters afterwards. A German colleague listening in mishears, leading to his newspaper revealing Gerrard declaring that 'Hamann should not squeal like a squirrel'. Nuts.

Euro 2000 is a strange, frustrating tournament to cover; instinctive respect for Keegan for a powerful, bejewelled playing career is offset by his obvious inadequacy as an international manager. In advance of the decisive game with Romania in Charleroi on 20 June, Keegan bemuses Owen by spending time in training at Spa working on the flier's hold-up skills, attempting to turn one of the best run-through strikers into a central beacon, bringing others into play. It's a joke. Few laugh, though. Keegan's tactics waste Owen's talents. After criticism from the manager in a team meeting in Spa, Owen is relieved to receive supportive words from Gary Neville and David Beckham. Although Owen makes a point to Keegan by scoring against Romania, England still board the first flight home when Phil Neville gets the wrong side of Viorel Moldovan, trips him, and Ionel Ganea converts to make it 3-2. Recriminations abound at the time, with subsequent reservations. 'I must admit when we heard Keegan was going to be managing Newcastle [in 2008] when I was there at the time, I thought: "Oh no, this is going to be difficult, I'm not going to get on,'" recalls Owen. 'I've never been so wrong about someone in my life. He was absolutely brilliant. What a fella, the best person, gave me so much confidence, a great man-manager, really funny and engaging with the lads. But not with England. I looked in the mirror and thought: "Was it just me? Was I low on confidence?" Keegan might not have been the same for England. He said he wasn't cut out for it.' Maybe it's the Impossible Job's old trick of emasculating incumbents. Martin Kcown, the Arsenal centre-back whose rugged style belies a contemplative mind, even calls Keegan 'tactically inept' in his *Telegraph* column. Midfield is too frequently over-run. The England role is clearly too demanding intellectually for Keegan. 'Yes,' Owen agrees. 'He might have felt a little bit out of place so he wasn't bringing his true value to the team, but as a club manager I thought he was absolutely brilliant.'

Keegan's patriotism is never in doubt but he takes too emotional an approach to international management, insufficiently cerebral. He's wobbling on his bike in an episode of *Superstars* when England crave a balanced chess grandmaster. On the eve of the important 2002 World Cup qualifier against Germany at Wembley, I join the Sky Sports discussion programme *Hold the Back Page*, and the main talking point is Keegan's plan to start Gareth Southgate as a holding midfielder. The idea is duly ridiculed. Over in the England hotel, the players are watching. So is an angry Keegan, who consults an FA official about the programme. After the ensuing defeat to Germany – who else? – Keegan resigns in the Wembley loos. Adding to the symbolism, a few days later bulldozers roll in to flatten the stadium.

Within an hour of Keegan's resignation, FA board member David Dein speaks to Sven-Göran Eriksson's adviser Athole Still. Many of the players want Terry Venables back but Crozier and Dein are obsessed with recruiting a foreigner to guide the Golden Generation, somebody with a reputation as a thinker, unemotional, a tactician, basically the antithesis of Keegan. Eriksson, widely admired in Europe at the time, is duly appointed. The Swede visits Bobby Robson, who warns him about the press. He takes tea and scones with Keegan. He

smiles a lot. So one of the most talented collections of English individuals is entrusted to a foreigner for the first time. Major mistakes
are made, such as using Paul Scholes wide, seemingly being in awe
of David Beckham, not confronting the penalty paranoia or using a
psychologist more, yet Eriksson's record of only 10 defeats in 67 games
(40 victories, 17 draws) is decent enough and those quarter-finals
look a golden era compared to recent labours. The fascination with
the private life of an unmarried man reflects poorly on the English
media; we need to be more adult about such matters, less prurient.
Sex sells newspapers but it shouldn't be allowed to dominate the
agenda, especially not on the sports pages, unless it affects dressing-
room respect. Apart from women, football and epicurean delights, it's
difficult to know what Eriksson's interests are. Finding myself seated
next to him at an FA dinner, I give Eriksson some background on the
road in Regent's Park, London he's bought a house in. Having grown
up there, I tell him about the time Goldie the Eagle escaped from the
zoo and terrorized local dogs, and about the local lady in the van, a
story eventually made into a film starring Dame Maggie Smith. It's
hardly Oliver Reed anecdote level but it offers some insight into the
neighbourhood. Eriksson nods and looks at his plate.

Players undoubtedly like the easy-going, undemanding Swede. 'I
thought Sven was good, a really nice fella who picked good teams,
tactically fine,' reflects Owen. 'He didn't do loads. There was a good
atmosphere at England with him there. You want to enjoy going
to England. The stakes are so high at club level now and obviously
managers don't necessarily want everyone to go, so it's good to have
a manager there who can make a nice atmosphere. I'd hate to be
bored to tears all week, don't particularly like the manager, and the
only release is when the whistle goes and you're actually playing for
England, and it's great because it's torture leading up to it.'

Jermaine Jenas plays fifteen times for Eriksson but is never convinced. 'I found Sven very weird, really difficult to work out,' says the
midfielder. 'Players respond to emotion a lot of the time. With Sven,
you never got that emotion out of him, never got that anger or happiness. It was just still. He would never get that involved with training.'

Eriksson keeps the tactics simple: 4-4-2 with the occasional diamond. He's hailed as the saviour from Sweden when Owen scores a hat-trick, Gerrard adds a skidding strike and even Emile Heskey scores in Munich on 1 September 2001. Here we go at last. Hallelujah. The Three Lions have claws again. Suddenly, the World Cup dream is back on. England could qualify. A month later comes Beckham's greatest moment in an England shirt: that late free-kick to equalize against Greece at Old Trafford. In the packed, smoky press box, Greek reporters choke on their cigarettes as the ball curls over the wall and in, sending England to Japan and South Korea. Last gasp indeed. A picture of Beckham's goal adorns a wall near the home dressing-room at Wembley, a reminder of class under pressure.

To some critics, Beckham embodies the lightweight, peacock traits of the Golden Generation, foolishly making mistakes like that dismissal in St-Etienne, jumping out of a tackle against Brazil in Shizuoka that leads to Rivaldo's equalizer in 2002, and the missed penalties at Euro 2004. He certainly stirs opinion, gushing but also unforgiving, as one letter I receive from a London address in 2003 highlights: 'To praise Beckham in your article (11/Oct) is just pathetic. This chap is an inarticulate, gormless moron with a girl's haircut. For you to idolize him is unworthy of the Telegraph. Get your act and your reporting together, you fool . . .'

What the stroppy scribbler ignores is Beckham's immense dedication. During a career laden with club trophies, Beckham proves a very good player, if never a great one, crossing superbly, deadly at set-pieces and working hard in preparing himself for games as well as his full application during the 90 minutes. He looks after his body well, ensuring he is in the best possible condition for matches. A story popular among journalists involves the news reporter who follows him into a restaurant to check on his professionalism, and all he learns from the waiter is not only how charming Beckham is but that he eats boiled fish without sauce and all washed down with a glass of water. Hardly refuelling madness. Beckham makes the absolute most of his talent, and for that quality alone, as much as his ambassadorial strengths, he stands as one of English football's finest role models. He also has a deep passion for the national cause. When named captain for the first of his 59 caps with the armband, for the November 2000 friendly against Italy in Turin, Beckham confides his concern about his singing abilities as he wants to do the Queen proud with his rendition of the National Anthem. He knows the cameras will be on him, picking up his words. Players reporting for England duty for the first time could do with heading into the film room at St George's Park and being shown a series of clips of Beckham, familiarizing themselves with the standards required. He fights hard to recover from injuries, including the metatarsal in April 2002 to make the World Cup, willingly fulfils all off-field FA diplomatic duties, and handles the astonishing attention levels with great patience and humour. He laughs at himself, too – always an endearing trait – as when an Israeli journalist suggests he has a Hebrew tattoo wrongly spelt. Beckham's an honest, frequently revealing interviewee. Following a robust game against Wales in October 2004, he tells me why he deliberately got himself booked: he damages his ribs in a challenge with Ben Thatcher, knows he'll miss the following qualifier against Azerbaijan, and as he's one booking away from a ban decides to trigger the suspension in a match he's injured for, so he kicks Thatcher, his aggressive opponent. Here's the type of streetwise act opponents turn into an art form, but as captain of England, seen as the guardian of the game's few remaining morals, Beckham gets lambasted. The FA's disciplinary department wants to charge him and requests my notes of the interview. I refuse (handing over notebooks is against many newspapers' policy) and the story duly runs out of legs and dies. It does, though, provide an insight into Beckham's cunning.

Very popular with England staff and players, Beckham stands as an uplifting example to the younger generation that it is possible to be a modest superstar. 'Becks was always very quiet, kept himself to himself, but he was really humble,' adds Jenas, recalling playing alongside Beckham for England. 'He was probably the only footballer I've ever been star-struck by when I first walked into the squad [in 2003]. He's a legend in his own right now but even then he was a star. He never made me feel uncomfortable. He always spoke to me. He especially spoke to the young lads, making us feel welcome and part of the squad. He was never one for ranting and raving or digging people out. He led by example day in, day out, with how hard he trained. I remember one occasion in South Africa when we'd finished training. Scholesy used to line up on the edge of the box with Phil Neville crossing balls in. Becks would line up on the edge of the box with ten balls, practising free-kicks. David James was in goal. The rest of us were sat there, stretching, relaxing, watching. We went through a sequence of Becks scoring a free-kick, then a cross would come in and Scholes would volley it in from the edge of the box. I'm telling you they both scored five in a row! We were all saying to Jamo: "You might as well come in, there's no point being there!" Watching Becks, I realized that's what it takes to get to the top.'

Japanese obsession with the glamorous Beckham is anticipated in advance of the 2002 World Cup but is still flabbergasting in its intensity. On a visit to the Hard Rock Café in Kobe, the Golden Generation are mobbed. FA security staff even fear one of the countless kids chasing the coach might slip under a wheel. England's preference for a base off the beaten track means a long trip to Awaji Island near Kobe, past the sobering sight of the mangled expressway kept as a memorial to the damage wrought by the Great Hanshin earthquake of 1995. For all the desire for privacy, Japanese kids permanently throng the pavement outside the hotel. A few hold up signs asking 'Beck-ham' to marry them. The more enterprising climb in the lift, ascend to the top, and press all the floor buttons so any England player getting in is trapped for a while on the descent, proving easy prey for an autograph or photo. England try to make their hotel media-proof but a photographer still snaps a picture of Beckham sunbathing, earning his paper a one-day ban. Security is otherwise tight for England. The glimpse of a frigate patrolling the sea alongside training generates much copy – 'Gunboat Protects Becks'. The story gets even better when it's discovered the vessel is atomic-powered. 'Nuclear Gunboat Protects Becks' runs very well in London.

Kobe proves a constant source of interest, not least the local radio station so fascinated by visitors that it records a group of us singing a tribute to the host nation and its star player Junichi Inamoto – 'Walking Inamoto Wonderland'. Somehow it fails to chart. One night we attempt to liberate six penguins from a basement bar. After lengthy and not entirely sober bargaining with the owner we agree on $1,000 per bird. What we consider a masterpiece of deal-making on our part is to negotiate six penguins for the price of five. Ultimately we decide the cost is prohibitive, let alone the logistics and cost of flying them home, or where then to house them. The serious coda to the story is the bar's treatment of the penguins, and at least this was highlighted at the time.

A tournament of late nights, partly to stay on British newspaper deadline time of course, is also one of early starts. Martin Samuel, award-winning chronicler of many sports and always engaging company, proves a regular companion on the dawn bullet train to Kyoto, exploring the temples, shrines and Zen gardens like Ryōan-ji with its soothing array of rocks and pebbles. A less divine experience occurs on a morning run up into the hills when I startle a monk meditating by a lake and he reacts with a kick. For any journalist, a tournament is about the occasion, the colour and the country as well as the football. It is about barriers breaking down between nations. One late night in Tokyo I encounter a group of Irish fans on the Guinness and Saudi Arabia supporters sipping Coke lites before their teams' meeting in Yokohama on 11 June. Within ten minutes they're all mixed up together, chatting away, friendships and memories made.

England slowly build momentum. Beckham converts a pressure penalty against Argentina for the key win in the group. 'That was for fucking St-Etienne!' screams an England player at the Argentines backstage in Sapporo. England progress to the knock-out stage where they destroy Denmark in rainy Niigata, reaching a quarter-final with Brazil in Shizuoka on 21 June. If England prevail they face Turkey in the semi-finals while Germany encounter South Korea. 'We were talking before that game, thinking we've beaten Germany, Turkey aren't much, South Korea were in the mix and we'd drawn with them [before the tournament],' recalls Owen. 'I remember being in the masseurs' room on the morning of the game with Rio Ferdinand,

Frank Lampard and a few others and people were basically saying: "Fucking hell, lads, if we win today, we're going to win the World Cup. This is our final. If we win this, who's going to stop us? The others aren't as good as us. There's no one left in the tournament. All the big boys are going out. If we win today, we're going to win the World Cup."'

Sadly, Owen needs that massage because he's struggling with an injury, the full extent of which is not widely known at the time. 'I tore my hamstring after half an hour against Denmark and knew it was almost "tournament over, I'm knackered here". I didn't train, I couldn't move, really.' Before Brazil, Owen approaches Eriksson, outlining his predicament. 'I'm just going to have to stay reasonably close to the box and not do any lung-busting runs,' he tells the coach. 'I can't sprint; it would probably snap in two if I go and sprint. I'm just going to have to finish. I can only offer goals.' Eriksson accepts the offer. Living up to his promise, Owen duly scores, seizing on some poor control by Lucio to race through and give England the lead. 'It worked, but I couldn't give the team what I wanted to,' Owen continues. 'If we'd got through I'd have been compromised because I had a fair old injury.' Rivaldo and Ronaldinho turn the game on its head and England tire badly. 'I was knackered,' says Owen. In the dripping heat, England run out of steam and ideas. Eriksson's too passive, failing to react sufficiently in the second half. In crunch moments, the Swede lacks decisiveness. Even against ten men, England struggle. When Ronaldinho fouls right-back Danny Mills – surely one of international sport's bigger role reversals – a couple of England teammates whisper 'the ref's getting a card out' and 'stay down'. Mills stays down. Ronaldinho is off. Who says England cannot be streetwise? Brazil still win.

Along with the usual complaint of surrendering possession too lightly, Eriksson's concern about his team fading after ten months of club exertions is borne out. The players undergo six months of saliva, urine and blood tests leading up to the World Cup. To counteract deficiencies, Mills tells me he takes six pills in the morning, and the same number in the evening – all legal, just magnesium and ginseng.

There's a price to pay: Mills reveals his body crashes a week later on holiday; he feels fluey and out of sorts. He advises the FA to warn players to wean themselves off the pills in the future.

After Japan, Eriksson's stock is still high, surviving howls of condemnation when he changes his whole team for the second half against Australia in a friendly at Upton Park in 2003. With a nod to the tour match's sponsors, Eriksson obviously couldn't give a XXXX for tradition. Mills ends up with the armband, which he proudly keeps at home in Harrogate. Amid the 'handing out caps like confetti' furore, it's abundantly clear that Eriksson does deals with club managers to keep them onside. 'Sven was a manager who experimented a lot,' says Jenas, who made his debut that night, coming on for Scholes in that stampede start to the second half. 'He'd give you one cap, and if he wasn't happy with you you wouldn't get another one. He'd give you one opportunity to prove you were a player with England capabilities, but after that there were a lot of players that came and went. Even though he chucked a lot of caps around – "you can have one" – he was tougher than people thought. He knew a player. A lot of the time there would be a lot of pressure put on him by a player in peak form, like Michael Ricketts when he came through at Bolton. He was having the season of his life, and people said: "Right, big lad, scoring goals, why can't he play for England?"' Taking the line of least resistance, Eriksson calls him up against Holland in February 2002. 'He gave him a chance,' adds Jenas. One chance. Eriksson's fortunate to have a breadth of options, far more than Roy Hodgson enjoys, but Ricketts struggles and is taken off after 45 minutes in Amsterdam, never to be seen in an England shirt again.

'You always found out who was an England international from training,' continues Jenas. 'You could see it a mile off. There are games where you are far superior to the other nation, San Marino, Andorra or Luxembourg, and you go out there and really look a star but the reality is they are easy games. In training, that's when you found out who was really good. There was always a call out from the press for other players in my position, like Nigel Reo-Coker, and my feeling was "bring them in, see if they can handle it", and a lot of the time they couldn't. The people who always stood out for me in training were Scholes, Gerrard, Rio, John Terry – a class above. Scholesy was out of this world. People used to find it hard enough to play against him in eleven-versus-eleven on a bigger pitch but in smaller sessions his brain went into overdrive. I'd come off with my body in bits. It was intense; everybody was at it, everyone wanted the shirt. When I went back to my club [Newcastle, and then Spurs] I could tell I'd been away with England: I was ahead of everyone at the club because of the level of intense training we'd been through.'

Analysis of the Golden Generation inevitably alights on a chronic capacity for own goals. A lesson for all professionals in the importance of concentration and time-keeping comes as a story of bed linen, mutiny and Battenberg cake unfolds on 23 September 2003, when drug-testers drive down the long lane to Manchester United's remote Carrington training ground. They want to test Rio Ferdinand but unfortunately he's gone shopping for sheets and pillow cases. United quickly contact him, he returns to Carrington, pleads his innocence, takes and passes the test thirty-six hours later. But an offence has been committed: the player was absent when the testers called, so the FA has to act. Ferdinand is summoned to the Worcestershire home of FA official David Davies and left to munch on cake as the FA decides to suspend him from England duty during the disciplinary process. Eriksson's aggrieved when informed he cannot select 'one of my best defenders' for the key Euro 2004 qualifier in intimidating Istanbul. 'This could only happen in England, leaving out one of your best players,' Eriksson wails to us. Once again, the FA finds itself trapped in a moral dilemma. It can hardly undermine the high-profile drug-testing campaign by allowing Ferdinand to play on, yet there is the old counter-argument of innocent until proven guilty. Whatever happened to fair play? The FA has no choice, though. The World Anti-Doping Agency is watching closely. England risk expulsion from qualifying if Ferdinand features against Turkey. Their media will skewer the arrogant FA if it becomes known that England are relying on a player under investigation for a drug offence. As often happens with the FA – and this is a lesson it is still trying to learn – it is not simply a decision's legitimacy that provokes most controversy. It's the way the decision is communicated to the England squad and the subsequent haste in imposing a new disciplinary code without proper consultation. Management by kneejerk never works.

In angry response, England's militant millionaires consider industrial action. The Great Strike Threat of 2003 is a crisis of leadership in all quarters: FA boardroom, England dressing-room and dug-out. The chief executive, Mark Palios, is an intelligent individual who should enjoy better rapport with the squad as an ex-pro with Tranmere Rovers and Crewe Alexandra yet he aggravates the situation with his prickly man-management style. Gary Neville, swiftly dubbed 'Red Nev', passionately defends Ferdinand, his United colleague. In siding with the players, Eriksson reveals a supine or pragmatic streak, depending on one's generosity of spirit. As ever with England, personality and tribalism hinder sensible debate and execution of correct policy. Soap-opera rules apply. Characters are defined: Neville versus Palios, polemicist versus bureaucrat. As ever, the media revels in the storm, hyping the hullabaloo further.

A toxic farce better suited to the theatres around the FA's West End quarters is all played out in a Jane Austen setting, the genteel surrounds of Lord Mountbatten of Burma's old abode Sopwell House. Peacocks peck at the grass outside England's hotel, ladies lunch inside, and tea is then served. So is insurrection. The Sopwell stand-off is astonishing, and another tutorial for the FA in player relations, although the regular turnover of executives makes continuity of thought difficult. Although the likes of David James and Steven Gerrard aren't enamoured with Neville's strike proposal, the clock ticks loudly towards the boycott of the Bosphorus. It's a PR disaster for the players, an exercise in egotism that still shapes some people's perception of the national team to this day. Neville, a conviction politician, blindly misreads the country's mood or simply does not worry about it. The backlash is immediate. Neville and the squad are pilloried on phone-ins and given the full 'TRAITOR' treatment by a scandalized press. A wretched, deteriorating situation is rescued only by texts from Ferdinand thanking comrades for their support but urging them to leave the picket lines and play on. The man whose accidental failure to fulfil his duties as a professional caused the chaos ends up as peace-maker.

Beckham's benign influence needs proper saluting; he talks common sense to the players and concludes a wearying day politely signing autographs for well-heeled diners at Sopwell. Close to midnight, an elderly guest stops a passing group of formerly rebellious players, gets them to sign her menu and then comes up to me and asks which scribbled signature belongs to which star. 'I'm just collecting autographs for my grandson,' she explains. It's all very English, very civilized. It just needs Noel Coward on the piano in the corner, crooning 'Mad About the Boy'.

Leaving Sopwell behind, the squad travel to Istanbul, still brimming with resentment at the public and press vilification, and step into a Şükrü Saracoğlu Stadium free of England fans after trouble in the first meeting at the Stadium of Light. 'You will drown in the Bosphorus' reads one welcoming banner, although the 'cauldron of hate' billing is slightly undermined when the PA puts on 'The Birdie Song'. It's a familiar occurrence at foreign stadia – menacing home fans undermined by fluffy pop. It's hard to scare with ABBA in the air. England's solidarity is tested and proven. Once again, England play best when they have a mission: Italia 90, Euro 96, Rome and Istanbul. After Alpay Özalan goads Beckham for missing a penalty, a ruck breaks out in the tunnel at half-time. England players will not yield to Turkish belligerence; a sign of their unity comes when even the mild-mannered Emile Heskey joins in the melee. A deserved point brings England qualification and respite from the storm.

Palios still rushes through a new player code of conduct, driving the FA further into a moral maze. 'James Beattie's banned from driving,' we chorus in union to Palios when he briefs the media on his new clampdown. 'So why's he just been called up, then?' Poor Beattie, a real character with an impressive array of super-hero answerphone messages whose column I ghost for a while, has scarcely checked into the England hotel when he's informed he has to go home. As with so many people at the FA Palios is well-intentioned, but insufficient thought has gone into such a major policy as this. Rules require discussion with senior players, proper communication and explanation to the whole squad, and ought to be introduced only at the end of a competition cycle.

And so to Portugal. Euro 2004 stands as the Golden Generation's golden opportunity. Midfield is imbalanced with Eriksson shoehorning in three players at their best attacking through the centre, Gerrard, Lampard and Scholes, with only one natural wide player, Beckham, who actually has designs on the centre. There's no orthodox holding midfielder, with Owen Hargreaves featuring only from the bench. It's the England star system gone mad. Eriksson should sacrifice one of Gerrard or Lampard and insert some natural width on the left. Few obvious candidates present themselves so Scholes is sacrificed, tucked in on the left. Hoddle voices his frustration. So do others. 'I always had an issue with the fact that Scholes wasn't playing central midfield,' observes Jenas. 'It's one of the biggest mistakes the country has ever made. To put him on the left wing just didn't make sense. The quality of the players we had was more than enough to go through.'

The squad's strong, bolstered by the tyro Rooney, as Owen notes. 'I was more aware of threats to my place in the Euros in Portugal and I didn't really enjoy that because I felt Wayne Rooney was taking my mantle as the main striker. Then if I have a bad game, I go to number three. Everyone was saying Darius Vassell should be starting.' Vassell replaces Owen in the second half of the 2-1 loss to France in Lisbon, and in the 3-0 win over Switzerland in Coimbra, but it's Rooney coming off for Vassell against Croatia in the final group game, partly to rest the youngster after his double in a 4-2 triumph. 'Rooney was fearless,' says Jenas. 'My first experience of Wayne came when he was 15 and Forest played Everton in an FA Youth Cup game. I was captain, and had been playing at higher levels, so I was far superior to a lot of the players on that pitch. I was taking the piss a little bit, scored a penalty to make it 1-1, and then I just remember Rooney coming off the bench. The ball was going out of play and I was trying to shield it. Rooney just came in and whacked me in the back, chucked me into the stand. I turned around, looked at him, and he just laughed and ran off, back up the pitch. We nearly lost the game when he came on. I came off, spoke to a few people, and said: "Who is this kid? He's outrageous." I watched him in a few England games, coming off the bench; he was rough around the edges; and then when he broke through I thought: "Yes, I definitely remember you."'

Unfortunately for England, Rooney fractures the fifth metatarsal in his right foot in the quarter-final against Portugal in Lisbon, depriving the team of much of their forward momentum, and the goalkeeper Ricardo finishes them off in the shoot-out. Penalties again. Leaving one tournament hobbling, Rooney limps towards the next. Covering Manchester United's visit to Chelsea on 29 April 2006, six weeks before the World Cup starts for England, I see Rooney's afternoon end in agony when he lands at speed and breaks the fourth metatarsal in his right foot. Eriksson tries to go down to see Rooney at Chelsea but Sir Alex Ferguson isn't having it. Half an hour after the final whistle, I position myself near the United coach, pulled up close to the players' tunnel. Rooney's on crutches, clearly in pain, and his World Cup dream seems over. Ferguson knows the looming head-lines, willing Rooney to play in the World Cup, whether fully fit or not. Even taking into account his focus on what's best for Manchester United, Ferguson also thinks of Rooney's long-term welfare not England's short-term need.

A nation's tournament hopes should not rest on one bone – and if they do, the whole structure of English football needs re-examining. There are hospital vigils and a Learjet flight to Manchester and back from England's World Cup base – purely for PR reasons: England's hotel in Germany boasts perfectly good medical facilities. Eriksson and the FA should be more clear-eyed about the situation; even if the calcification of the bone is sufficiently advanced, and Rooney's desire to play is strong, he will still lack match sharpness when he returns to the fray in Germany. Ferguson's warnings should have been heeded. Rooney does help England to the quarter-finals but Eriksson's deci-sion to start him in a lone striker position in Gelsenkirchen on 1 July, battling canny Portuguese defenders like Ricardo Carvalho, feels risky.

Short of fitness and frustrated by the opponents, Rooney's fuse blows and he stamps on Carvalho. The Portuguese protest theatrically, particularly the shameless winker Cristiano Ronaldo who accelerates his club-mate's expulsion. England battle on manfully but it's penalties again. A couple of German reporters in the press box look over and offer support. But it's the look of a sympathetic hygienist when the dentist appears with a drill. Nothing can reduce the inevitable pain. I shake my head. Everyone knows what's coming: death by shoot-out. The day leaves a bitter taste. Rooney should never have been rushed back. It's an episode that needs to be logged in the memory bank at St George's Park: don't take injured players to tournaments.

Do, however, research the proliferation of certain types of injuries. Rooney is joined by Beckham, Gerrard, Gary Neville, Ashley Cole and Michael Owen of the Golden Generation with cracked metatarsals. Manufacturers dismiss claims that boots are too flimsy, although John Terry has the soles of his boots strengthened. Pitch manufacturers dispute suggestions that the new style of surfaces, lush on top, harder underneath, lead to bones snapping on impact. Plenty of conjecture exists but no real conclusion. Representatives of boot companies and pitch experts should all have office space at St George's Park so they can have regular discussions with England medical staff.

Rooney is staunchly defended by Eriksson, who bows out a disappointed figure, ultimately mocked and castigated as a flirt. During his England reign, Eriksson talks to potential club suitors in Manchester United and Chelsea. He attracts women attracted to publicity, much to the embarrassment of the FA. He tried to impress a stranger dressed as a wealthy Arab pretending to be fronting a take-over of Aston Villa who turns out to be a noted *News of the World* reporter. After the Fake Sheikh farrago, the FA calls Eriksson in to Soho Square for two long meetings to discuss his future, which he neither forgets nor forgives. Ultimately, the verdict on the Swede is that he's likeable, civilized, a bit naive, too trusting of the wrong people, too in awe of English stars and tactically not flexible enough. Eriksson's reputation begins to be rehabilitated only when people realize the weakness of his successor, Steve McClaren. As the squad gathers in the hotel before leaving Baden-Baden, Eriksson fumes when McClaren, his erstwhile assistant, gives a speech and invites the Swede to be a special guest at the Euro 2008 final. Because of course England are going to reach it under McClaren. Eriksson's speechless.

To few people's surprise, England swiftly nosedive under the matey McClaren, an outstanding coach who tries to make himself look strong as a manager by dropping Beckham, and then totally undermines himself by recalling him. 'I wouldn't say McClaren was out of his depth but he was one of the best coaches we've had, definitely,' says Jenas. 'Me and Steve had a relationship where he always really liked me as a player, and was always pushing me when I was with Sven. When he got hold of the reins himself he made really weird decisions that I didn't really feel was him, like playing Alan Smith or Ledley King in midfield.' Against Brazil in the first game at the new Wembley in June 2007, Smith drops back from attack and King steps into midfield. 'Me and Michael Carrick were looking at each other and saying: "What's the point of us being here?" If you're going to play a striker in midfield ahead of me and Michael Carrick I don't get it. There was one game, when we played Croatia away, when the ball went over Paul Robinson's foot [the Euro 2008 qualifier on 11 October 2006], and I went to see him. I said: "What's going on?" Somebody got injured [Gerrard] and Steve called in Scott Parker and started him. I said to Steve: "What's the point? Why bring me if that's your mindset?" "You're different players." "Well, there's a reason why he's third down the list behind myself and Michael." With these decisions, me and a lot of other players started to lose faith a little bit. From Steve's perspective as a manager it was a massive learning process.' An expensive one for England. The return against Croatia in the rain of Wembley on 21 November 2007 brings the inevitable *coup de grâce*, McClaren's dismissal, a slump in brolly sales, and the arrival of the strict Italian Fabio Capello.

Despite repeated failure, fascination with the Golden Generation lingers. In Almaty in June 2009, Kazakhstanis queue for hours to glimpse the celebrated visitors. A taxi driver rolls down his window, shouts 'England!' and kisses his match ticket. Police insist on having their pictures taken with Gerrard, Lampard and Rooney outside the away dressing-room. As Gerrard tries to warm up, a local pesters him for an autograph. The Central Stadium probably holds the record for number of drummers in the stands, and even a 4-0 defeat fails to silence Kazakhstan's magnificent fans. England cruise to the 2010 World Cup but problems proliferate. Capello insists on 4-4-2 when senior players privately urge 4-3-3. He arrives with a regal reputation owing to his acclaimed work at AC Milan, Real Madrid and Roma but shrinks as the reality of the Impossible Job grips. Everything gets magnified with England. Tiny issues become stumbling blocks. The Capello Index, his money-making player-rating service, seems gratuitous, especially for someone paid £6m a year to focus on one thing. Capello's pre-tournament contract negotiations annoy some players as he's told them to avoid such distractions. His English seems to deteriorate rather than improve. Originally well received post-McClaren, Capello's tough man-management methods grate. 'Capello was very cold, but what I really liked about him was that everybody was on a level playing field,' says Jenas, who played four times for the Italian disciplinarian. 'Reputation meant nothing to him. I remember JT was late for a meeting, and he was our captain, and Capello wouldn't even let him in the room. Even simple things. He used to take the midfielders for this session. He was talking to us and Lampard bent down to tie up his lace. "Get up." He was just tying his lace! But for Capello it was an authority thing, a discipline thing. Everyone had to wear the same items of clothing when we came down to dinner, to the point where if he said the T-shirt was a round neck and somebody came down with a polo on they would be sent back to their room. It got borderline ridiculous towards the end.' Treating adults as children is rarely wise.

'I'd heard he really liked me as a player,' Jenas continues. 'He started me [against Switzerland on 6 February 2008], I scored for him, and then he didn't pick me for the next game [against France at the end of March]. I was playing really well for Spurs, scoring goals, had just won the League Cup. [Tottenham manager] Juande Ramos told me he and Capello had had a chat. I had a dodgy ankle at the time. Ramos said to me: "Go easy now throughout the rest of the season, concentrate on your England career for the rest of this season. I'm going to dip you in and out of games, maintain your ankle, so when the England games come you are ready to go."' This seems remarkably generous for a club manager, but anyway. 'We were playing France in the next game and I was sound with that. I thought this is the start of my England career. I've been in the squad for so many years, just scored, playing just off Wayne Rooney, and then he named the squad [and] I wasn't anywhere near it. France away I was really looking forward to. I got the message to him: "Why aren't I in the squad?" The message back was: "Any player that doesn't play for their clubs at the weekend doesn't play for England." I thought we had an understanding. Later that whole situation relaxed, and you saw Gareth Barry go to the [2010] World Cup when he was injured. I felt hard done by. I'd waited all this time to kick on with my England career, I had a manager who was prepared to start me, a position that suited me, I'd got the goal, and then it was like "grrrrrr". It never stopped me wanting to turn up. Definitely not.'

The disciplinary touch, ranging from banning sauces to prohibiting visitors to the hotel, is fine in short bursts of qualifying gatherings. During tournaments, England players need a lighter touch, easing the tension, especially those who suffer homesickness. Capello just does not understand. Little things, like calling Joe Hart 'John' at training at the secluded Royal Bafokeng Sports Campus during the World Cup, are mistakes with a painful resonance amplified in a soulless camp miles from anywhere. Robert Green is deemed too quiet by certain influential players, James is too old at 39, so it is crazy of Capello not to pick the in-form Hart. Green spills a routine shot from Clint Dempsey in the opening 1-1 draw with the US. England's habit of travelling with injured players also costs them: Capello's gamble on Ledley King's fitness does not even last a half; Gareth Barry labours. Distraction from England's woes is provided by the wildlife. At the media's Sun City base a few miles from the squad's, baboons lurk in trees and drop on to breakfast tables in high-speed food raids. The local self-styled Baboon Squad goes round with small pellet guns trying to deter the primate pirates. 'I aim for the arse,' one guard explains. A group of us head out on safari and get charged by a bolshy elephant. YouTube footage proves popular among England fans unimpressed by press criticism of the team.

England's stuttering start brings increasing derision. One South African paper accidentally bills England's coach as 'Fabio Costello'. After the abject 0-0 against Algeria in Cape Town, Rooney rages at dissenting supporters and the players hold an inquest over a couple of beers. Back in Rustenburg, John Terry is put up by the FA to face the media. Good news. Terry, always defiant, will talk and talk. Probably too much. Rubbing our hands in gleeful anticipation we troop into the media marquee and listen to Terry declare that home truths need airing, and if it upsets Capello "then so what? I'm here to win it for England." Terry wants Joe Cole to start. This is immediately construed as a Chelsea unity thing when many people, players and supporters, want Cole in the side. Even the England fans' *Three Lions* fanzine has a front cover picture of Cole with the headline 'Has Anyone Seen This Man?' Terry's full of swagger. He'll be telling Capello a few things at the team meeting later, he promises. His outburst has us looking at each other, raising eyebrows, knowing how this will play out, in public and in private. Here's a player wanting to pick the team. Terry's gone rogue. This is front page, let alone back page. He has no right to speak on behalf of the dressing-room. That's the sole prerogative of the captain, Gerrard, hugely popular among the media because of his humility and wry humour. The armband's such a sensitive fabric and has just been changing owners. In classic England pantomime fashion, Terry is stripped of the captaincy after sleeping with Wayne Bridge's ex; Rio Ferdinand is given the honour but falls lame; so the responsibility now lies with Gerrard. Has Terry simply been biding his time, wanting to show who is the real leader of the Three Lions? Putsch-and-run tactics? 'Insurrection!' screams the press. Dressing-room divided. Creative departments of newspapers itch to use an image of the Three Lions crest cracked down the middle – the staple of crisis situations. Terry's stance is seen as an attack on Gerrard's regime as well as Capello's. Nothing beats the adrenalin running on a huge story. I go for a stroll, talking to the office, and bump into other reporters breathlessly updating their bosses. 'It's all kicking off . . . Terry . . . Gerrard . . . Capello . . . Cole . . . mutiny . . . twelve hundred words? Done.'

Calls are put into the England camp, the mood assessed, soundings taken. Gerrard is known to be upset with Terry. Jamie Carragher too. The presses roll, and we know they will roll over Terry. The morning headlines will slaughter him. He's undoubtedly foolish to voice his frustrations in public, and certainly to suggest that the dressing-room's behind him in challenging Capello. As dusk falls, so does Terry's standing. The word quickly comes back from the England management that the subsequent squad meeting is pretty amicable and nobody stands up to Capello. Terry's threats ring even more hollow. A big beast of the England jungle is tamed. Chelsea's controversial captain possesses so many character flaws that it is hard to summon much desire to defend him, but I have some sympathy. Thank God a player at least confronts England's predicament. Why can't players be grown up, take criticism and collectively find a solution? Terry is simply being honest. England are miserable on and off the field. Some in the England camp privately feel supportive of Terry, not believing he's trying to snatch back the armband from Gerrard. Within the FA, Terry's challenging rhetoric is perceived more as a threat to Capello's authority – until the meeting and the silence of the lions. Terry apologizes to manager and players.

While using the gym in Sun City I fall into conversation with some Australians. 'Your boys need to pull their socks up,' one concludes. They do, briefly. Against Slovenia in the pretty city of Port Elizabeth, England fans hold up a banner reading '6,000 miles for what?' in protest at how far they've travelled for no reward. Their faith is repaid with an improved display and they're soon chanting, 'We're not going home!' and 'Rooney!' Yet England are still not firing, Germany lie in wait in the round of 16, and Götterdämmerung duly arrives in the heat of Bloemfontein.

I travel up in the lift at the Free State Stadium with some German politician, hemmed in by bodyguards. He is totally convinced his country will win. His belief is unshakeable, and correct. Mesut Özil,

Thomas Müller and the rest of the Germany side are too good, too intelligent, too quick and fluid in their attacks. The English berate the referee, Jorge Larrionda, and his assistant for failing to spot Lampard's shot crossing the line after rebounding down off Manuel Neuer's crossbar. Rooney argues with the Uruguayan official, so do Jermain Defoe and Capello. The man from Montevideo needs video technology. At least Larrionda's aberration sets in motion the Goal Decision System as Fifa finally begins bowing to technology. Terry, meanwhile, is screaming at the German bench. He could direct his spleen at England's. Capello's insistence on 4-4-2 gifts Germany superior numbers in midfield and Özil runs amok. Müller rips England apart off the pitch as well as on. 'It's difficult to have so many alpha males in the same team and expect them to row in the same direction,' he says. The words of Müller, a footballer who grows in stature the tougher the task, should be painted in large letters on the walls of the coaching department at St George's Park. He's right. Teams require a blend. England lack balance and duly topple over, losing 4-1.

There are angry calls for Capello's dismissal. Those close to him say he looks a broken man. Sources reveal that the proud Italian is prepared to leave the morning after the Germany defeat. There will not be any additional cost as he would walk on the original terms of compensation, on what is called 'liquidated costs' for removal. The current FA chief executive, Martin Glenn, tells the 2015 Soccerex convention that the decision to award Capello a new deal on the eve of the 2010 World Cup was 'slightly unsavoury'. But is it a new deal? Capello's contract runs from 2008 to 2012; and it gets adjusted because Inter Milan are sniffing around. The FA privately disputes it would have cost them an excessive amount to sack Capello. Dave Richards, the acting FA chairman, tells the England manager to go home and take a few days to think about it. The FA, meanwhile, an organization riddled with uncertainty following the departure of senior figures such as Lord Triesman, decides to back Capello, who agrees to stay on.

Capello is viewed among FA staff as an honourable, caring man who will have arguments, and there are four-letter-word exchanges with FA staff in South Africa, but he quickly says 'no problem' and everyone moves on. The main problem is that many players, like Gerrard, find him cold and note his English failing to improve, particularly after he has been back in Italy for a period. Capello returns from his post-World Cup holiday not so much refreshed as ready for a ruck, unleashing all his venom and frustration at one of the most entertaining press conferences in England history at the Grove Hotel near Watford on 3 September. He rails against the fickle press, accusing us of hailing him one moment, assailing him the next. 'You create the God, and you create the monster, no?' Capello shouts at us. He has a point. England managers are built up as world-beaters after a win then ridiculed as hopeless after a loss.

Capello manages to steer England to Euro 2012 but resigns, to much relief and celebration, after being angered by the FA's refusal to let him pick Terry, who is accused of making a racist remark towards Anton Ferdinand (he's eventually cleared in court but found guilty of making a reference to Ferdinand's 'colour or race'). Capello tries to defend the player he fell out with in South Africa and it costs him his job. The Golden Generation is ending with a whimper.

13

The Knowledge

To LOUD FANFARE in 2007, the FA erects a magnificent statue of Bobby Moore outside Wembley, puts up dramatic photographs of the late, great England captain inside the stadium and contributes funds and publicity to cancer campaigns run in Moore's memory and name. Guilt stains such monumental munificence. Moore gives the FA its most iconic, historic and lucrative moment yet the governing body, at the time shot through with snobbery, snubs him during his lifetime. 'Moore was treated appallingly,' admits a senior figure at the FA. Fortunately and belatedly, the Blazers learn from their predecessors' disgraceful behaviour. Moore is now properly celebrated at the headquarters of English football. The FA still needs to embrace quicker and more fully those who serve it well, creating a better environment for England. Members of the Golden Generation like David Beckham, Rio Ferdinand, Steven Gerrard and Frank Lampard need to be offered substantial roles at the FA. They have the knowledge.

The Moore fiasco must not be repeated. His reading of the game, timing in the tackle and calm, accurate distribution made him an exceptional player yet he was also a special person. Those who say never meet your heroes – for fear of disappointment – never met Bobby Moore. Covering an England schoolboy international at the old Wembley in the late eighties, I walk into the press box, glance around and take in the presence of a few agency men and a radio crew sitting at the far end. It's Capital Gold. With them is the golden one, Bobby Moore, well dressed, polite and modest, and radiating class. I introduce myself and, as he does with so many, the England legend immediately puts me at ease. Where many stars hold court, Moore converses, engages, listens. He's even more impressive and heroic in person. His humanity shines through. Grace characterized Moore's movement as a player and defined him as a man.

A couple of cherished minutes in Moore's company left an inevitable question: why is a Wembley king residing in a largely deserted press box reporting on a kids' game? From the moment he finished playing at Fulham in 1977, Moore should have been embedded in the England dressing-room by the FA, imparting wise counsel to those who aspired to his sporting heights. Moore had the knowledge, the appreciation of what it takes to end the years of hurt. He could have advised the FA on how he was inspired by the most daunting occasion, rather than feel constrained as so many of his successors do. Moore should have been directed to the dug-out by the FA and invited to coach the schoolboys, passing on the encouragement and instructions that worked so well back in 1966. Moore was so handsome, so humble, so appealing that a generation would have fallen further in love with football. He could have instilled durable principles, showing why sportsmanship should always conquer gamesmanship. He could have explained why his innate respect made him wipe his hands clean of dirt and sweat when ascending the thirty-nine steps upon espying the spotless white glove on Her Majesty the Queen's right hand preparing to stretch out towards him. Moore should have been led up to the royal box by the FA and shown to the best seat in the house. He should have been used in campaigns by the FA, promoting respect, forthcoming internationals or urging youngsters to start or stick with the game. Moore should have been driven to school after school, educating pupils in his profession, talking about the famous picture of him and Pelé swapping shirts at the 1970 World Cup. This sepia celebration of mutual respect should be hung in every school sports hall or dressing-room. It's what the game should be about, respect – a value largely lost in the modern era. Moore should have been ushered into the boardroom by the FA, given a seat next to the chairman, and asked to help shape the future of the national game. He should have been given a blank cheque and told to build the facilities and rewrite the coaching philosophy to nurture a crop of players capable of repeating 1966. Moore should have been recruited to work with young defenders, teaching them to pass the ball out rather than hoof clear. The FA should have employed this golden asset as ambassador, coach and sounding-board. Instead, a deep understanding of the game acquired over many years and many, many matches was passed on only to listeners of Capital Gold and readers of the *Sunday Sport* tabloid.

For a defender adept at moving upfield, Moore never pushed himself forward off the pitch. Talks with more enlightened members of the FA give me the impression that some of those in the corridors of power in the eighties and nineties were jealous of him. It takes recent regimes, populated with those who grew up eternally grateful to Moore for the most precious sporting moment of their childhood, to atone for the organization's sins of omission. The FA has made partial amends, campaigning to Fifa to get medals for those of Sir Alf Ramsey's squad who didn't play in the final. It also takes the lengthy lobbying of journalists like Jeff Powell, Moore's close friend and *Daily Mail* writer, for the Boys of '66 to be treated with the respect they deserve. Five of the eleven – Alan Ball, George Cohen, Roger Hunt, Nobby Stiles and Ray Wilson – are not appointed MBE until 2000. Ordinary men who achieve something extraordinary should be feted more.

Sir Bobby Charlton is the FA's Franz Beckenbauer, but Moore should have been as well. Charlton gets deployed by the FA during World Cup-bidding charm offensives, but why has he never been on the FA board? Charlton's been an amazing ambassador, always willing to turn up, presenting caps and attending conventions. He takes his England responsibilities very seriously. He is properly venerated, and his acumen appreciated, but that's mainly because Manchester United possess more soul and conscience than the FA. A shocking institutionalized antipathy towards Ramsey and his men pervades parts of the FA, so they seek earnings elsewhere. It feels slightly demeaning that many of the Boys of '66 should rely on corporate work – I once found myself fielding questions in a Stoke car showroom with Gordon Banks – when they should be given jobs for life at the FA. The governors parade Sir Geoff Hurst on occasion, especially when campaigning to host World Cups. I've done corporate events with Hurst and he's brilliant value. He turns up, punctual and immaculately dressed, reminisces engagingly for fifty minutes to an hour, gets paid a couple of grand, and moves on to his next job. Hurst is so eloquent and interesting, and the corporate clientele are so captivated, that he could probably charge more. The hat-trick man has cracked the system.

Good. He deserves every penny. Back in 1981, Hurst eventually went on the dole after being dismissed as Chelsea manager, where he was earning roughly £28,000 a year. Hurst shouldn't have needed to tout for employment, to join a dole queue, for heaven's sake. He won England the World Cup. He should have been set up for life, tended by a grateful nation. Tears rolled down Nobby Stiles' face as he sold off his '66 medal, that gleaming reminder of his greatest moment. How demeaning is that? How depressing is it that the country that invents the game cannot look after its most celebrated champions? It's pathetic. They are treated with more reverence now and are rightly taking centre stage on the 50th anniversary of their World Cup heroics. But all the Boys should have been employed en masse after the World Cup, dovetailing with their other commitments, to tour schools and clubs, inspiring the next generation. The likes of Banks and Cohen felt let down by the FA. In the past, understandable resentment lingered at the modest bonus paid to them by the FA in 1966: the £22,000 pot was shared equally between the twenty-two players – a touch of class from the starting eleven. They played for the glory, and felt privileged to wear the Three Lions, but they deserved a larger, more nourishing slice of the pie the FA still gorges on. The one star on the shirt, denoting World Cup success, continues to generate substantial riches for the FA.

Some inside the FA admit to a frustration over certain of the '66 Boys slating the current generation. Hearing the old 'they're not fit to lace our boots' narrative is deemed unhelpful to the team's development. Listening to the lament that 'we'd have done things differently under Alf' is difficult for the current England management. They have a phrase for it in the FA: 'The '66 Overhang'. Some at the FA are keen to escape the shadow of '66.

Yet it is to the shame of the FA that its treatment of Sir Alf Ramsey was so shabby. It is not simply the manner of his dismissal, which he discovers via television, that reflects badly on the governing body. It is the organization's subsequent refusal to draw on the sagacity of the only English manager who knew what it took, tactically and temperamentally, to win a World Cup. Ramsey should have been part of the appointment service, selecting managers. He was largely ignored, an outrage heaping more infamy on the FA. Ramsey's bust in the tunnel at Wembley is only a recent addition from a newly contrite FA.

The FA needs to make Wembley more of a home for England rather than a major municipal arena frequently associated with gridiron and concerts. When The Killers play Wembley in 2013, the band's lead singer Brandon Flowers hits the right notes throughout, especially halfway through his set. He sings, 'Whether a hot-blooded win or a heart-breaking loss, those Three Lions proudly play under the St George's Cross,' as the Wembley screen shows the England crest. The picture is soon replaced by the iconic photo of Moore being chaired by the other players. 'Sixty-six – the winning team,' Flowers sings. Wembley roars its approval of this homage to 1966. Saying it with Flowers, singing it with respect.

In September 2015 the public is given a rare peek inside the England dressing-room when the FA releases footage of Wayne Rooney giving his short thank you speech to team-mates after reaching a record 50 goals on scoring against Switzerland. It is noticeable that there are no emblems on the walls, no stirring slogans, no photographs of the players. The space is functional. There's no sense of belonging to England, barring the pictures of iconic moments and quotes on the walls outside, Ramsey in the tunnel and Moore outside. When Middlesbrough visit Wembley for the 2015 Championship play-off final, their manager Aitor Karanka sends in a Teesside company,

Shutter Media, to make their dressing-room truly Boro's. They cover the floor with the club crest, the famous lion and the year of their founding, '1876'. Each player's cubicle is adorned with a large photograph of the occupant in action. The graphics don't help in the end – Boro freeze, Norwich win – but little details can count, can inspire players. After a Chelsea game at Napoli, I wander around the dressing-rooms and the home quarters are a monument to the *tifosi*, with photographs of the people, the club's heartbeat – the mission statement being to serve the community.

Ultimately, the FA will always be best represented by people, not pictures on the wall. With Charlton less mobile, the FA looks at more recent generations, calling on the trusted Sir Trevor Brooking and Ray Clemence. Determined not to repeat the mistakes post-'66, and especially its Moore travesty, the FA operates an accelerated ambassador programme and holds regular meetings about what to do with Beckham, Ferdinand, Gerrard and Lampard. They want to respect the knowledge and utilize their expertise and role-model status. Yet even in an age of relative enlightenment, the FA can cock up spectacularly. Beckham is the FA's global ambassador, a huge draw around the world, and with residual footballing qualities in 2012 when Stuart Pearce decides on his three over-aged players for Team GB at the London Olympics. Pearce chooses Micah Richards, Ryan Giggs and Craig Bellamy. No Becks. Pearce insists it's for 'football reasons'. By FA standards this is only a minor car-crash, but it's still damaging. It's a snub for a popular footballing figure whose persuasive qualities helped bring the Olympics to London. It's a no-brainer, a tap-in. Beckham will bring substance to GB football, an crsatz operation at the best of times. The former England captain deserves a place on footballing grounds; a year after the Olympics, Beckham can be found competing in the Champions League for Paris St-Germain. FA wrath at Pearce needs placing in context, though; the governing body is itself blameworthy. Knowing Pearce would bristle at the thought of Beckham's involvement, the FA should have broached the subject when offering him the job as coach of Team GB.

On 24 June 2012, the FA holds a meeting at a hotel in Kiev to debate the Psycho–Golden Balls impasse. England's players are asleep upstairs, preparing for what will prove a frustrating evening against Italy (extra time, penalties, you know the scoreline). Back in London, the FA approaches football's biggest Sex Pistols fan. Never mind the Blazers, Pearce is not for turning. 'Terrible call,' confides an FA official when asked about the organization's verdict on Pearce, and that's the polite version. Pearce at least has the courage to phone Beckham and explain why the man who features heavily in the Olympics' global hit of an opening ceremony will not then feature in a sporting drama he has helped script. The squad hardly overflows with talent and quickly bows out. On penalties, inevitably. Beckham handles the rejection with typical dignity, wishing everyone well, as steam comes out of FA ears.

Pearce unintentionally shreds an FA plan. Painful memories of their predecessors' aberration with Moore drives FA officials to make a proper plan for Beckham, another East End boy with West End glamour. 'The Olympics was the perfect time to get Beckham into the FA, making him a vice president, attending events when the president is otherwise engaged,' admits a frustrated FA official. The president is HRH Prince William, Duke of Cambridge, who is occupied with weightier royal, military and air ambulance commitments but still turns out for between four and six FA events a year. The people's prince, David Beckham, his playing days soon over, would be the dream understudy. The FA is desperate to have a respected captain on board, to see the Olympics as a stepping stone to the boardroom, and will push for him again. Those around the England camp respect Beckham for his passion for the team, and just for being him, a polite, grounded individual. As officials consider conferring vice president status on Beckham, they constantly express wonder about his natural, relaxed feel despite his life being hemmed in by showbusiness. They know all about Beckham's motivational effect on younger players, helping them settle in. They know how hard he worked during the World Cup in South Africa, operating in a slightly nebulous role in training as he recovered from a torn Achilles. Beckham doesn't have his badges, so he cannot coach. The FA regrets not making his role more defined, and winces when made aware of LA Galaxy's displeasure at pictures and reports of their convalescing star smashing a ball into the net in training at Rustenburg. At least the FA has learned from its blundering over Moore and is attempting to incorporate Beckham, drawing on the knowledge.

The FA needs to build a proper programme, including notable alumni like Beckham, Ferdinand, Gerrard and Lampard, and get them involved in the development teams rather than pontificating from afar. An FA source reveals that some of the organization's coaches are sceptical about the motives and potential of England alumni. 'The coaches say that "just because they are ex-internationals doesn't mean they'll be good as coaches",' says the source. 'But a link with the past is vital. Other countries feed former players in, talking to them early, integrating them. The FA should have been wooing Paul Scholes years ago, getting him working with the younger age-groups, and doing specialized midfield lessons. Put him in with Jack Wilshere. Gary Neville was asking from a long time out whether he could be involved.' When Neville retired in September 2009, the FA should have found a place on its main board for this deep thinker about the game. At least he's involved with England.

Managerial knowledge, as well as playing erudition, needs absorbing. The FA has embraced the dressing-room diaspora before, welcoming managers, giving them exposure to international football. Ron Greenwood happily helped Bobby Robson, Terry Venables, Howard Wilkinson and Dave Sexton. Brian Clough was involved in the B team, although sadly not the senior. England need to reintroduce a similar programme, initially using possible future international managers like Alan Pardew, Eddie Howe and Garry Monk as scouts, just integrating them into the England system. As one FA source points out: 'It would be useful if an England manager hits a sticky patch to have Premier League managers supporting him in their Thursday or Friday press conferences. It also gives them exposure to international football, gives them a taste.' It gives them a chance of succeeding if they ever take the main job in the future.

Gordon Hill, six times an England winger, wants old pros involved.

'Look at Holland's coaching bench,' he writes via email, thinking of Ruud van Nistelrooy and Marco van Basten assisting Danny Blind. 'Most of them are former top internationals with a new batch ready to step in when they finish. That is all the experience you need to win. It does not take a genius to look at all the countries' coaches who have played and know what the game is all about. What do England have? A bunch of coaches that are yes men, played the game but not at a high level, and most of them defenders – same old story.' The FA needs to do the knowledge. It could also do with encouraging greater acumen and accuracy from 12 yards out.

14

Spot of Bother

DEAR ENGLAND: TO lose one penalty shoot-out may be regarded as a misfortune, to lose six looks like carelessness. Fifty years of hurt are pockmarked by 12 yards of hurt. Names and shoot-out dates hang like tattered regimental flags over the battlefield of tournament football: Stuart Pearce and Chris Waddle at Italia 90; Gareth Southgate at Euro 96; Paul Ince and David Batty at France 98; David Beckham and Darius Vassell at Euro 2004; the carnage of Germany 2006 with Frank Lampard, Steven Gerrard and Jamie Carragher; and the Euro 2012 aberrations of the Ashleys, Young and Cole. Despair is the only emotion. The profligate dozen are good players, sharing 824 caps between them. Seven captain their clubs. Six captain their country. A half dozen feature in European Cup finals. Lampard and Cole even convert two penalties each in Chelsea's finals. But put them in an England shirt, and they can stumble.

Little romance is in the air in Casablanca too as England also trip up in the pre-France 98 King Hassan II International Cup in Morocco. The penalty misses of Rob Lee and Les Ferdinand mean England's current shoot-out record is seven lapses out of eight. Only Spain at Wembley in '96 are vanquished on penalties. The road to redemption has a sink-hole under a whitewashed spot, one needing urgent repairing. To discover how England can last longer at tournaments I first have to find the country's king of the shoot-out. Word reaches me that Alan Shearer is now addressing another still ball, a smaller one, out on a golf course in his native north-east.

A devoted supporter of the Sir Bobby Robson Foundation, Shearer is somewhere on the magnificent Rockliffe Hall course for the annual Sir Bobby celebrity golf bash. I've just talked to Lady Elsie about her late husband; now it's time to look for one of his favourite players. It's a glorious day, the summer heat mocking the autumnal date. I climb into a buggy with Liz Luff, a Toon obsessive who works tirelessly for the Foundation, and we stop-start our way from the club-house on a Shearer safari. What Liz lacks in height she makes up for in personality and noise. As I drive, she consults ex-players out on the course about Shearer's possible whereabouts. Michael Gray shouts directions to the last sighting. 'Desperately seeking Alan,' Liz tweets. 'With @henrywinter in search of @alanshearer.' We steer quietly past Steve Howey taking a putt at the fourth before Liz resumes her running commentary on the weather, the joys of the north-east, and could that be Alan over there? Or there? Finally, and after a near-accident with a water hazard, my faithful tracker spots Shearer's blue shirt on the 14th. At 45, he still cuts a powerful, athletic figure, smacking the ball an almighty distance. Abandoning the buggy, we catch up with our quarry on foot. I've interviewed Shearer all over the world, in Hong Kong when England played there before Euro 96, in St-Etienne when England bowed out of the World Cup, in Venice when visiting a boot factory and in Spa when he retired emotionally from England, but never walking alongside him as he contemplates his next golf shot. Typically, he talks sense, revealing his passion and concerns for England.

Shearer is now an acclaimed studio analyst on *Match of the Day*, his output improving after stepping out of the sizeable shadow of Alan Hansen, the Liverpool icon whose opinions were conveyed like statements to the nation. Shearer delivers, just as he did as a player. Even when Terry Venables' Christmas tree tactics has him playing with his back to goal, holding the ball up, taking a bruising from centre-backs, Shearer stays physically strong. Even when mercilessly mauled by critics for not scoring in the interminable run of friendlies before Euro 96, Shearer remains mentally strong. A couple of times on leaving Wembley in that phoney-war period I encounter Shearer hobbling to his car. He's taken so many whacks but never complains. That resilience serves him well. England never feels a burden.

The shirt weighs like chainmail on many players. 'That's right,' says Shearer walking and talking. 'Particularly with social media, newspapers, television, the scrutiny. The scrutiny when we were playing was massive because of England not winning anything since '66. That turns that desire and hunger into more pressure; the longer we go on, the more it churns up. You have to be able to handle that pressure. We all tried our best to get to where we wanted to be, which was ultimately to win something. Euro 96 was the closest we've come. Nobody can say it didn't work out because of a lack of effort or professionalism. That didn't happen in my era. I'm quite happy with what we did.'

Shearer misses only one penalty during his 63 internationals, shooting against a Polish post in Katowice in 1997. Otherwise, he converts six kicks, including three in tournaments: against Holland at Wembley on a special night during Euro 96, against Argentina after Owen is fouled in St-Etienne two years later, and then in his final international, against Romania at Euro 2000, his 30th goal for England. He converts twice against Luxembourg (in 1998 and 1999) and versus Hungary (in '99). He also holds his nerve in three shoot-outs, starting with Spain in the quarter-finals of Euro 96. Shearer targets the left corner. Andoni Zubizarreta guesses correctly but the strike, as so often with Shearer, is just too powerful. He again leads the way in the semi-final against Germany, driving the ball into the top-right corner as Andreas Köpke travels the wrong way. Two years later, Shearer's again first up for England, again demanding responsibility, again driving the ball into the roof of the Argentina net, left of centre, as Carlos Roa dives low, underneath the ball. So what's his secret? 'No fear – and I practised penalties every day,' he replies. Gone is the smiling Shearer joking with friends and corporate guests on the fairway. He has his game-face on again, all serious, all prepared for the challenge.

He's heard the doctrine that penalties cannot be practised, a creed espoused by his former manager Glenn Hoddle, who argues the match-day noise and tension cannot be reproduced in training. 'I understand where Glenn's coming from because you can't replicate the stress and pressure you're under,' Shearer says. 'I agree with that with the players who don't take penalties and are not used to the situation, it's pressurized; but if you've taken them all your life like I did, then the pressure didn't mean that much. It was: "Right, I've been in this situation before. Do what you practise, do what you've been taught to do. And stick to it, and never do anything different."'

Shearer's train of thought is briefly interrupted as he watches a fellow golfer steering a Segway towards some rushes and almost into a lake. 'Because I took penalties at a young age, and I took them all my career, when I had to take them in bigger tournaments, I knew how to handle it. It's different for the guys who have to take the third, fourth and the fifth penalties because they've never been in that position. They might change their minds. The first two or three might be used to it and can handle it. I always picked my spot and don't change my mind. If the keeper manages to go that way, then make sure he doesn't get it.' Hit it hard. 'You have to change your mind now and again because if you go the same way every time, they'll know.'

Throughout his penalties, Shearer exudes confidence. In St-Etienne, he chats to the Argentinian Roberto Ayala as the ends are decided. He pats Michael Owen on the head, reassuringly. 'I'm nervous,' Owen recalls. 'I say to Alan Shearer: "Which way do you think I should go?" He says: "Do what you fucking normally do and put it in the back of the net." Which was fine, but I wanted a bit of guidance . . . stick it to his [Roa's] left or right? I could have gone either [way]. I didn't have a preferred corner. I was looking over to my mum and dad, and going: "Which way?" I was fourth, so I watched the next penalties and realized the goalkeeper went the right way every time. I thought: "He's looking at something in the run-up. He's gone the right way in normal time with Shearer's, and then the right way again."' Roa does the same for Shearer's shoot-out penalty, but it's too good, then saves Paul Ince's before narrowly failing to keep out Paul Merson's. 'So I thought: "Right, I've got to kid him with my run-up." I ran towards the ball and opened myself out to push it to my right, his left, and thought, "I'll pull it to the left and pull it across myself." It worked. I sent him the wrong way.' The ball swept in high off the left upright. Cool analysis in fraught circumstances brings due reward. 'It was my mental attitude. I never thought I'd miss even though I didn't think I was naturally a great penalty-taker.'

Owen never misses a penalty with England, whether during a match (against Slovakia at the Riverside on 11 June 2003) or in shoot-outs (in St-Etienne, and down the middle against Portugal in Lisbon at Euro 2004). In the King Hassan II International Cup in Casablanca, Owen also scores high into the left-hand corner during the shoot-out with Belgium. 'I had a good record for England but I didn't have a great record for Liverpool,' he says, thinking of his ten misses in twenty-three attempts during his career with the Merseysiders. 'I always took penalties as a kid. I had nerves of steel. I don't think anyone could have been in a better frame of mind than me. Goalkeepers can move beforehand, so even if you knocked one in the corner, it wasn't necessarily guaranteed. You need to really knock it in with pace into a corner to be guaranteed a goal.'

Back in St-Etienne, Roa saves the next spot-kick, a feeble one from David Batty, and England are out of the 1998 World Cup. Shearer sighs. He's done all he can.

The penalty professor offers advice that should be sent to the iPads of every one of Roy Hodgson's expected penalty-takers at Euro 2016 – Wayne Rooney, Harry Kane, and others confident enough to volunteer. 'In international football, I knew if we trained in the stadium the night before the game there would be a spy from the opposition somewhere in the stand watching. [Just as Gary Lineker had noticed in 1990.] I always used to practise penalties the night before knowing I was being watched. So I'd always take ten penalties to the opposite side I was going to go the following night. The night before Romania in Euro 2000, I knew there was somebody in the stand there so I hit every one to the keeper's left, knowing he would go back to the goalkeeper and say: "I saw him practising last night and he's put them all to the left [of the keeper]." I took a penalty the next night and put it to the right and it went in.' Bogdan Stelea dives the wrong way. 'Little things make a difference.'

I follow Shearer down the fairway, enquiring whether any of those hoping to end the fifty years of hurt have contacted him about his penalty prowess. 'Er, no,' he says, stopping in the middle of the fairway, yards from his ball, clearly distracted by the question. Does that lack of contact surprise you? I ask. 'Yeah, it does. I'd like to think I'm always open to anyone to get hold of me. So if someone asked I would gladly give that advice, definitely, but no one's ever asked. No manager's ever asked. No one from the FA's ever asked. It's such a fine line. When you consider how many times England have gone out on penalties . . . Mad, it's crazy. You'd think it would be a simple thing, to ask. And that's why we haven't been successful.'

Leaving Shearer to his golf, I round up Liz, who's swapping jokes with the rest of the party, board the buggy, and crawl back to the club-house. Finding a quiet moment, I contact the FA to set up a meeting to discover more about their penalty philosophy. In denial? Or actively researching a cure for the affliction? It appears the theory and practical study of transferring a still ball 12 yards past one opponent has become part of the footballing curriculum for England age-group players. 'I'd be lying to you if I said it was every tournament, every event, but there are quite a few events through the players' pathway where we deliberately make sure we practise penalties at the end,' says the FA's technical director, Dan Ashworth, when we meet up in London. 'We'll host a Uefa tournament at Under-16s and at the end of the game if we've beaten France 3-1 it still goes to penalties. With our Under-20s against Mexico at Barnet, we pre-agreed penalties with Mexico. We told the fans: "Stay on after the game, make some noise for the shoot-out." There's practice and real life. Hopefully we can reproduce a little bit of pressure taking a penalty in front of a crowd in something that matters. The difference between success and failure is tiny and sometimes it is a penalty.' He pauses. 'Six tournaments.'

The suffering commences at Italia 90. 'We were the first ones,' sighs Gary Lineker. 'We weren't mentally scarred by previous teams' debacles! I felt quite confident we'd win it. We had good players.' The sequence of events is so familiar that England fans probably recite it in their nightmares. Lineker, having practised fifty penalties in private the day before the semi-final with West Germany, makes no mistake. Andy Brehme, Peter Beardsley, Lothar Matthäus, David Platt and Karl-Heinz Riedle all convert theirs. 3-3. Up steps Pearce, striking the ball hard and low. Bodo Illgner dives the wrong way but the ball hits his legs and flies to safety. England's world begins to lose its motion. Bobby Robson falls back in his seat, deflated. When Olaf Thon, putting in a little shimmy, beats Peter Shilton, Waddle has to score. He shouldn't have been taking it. Waddle takes up the tale. 'The fifth penalty was Gazza's,' Waddle says, recalling the tearful Gascoigne who's an emotional wreck after receiving a booking that means he's out of the final if England progress. 'He was trying to get a sponsorship with Kleenex at the end. Gazza always tells the story about me missing but I always say to him: "Yes, but it was your pen." He was in such a state. To miss the World Cup final if we'd got through would have been the end of the world for him, by the way. If you think he's had problems since, God help him if he'd missed that game. I remember Bobby Robson saying: "He can't take it. He's in a state. Does anybody want to take it?" Nobody put their hand up. Bobby looked round. I was never a penalty-taker. I enjoyed the game, so I put my hand up and that was it.'

Some planning has gone into the eventuality of a shoot-out. 'We talked about it,' adds Lineker, 'who would take one, but things transpire in the match where who knows who's going to be on the pitch, what state you're in, probably tired? But obviously with what happened to Gazza, he didn't fancy it. Chris didn't really want to take one but someone had to. You had to have five – at least. We were all in the middle of the pitch, the four volunteers and Chris Waddle.'

Waddle runs in. Contact. The ball flies over. Waddle drops to his haunches. Pearce weeps. England are out. Showing a touch of class never to be forgotten by England fans, Matthäus consoles Waddle. 'Matthäus was brilliant,' recalls Waddle. 'They were all good, the Germans. They could easily have run off to the fans, and gone "see you later, mate" to us. We probably would have. They all came up and said it was a great game and that it should have been the final.

We said: "Good luck to youse." They said: "It could easily have been you going to the final." They were regarded as the best team in the world at the time and there was nothing between us.' Just a couple of wayward penalties.

Typically with a coach as well-prepared as Franz Beckenbauer, the Germans are clinical, unemotional, going to work with precision and ruthlessness. Illgner kisses the ball during the shoot-out, a symbolic act twisting the nerves of the English. The Germans stride confidently to the spot. A sense of inevitability pervades their approach, again intensifying the stress levels of the English. The Germans embrace pressure. Shilton tries hard but the penalties are too good. The first two go to Shilton's right, the second two to his left. He doesn't get close; it looks like he's reacting late but clearly his hope is for one down the centre. 'My fault,' explains Lineker. 'I roomed with Shilts. We watched a lot of games. And there were a few penalty shoot-outs at that World Cup.' The Republic of Ireland beat Romania while Argentina pip Yugoslavia and then Italy. Some eminent names miss, notably Diego Maradona, Dragan Stojković and Roberto Donadoni. Lineker resumes his story. 'Every shoot-out there were at least two or three penalties where if the keeper waits, you think: "God, the keeper's going to save that." There are always one or two who go down the middle, and always one or two which aren't very good. So between us we thought if there's a penalty shoot-out, wait and see where it goes. Of course with the Germans, everyone hit the stanchion. Shilts went the right way every single penalty but never got near one because they were really good penalties. I felt it was partly my fault. They were such good penalties that I'm not sure even if Shilts had known where they were going he would have saved them.'

The Germans make no mistake in planning or execution. 'Every one was hit like a rocket,' Shilton says. He shrugs off English mistakes. 'Stuart Pearce more or less hit it at the keeper and Chris Waddle missed the goal. That was the difference. I don't know what it was like in the dressing-room because me and Stuart Pearce – typical of Pearcey – had to go and do the drugs test. We didn't get back to the hotel until two hours afterwards. Everybody was down. But it was strange. We knew we'd done everything we could. But we also knew we'd done the country proud. When you're so close, you always think, "What could have been."'

After losing the pointless third-place play-off, England return home, drowning their sorrows, before dispersing to family and friends. Waddle provides insight into the experience of Those Who Miss Penalties. 'I had two weeks back in England first and then I went back to France,' says the winger, then a firm favourite at Marseille. 'Franz Beckenbauer took over Marseille just after the World Cup final, so when I got back to France I walked in the dressing-room, and Beckenbauer was stood there. He went: "Ahh, Chris, my FAVOURITE English player!" He was just having a laugh. Dragan Stojković said: "Come on, we'll have a competition."' Two of the most technical footballers at Italia 90, two players who missed penalties, now duel in training. 'I got four out of five and he got three.' Waddle agrees with Hoddle, his old singing partner, that practice does not necessarily make perfect. 'You can't recreate the atmosphere, the day, the event. You can practise as much as you like but it's a lottery. It's luck. If you hit it well, and the goalie goes the wrong way, it's in. People always say: "You shouldn't miss." That's rubbish. I saw Maradona miss a penalty. Lionel Messi and Ronaldo have missed four or five.'

Talking at Wembley, Waddle's voice surges with a frustration bordering on anger. 'We go on about penalties far too much. Before the Euros in France, somebody will be writing now: "Go to the bookies and say England to lose on pens in the quarter-finals." It's a constant thing. Italy and Spain were terrible at them for years and Italy won a World Cup on one. They got knocked out of three World Cup tournaments in a row [Italia 90, USA 94 and France 98]. In Italy, they don't go: "Oh no, we're going to lose on pens again." It is more, "What will be will be."' *Che sarà, sarà. Calma.* Italy practise, keep their nerve and grasp the World Cup on penalties in 2006 when Andrea Pirlo, Marco Materazzi, Daniele De Rossi, Alessandro Del Piero and Fabio Grosso convert against France in Berlin. Italy conquer their demons. They lose on penalties to Spain in Vienna two years later but Pirlo's exquisite Panenka to beat Joe Hart at Euro 2012 shows that little scar tissue remains from Euro 2008. Waddle again: 'We seem to have this build-up to a tournament: there'll be a lot said – "Second phase, we'll lose because the game will be that tight, a draw, go to pens, and we know what will happen." That places doubt in players' minds. It's 1990. Ever since then every tournament people harp on about me, Pearcey, Southgate, Batty, Ince. People bring it up all the time. Just let them take the pens. If they score, they score. It's strange. When you go to Italy and talk about Franco Baresi, they'll all go: "Oh, fantastic player." They never say: "But he can't take pens."' Baresi skies his in the 1994 World Cup final shoot-out loss to Brazil. Roberto Baggio also misses. Both are revered players in Italy for their gifts, their careers.

So why the constant English sniping about players' failures from the spot? Is it jealousy? 'Yes,' Waddle replies. 'The general public love to have a dig.' Schadenfreude? Makes them feel better about their own lives? 'Yes. We are the only country who do that. Italy didn't, France didn't. At Marseille we lost a penalty shoot-out against Red Star Belgrade.' The 1991 European Cup final is far from a classic, stained by Red Star's caution, nullifying Waddle, Jean-Pierre Papin and Abedi Pelé, and remains goalless after extra time, with all the drama at the start of the shoot-out. 'Manuel Amoros missed. Nobody harped on about that. I remember going back to France and a few people said "unlucky", "should have won the game", "cruel way to end", but that was it. I can't remember going around stadiums and a fan going: "Amoros – you missed!" Never, ever heard it.'

In England, it's different. The twelve who missed seem to have been immediately co-opted as members of a club of shame, Les Misserables, forever condemned as targets for cheap shots. 'You let your country down!' goes the merciless melody. 'I still get it every week,' shrugs Waddle. 'I'll be out somewhere, in a restaurant, bar, and people will come up to talk. They say: "I like the way you played, Sheff Wed, liked you at Tottenham." But then somebody will shout: "But he cannae take pens, can he?" It always happens. The other day, some-body said: "How much is he worth, Sergio Agüero? He must be worth £100 million." I was stood there, and the bloke pointed at me and went: "He's as good a player." Then another bloke went: "Ow, but he cannae take pens." I went: "I missed less than Agüero. How much am I worth now, then?" He went: "Oh, em, but I thought . . .'" Silenced.

Waddle lives with the insolence and the ignorance of lesser men. 'It doesn't bother us because it made us stronger. I came back, got Footballer of the Year [in '93, with Wednesday], won two more leagues in France, got to cup finals. I didn't go back from the World Cup thinking: "That's the end of my life." If people say it to me, I reply: "Yeah, I did miss."' Turin's legacy is borne by more people than Waddle himself. It inevitably places pressure on his family. 'They never showed it. If somebody says to my son, "Hope you take penalties better than your dad," he says: "I probably do, but you've got to be there to miss it." It doesn't bother them. It doesn't bother me. It bores me, to be honest.'

It fascinates us rubberneckers. Of the seven shoot-outs I've covered, including a very unromantic Casablanca, the only time the players' body language seems filled with confidence is against Spain. The five milling around, looking like Terry Venables' chosen ones, are in form: Shearer, Platt, Pearce, Gascoigne and Robbie Fowler. The pressure is immediately eased by Fernando Hierro crashing Spain's first against the bar, and belief rolls through England. The services of Fowler aren't even required. Four days later, Venables' opening quartet all score against Germany and Sheringham adds the fifth. The Germans, inevitably, are clinical. At 5-5, England move from experts to willing volunteers. Southgate, ever the team player, offers to take the sixth. More technical players can be found among the alternatives – Paul Ince, Tony Adams, Darren Anderton and Steve McManaman – but they're reluctant. Anderton and McManaman have shone during the game and should really step forward; whatever their personal misgivings, they should look at Southgate, a centre-half unfamiliar with such tests of character and technique. Again, one of the themes of the fifty years of hurt is a failure for some to take responsibility when required most. Anderton is on the seventh pen. Ince refuses. A lamb to the slaughter, Southgate cannot be blamed for his hapless penalty, even if he subsequently receives a letter from a jail-bird holding the defender accountable for his meltdown, offence and incarceration.

More thought needs injecting into penalty preparation, even over-loading the 23-man squad with regular penalty-takers, such as Mark Noble, who could come on for only one touch. 'Mark Noble would never want to practise a penalty in his entire life,' says Sam Allardyce, who worked with the midfielder at West Ham. 'He'd say: "Don't ask me to practise a penalty, Gaffer. It'll put me off. Don't tell me, don't ask me, don't distract me, don't instruct me." He's missed one in twenty. He's got that confidence. Mark says: "When I'm on there, I have a plan and I can't replicate that plan in training where there's no pressure, no crowd. But there on the pitch, I can handle it. I know I'm confident enough to do it."' I check with Noble. 'I've never practised penalties,' he confirms.

England's woes continue at France 98 where Beckham's dismissal proves doubly damaging, robbing Hoddle of a dead-ball specialist and meaning his substitutions are cautious (Southgate and Batty coming on for Le Saux and Anderton to shield David Seaman's goal, as well as the more attacking Paul Merson for Scholes). Ince's nerves ensure England make him take an early penalty, the second, which he promptly misses. Batty falters with the fifth and England are out again. England require those with the mindset of Ian Wright, whose omission from the Euro 96 squad and injury before France 98 still grate. Wright believes in himself so much that he would demand the fifth penalty, frequently the killer one (although not at Wembley). 'Any penalty shoot-out I want to be involved and say, "I want to take the fifth penalty,"' he says. 'It's the jeopardy. You could get to that penalty and have to score just to stay in. You could score that one to win it. I'll always take the fifth. In '98, I would have got on the pitch to take a penalty instead of Batty or Ince.' Sadly for England, injury prevents him.

'I practise a lot,' continues Wright. 'That is the ultimate shoot-out, you against a top goalkeeper in a top competition. I thought Michael Owen's and Alan Shearer's penalties in '98 were absolutely brilliant. I just wanted to go on and show I've got the bottle to take that penalty. Euro 96? Gareth Southgate? I'm a penalty-taker for Arsenal. Why didn't Robbie Fowler get on? He took penalties. I would have been naturally somebody who says, "I'll take a penalty." When I then see

Gareth Southgate missing his penalty, I was thinking: "Fucking hell, I could've been there taking that."'

On returning home from France, Hoddle finds his son asking him to play shoot-outs. The passing of the years has seen little improvement or sufficient forethought. Before England set off for Euro 2004, the rugby coaching legend Sir Clive Woodward emails the FA's then chief executive Mark Palios with an idea. 'Why are you not having penalty shoot-outs after each of the warm-up games?' writes Woodward. 'Think you have missed a major opportunity of rehearsing this in a pressure situation with crowd and TV all watching. Should somehow have built this into the friendlies. Vital you go into the tournament with the mindset you have the best penalty-takers in the business. It can be clearly rehearsed in training in a variety of ways but even better to expose players whenever possible to this.'

England's keeper, David James, later voices his annoyance that they lack sufficient detail on opposition takers. In the Lisbon shoot-out against Portugal in June 2004, James dives the wrong way for the kicks of Deco, Simão and Maniche, and is bemused by Cristiano Ronaldo's stop-start and Hélder Postiga's Panenka. England's successful kicks from Owen, Lampard, Terry, Owen Hargreaves and Ashley Cole are bookended by misses from Beckham and Vassell. Ricardo removes his gloves when Vassell walks up to spot the ball, unnerving the taker. Nobody in the England camp really expects Ricardo, Portugal's keeper, to drive in the decisive penalty. He does. England should consider working on the keeper as an option. Joe Hart swept in England's second for the Under-21s against Sweden in Gothenburg in the 2009 Euros.

And so to the 2006 World Cup, which culminates for England in another shoot-out against Portugal. 'You can practise penalties, yes,' says Jermaine Jenas, one of those working on shoot-out technique in training at the Mittelberg stadium in the Black Forest in 2006. 'It's about repetition. That's why people who take penalties regularly inevitably score. Like when Lineker stepped up, he knocked it away. When Shearer did, he knocked it away. We religiously practised penalties. In Germany after every single session we had a penalty shoot-out. You'd take five each. It took ages for a whole team to take five penalties each. It was to get that repetitiveness.'

The players are stalked by fear of another repetition, the very real fear of history repeating itself. Lampard, Gerrard and Carragher all miss against Portugal in Gelsenkirchen, where the only success is Owen Hargreaves, whose footballing education came in Germany. Beckham's injury and Rooney's dismissal limit Eriksson's options but there's still sufficient talent there. Carragher scored in Liverpool's 2001 League Cup shoot-out victory over Birmingham City, coming in off a long run-up. With England, expectation and nerves engulf the takers, although Carragher's unfortunate to be made to take his kick twice as Horacio Elizondo has not blown his whistle. Watching from the bench, Jenas understands the tension. 'All the players weren't just aware of the history but the wrath of what comes with missing. Not just the wrath of the press, but more the fans and that feeling of "it's my fault, I let the whole country down". No one talks about it. It's just there.' Fear accompanies them on the walk from the halfway line. It's in their mind as they place the ball down on the spot. It steps back with them as they prepare their run-up. It runs in with them, these ghosts of the past haunting them. When interviewed by FA chief executive Brian Barwick about succeeding Eriksson in 2006, Allardyce is asked about his approach to penalties. 'Make sure we don't have to take them if we can,' Allardyce replies. Win in normal or extra time. Spare the familiar agony from 12 yards.

Maybe the amateur ethos of the game's roots lingers on in the English psyche, that it is somehow unsporting to prepare forensically and physically. Rather than hide behind the sofa and pray the recurring bad dream goes away, other nations confront their fears. On 8 June 2008, FA staff absorb a fascinating article by Leila Abboud and Max Colchester in the *Sunday Times* headlined 'Send for the Shrinks', detailing the Dutch FA's response to going out on penalties in four tournaments between 1992 and 2000. The KNVB decides to tackle the problem, instructing kids as young as six to practise penalties routinely. Having consulted Geir Jordet, a sports psychologist at the Norwegian School of Sport Sciences, the KNVB recommends penalty-takers maintain eye contact with the keeper, showing poise. Don't rush. Adjust socks, tighten laces, raise the keeper's anxiety levels. As reported in the *Sunday Times*, those who hurry their kicks, taking an average 1.7 seconds to place the ball, manage only 58 per cent accuracy. Those who take their time, using up 2.8 seconds, score 77 per cent of the time. Breathe deeper, stay calm, concentrate, believe. Mind games are vital; wildly celebrating a successful kick cranks up the pressure on the next, opposing taker stumbling towards the box of horrors.

Penalties fixate the FA, England and all around. When Barwick holds his leaving party from the organization in 2008, he tells a story of his secretary always pleading with him to stop chewing his pens as they spill ink on his shirt. 'It always ends messily with pens and England,' I whisper to David Gill, the Manchester United and FA stalwart standing alongside. But it's no laughing matter. England evoke pity at tournaments.

Craving further insight into the pressure of shoot-outs, I go to see Gareth Ainsworth, whose Wycombe Wanderers side lose 7-6 to Southend United in the League Two shoot-out in 2015. 'You can prepare for penalties,' insists Ainsworth. 'I always wanted to go left foot, right foot, left foot, right foot, left foot, alternating. I had this strategy when I was younger. Jim Furnell, the goalkeeper at Arsenal [in the sixties], was my youth-team coach at Blackburn, and the only shoot-out we got to was a tournament in Holland, against top teams. We won it on penalties. I was 17. I remember Jim Furnell going right foot, left foot, right foot, left foot, and it worked. I believe there's something in that. I didn't have that [capability] on the pitch in the final at Wembley. The emotion takes over. Calmness comes into it. Experience comes into it. At the next penalty shoot-out, I'll be a calmer and more decisive manager. It was chaos, players stretch-ered off, players playing through injury, couldn't take penalties, it was almost the five fittest lads. In an ideal world, I will try to do what I saw in the youth team. But it is a total lottery.'

Psychology counts. The Germans even put up their goalkeeping coach Andreas Köpke to talk to the media about penalties on the eve of their 2010 World Cup knock-out game with England in Bloemfontein. Köpke has plenty to say, having been in goal at Wembley at Euro 96. Penalties are not required in South Africa.

They are two years on when England's hoodoo continues. On the eve of the Euro 2012 quarter-final against Italy in Kiev on 24 June, Roy Hodgson is found sitting in an elegant hotel, sipping coffee, and not enjoying the incessant focus on penalties. Hodgson's side prepare for them, and Joe Hart quickly goes through some iPad imagery of Italian kickers at the end of extra time. He's promptly beaten by Mario Balotelli, but Gerrard levels. 'I took my first penalty for England [in 2006] and I missed it but I wasn't a penalty-taker for Liverpool then,' Gerrard tells me during our talk in LA. 'The stage and the moment were almost too big for me. The second time I took one I was Liverpool's penalty-taker, I was used to the situation. I was used to the pressure. I almost knew I was going to score when I walked up.

'People have to walk up when they go to take a penalty who are used to taking a penalty in the Premier League. For example, if we are ever in the situation again at Euro 2016, Roy has got to have natural penalty-takers in those positions to do the job. They're used to the feeling. You cannot get the feeling as a penalty-taker overnight. You can't get it after a week, two weeks, three weeks.' It's acquired over time. 'You have got to be able to accept that responsibility and not be scared to miss. That's when you'll score. It's experience. I believe I became a better penalty-taker the more times I faced that pressure situation. Taking the penalty the second time round, I didn't feel out of my comfort zone. I didn't feel nervous. I didn't feel scared. That felt good. I was happy. I enjoyed the walk up. The first time I walked up, it was horrible. The second time I walked up I just put my shoulders back, believed in myself. The feelings I was getting weren't a shock to me. Because I had it for Liverpool on so many tough occasions, I felt used to it. The first time I wasn't.'

When Riccardo Montolivo misses and Wayne Rooney scores, England are 2-1 up, but nobody is getting the bunting out in our part of the press box. The stigma is too ingrained. The pressure's on Italy but up steps Andrea Pirlo, the man who never feels the heat.

Hart decides to dive when footage of the midfielder's 2006 World Cup penalty shows him striking it down the middle as Fabien Barthez leaps right. Pirlo executes the more subtle Panenka technique in Kiev, waiting for Hart to dive before dinking the ball down the centre. It's psychologically inspired, crushing England. Why isn't it anticipated? Pirlo has tried four Panenkas previously, scoring three. Ashley Young hits the crossbar and Ashley Cole is denied by Gianluigi Buffon. With Antonio Nocerino and Alessandro Diamanti converting, England are going home. Venom spills out. Cole and Young are racially abused on Twitter. One troll posts that the pair are 'worthless n******' who 'should be deported to Africa'. An outraged FA calls the tweets 'unacceptable and appalling' and demands the police investigate. As the inquest continues, Southgate pleads for England to bring a psychologist to future tournaments.

'We've become obsessed because we keep losing them,' concludes Gary Lineker. 'It becomes like a mental block. It's bloody annoying. It goes back to: "Are we technically brought up in a way to deal with those circumstances?" Under this extreme pressure, the better your technique, the more you are likely to score. Balls of steel very much come into it.' England need more balls of steel. Practise more. Take longer to walk up, breathing deeply, and place the ball slowly, perhaps even take time to re-tie laces. Stare at the keeper. But perhaps first phone a friend. Give Shearer a call.

15

Bubble Trouble

NOTORIOUS FOR MISSING penalties, England are also associated with aloofness, holing up in five-star luxury, disappearing for hours into PlayStation or Xbox combat and failing to embrace life at tournaments. 'It's embarrassing to see the scale of the games room,' confides a senior figure at the FA. 'Are the Germans doing this? Are the Italians?' It's an unfair reputation for certain players; some are grounded individuals, curious about their surroundings. Others just need their eyes opened. The FA attempts to make them 'better tourists', engaging more with host nations and not cutting themselves off in precious isolation. England's Bubble still needs pricking. Closeted and cosseted in Academies from an early age, these starlets must be enticed into the real world, making them appreciate their good fortune, seizing the moment in games and tournaments.

The journey towards enlightenment begins eight miles from England's deluxe training base at St George's Park, near Burton upon Trent. Conscientious individuals like the winger Theo Walcott, whose father Don was in the RAF, have already visited the National Memorial Arboretum, 150 acres of Staffordshire woodland dedicated to those who serve. Anyone reading the countless tributes to those who lay down their lives for their country inevitably leaves with perspective enhanced. More players should make that short drive to the Arboretum after training, appreciating the sacrifices of those of a similar age and often background. Players should also occasionally escape their gilded fortresses at tournaments and experience a different land. Get some fresh air and a fresh outlook. A little less condescension, a little more interaction, please.

The Arboretum is found on a slightly winding road off the wind-swept A38, seemingly heading to a quarry before opening out to a couple of car-parks, a visitors' centre, thirty thousand trees and more than three hundred memorials, including the imposing Armed Forces Memorial atop a huge mound. It's an historic, humbling place, home to a particularly poignant footballing shrine, the Christmas Truce. According to legend and a few letters home from the Front, the Germans and British played a game in no man's land in 1914. On the day I visit, making a pilgrimage to the Truce memorial, the rain adds to the sepulchral air clinging to the Arboretum. Passing small groups of veterans clutching mugs of tea in the restaurant, I step out into the extensive grounds, past the memorial to Gallipoli and on past the chapel.

It is a place to reflect and pay respects. I think of players' past failures to open their eyes to the world outside the Bubble, embarrassing episodes like Durban in May 2003. Eight of Sven-Göran Eriksson's players – Paul Scholes, Gareth Barry, Joe Cole, Danny Mills, Phil Neville, Steven Gerrard, Gareth Southgate and Paul Robinson – decline the invitation to fly to Johannesburg to meet Nelson Mandela. The FA makes the trip 'optional' because it fears players being tired after the long haul from England. Southgate, one of the more thoughtful members of the squad, argues that at 32 and with his international career coming to a close he needs to focus fully on the imminent friendly against Bafana Bafana (and he does score). But I recall a recent conversation with one of the players who did board the plane to see Mandela. 'It did surprise me,' Jermaine Jenas says of the refuseniks. 'I'm pretty sure they regret it now. I never under-stood it. That's crazy. We got invited to Nelson Mandela's house. When you think of the struggle he went through, the last thing on my mind was resting for a game which meant nothing. When you do get to that stage of your career like Gareth . . . he was still probably holding on to any type of England recognition and really felt it was important he rested. I was 19. I could have played the day after anyway.'

The Mandela debate reopens seven years later when England stay in glorious Cape Town during the World Cup. Fabio Capello gives his players a day off after the stalemate with Algeria at Green Point Stadium, a stinker of a game appealing only to masochists. England certainly don't deserve time off; some candid team meetings and reviewing the video nasty might be more appropriate. Presented with a few hours free, Capello's men head for the shops, the golf course and hotel reception for chats. A handful venture further afield. David James gets part of the way up Table Mountain. John Terry visits a township. Surprised? Chelsea's controversial captain is few people's idea of a role model but he occasionally goes to the Defence Medical Rehabilitation Centre, Headley Court, near Cobham, arriving quietly, avoiding publicity, simply wanting to show his respect for injured military personnel. David Beckham, ever the ambassador, presses flesh on 2018 World Cup bid duty in Cape Town. The rest have no excuse for not joining countless England fans boarding the ferry for the choppy crossing to Robben Island to see where Mandela was incarcerated in a tiny cell for eighteen of his twenty-seven years in prison, to visit the quarry where he laboured, where the dazzlingly bright limestone harmed his sight. Dutch players find time to make the journey to honour Mandela and they reach the final. Germany visit. Dutch Wags are looking round Robben Island when the English press attend, listening to the guide, an ex-prisoner, talk of how the censors cut holes out of newspapers 'although they left the sports pages alone'. The Little Englanders stay in the Bubble. The mood in the camp borders on the fractious after the fans' and media's caustic reaction to the Algeria game. The FA confides it would facilitate a trip but none of the players mention the possibility. The FA should take more of a lead, telling the players they are going to Robben Island. It needed to prepare earlier, to convince the sports scientists that the expedition the day after the game is advisable, and not to worry whether the whole thing might appear like forced PR. Just do it. They're not there long.

I continue my way through the Arboretum, passing the tributes to the Falklands Task Force, the Battle of the River Plate, and the Castle Class Corvette convoys that endured such ferocious seas and

U-boat attacks in the Atlantic. I think of the attempts made by the FA to inform and edify players. On the eve of the European Under-19 Championship in Normandy in 2010, the FA shows Noel Blake's youngsters clips from the opening scene of *Saving Private Ryan* before the coach takes the squad for a walk on what was Gold Beach at D-Day. They talk of the sacrifices made by those leaping into the spray and zigzagging across the beaches on 6 June 1944. Blake's group, including Nathaniel Clyne, Steven Caulker and Declan Rudd, are shocked to hear that many of those storming the beaches and neutralizing German gun emplacements are of a similar age to them. It makes them think. However briefly, it presses the pause button on chatter about cars, women and money, helping them become more rounded people.

I think back to Euro 2012 and the squad's base in Kraków where England and FA staff debate whether they should take the players to visit Auschwitz-Birkenau. Some around the camp express concerns that the visit will distress and distract the players. The main worry is the distance – an hour each way from England's base in Kraków. The traditional mantra is that players are there 'to do a job' but the counter-argument voiced in discussions between FA and England coaches is that it is important to venture out of the Bubble at times. It's what grown-ups do. So many of the national team's woes come down to psychological frailty, as if the Academy and England Bubble system keeps some in a state of suspended adolescence. Roy Hodgson is very keen on going. The FA chairman at the time, David Bernstein, is hugely influential in the decision to take the players. Only those outfield players definitely not starting against France three days later are allowed on the team bus to Auschwitz-Birkenau: Andy Carroll, Phil Jagielka, Jack Butland, Theo Walcott, Leighton Baines and the suspended Wayne Rooney (Joe Hart insists on going too). The rest of the squad head off to the Oskar Schindler museum in Kraków.

The players listen intently to the talk given by the Holocaust survivor Zigi Shipper, who visits the squad at the Grove in advance of the Euros, but nothing can prepare them for the hell of Auschwitz-Birkenau. I travel with the seven players, covering the 8 June visit with two other reporters on a pool basis for all the newspapers. I've visited Auschwitz-Birkenau on six occasions when England, seniors and Under-21s, are stationed nearby for games. Squads have gone in the past but Euro 2012 is the first time I feel England truly register the right respectful note throughout, from sombre attire to wreaths and lit candles, and particularly the intelligent questions asked of the guide Wojciech Smolen. Standing on the railway platform where the SS doctor Heinz Thilo selected which new arrivals went to the gas chambers and which went to hard labour, Rooney debates the mentality of this murderous figure. The gist of his question to Smolen is how Thilo, who lived nearby, could dare try to lead a normal family life having destroyed so many other family units. I walk with Jagielka, the thoughtful Evertonian with Polish forebears, back towards the gates of Birkenau. He speaks movingly of being a father and standing on the spot where so many families were torn apart by Thilo. Jagielka finds it particularly traumatic seeing a suitcase belonging to two-year-old Petr Eisler, gassed at Auschwitz. Also present is Avram Grant, who lost fifteen relatives in this human slaughterhouse. The former Chelsea, Portsmouth and West Ham manager delivers a short speech to the players. 'It's very important you came here; it's so good that you came here,' Grant tells them. 'It's important to talk about this and spread the message of what happened here.'

On the journey back to Kraków, Baines just stares out of the window, his William Boyd novel unopened by his side. Rooney, a player with more personal hinterland than most appreciate, talks of studying events at Auschwitz through watching the box set of *The World at War*, narrated by Lord Olivier, during Manchester United's away trips in Europe. On re-entering the Bubble, the seven players are asked to recount their experiences by the rest of Hodgson's squad. Scott Parker and Glen Johnson visit subsequently. Rooney informs FA staff he wishes to return the following day and adds that he wants to go back with his sons when they're older, teaching them about the most evil period in world history.

That evening, elsewhere in Kraków, a few of us go out for dinner with Grant. I'd never got on with Grant, never understanding why he's given good jobs when better talent's ignored, believing it's simply his networking skills that win him favour. Past disagreement is placed in proper perspective on such a day. Such visits are vital for all involved, also demonstrating to onlookers that England are not remote and self-important. Two years later, Hodgson sends Zigi Shipper a congratulations card on his belated bar mitzvah. Gerrard and Hart contribute to a Holocaust Educational Trust video still being shown in schools. It's important that England do not disengage.

Keeping on towards the Christmas Truce memorial, I weave through the grassy domain housing tributes to Allied Special Forces and the Dieppe Raid Memorial Garden. I detour away from the Pegasus Bridge Memorial so as not to disturb two Parachute Regiment veterans paying their respects to 7 Para, Lieutenant Colonel Pine-Coffin's group who assisted in repelling German attempts to regain the bridges in Normandy. Maybe the players remember it from *Call of Duty* (2003). As I continue, I remember a conversation with John Barnes, the son of Colonel Ken Barnes, about the days when England players would leave the hotel, experiencing life during tournaments, encountering locals not alienating them. Bobby Robson gave his players some freedom at Italia 90. 'It was strict but we could go out,' Barnes recalls of their time in Sardinia. 'We went to the beach, snuck out to the pub, and got pissed. OK, times have now changed. When we played Home Internationals everyone wanted to beat England because we're England. Now everyone wants to beat England because they believe England have this arrogance. They're not the best team but they behave like the best team: the environment created for them in terms of keeping them away from everyone, the press, the Wags. But then Costa Rica are going through at the World Cup in 2014. We have to have a much more humble experience about England.

'When Holland got to the World Cup final in 2010 they were in Sandton [Johannesburg], walking around the shopping centre the day before the final, mixing with people, and that's what we have to do.' Four years later, the Dutch stay at the Caesar Park Hotel right on Ipanema Beach and 100 metres from one of Rio's liveliest bars, Empório, where revellers cram the small rooms or spill on to the pavement until 5.30 a.m. Being in the noisy, merry centre of the World Cup does not stop the Dutch reaching the semi-finals. England are away from the caipirinha crowd, billeted briefly in a hotel on the far quieter São Conrado beach.

English press representatives being inquisitive souls, a couple of us book in for breakfast at the Royal Tulip as the FA check out, England having failed to make it past the group stage. I ask hotel staff whether they expected England to stay long. They admit they were accepting advance bookings from elsewhere for the knock-out round. Our years of hurt had reached their ears. There's time for a brief look around a hotel updated substantially in 2010 after guests posted unfavourable reviews such as 'a good hotel for the Soviet Union in the 70s'. As usual, the FA spares little expense in seeking to keep amused a group known for sliding swiftly into torpor. A games room is installed. The beach and a shopping mall are yards away. For those of Hodgson's players with a social conscience, the sprawling Rocinha favela is close by, and Daniel Sturridge, Danny Welbeck, Adam Lallana, Jack Wilshere and Fraser Forster do visit with the FA. Unexpected pleasures present themselves for the likes of Leighton Baines, a Smiths devotee, who bumps into Morrissey in the hotel bar. Baines also wiles away the free hours playing his guitar, listening to music from The Doors to Arctic Monkeys, The Beatles to Kasabian, and reading the surrealist Japanese writer Haruki Murakami, whose depiction of love, loss and the quixotic chimes with England. Baines is more adept than most at filling the down-time, but the general consensus among staff is that Hodgson's players have not suffered their usual ennui. Hardly surprising: Baines and company are on a magnificent beach staying in one of the most charismatic, photogenic cities on the planet, and playing in the land of Pelé, Romário, Ronaldo and Neymar. Besides, they aren't there long enough to get bored.

Encouraging signs of England embracing a tournament are actually detected two years earlier, at Euro 2012. In Kraków's scenic main square on 17 June, ten young men gather in front of a TV showing the Dutch losing to Portugal in the final Group B game in Kharkiv. They're eating pizza, sipping soft drinks, loving the drama on the screen, frequently cheering. They're ten England players, spending some spare time getting involved in the tournament, in a public space, politely dealing with a few selfie requests but otherwise just enjoying each other's company as well as the game, creating more camaraderie. The way it should be.

England chose a city-centre base in Poland after a wretched experience in 2010. The Royal Bafokeng Sports Campus in Rustenburg causes consternation. A retreat surrounded by high-wire fences, it is so cut off from the tournament in South Africa it could be South Mimms. 'Breakfast, train, lunch, bed, dinner, bed' is Rooney's verdict on daily life – and repeat. No wonder the players go stir crazy; it isn't just Fabio Capello's tactics depressing them. England want seclusion, to be able to train in peace, but they miss out on the World Cup party, on feeling life in one of the most beautiful if complicated countries on the planet.

The day after England vacate their Rustenburg base and head back to Blighty following defeat to Germany, I don blazer, tie and semi-ironed chinos and walk purposefully up to security, who kindly wave me through. All around are signs of FA investment, including a well-stocked library, although only David Peace's *The Damned Utd* and Lance Armstrong's *It's Not About the Bike* seem to have been borrowed. The FA has provided players with laptops, flat-screens and Wii games. While exploring, I text a friend in the Forces, who replies that one frustrated soldier in Afghanistan watching the TV as Capello's players succumb limply to Germany observes: 'The players should try coming out here for six months.'

Rustenburg seclusion is a major mistake. 'Who takes these decisions?' John Barnes asks. 'It's not only just about experiencing life. It's more to do with the perception people have of you. They believe we're arrogant anyway because we're English, and then you're actually proving it by demanding better protection, better hotels, nicer training facilities, whereas everyone else is getting on with it. We are detaching ourselves from the brotherhood of football at World Cups.'

The FA feels a duty to clubs to protect their valuable employees, understandably so, and club-versus-country tensions make the FA even more sensitive. England's hotel swiftly becomes a palace of paranoia with heavy security. Press and public are kept at arm's length. It fosters a culture of suspicion and superiority with little on the pitch to justify it. England are heading to Chantilly for the 2016 Euros and their hotel, Auberge du Jeu de Paume in Picardy, will be part Fontainebleau, part Fort Knox. Le Bubble. 'The players now expect that because it is what they've become used to, which is sad,' adds Barnes. 'The rest of the world doesn't behave like that. What happens now with the Premier League is everything's perfect: pitches, training ground, food. Young English players get everything done for them. When they're taken out of their comfort zone, going somewhere else, they have excuses now to lose.'

Barnes hooks another carriage-load of ideas to his train of thought, mentioning the Azzurri's collective desire to improve the image of Italian football in the wake of the *Calciopoli* referee-fixing scandal. 'Italy had a mission in 2006, saying, "We don't care what's going to be thrown at us",' says Barnes. Italy just drive on through, ignoring any imperfections in hotels, training and travel, to reach the final in Berlin, win the World Cup and show their pride in *calcio* and their country. In 1992, when Yugoslavia are excluded from the Euros because of their civil war, the Danes are scrambled from beach holidays and DIY duties, grab their boots, gratefully accept whatever accommodation is available in Sweden, and become European champions. In Brazil in 2014, some annoyance is expressed privately at the nine-mile trek from the England team hotel to training at the military base at Urca, a beautiful secluded spot at the foot of Sugarloaf Mountain. Wayne Rooney, among others, certainly feels the drive is excessive; it can take an hour when the few major road arteries through Rio are clogged with traffic. So does Gary Neville. 'Gary complains more about the journeys than the players do!' Roy Hodgson remarks with a smile. A few England players in Brazil even complain about having to walk a short distance for a massage. For the triumphant Danes in 1992, there is no moaning about queueing to have their muscles loosened or journey times to training; the Danes feel fortunate to be at the

tournament, love their underdog status, perform free of expectation, and rely on their team spirit (plus exceptional players in Peter
Schmeichel and Brian Laudrup). They seize the moment. And that
is why England's seventeenth most capped player of all time worries
about his country's latest representatives. 'Now we give players excuses
to lose by saying to them ,"We are going to give everything to make it
perfect for you,"; then if that isn't perfect, the players will blame the
food, the training pitch, the hotel – "There was noise outside, they
kept us awake,"' Barnes concludes.

The concept of embracing the tournament, as well as playing in it,
of exploring the world, finds an echo with another footballer with a
deep affinity with Sir Bobby Robson. As he does with Barnes, Robson
improves Jermaine Jenas as a player and a person. He invites his lads
outside the Bubble. 'When I was at Newcastle, that was a big part
of what Sir Bobby believed in because it developed the players,' says
Jenas. 'He was so well travelled with the clubs he managed. We played
Barcelona in the Champions League [in 2002] and my mindset is that
I'll be having to chase Xavi on this massive pitch tomorrow. I was
already crapping myself because I'm 19, about to go on this pitch in
the Champions League, and I want to rest.'

Robson has other ideas. 'Everyone, we're going out!' he informs his
Newcastle squad. 'I used to live in this city. I've got to show you the
unbelievable architecture.'

They start with the Sagrada Família, Antoni Gaudí's elaborate
basilica, and go on. 'Everywhere!' Jenas laughs. 'To the point where
we were walking around for an hour and a half, and even the coaches
were going, "Bobby!"'

'"No, they'll be fine."'

'"Our backs are killing us!"'

'"Take it in!"'

'I could see Sir Bobby was annoyed at people on their phones.
Anywhere we went, he took us for a walk. When we went to Basel one
year [2003], he took us on a walk that long we got lost. And we had a
game that night. He was a god.'

On duty for club or country, simply escaping the confines of the hotel is worthwhile, especially with England, for the scrutiny can be suffocating. From 2003 to 2009, Jenas goes on England trips all over, from the Algarve to Zagreb. 'You've got security outside your door,' he says. 'You can't really move. You couldn't do anything when you went away, especially in the squad we were in. We had Becks and he was a world star. I remember some nights when we would be in bed and there would be hundreds of people outside the hotel chanting his name, chanting, chanting, and I'd be thinking: "What the hell's going on?" I'd look out the window. And there were all these people chanting for Becks. I thought: "This is mental." It was like travelling with The Beatles.'

My short and winding road through rural Staffordshire continues, past the 'Home Run' memorial 'dedicated to the Allied escapers and evaders of WW2 and to their helpers of all nationalities and faiths who assisted them in returning to Great Britain to continue the common fight for freedom'. I trudge on, past a tree dedicated to a Harry Hudson by his friends and family on his death in 2012, marking his work in clandestine operations in Japanese-held territory. His war is so secret that details 'cannot be revealed from the National Archives until 2025'. Later, I ring an army friend about what sort of work Hudson might have been engaged in. 'He wasn't in uniform,' comes the simple reply. And he was a hero. At 20.

I think back to times covering England Under-21s, when one player is reprimanded by FA staff for laughing, nervously, when seeing the room full of spectacles at Auschwitz. I think back to another Under-21s finals, the 2000 version in Slovakia. England share a Holiday Inn on the outskirts of Bratislava with the Italians and Turks. Andrea Pirlo and Christian Abbiati sit in reception, lost in their books, sipping occasionally from little bottles of water. Helped by a goal from Pirlo, Italy defeat Frank Lampard, Jamie Carragher, Ledley King and company in the opening game of Group B. Elsewhere in Bratislava on the same day, 27 May, Slovakia beat Turkey. All four squads are invited by the Slovak Football Association to an evening of culture and entertainment in a local castle for the usual folk dancing and falconry displays. The Italians and the Turks walk around, experiencing the event, engaging. Most of the English group huddle in a corner, like truculent children unhappy to be dragged somewhere.

I think back to the Championship in the Czech Republic in 2015 when Gareth Southgate's players are driven from their Olomouc hotel to the stadium. As the players peer from the coach window, a colleague and I pace out the distance of the journey: 127 yards. FA claims about 'Uefa protocol' are laughed off by organizers. The players also see the absurdity of this molly-coddling and stroll back post-match. It doesn't take long. They survive.

The coach story from Olomouc rouses memories of the bus stop from Spa in 2000. More Bubble trouble. A photograph of the card-school staying on England's parked-up bus outside the team hotel, refusing to halt their gambling simply because the journey is completed, prompts criticism of the regime under Kevin Keegan. Certain players are undoubtedly uneasy about the card-school, believing it affects squad dynamics simply because of the time involved. It's deemed a distraction. Most players feel there's nothing wrong with wiling away down-time between games and are exasperated by the media's fascination with stars, their money and how they should be spending their tournament time.

Two years later, after Sven-Göran Eriksson's side return from the World Cup in Japan, the *News of the World* publishes a photograph of a cheque for £30,000 written by Michael Owen to Kieron Dyer as part of the settling-up of the six-week card-school playing thirteen-card brag with Wayne Bridge, David James and Teddy Sheringham during the preparation camps in Dubai and South Korea, and then at the competition itself. Annoyed at the suggestion he has a gambling problem, Owen points out he has more than £15,000 coming *in* from card-school debts; his outlay is effectively £2,500 a week, a fraction of his Liverpool salary, let alone endorsements. A man with experience of five tournaments with England, Owen remains resolute in defending his behaviour on the road, opening up on life in the Bubble. 'It's easy for someone to look in and say, "Oh, they're playing cards," but what else do you do when you're away?' he asks when we meet at his Cheshire stables. 'We didn't have computers back then. There's television that's foreign. If anything, it's good getting the lads together having a card-school. I wouldn't say it was small sums. We're getting into the realm of "what's small?", "is gambling right?" and "is it going to cause friction because someone owes someone five grand?" If any figure gets out into the public domain, losing five grand or ten grand would upset the vast majority of the population. It is totally understandable.' But as a percentage of a wealthy footballer's wages is it not also totally permissible? I enquire. 'Exactly. It was also a way of passing the time, being with each other, bonding. Try being in a hotel for six weeks. You train for an hour and a half, and there's matches, but apart from that you're going stir crazy. If there hadn't been a card-school, people would be stir crazy. It's got to that stage where people are not as keen to go [with] England as they always were. It's so boring. It's not playing for England but the lead-up . . .' His sentence collapses into a sigh. Surely there's always a round of golf? 'Who plays golf nowadays of the England team? Maybe five or six. Yes, you can play golf, but you're not allowed to play golf a day or two before the game.'

Owen pauses, realizing he needs to place the footballer's five-star existence in perspective. 'It is laid on. You can act like a spoilt brat. There's people with no food out there. There's people with nothing out there.' As unpalatable as it may be to many, Owen provides an insight into the Modern Footballer's Thinking, into the downside of life in the Bubble, a reality that some players struggle with. 'If I was at my club, all my home comforts are there, my family's there, my house is there, and I go into the club and the food's normal,' Owen explains. 'With England, you're taken out of your perfect normal routine and, OK, shoved in a nice hotel room. [But] I don't care how nice your hotel room is if you wake up at seven a.m. [and] you're in there until ten, you're stir crazy already. OK, you go out training for an hour and a half, but then you're in there from lunchtime until eleven at night, looking at four walls for six, seven days. You're basically counting the days when you're with England until the game.'

Hold on, Michael, other nations manage to combat world weariness at tournaments. 'I'm just sticking up for the card-school or going round to rooms and playing computer games, just whatever England players want to do to pass time. I wouldn't say, "Ban card-schools because you can lose a couple of grand and that might upset you, and you won't play well for England on a Thursday night in the World Cup." It's a good story but it's all very far-fetched. A card-school wouldn't distract from your concentration in the bloody World Cup. We were so focused.'

Back in Staffordshire, I continue past the commemoration of the Cockleshell Heroes and past a pill box, a reminder of the threat of Operation Sea Lion, Hitler's planned invasion of England. As I keep going, I think of footballers with military connections, goalkeepers like John Ruddy of Norwich City and, briefly, England. Ruddy's father did a tour of duty in Northern Ireland. His grandfather and two uncles served in the RAF. When Ruddy marries in 2012, his best man flies back from Afghanistan and the wedding list requests that guests donate to Help for Heroes. Ruddy's someone with his profession in the right perspective. Not all footballers inhabit the Bubble.

Scarcely 100 yards on, a man painstakingly cuts the grass, snaking in and out of a line of conifers. Here stands the Christmas Truce memorial, a statue of a handshake and a football designed by a 10-year-old Newcastle United fan called Spencer Turner and dedicated by Prince William, the FA president, on a chilly December day back in 2014. For all the doubts expressed about the occurrence of one Truce game in no man's land – some suspect there was a series of smaller games along the Front at Christmas 1914 – the concept alone is powerful: football uniting warring foes. The small museum adjacent to the memorial gives an insight into the harrowing events preceding and following the Truce match. Bloodshed on an industrial scale. As I retrace my steps, I think of the looming hundredth anniversary of the start of the Battle of the Somme on 1 July 1916. England representatives will commemorate the event with a 160-mile round-trip visit from their Chantilly base to the sites of the muddy, bloody trenches where the British Army suffered 19,240 deaths and 38,230 injuries on the first day alone.

Among those who fell in Flanders that Godforsaken day was an England international, the former chairman of the Professional

Footballers' Association, Evelyn Lintott. I recall the words of the PFA's Gordon Taylor when we visit the Somme in 2014 as football honoured the centenary of the start of the First World War. 'The very idea of footballers going over the top, marching towards the enemy, being shot, being gassed is beyond belief,' says Taylor as we stand by the grave of Donald Bell, the only English professional footballer to be awarded the Victoria Cross. We're near Arras, treading carefully past piles of old ordnance ploughed up by farmers in their 'Iron Harvest'. Reasons other than the wind and the cold cause Taylor's eyes to moisten at the memory of 1 July 1916. Lintott, a sturdy half-back, is capped seven times by England, and proves so popular among his peers that he's voted PFA chairman. Five days after Lintott succumbs, Bell storms a German machine-gun nest, earning that VC. Five days further on, the former Newcastle United and Bradford Park Avenue player is shot in the head, his helmet giving no protection from the ferocity of the fire-fight at Contalmaison, the spot now revered as Bell's Redoubt. 'It is Dante's Inferno,' Taylor tells me. 'Then you heard the way they talked about it: it was a matter of duty and honour, King and country, death or glory. Your Country Needs You. Men like Lintott and Bell were the founding fathers of the professional game, acting with bravery and dignity, real leaders. They were heroes on the football field and heroes to the tune of a different whistle here. We hope that what was in the genes of those heroes remains in the genes of sports men and women today.' Amen to that.

As I leave the Christmas Truce memorial behind, I remember my visit a month before to Wycombe Wanderers' training ground to see their charismatic manager, Gareth Ainsworth. Towards the tail-end of his twenty-four-year playing career, Ainsworth represents his peers at the unveiling in 2010 of the Footballers' Battalions memorial in Longueval close to Delville Wood, nicknamed Devil's Wood such is the carnage. Ainsworth blows a whistle as if to echo those going over the top and delivers a moving elegy. 'I read the epitaph "for your tomorrow we gave our today",' recalls Ainsworth. 'Even now, now you've just reminded me, I get the hairs standing up on my arms, just thinking about that, blowing that whistle, a whistle that was around in those days, saying those lines. I was humbled, I was honoured, and I will never forget.' He cherishes this chance to salute those professionals who lie buried in French soil. 'I'll keep their memory alive. I felt something out there on those fields, standing there on the cold morning, looking across the fields; even though they were beautiful fields, standing in the cemetery, you still feel something. You go there and breathe it in. There don't seem any birds flying around. It's quiet. You can feel what the men went through. Maybe there's something still knocking around with the amount of casualties, the amount of death. There's something about that place that will affect anyone. It was almost an epiphany. I felt I have to bring someone back here. I've got a son, 8 years old, and I'll take him when he's old enough.'

Those of the England squad who visit the Somme during Euro 2016 will be similarly moved. 'Every single person, no matter how old, what colour, what intelligence level, will have somebody out there in the same shoes who fought and died,' says Ainsworth, who took his Wycombe players there in 2014. 'You just have to find them, hear the stories, and realize "that could have been me". You'd find a story that was you: the life and soul of the party, the quiet one, the one who had turmoil in his life. They were all out there fighting, and that's what hit home to me. My players understood it. Thirty per cent probably knew what they were going to. Seventy per cent were shocked when you go to Lochnagar, see the crater, hear about the devastation [caused by a mine]. Such a big conflict. Such a big moment in history. It's important that we go there and be shocked.'

Leaving briefly behind such ruminations, I pass the Children's Woodland, a play area for visitors' younger offspring, and my mind immediately turns to the remarkable work performed by a former England centre-half, one of the stars of Italia 90. Mark Wright would love to talk to the current wearers of the Three Lions and explain how they can step out of the Bubble and make a difference. Wright and his wife Sue foster children and campaign for others to follow suit. 'In football, you're in a bubble, so driven to succeed that fostering never even entered my head,' says Wright, sitting next to Sue during our conversation in Manchester. 'Meeting my wife, who was a child protection barrister, some of the stories that came home, about the abuse and neglect, the horrors that could happen to a child, I couldn't believe it was happening here. It broke my heart. We've had six children come through the door to look after, and adopted one of them. Our daughter Sonia, who was adopted, is treated no differently. It is the most remarkable thing you can do. I always felt I was a very good father, always looked after them, always wanted to be with them; I wasn't one who went out drinking every afternoon, or going out nightclubbing all the time. I liked to go home and be with my children. They get older, they move on, and another one comes in. We wanted to make a difference in this country, to raise awareness for fostering and adoption. There's a ten thousand deficit of foster carers.

'I trained morning, noon and night to get to the levels I did as a footballer and I loved every single minute. From being an uncompromising centre-half, playing alongside Terry Butcher with England, and brought up by Gary Briggs and Malcolm Shotton at Oxford United, I've gone real soft because all I want to do is help the kids. If we can, I'll regard myself as a success. The challenges in fostering are more than when you play football by a mile, but more rewarding as well. In loads of cases these children are coming from broken backgrounds, whether [it's] neglect, abuse, physical or mental, and they have nowhere to go. Then they're picked up from school, clothes thrown in a bin-liner, and off they go and plonked with you. They're petrified. They don't know whether they have a bed, a home, when they're going to see their parents again, wondering what they've done wrong. They don't smile a lot because they're missing their parents, brothers and sisters. The day they start to smile you know you're on the right track. There's nothing better than the laughter of children.'

I walk on past the Anglo-Japanese Peace Garden and thoughts fly back to 2002. During the World Cup finals in Japan, some of Sven-Göran Eriksson's players staying on the secluded Awaji Island, Kobe, discuss taking the bullet train down to the Hiroshima Peace

Memorial Museum. Some of us reporters visit, reading the survivor testimonies from that August day in 1945, and chronicle our experiences of the trip. 'What's Hiroshima?' one of the players asks. Such ignorance is even more reason for making the trip. None do in the end. They stay in the Bubble. Pity.

The FA wants to make players stronger, to cope with the tournament crucible. 'There are things we can do internally around mental resilience, dealing with pressure,' says technical director Dan Ashworth. 'With clubs, players go back to normality, back to families, back to homes. When you're in Brazil or the Czech Republic, you're in a bubble and can't replicate the players' normal lives. I talk to the senior players and they're all used to going away on a Friday, playing a game on a Saturday, and coming back, but not many would have experienced a period of time away from families, and are in danger of going stir crazy.' Capello could never understand how players just couldn't entertain themselves. 'They do have to deal with it,' adds Ashworth. 'We've got to use that time more wisely.'

Visiting the Christmas Truce memorial is time spent wisely. Nearing the end of my visit to the Arboretum, I climb up to the Armed Forces Memorial and look at the engraved names of those who've fallen in the service of their country. Space on those slabs of stone awaits those who have yet to fall. It's a poignant sight, one that will make players, anyone, everyone, think. It might even prick the Bubble.

16

Press and Pressure

STANDING IN THE tunnel at Wembley, awaiting the referee's call to arms, must be one of the most vivid sporting experiences imaginable. Representing England, lining up with revered peers and good friends, must be so emotional. Hearing the fans' rising roar, anticipating the drama in store, must quicken the pulse further. So I ask one experienced former England international to describe the feelings gripping him as he prepares to walk out at Wembley. Pride? Patriotism? Excitement? 'No,' he replies without hesitation. 'I just think about what mark I'm going to get in the ratings in the papers. If it's bad, my life's shit for a bit.' He insists his words remain unattributed. He's even sensitive about revealing sensitivity to press criticism.

A grievance of those dwelling in England's dressing-room, as well as those residing in the FA corridors of power, is that the media medusa, and particularly its written strand, can harm the national team. Another player confides that complaining about the English press is like 'moaning about the English weather – get on with it'. Scrutiny is far fiercer with England than with clubs, even Manchester United.

Managers rarely escape Fleet Street's cross-hairs. Much of the excess is well chronicled: the vilification of Bobby Robson before Italia 90, dragging Graham Taylor through the vegetable patch three years later, and that unpleasant back-page mock-up of Terry Venables with his head in a noose in the run-up to Euro 96. Even during that brief summer of hope, Venables' press conferences are split down the middle between admirers and adversaries. How he keeps his sangfroid to lead England to within a penalty-kick of the final is remarkable, especially as his business dealings attract so much media interest, not least investigations by such respected programmes as BBC's *Panorama* and Channel 4's *Dispatches*. The focus on Venables is intense, certainly compared to misdemeanours occurring elsewhere in the financial world, but it reflects a media absorbed by his dispute with Alan Sugar over Tottenham Hotspur and public obsession with all matters England. Venables himself is so intrigued by print coverage during his spell as England manager that an FA emissary checks for him the first editions of the newspapers when they get dropped at King's Cross Station at midnight.

On succeeding Venables, Glenn Hoddle is initially friendly with Fleet Street but becomes wary, particularly on discovering its sharper edge. Moments of levity do occur. When he throws out the cliché that England prepare a certain tactical way for the visit to Katowice in May 1997 – 'when it's horses for courses' – the revered *Guardian* correspondent David Lacey immediately replies: 'No, Glenn, in Poland, it's horses for main courses.' It's not always so relaxed. Later that year, within thirty minutes of the FA releasing a statement about Hoddle splitting from his first wife, photographers and reporters camp outside his house. The announcement comes shortly after Hoddle masterminds England's World Cup qualification in Rome. That clash of contrasts, professional pleasure and personal pain, is always fertile territory for the press. Newspapers hate plateaus in form and fortune; we're like stockbrokers, profiting from movement either way.

Before the 2002 World Cup, England are training in Dubai when Sven-Göran Eriksson calls a team meeting to apologize for the media hysteria over his paramour Ulrika Jonsson. 'Welcome to England!' laughs Robbie Fowler. Eriksson's always a mixture of the sanguine and the bemused over the prurient press; he simply cannot understand the interest in his eventful private life. He rarely gets angry with the media, though. He rings one day and we chat about England's qualification for Euro 2004. It's all very polite. It takes a while before it sinks in he's actually gently admonishing me over the quizzical tone of my newspaper's coverage. As storms go, it's a summer breeze compared to the Alex Ferguson hair-drier. Eriksson even telephones Urs Meier to say sorry for the abusive 'Urs Hole' headlines in the English press after the Swiss referee rules out a Sol Campbell goal that would have guided England towards the semi-finals of Euro 2004.

Eriksson's successor, Steve McClaren, manages to fall out with some of the hack pack before even taking the job in 2006 when he's still assisting the Swede in Germany. Over afternoon tea with three reporters he trusts in Baden-Baden, McClaren reveals he's interested in bringing in an England legend, Alan Shearer, as a coach in his new regime. Good story. When the first editions drop of those three newspapers, with the story splashed over the back pages, my blood goes cold. I swallow my pride, quickly file the story for the *Telegraph*'s second edition and hit the phone to television and radio contacts. Within ten minutes I'm outside the town hall in Baden-Baden, going live and pouring scorn on McClaren's plan. He's watching in the team hotel, Schloss Bühlerhöhe, as a steamed-up reporter fulminates that he'd rather have Shearer in charge and McClaren, a first-rate coach, as number two. At training the following day, McClaren marches across to demand an explanation. The only explanation, and apology, I owe is to three colleagues, for reacting pettily to their excellent story, commandeering the airwaves and having a rant. But not McClaren. 'Feed three and you starve the rest,' I tell him. Others, equally piqued, wade into the argument.

Players notice immediate changes. 'When we drifted into the McClaren era, it was "don't read anything"; it was another kind of method of how to deal with the pressure of playing for England,' says Jermaine Jenas. 'All of a sudden there were no newspapers.' McClaren is soon dubbed 'likeable but limited' by the papers. There is a likeable individual somewhere in McClaren but he seems to have taken advice on PR from so many quarters, friends, journalists and gurus, that it's not clear what's the real McClaren. Wooing the press, as McClaren briefly tries, is a dangerous game. England managers should remember how Icarus fared when flying too close to the sun. McClaren is soon nicknamed 'Bungle' after failing with one of his folksy aphorisms. Before a Euro 2008 qualifier with Israel, McClaren observes: 'That was the pre-season friendlies, now for the rainbow.' It sounds plausible, the prospect of sunshine coming out, crock of gold, that sort of thing. Of course, the newspapers go to town on 'rainbow', immediately lining McClaren up with Geoffrey, George and Zippy from the popular ITV children's series. McClaren goes ballistic, demanding the FA contacts reporters to ascertain where on earth 'rainbow' came from. We explain patiently, and FA staff go back through the tape. Even they hear 'now for the rainbow'. In fact, as a furious McClaren explains, he said: 'Now for the real bull.' Real bull or rainbow? Neither makes much sense. When he eventually calms down, McClaren enlightens us: apparently the 'real bull' emerges in a bull ring when the warm-up bulls have gone. Anyway, it's a new one on us and 'Bungle' sticks. Almost a decade on, England correspondents routinely refer to McClaren as 'Bungle'.

The nickname proves prescient. McClaren's dismissed after the rain-lashed Euro qualifier defeat to Croatia in November 2007, awaking to headlines ranging from the *Mail*'s famous 'A Wally with a Brolly' to 'The Man with No Shame' in the *Daily Mirror*, and has to brave a brutal farewell press conference at Sopwell. A word of advice to departing managers: don't make photographers' lives easier by lingering under a sign reading EXIT, especially EMERGENCY EXIT. A security man pulls the curtain back from the door as McClaren enters and departs, giving the snappers ample opportunity for pictures inevitably captioned 'Curtains for McClaren'. 'Bungle', 'exit' and 'curtains' are all stories mentioned on the coaches' media training day on the Pro Licence course at St George's Park.

P45 press conferences are the ultimate in demeaning. I'm in the front row at Sopwell, ringside. Sitting in the back row is Kathryn McClaren, listening to her chastened husband talking of his 'saddest day', 'my failure', and accepting 'full responsibility'. The prospect of £2m compensation only partly softens the blow. McClaren is forever associated with one of the bleakest periods in England's history yet the presence of Mrs McClaren is a timely reminder of the human side to public figures. Having children of school-age makes the headlines and fall-out even more painful.

McClaren's replacement, Fabio Capello, settles in quickly, bringing real authority, and his press conferences initially border on the reverential. But he apparently resembles Postman Pat, according to a couple of players at the 2010 World Cup, and the nickname's leaked to the press which keeps some back pages entertained. In the usual flip-flop way of the English media, the Italian is praised as a much-needed disciplinarian when he arrives yet an out-of-touch martinet when he departs. Capello leaves shaking his head at the inconsistency of the media.

Next to step into the coconut shy is Roy Hodgson, whose slight lisp is cruelly lampooned in the *Sun*'s 2012 front-page headline 'Bwing On the Euwos'. The personal nature of this attack wins him sympathy. Subsequent treatment of Hodgson is, by and large, relatively kind. He is clearly a decent man and the alternative English options are few. Harry Redknapp enjoys the support, and frequently the company, of many reporters but Hodgson proves popular among the media, partly because he doesn't have favourites. Players tell reporters regularly on and off the record that they like Hodgson. They would say that, wouldn't they? Not always. When dressing-room support for Capello waned, concerns are voiced discreetly.

Those who take on the 'Impossible Job' may be the main lightning conductors, but the players too suffer vitriolic headlines, for missed penalties, strike threats and goalkeeping gaffes. When John Barnes is targeted by thousands of England fans during the San Marino game at Wembley on 17 February 1993, he believes the boos and shouts of 'Fuck off Barnes' spring from an article that morning in the *Daily Mirror* which sputters: 'How can John Barnes play for England when he wants their cricket team to lose to the West Indies?' The Jamaican-born Barnes, who was joking about the cricket, is outraged at the time but is phlegmatic now. 'I was very fortunate that Graham Taylor would always say to me: "Whether it's positive or negative, ignore it. If people are going to say how great you are, ignore that. I will tell you, your team-mates will tell you, the people who care about you will tell

Thirty Years of Hurt. England fans get behind the team in the unforgettable summer of 1996.

Shearer, Darren Anderton, Gascoigne and Steve McManaman celebrate Teddy Sheringham's second goal (*right*) as the Dutch are thumped at Wembley, but the reign of Terry Venables (*below*) was lamentably short and a home victory eluded us.

England did taste tournament success in 1997, as Paul Scholes's goal against Italy set them on the way to victory in Le Tournoi. It may not have been the world's loveliest trophy, but David Seaman still got to lift some silverware.

Glenn Hoddle went on to mastermind another crucial result against Italy in World Cup qualifying that year, with Ian Wright at the forefront of his plans and giving everything for the shirt, alongside Paul Ince (*right*), captain for the night in another brilliant piece of managerial thinking.

Diego Maradona may be painted as the arch-villain for his antics in 1986 (*left*), but England players need to be more like Michael Owen, below making contact with Mauricio Pochettino to win a penalty in 2002, in exploiting challenges of those like Argentina.

Owen's goalscoring expertise, famously at France '98 and (*bottom*) in vain against Romania at Euro 2000, needs to be tapped into by the FA for the optimum development of emerging England footballers.

The Golden Generation. David Beckham, Scholes, Wayne Rooney, Steven Gerrard and Frank Lampard congratulate Owen on opening the scoring in the Euro 2004 quarter-final against Portugal.

In Lisbon, though, Beckham was unable to replicate his penalty success of two years previously in Japan. The fans travel the world to fly the flag for England — they deserve so much more.

Bad luck, or poor decisions, can play a part. Manuel Neuer is beaten by Lampard at the 2010 World Cup, but no goal is given.

Dejection, thy name is Stevie. Gerrard after his mistake against France in 2004 (*top*), penalty miss against Germany in 2006 (*above*), and mugging by Luis Suárez and Uruguay in 2014 (*left*). Who will ultimately captain England to glory?

The National Football Centre in Burton upon Trent, opened by the Duke of Cambridge in 2012, is where the masterplan must be made. Many aspects of football in this country need to change, including learning from past mistakes and empowering more young English coaches.

Another long-overdue inauguration, this time of Bobby Moore's statue at Wembley in 2007. As Gary Lineker told me, that tribute to the 1966 captain can become the symbol to show that it is possible to end the years of hurt.

BOBBY MOORE OBE
1941 · 1993

IMMACULATE FOOTBALLER · IMPERIAL DEFENDER
IMMORTAL HERO OF 1966 · FIRST ENGLISHMAN TO RAISE
THE WORLD CUP ALOFT · FAVOURITE SON OF LONDON'S
EAST END · FINEST LEGEND OF WEST HAM UNITED
NATIONAL TREASURE · MASTER OF WEMBLEY
LORD OF THE GAME · CAPTAIN EXTRAORDINARY
GENTLEMAN FOR ALL TIME

Rooney on his way to becoming England's record goalscorer (*top*) as England win in San Marino to seal their qualification for Euro 2016 under the management of Roy Hodgson and Gary Neville, with a new generation of talented players like Dele Alli at their disposal.

you how well or badly you are doing. The fans, for whatever reason, may love you or hate you, so ignore them." It was difficult, obviously. I was very fortunate that I didn't take the praise too greatly either. You know what Gazza is like with the press: you say he's "great", he loves you and speaks to you; you say he's "crap", he doesn't want to talk to you. It affected me, so I was fortunate I had good people around me.'

A Liverpool team-mate of Barnes', David James, is ridiculed for letting Andreas Ivanschitz's shot slip under him in a disappointing 2-2 World Cup qualifying draw in Vienna on 4 September 2004. He's promptly depicted as an ass. The *Sun* immediately scrambles Mavis the Donkey, saying she's a better alternative. Eriksson decides on Paul Robinson, instead of James or Mavis, for the tie with Poland four days later. Angry about the treatment of the affable James, England's senior players decide to boycott the press. The vow of silence lasts during the trip to Katowice. More recently, FA staff and players are aggrieved at press reaction to the Andros Townsend 'space monkey' episode that dampens celebrations over qualifying for the 2014 World Cup finals. Hodgson is accused of telling a story with racist connotations when it's just a rather odd joke.

In Rio in 2014, the FA fumes when two reporters are caught watching the private section of training at Urca. England feel that crosses the line and they also fear footage being taken of their set-plays on camera-phones – something that no England reporter would ever do. England staff are convinced Italy know their set-plays in advance of the meeting in Manaus. There's no suggestion the Azzurri are spying on England training in Brazil but it has been known with other countries. On climbing up a tree in the Black Forest in 2006, one English reporter finds a spy from the opposition FA higher up. Few secrets exist. England never get the other team's line-up wrong.

I've certainly spied on England training – anything to acquire information on the starting eleven for my newspaper. A-level German serves me well when chatting to German police patrolling the training-ground perimeter at Baden-Baden in 2006, and a quick-ish pair of heels helps to escape security in Saitama in 2002 and Moscow in 2007. Seeking vantage points, I've hidden in corporate boxes and up trees. I dare a stoned security guard at one venue to show me training and he willingly accepts the challenge, leading me to a fine viewing gallery. I'd never run anything tactically, only the identity of the eleven starters.

Despite tensions over spying and occasional stories, relations between England press box and dressing-room are fairly civilized currently, certainly compared with previous eras. 'Honestly, I'd say over the last three and a half years that I've been with England the press coverage has been entirely fair,' says Gary Neville, Hodgson's assistant. 'There might have been the odd moment, maybe the Andros Townsend thing, or watching training in Urca in Brazil. But it is probably the most calm and tranquil it's been. In the past there have been moments, back in the late nineties and early 2000s, where I thought it got far too personal, far too intense. The David James thing became too personal. It became a critique of personality, rather than a critique of performance. That's too far. We should stick to football, stick to criticism of selection and method. What we should stay away from is depicting people as animals, or depicting people as vegetables. That's where it becomes humiliating. It can damage particularly young players. It can put them in trepidation.

'But it has calmed down. The reporting has become a lot more mature; there's a different type of reporter now. People are more interested in tactics, team selection, why did he pick him?' The focus on tactics is even keener in Spain where Neville works for four months at Valencia. 'It's very, very intense over here. I go into a press conference thinking they are going to ask me about how I lost the game and keep it general but it's very different. They'll dig into the game. They'll ask questions like, "Why did you bring Santiago Mina on on the left, and move Rodrigo Moreno to the right? I couldn't see the logic behind that." I'm thinking: "Oh, right, good question." In England, I'm not sure you'd get asked that that often. In Spain, they're asking that level of detail twenty minutes into a press conference. They won't focus on the referee or sensationalism. They're very much into, "Why did the coach do that?" It's getting more that way in England: analysis is becoming more tactical, match reports are becoming more analytical, rather than the more sensational types that you'd see ten to fifteen years ago. We're getting a more mature press now.'

Quality abounds in the work of journalists like Martin Samuel (*Mail*), Paul Joyce (*Express*), Paul Hayward (*Telegraph*), Sam Wallace (*Telegraph*), Danny Taylor (*Guardian/Observer*), Jonny Northcroft (*Sunday Times*), Matt Dickinson (*Times*) and Oliver Kay (*Times*), among many others. They write eloquently against the clock, calmly hitting deadlines, delivering strong copy in 'runner' match reports when up to 1,400 words are filed in chunks during the game. All of us want England to win. We get to know the players, ghost their columns and books, meet and interview them in far-flung places. We're like weathermen: if it's raining, we can't kid anyone it's sunny. If England are poor, as they have been for too long, we'll say so, but with a glimmer of hope for the future. We're critical friends. There is genuine excitement at the fearless football of Dele Alli, Harry Kane and Jamie Vardy in Berlin in March 2016.

Fallings-out still occur. Players object to the 'Moldova Legover' story at the Grove when some of the Wags stay in part of the team hotel, far from the locked-down players' section, on the eve of a World Cup qualifier in 2013. The whole Wags phenomenon is largely a media obsession, reaching its apogee amid the cobbled streets and bijou eateries of Baden-Baden in 2006, partly because they're staying in the same hotel as many of the reporters. The FA should never have mentioned that Baden-Baden's a spa town. It's difficult to escape them: Carly Zucker, Coleen Rooney, Cheryl Tweedy and their glitzy company get dressed up and go dancing in Max's nightclub, where Lampard's then girlfriend, Elen Rives, is spotted on a table singing 'I Will Survive'. A group of journalists is asked by the owner of Garibaldi's restaurant to vacate the table mid-meal – bill paid on the house – as it's needed for the wealthy Wags. At the high tide of the high heels, the *Telegraph* asks me to go shopping with the Wags and chronicle the experience. I hit the high street in Baden-Baden with one friendly family, admiring their insistence on paying for everything with €500 notes however small the purchase, and don't file a word. They're families enjoying themselves, desperately proud of their footballing loved ones, and have made many sacrifices them-selves to facilitate their careers.

The Spanish paper *ABC* calls the Wags 'hooligans with Visa cards'. Thank God it's Visa – Fifa-approved. 'Wags' even enters the *Oxford English Dictionary* in 2007. Rio Ferdinand subsequently acknowledges that Baden-Baden became 'a bit of a circus in terms of the whole Wag situation'. The Wags are undoubtedly a distraction, but also a symp-tom of a deeper malaise: a narcissism in the 'Golden Generation' at that time, overly puritanical media mores, and the clamour for glamour. Deeper reflection is required. English football needs to be more grown up. England don't go out of the World Cup in Germany at the quarter-final stage because of the Wags, but because they prove brittle in stressful situations and poor at penalties. The missus isn't responsible for the misses.

On arrival in the Premier League, two highly intelligent foreign coaches, Louis van Gaal and Jürgen Klopp, soon realize that the English media is more obsessed with personality than philosophy. They make sensible points about the need for a winter break, but it's rarely debated at length. Playground rules apply. When Paul Scholes delivers a thoughtful appraisal of Jack Wilshere, arguing that he needs to impose his talent more, it's whipped up into spiky Punch and Judy headlines. Fortunately, Wilshere sees through the storm and contacts Scholes to try to learn and improve.

Players and managers are increasingly wary of the press. Changing dynamics loosen the bonds, not least Glenn Hoddle decreeing that the press will not travel on the England plane any more (some nonsense to do with numbers), immediately ending the 'carousel culture' where players and reporters mingle and chat, address issues, even settle scores in some distant airport while awaiting luggage. Also accelerating the divide is the click-bait nature of some websites, the media's focus on wealth and Wags as much as the football, and the desire of clubs (and occasionally the FA) to channel exclusive content towards their own websites. The schism damages England; players need to engage more with the media, leaving their Bubble, dealing with criticism, being tougher and taking responsibility more. It's confronting the fear factor. 'There's too much fear with England,' says Peter Reid, getting to the heart of the problem.

More contact with the dressing-room, more mutual respect, might soften some of the post-defeat assaults. Some players are excellent with the media: Jack Butland, owner of nine GCSEs, earns regular praise for his goalkeeping and ambassadorial qualities. There is genuine sadness amongst the England press corps when Butland fractures his ankle in Berlin on 26 March 2016. He's very popular. On the eve of an FA Cup weekend in February 2015 I have an interview set up at Stoke City's training ground with Charlie Adam, but unfortunately he gets injured in training. Butland willingly steps in at the last moment, filling a double-page spread. Journalists won't forget that. While I'm waiting in reception at Clayton Wood, Ryan Shawcross walks past with what seems an air of disdain towards the press. Journalists don't forget that. Shawcross is a highly capable centre-back but receives little support in the media. Controversy still lingers over his 2010 tackle that broke Aaron Ramsey's leg. The image also remains strong of Shawcross being outfoxed by Sweden's Zlatan Ibrahimović in Stockholm in 2012. Better communication with the media might address these issues, improving matters. That contrasts with Owen Hargreaves' intelligent response to criticism, namely over his right to play for England having been born in Canada and educated at Bayern Munich. Hargreaves and the FA call a meeting with England correspondents at the Lowry in Manchester. For forty minutes Hargreaves speaks eloquently about his love of representing England, his parents' roots in the country, and he changes the views of the sceptics in the room. Contact helps.

Social media also assists dialogue. Direct messages, even simple tweets, maintain contact. I get a fact wrong about Wayne Rooney's choice of shirt number which he helpfully clarifies for my benefit. When I mistakenly suggest Michael Owen commuted to Newcastle United by helicopter, he points out this is a myth and I could correct my mistake. One day I receive a DM from a (now former) England international looking to change clubs, so I make a discreet call on his behalf (while also suggesting he tell his manager). Information and assistance still flows between dressing-room and press room but sadly not with the regularity or rapidity of before. The likes of John Cross of the *Mirror* and Neil Ashton of the *Sun* still have exceptional contacts with the dressing-room.

It's not just the headlines angering players, it's the reverberations. It's not just the star's life being 'shit for a bit', it's the collateral damage to those around them. When Rob Green errs embarrassingly against the US at the 2010 World Cup, being beaten by Clint Dempsey's daisy-cutter, his family's besieged. Green's sister has only recently given birth and reporters are climbing into her garden. His ex-girlfriend is door-stepped. Talking to FA officials in Rustenburg, they despair of the treatment of one of the most well-liked members of Capello's squad and his family. When players do manage a few hours out of the claustrophobic Royal Bafokeng Sports Campus, visiting a safari park, they find themselves the ones stalked – by photographers. 'A couple of the lads would have liked to see them eaten by lions!' laughs Joe Cole at the time.

Further corroboration of the madness of St George comes with Operation Orphan. When Michael Dawson flies in to Rustenburg, replacing the injured Rio Ferdinand, I call the FA to remind them that the incoming centre-half sponsors a 12-year-old called Aubrey at a local SOS Children's Village orphanage through one of Tottenham Hotspur's admirable community schemes. Sensing some useful PR and a feelgood moment, the FA duly sets off for Tlhabane township with Dawson – and more than ten camera crews. Everyone's keen on a photo-opportunity. The FA wants Aubrey in an England shirt; Spurs, understandably, want him pictured in one of their shirts. Fair enough. It's their initiative funded by first-team players' fines. When the rolling media maul arrives at the orphanage, a problem immediately presents itself: Aubrey's standing there smiling, wearing a Manchester United ROONEY top. A United fan. They're everywhere. Fortunately the FA has brought an England shirt while an enterprising photographer nips out to buy a Spurs top. Three separate wardrobe changes and photo-shoots later, everyone's happy. The down-to-earth Dawson's brilliant, spending time with Aubrey, and everyone hails Operation

Orphan a success. 'You must come and meet my orphans now,' one of the FA overlords instructs me the following morning. The episode sums up life with England: assorted agendas, not least club versus country, and the ravenousness of the media.

For all England's flaws, interest in the national team remains huge. I cannot think of one press-box regular who does not want England to succeed. Such is the disgust felt towards Argentine players for taunting the defeated English and their families in the St-Etienne car-park at France 98 that four years later Steve Howard, chief sports writer for the *Sun* at the time, takes vocal revenge. Howard, who has a stronger constitution than the United States, stays up all night in the reception of a Sapporo hotel to serenade Diego Simeone and Gabriel Batistuta as they check out the morning after losing to England. 'Don't cry for me Argentina,' sings Howard, mostly in tune.

It's a privilege covering England, and there's colossal respect for many of the players, past and present. No reporter on the England beat will ever forget Steven Gerrard's support for one of our number, Danny Fullbrook, when the *Daily Star*'s exuberant chief football writer fights cancer. Known as 'Fearless' after his byline 'Frank and Fearless' Fullbrook, Danny passes away in London aged only forty while we're all out covering Euro 2012, plunging the whole press corps into mourning when the news comes through as we wait at Kraków airport for a flight to Donetsk. On hearing of his death, Gerrard gives a moving tribute in his pre-match press conference and promises England will be 'fearless' against Ukraine the following day. This allows the *Star* to run the huge back-page headline 'Fearless', giving some comfort to Danny's grieving family. Frank Lampard, who visited Danny during his illness, was immediately in touch with the family. Like Gerrard, Lampard is another admired by the media who can expect support wherever his career takes him.

Sadly, England's most consistent performer of the post-Millennium era, Ashley Cole, rarely receives many flattering column inches following a lengthy period of froideur between player and press. Olive branches from the England press corps are extended to Cole via caring people at Chelsea and repeatedly via the FA but the left-back refuses to speak or come in from the cold. He remains sulky over front-page coverage of his private life and back-page condemnations of certain antics, such as accidentally shooting a work-experience student at Cobham, Chelsea's training ground. The stand-off between press and player is a pity, really. Cole deserves to be revered as England's most accomplished ever left-back. Nobody played Cristiano Ronaldo better.

Rooney experiences similar spells under the media's unforgiving magnifying glass, with every imperfection noted, but the captain is popular and respected. He always reports for duty, even if nursing a slight injury, and usually presents himself for interview, even if holding a grievance about a story on the news pages. Rooney's a good, honest talker, far better than perceived, partly because he relaxes more in the newspaper briefings. Savvy too. He handles adroitly some tricky questions about Old Firm rivalry when England play in Glasgow in November 2014. A year later, Rooney applies compassion and intelligence to all the questions about the Paris atrocities in the build-up to the friendly with France at Wembley. He understands and accepts the constant analysis. This is England. The years of hurt simply add to the forensic examination.

Some consolation for pained players can be found in the appreciation that the press is also very open to criticism. 'It goes without saying that all you hacks in this now degenerate country are whores of the race-mixing, sexually depraved, traitorous establishment,' reads one letter I receive in 2004. 'It comes as no surprise therefore to read your bone-headed piece . . . I was attending football matches both amateur and professional in this country before you were born when players had far more technical skills than the pass and gallop clowns now disgracing today's game. Yours faithfully . . .' Leaving aside that 'pass and gallop' should be hyphenated, it's pretty strong, but I've received far worse. I've had death threats (and a marriage proposal) on Twitter. Every morning at ten I used to receive the same one-word tweet from a follower – 'cunt'. It stopped after a while. I always wondered what happened to my clockwork troll.

This is the English press, and it's a highly competitive field.

Friends over a drink are rivals over a story. Scoops are saluted and envied. Although information-sharing occurs among the press coterie, and there's plenty of camaraderie with some of the most amusing characters imaginable, the business is cut-throat. There's a spot on the A1 near the Black Cat Roundabout in Bedfordshire where I nearly pull over and vomit on learning that *The Times* is reporting that England are set to strike in 2003 over Rio Ferdinand's exclusion over a missed drugs test. Even now, thirteen years on, my stomach turns every time I pass that spot. Nothing drains the blood more than screaming England headlines in a rival publication. We're fairly driven beasts, and there is a desire for strong stories or opinion pieces that may upset players, managers or the authorities. During the Ulrika Jonsson saga, I lock the doors on one tense Eriksson press conference to keep TV and radio out, ensuring what's uttered within stays fresh for the morning's newspaper headlines.

Some players are too sensitive. We always note when a player goes off Twitter because he cannot stand the trolls any more. Have they the backbone to survive with England? Certain Under-21 starlets admit privately that they are startled, some even scared, by the intensity of interest shown in them by the press at the 2015 Uefa Championship. 'This is not a dig at you and your industry but the Under-21s go through their two-year qualification campaign, and you [the football correspondent] don't go to their games,' says the FA's thoughtful technical director, Dan Ashworth. 'Then all of a sudden the big hitters are there for the 21s tournament. It's like a senior game.' The scrutiny, the caustic headlines when they slip up, the requests for an inquest duly follow. 'Expectation is high and they failed to get out of the group stages,' acknowledges Ashworth. 'It's tournament preparation, it's handling the pressure, it's getting the players psychologically to have the freedom to play while handling the pressure of the media. You guys have your jobs to do and I remember saying to you in the Czech Republic that I don't expect the headline "oh, everything's rosy", but let's take the pressure off the players. It's in your interests that we win it. Uefa said to us: "Why do you do so many interviews? You do that TV one, Sundays, dailies, radio, why so many? None of the other countries do." They do what they are bound to by Uefa.' One major set-piece with coach and player before the game – Uefa's beloved Match-day Minus One – and one post-match. The insatiable English newspaper industry demands more.

England understand and expect public obsession with the Three Lions and really need to rise to it, not shrink or sulk. The press reflect that fascination. Semi-finals are reached at Italia 90 and Euro 96 following two of the most acerbic build-ups, including spells of dressing-room omertà. Bobby Robson's squad are furious about the treatment of their manager and also a story about a player alleg-edly enjoying a dalliance with an Italia 90 hostess – a tale never substantiated despite offers rising to £25,000 from newspapers chasing info. That creates a siege mentality that bonds the players even closer together. Fast forward six years and Terry Venables' squad are angered by coverage of their drinking session in the Dentist's Chair in Hong Kong and also reports of extensive damage on their Cathay Pacific plane coming back. Unwilling to name the guilty parties, England eventually come up with the clever phrase 'collective responsibility': all for one and one for all. That unity, and anger against a hectoring media, helps drive England on. 'We grew out of the adversity in Euro 96 as a group – us against the world,' says Neville. 'I liked that. I like it to this day. You need a cause, something to bring you together.' Strong players responded powerfully to denunciation by a moralizing media.

Maybe we should fall out again. 'You can joke there that the best two tournaments have been had on the back of the worst media relations,' says Ashworth. 'So we could go: "Right, that's it, we'll do the bare minimum of media work." That antagonizes, but does it manage expectations? Or do we go: "No, we're going there to win it, let's take the pressure right off the players together internally and externally of the Bubble." I'd like to think we would come up with it [more media access]. Whether everyone would stick to it is another matter.'

The FA holds meetings discussing how to bring press box and dressing-room closer together. One idea might be reopening the flight to the media, especially in the cash-conscious era at the FA. It might help if people like me appreciate more that players are human beings, and put the digital or print pitchfork down at times. A lesson can be taken from England's women's team excelling in reaching the semi-finals of the World Cup in 2015. 'There was no media pressure,' observes Ashworth. 'Not many journalists went out, no high expectations. What was the pressure on Greece at Euro 2004? What's the pressure on Costa Rica players in 2014? But we can't be a big footballing nation with fantastic history and great resources and then expect not to have any pressure. It's a bit like playing for Manchester United, I'd imagine. You've got to play well and you've got to win. Anything else is not good enough. That's England. We've got to accept the pressure is there; pressure from the media, the expectations of the supporters are there. We are a big football country with a hugely well-resourced league and there's a pressure to do well. We have to become better at dealing with that pressure.'

In 2016, the media are inevitably focusing heavily on the fiftieth anniversary of World Cup glory. Ashworth does not see '66 as a burden. 'I embrace it,' says the FA technical director. 'I'm proud of the history. If Wayne Rooney is England captain and we win the World Cup in Russia, he's a sir, gets a statue at Wembley. We can't give him the financial rewards that the club can but there's something [special] he can get from us. I'm sure Wayne's motivation is not so he can have a statue. But, too right, we've not got much to celebrate in our time. But '66 is so far removed from the current players' generation now. I don't think it's rammed down their throats. I think we should celebrate the fact that we've won a World Cup, celebrate the people involved. It's a remarkable achievement and one that I hope during my lifetime we can match again.' The press, the pressure-bringers, will love that, even if the player ratings are harsh at times.

17

The Hunger Games 1:
Too Much Too Young

IT's THE LOUIS Vuitton wash-bag that gives the game away. It's the £465 lavished on the much-desired designer deodorant-holder that's the early warning sign of an impressionable young professional signing his first real contract, and the rewards going to his well-groomed head. Make a statement. Show off the money. Get the car. All hail Roy of the Range Rovers. The most talented footballing tyros in the country can make £2m a year. At 17. Unless they are strong-willed, adolescent millionaires risk their hunger being sated. Some inhabit roped-off areas of nightclubs, drive black 4×4s, and swagger into grounds with these wash-bags tucked under their arms, walking past fans and cameras, and then find a place on the bench at best. A footballing visionary in Worcestershire has long lobbied the FA to tackle Generation Xcess. Continuing the quest for more answers to the years of hurt, I head for Aggborough, abode of non-League Kidderminster Harriers and home to a man who wants starlets focused on glory, not the glamour or the cash. I drive into Kidderminster's small car-park, note the hoardings for Wyre Forest Pest Control and UKIP Worcestershire, and seek out Colin Gordon, one of the more forthright citizens of planet football.

If Hollywood ever makes a film on life outside the major leagues of English football, Kevin Costner will play Gordon. His career's got a touch of the Bull Durhams about it. After a decade as a bustling centre-forward with clubs from Swindon Town to Fulham, Birmingham

City to Leicester City, Gordon co-founds the Key Sports agency, helping nurture Theo Walcott, Josh McEachran, Ravel Morrison, Phil Jones, Saido Berahino, Izzy Brown and Jamie Vardy. He represents Steve McClaren, offering constant support during the coach's benighted England spell. A Uefa A-licensed coach, Gordon is director of football development at Kidderminster, even caretaker briefly, and is passionate about confronting the ills that obstruct youth development and extend the years of hurt. His words need heeding by the FA, Premier League, Football League, Professional Footballers' Association and also by parents of those who aspire to the heights.

After a cheery welcome, Gordon guides me through Aggborough, his movement unimpeded by hips battered during two decades of leading the line, until we find privacy in the deserted directors' box. He eases himself into a seat and lets rip about the Too Much Too Young brigade. 'These huge contracts destroy them,' Gordon says of some young players. 'I've seen that first hand for twenty years. Only one in twenty have a good support network around them like Walcott. It's the "wash-bag mentality". The first thing you do is get a Louis Vuitton wash-bag, then it's the Range Rover, then the girlfriend, then the watches. The lads are cocooned. They go from training ground to expensive apartments to the VIP areas of nightclubs. That's their mentality now. They phone up agents and say: "Can you get me on the guest-list of this club?" They don't mix down the pub like it used to be. They don't know what the average man does for a living. They can't relate to them. They don't develop any social skills whatsoever. I'm not saying *all*.' Definitely not all. Dele Alli, Eric Dier, Harry Kane, John Stones and Ross Barkley, among others, are grounded individuals.

Certain others aren't, though, and will struggle to get near England. 'Technically we are far, far superior than we've ever been,' Gordon continues. 'They can play. Our failing is we are not getting the kids through to the first team because of the distractions. We're creating the distractions. We're creating wrong values, wrong ideas on the game. It's like *Animal Farm* – we're all equal but some are more equal than others. Chelsea come along and distort it. A dad thinks: "I'm working forty hours a week driving a bus, my lad signs for Chelsea, I can retire." The agent's happy, the dad's happy, the kid's going to get a nice few quid and he's got a lovely crest he can walk round town in. He's got no chance of ever being a player. You have to strive to achieve something. The old system where the kids used to do the boots, knock to enter the first-team dressing-room, there was a pecking order. A top kid now would get £2m a year on a four-year contract – £8m, and never need to work again. That kills England.'

Kills England. It's scary and sad. Too many chase the money. Too many parents forget long-term considerations for short-term gains, signing for the agent who offers cars, houses, cash. It's a cattle market for 12-year-olds. Soft courting begins far earlier with clubs pursuing 8-year-olds. Gordon, the poacher turned gamekeeper, rails against some agents. 'I had to ask the FA: "Are you allowing inducements now?"

' "No, of course not."

' "Are inducements still against regulations?"

' "Absolutely."

' "Well, why aren't you stopping them?"

' "They don't happen, do they?"

' "You're kidding me! Parents are getting jobs, cars and houses. Kids are getting cars from agents."'

Gordon shakes his head in frustration. 'It's ridiculous. You tell me the moment a parent takes an inducement, who's got the power? The club? No. The agent. We saw in the transfer window kids go on the transfer list at the request of the agent. You don't go on the transfer list! That is absolutely the last resort. Raheem Sterling went on the transfer list – you can't do that to Liverpool supporters. John Stones – lovely kid. Transfer list? Are you kidding me? Saido Berahino goes on the transfer list. But you don't do that. That means you can't sit in a room with a decision-maker and work a way out. So what you have to do is throw all your toys out, rub your supporters' noses in it like Jermain Defoe did the day after they got relegated at West Ham [in 2003] and went on a transfer list. He's despised [by the Hammers fans].

'The FA are naive, head in the sand, and the Premier League are the same. They have to educate parents, explaining what a good agent should do and the pitfalls of taking the inducement and then being completely in the control of an agent. I'm not just talking about dodgy one-man bands, I'm talking companies. They'll offer jobs, cars, houses, money. They'll message 14-year-old kids: "What's going on? Have you got an agent? We've got so-and-so, will you meet us?" That's the first contact these days.' The fluid, poorly policed social-media world allows agents instant access, presenting a cyber calling card. They don't need to hang around training-ground gates nowadays. Introductions take place on Twitter and Facebook; they get their claws in, offer the world, then tempt the parents.

'Why are we losing players?' Gordon continues. 'Because a parent can retire from work if he has a good 15-year-old kid. It'll be worth £200,000 to the parents at 15 and then however much they can make off the kid going forward. It changes the dynamic between father and son. The power is with the breadwinner. Traditionally the father's been the breadwinner. Now the kid is. Some of the dads love it, wearing the good gear, driving in the cars; they love the association, the lifestyle. The parents are getting involved in that "wash-bag mentality" now.'

Theo Walcott's parents, Don and Lynn, have always done the right thing, keeping their son's feet on the ground, nurturing a good citizen. Polite and eternally positive, Walcott's a credit to his parents, and to advisers like Gordon. For all the controversy over his transfer request, Stones has been brought up well by his parents, Janet and Peter. Ditto Dier and Kane. Alli hails from a fractured background but surrounds himself with good, caring people. Some others need guidance. This is the speech Gordon gives to parents:

'Be a father, be a mother. Watch your son play, enjoy what he does. Leave the work to experts. Support him because it's tough. He's not guaranteed to make it. Keep the family unity tight. Take care of the other siblings who're not footballers. They might feel left out, not as important, and that can create divisions.'

Gordon sighs as he recalls his first visits to families with a prodigy.

'You're talking to the dad, and the lad's got his baseball cap on the wrong way round and watching Sky Sports News. He should shake hands, look people in the eye, contribute. He should be interested in how you can help his career. Some have no social skills what-soever and are excused for it. They wouldn't know how to open the door for somebody, they wouldn't give their seat up on a train for anybody. They don't understand basic decency. We've had lads who we thought are not for us, like Saido Berahino.' In mitigation, the England attacker has endured a tough upbringing, losing his father in the civil war in Burundi, fleeing the country, following his mother to England and needing to take a DNA test to prove he's her son. He settles in a foreign land before making it at West Brom where he comes under the guidance of Dan Ashworth, now technical direc-tor of the FA. 'Saido's been through a lot,' says Gordon, 'but he's had good people around him – Dan Ashworth, Mark Harrison [Albion's Academy manager], ourselves. Dan sacked him.' This occurs while Berahino's on loan at Brentford and falls out with their manager, Uwe Rösler, after being subbed against Leyton Orient. 'I begged Dan not to sack him. Three weeks later I got a call from Saido saying: "I want to leave because you're not doing enough for me." "I've just saved your fucking career!" I told him.' That career now seems back on track.

Ravel Morrison's a more extreme case with more skirmishes with the authorities than medals. He has a police caution for assaulting his mother. In 2011, he pleaded guilty to witness intimidation and a year later posted a homophobic tweet. Talk to England age-group coaches, mention Morrison's name, and a look of sadness flits across their faces. What a waste of talent. Having written about this prospect emerging from their Academy, Manchester United allow me to watch Morrison play behind closed doors at Carrington when he's 15. I sit next to Paddy Crerand, the club legend, huddling under an umbrella as the rain sluices down, and just marvel at this silky zephyr. Morrison absolutely tears a visiting Inter Milan side apart. Box to box. Head up. Always wanting the ball. Loves a nutmeg. Fearless. Sadly for club, country and player, a thoroughbred colt never trains on. Too many scrapes. Sir Alex Ferguson tries so hard. Ruefully, United give up on him. West Ham hope the troubled teenager might settle down away from his Manchester mates but eventually offload him on loan to Birmingham, QPR and Cardiff. I talk to West Ham staff and they really tried with him, they really cared for a wayward kid. Whether it's an indictment of the nation's education and welfare system or whether it's just the faulty hard-wiring of Morrison's mind, it's a frustration bordering on tragedy for England. Echoing some of Gascoigne's play, Morrison's supremely gifted technically, beautifully balanced in possession, floats across the pitch, the type of midfielder who leaves no footprints and scores breathtaking goals. Dribbling from his own half when West Ham defeat Spurs in 2013, Morrison sashays past Michael Dawson and Jan Vertonghen before lifting the ball over Hugo Lloris. 'Genius,' Sam Allardyce purrs afterwards.

Morrison heads to Rome, signing a four-year deal with Lazio, trying to rebuild amid the ruins. Maybe he never stands a chance. His family background is best described as dysfunctional. Some friends lead him astray. Problems also stem from learning difficulties. He's a poster-boy for Broken Britain when he should be a pin-up for England.

'Ravel's a unique case,' Gordon sighs. 'John Colquhoun, my partner, looked after him for a number of years at United's request. It was nigh on impossible because of his background. He's educationally challenged. From the background he came from, he didn't see what he was doing was wrong. At times, he was such a lovely kid. He's not got a bad bone in his body but he never really understood what he needed to do to be a footballer. It saddened me.' Gordon recalls receiving an urgent SOS from the then England Under-17s coach John Peacock in October 2009 when Morrison was out with the squad in Baku, trying to qualify from a four-team group for the European Championship.

'Are you coming out?' asks Peacock.

'Yes.'

'You've got to bring Mars bars and Lucozade.'

'Why?'

Peacock, who's seen most things in player development, explains Morrison's issue with the food in Azerbaijan. 'Ravel wouldn't touch the food,' Gordon tells me at Aggborough. 'We had to go straight to the hotel when we landed with a crate of Lucozade and a box of Mars bars. He could play only twenty minutes in each game because he didn't have the energy to see it through. He convinced himself that if he ate foreign food he'd be poisoned. That's what you're dealing with. But Ravel could do things with the ball that no one's seen. He should have loads of caps for England but he never had a prayer, because of his background. You have to remember the people he was under at United – Brian McClair, Fergie. He's not going to get better people than that. They gave up on him in the end. He just couldn't tell right from wrong. He broke everybody's hearts. He broke ours. He told us he was leaving.'

Clients are friends to Gordon. 'We've had some failures but invariably the most successful kids are kids who have very good support structure. Phil Jones, Theo, Izzy Brown and Josh are good young kids who do have good standards. Izzy will stay hungry because he wants to succeed.' Gordon thinks of the Manchester United Class of '92 driving each other on, and being shepherded skilfully by Ferguson. That's Shangri-La for Academies: finding another crop of low-maintenance, high-yield kids like Scholes, Giggs, Butt, Beckham and the Nevilles. 'They were a group. They policed themselves, and the manager was at the head of that, clipping people around the ear, keeping [Lee] Sharpe, Beckham and Giggs in line. Now it's down to the strength of the players.' It's player-power. Some youngsters have egos inflated by Instagram and constant exposure on clubs' in-house television channels broadcasting youth games; they're stars in their own minds. An increased turnover of players in the first-team dressing-room means fewer well-established stalwarts to advise and control the teenage kickers. 'It's football's problem, not society's,' says Gordon. 'You don't see it in other sports. It's purely football's problem. When the senior players are driving round in the big cars, got the girlfriends, that's what the young players aspire to. They don't aspire to the performances of the senior players. They aspire to the wealth.'

Money talks loudest. 'It's dreadfully sad but we've created a position now with the Elite Player Performance Plan [at English Academies] where even 9-year-olds have a value. Could we be so stupid? If he's been in a club for a year there's a value on him. If someone wants to come and take him they pay a fixed fee.' For a pupil in the Foundation Phase (Under-9 to Under-11), compensation is set at £3,000 per year. For a player in the Youth Development Phase (Under-12 to Under-16), compensation ranges from £12,500 per annum (Cat 3) to £25,000 (Cat 2) to £40,000 (Cat 1). Parents know that if their 16-year-old child has been in a Cat 1 system since the start, he's valued at £286,000 (plus £150,000 for every 10 appearances in the Premier League up to 60 appearances, and then £100,000 for every 10 appearances up to 100). Gordon sighs again. 'Parents go: "My lad is worth this much."'

Money pollutes. 'We get to a position now where clubs say: "What's the point of us having an Academy when Chelsea, Man United, City and Arsenal can turn up and just take him away for a set figure? We may as well scrap the Academy and invest later on, picking these boys up when they get released." It's killing England now. We can't win an Under-21 tournament. The gross salaries of the England squad in the last Under-21s tournament [in 2015] would have been six times the next group, Italy, and twenty times the worst-paid group [probably Serbia].' And England get knocked out in the group stage. 'Where's the desire? Where's the coaching? Where are the mentors? Where's the morality? There is none.'

Gordon looks to Germany, home of the current world champions. 'They don't pay them over the top until they start producing, even in their first team. I went over with Steve [McClaren], did his contract at Wolfsburg, and it was all incentive-based. They need to be winning to earn great money. A lot of the kids are kept on amateur contracts until they prove themselves. They could be on £60,000 a year and playing in the Bundesliga. They've got it right.'

Making wages more performance-related, as Southampton do with their younger players, would be a start. 'Trust funds are possible but everyone has to agree to it,' says Gordon. 'I'd put it together with a fund in Jersey that every boy would receive an allowance. Some of the boys only earn peanuts but there are clubs who are paying ridiculous amounts of money. Kids of 17 are on £2m a year – that should be put in trust for them until they're 21. If they make it, and are still playing at 21, keep it in trust. If they don't make it, then there's a nest egg for them, an annuity that gives them an allowance that allows them to invest in another career.'

During a two-hour meeting at Wembley, Gordon proposes the trust fund idea to the FA chairman. 'Greg Dyke loved it,' recalls Gordon. '"Fantastic, brilliant," he said. "Send me an email." I said to Greg: "We're losing players hand over fist, we're bringing foreigners in like nobody's business. I should take this to the Premier League but I want to come to you first because you look like you're saying the right things, and you can lead this." But then I didn't hear from him. I spoke to a friend at the FA and said: "What's going on?" "You've got to realize Greg only works two days a week." "What? It's a twelve-day-a-week job!"'

Stop Press: progress is made. Gradually, the FA and Academies place more emphasis on skill, encouraging youngsters to complete the ten thousand hours deemed requisite to make the grade. The game needed to build St George's Park earlier, creating this vital coaching hub where people get badged up before heading out to develop kids. 'Without good coaches, we cannot expect to produce good players,' emphasizes Dyke's May 2014 England Commission report into the national set-up's defects. (On page 48. Should be page 1.) Dyke tightens work permits, making appeals trickier. He launches the building of 150 football hubs in thirty cities in a £230m scheme with more artificial pitches and thirty-five new full-time FA coach educators. He aims to 'increase the number of Pro Licence holders from 200 to 300'. Football still needs more inspiring coaches like Steve Heighway, who developed Steven Gerrard and Michael Owen, and Karl Robinson, who nurtured Dele Alli, the latest afforded saviour status. The game needs more inspired initiatives too, like Lancashire FA's 'Silent Weekend' when all adults, coaches and watching parents are asked not to shout anything during kids' games. The feedback from the youngsters is ecstatic. They can express themselves without distraction. Silence is golden.

Football also owes a debt of gratitude to Gareth Southgate and FA coaches Nick Levett and Roger Davies for their tireless travelling up and down the country, talking to counties and clubs, persuading them to agree to age-appropriate small-sided matches. The game similarly owes thanks to the FA Council, a frequently belittled body, for voting in the reforms on 28 May 2012, making a five-a-side format mandatory for Under-7s and Under-8s while Under-11s and Under-12s play nine-versus-nine on appropriately sized pitches. England could go further. Belgium promote two-versus-two at Under-7s and Under-8s. Manchester United's Academy has long been in the vanguard of small-sided football, promoting four-versus-fours, including the Danny Welbeck–Tom Cleverley generation with skills coaches like René Meulensteen. Back in 2005, I watch one of the Dutchman's sessions at Carrington and it's full of 10-year-olds working on their technique, trying tricks, rolling a foot over the ball like Zinedine Zidane or pirouetting à la Thierry Henry. Drag-backs and step-overs pepper the play. It resembles a homage to Cristiano Ronaldo, who's starting to show his skills at United at the time. At the end of the session Meulensteen calls the kids into the middle and I listen in. 'You all have the ability,' he tells them. 'But do you have the confidence to play in front of ten thousand people, twenty thousand, thirty thousand? Use all your time training. Don't waste it. Learn. Train hard, work hard. Take responsibility.' Ten years on, how many have come through? A few, but United want to nurture more like the promising attacker Marcus Rashford.

United foster talent and have a reputation for giving them a first-team chance. 'You've got a bleeding dwarf,' somebody shouts at Brian Kidd, United's then youth-team coach, when a short, asthmatic ginger-haired kid struggles for breath in an Under-16s game. 'You'll eat your words,' comes the reply. The kid is Paul Scholes. Clubs have to be patient as teenagers develop at different ages. Photographs at Liverpool's Kirkby Academy show Gerrard the same height as Owen at 16. A growth spurt causes problems and Gerrard hits his stride only around 20. The better Academies like Liverpool tend talent well.

Good work takes time. As Dyke immediately concludes in his Commission report, the chief glitch in the system is the blocked pathway from 18 to 21. The kids are getting the money, but many aren't getting the games – a massive long-term hindrance for England. Some are happy just taking the cash, playing the occasional Under-21 game, being on the fringes. Most crave action, but the Premier League's foreign fixation stymies local ambitions. They need games and toughening up, so the loan system is vital. 'We have three lads in from West Brom,' says Colin Gordon of Joe Ward, Alex Palmer and Kyle Howkins. 'I went to see Tony Pulis, had a cup of tea, and he said: "Sod this Under-21 football, get them playing men's football, make them realize what it's going to be like, washing their own kit, then they can come back up to us when they've grown up a bit." It's a shock to some of them. West Brom are good. But we had one lad who came down from a local club who lasted one day. He said: "I couldn't handle the facilities." The ones at the top clubs are the worse. They don't want to leave. When they go on loan to someone they invariably come back early because they don't want to knuckle down, don't want to learn. The West Brom boys have been good; they have good mentors, not just Tony, but Mark Harrison. Dan Ashworth started all of that. They don't over-pay at all. Far from it. You have to earn it. Jeremy Peace [Albion's chairman] is not giving you nothing for nothing.' Berahino's on £850 a week before his contract's improved in 2013.

Berahino's long gone from Gordon's books. One of his clients is Josh McEachran, whose tale is oft-lamented within FA circles. The midfielder comes through the ranks at Chelsea's richly resourced Academy, stars as England win the 2010 European Under-17 Championship, and makes particular strides under Carlo Ancelotti at the Bridge in 2010/11, playing 17 times. McEachran uses the ball neatly, rarely wasting possession, can see a pass and looks all set for a successful career at the highest level. When I bump into him at the time at Cobham he seems slightly diffident, but that could just be wariness around a reporter. Those who've worked with McEachran speak glowingly of him, mocking any suggestion that he's a paid-up member of the Too Much Too Young glee club. 'Josh was breaking into the first team under Ancelotti, and doing really well,' says Gordon. 'Ancelotti – top manager – trusted him. He said we don't need anybody else. Players trusted him with the ball. But then they changed the manager. They signed Oscar. What have they done that for? That's Josh's position! He was involved in 22 games [including the start of the following season]. He needs to be playing at that level with those people. He sees things that most people can't see. Money wasn't the issue with Josh, it was opportunity.' André Villas-Boas arrives, McEachran is largely limited to Carling Cup action, then Oscar is signed, and a home-grown contender's hopes recede further. McEachran is off on loan, joining the three teams' worth of Chelsea players scattered away from the mother-ship, and has now been sold to Brentford for £750,000.

'We still have a tendency in the boardroom to go overseas because it looks better,' continues Gordon. 'Football's ills are from the boardroom. If I had to put my top executives, chairmen and directors on a pitch we'd have to play five-a-side. So few. The FA too. We don't have twenty Dan Ashworths in the Premier League. At Wolfsburg, I dealt with one of the toughest in [general manager] Dieter Hoeness [the former Bayern Munich and West Germany striker]. Germans have people run clubs from football backgrounds. We have no football knowledge in the boardroom. These people are wealthy but their egos stop them thinking correctly. They do no due diligence.' The bloated summer transfer window of 2015 particularly exasperates Gordon. 'There was £800m spent and with proper due diligence I could have cut that down to £500m, paying the right transfer fees, the right agents' fees to the right people, where it should go, not where it shouldn't disappear to. I said to Greg Dyke: "There are two problems in football: incompetence and corruption." He said: "Is that still going on?" Shambles. With all due respect to the head of the FA, I'd have him fix my telly [as an ex-BBC Director-General] but I wouldn't let him tell me how to run my football club.' In February 2016, Dyke decides against staying on at the FA. He tries to force through changes but encounters too many obstacles.

Chelsea similarly frustrate Gordon. 'This summer they signed Radamel Falcao. They've got Izzy Brown, [Patrick] Bamford and Dominic Solanke. What does that say to them? It was difficult for

Izzy, he's on loan in Holland, trying to learn his trade.' Chelsea hope Vitesse Arnhem serves as a finishing school for their youngsters like Brown, rather than a year out. 'It is good experience for him,' continues Gordon. 'Steve [McClaren] always said the Dutch are very, very deep thinkers about the game. If you put a problem on the pitch, the Dutch kids would explain to you how they would work it out tactically. They all knew their roles on the pitch. They can solve problems. It'll be good for him to learn, good responsibility off the pitch as well, away from the bright lights.'

Job insecurity among managers breeds a resistance to gambling on youth and to playing a possession game. 'Technically, you watch them in possession before kick-off, you'd not be able to tell whether you were in the Nou Camp or at Morecambe. The ability's there. But the difference is that when Morecambe kick off, the ball gets lumped up there [in the air], and people in the stands are sitting in neck braces. There's a fear to take a player on when five minutes ago you looked like Lionel Messi. Now you look like Lionel Blair. They're great in the [pre-match] grids: ping, ping – wow. Kick-off – deflate. You might as well be in the Somme. The players are more worried about what the fans are saying – are they getting on my back? – and the manager is telling me to get the ball forward. Brian Clough wasn't a coaching genius. He just took the fear out of playing, made players feel ten foot tall. There's fear in the dug-out now. How long am I going to last? Eight months in the Championship. When our players are being loaned out by top clubs to the Championship teams playing with pure fear, no wonder they look average. They can't play at the tempo and style. It's good that our players are going over to Vitesse, and [Chelsea youth] Nathaniel Chalobah to Napoli, where you play a different style and with an absence of fear.'

Fearful of some drifting out of the game through lack of opportunity, Gordon establishes a football college at Aggborough. Players discarded at 18 by clubs like West Brom, Walsall, Villa, Leicester, Derby and Bristol City can study for a degree in an area of football such as the media, scouting or recruitment while still playing. 'There's such a vacuum around 18 to 21. How much talent are we going to lose?

People give up a little bit early.' That 18 to 21 problem period is an area Dan Ashworth is attempting to tackle. Colin Gordon's frequent commendations of Ashworth's work demand further investigation. I thank him for his insight, leave Aggborough and head south to London to meet the FA's energetic technical director.

18

The Hunger Games 2: The Hope

IT'S RUSH-HOUR IN London and it's lashing down with rain – never the most appealing of combinations. Stepping nimbly between puddles and side-stepping pedestrians, the purposeful figure of Dan Ashworth marches into the restaurant, wheeling an England case behind him. The FA's technical director has agreed to meet in a pizza place opposite Euston Station, a familiar haunt as he dashes between Wembley and the National Football Centre at St George's Park. He's always on the move, knowing the size of his youth-development mission, fostering appetite and opportunity. Almost messianic in his desire to revive England, Ashworth hears the debate over young players enjoying 'too much too young'. He's seen the softening impact. 'Having been on the inside, the clubs know it is an issue,' says the former West Brom youth-team manager and technical director. 'There's talk of capping salaries at a certain age. There's an issue that a young player can potentially be made for life on signing [his] first contract. Trust funds will help. They get too much money too soon, and if the money comes at 25, rather than 18, they're in a better state to "waste" it.'

Like many working in the English talent factory, Ashworth admires much of the German system. 'I've heard a lot about the Xbox and iPhone generation but they have those Xboxes and mobile phones in Germany,' he says. 'Danny Collinge is in the Under-17s, plays for Stuttgart, really articulate. It's really interesting to hear his theories on the difference between the German and English system. One of the things for him is that he's in education more than he would have been if he'd stayed at MK Dons.' World Cup winners like Thomas Müller, Per Mertesacker and André Schürrle complete their *Abitur*, Germany's equivalent of A-levels. More and more pupils in German academies study hard for their *Abitur*, believing it helps their footballing intelligence and ability to absorb information, as well as giving them an avenue into another profession if football doesn't work out.

So how do the English catch up with the Germans? That's Ashworth's task. Originally on Norwich City's books, the defender spent part of his career in the shadowlands, playing non-League for Wisbech Town and Diss Town before making his name in talent development and recruitment at Peterborough United, Cambridge United and West Brom. Drawing on his understanding of the Academy system, Ashworth wants movement restricted between Cat 1 Academies, reducing the opportunity of inflated remuneration at a young age. 'That would dampen down the opportunity for finances to change hands. I don't buy the idea of moving from Manchester United to City, or Tottenham to Arsenal, at 14 or 15 "for football reasons". The facilities are the same.' Ashworth worries about the advice some younger players receive, and whether the size of the salary is the main motivation, especially for the agent taking a cut. Now that agents have been deregulated by Fifa, fears proliferate that the player-representation world will be engulfed by Wild West scenes. 'I don't think it's good news,' says Ashworth. 'Anybody can now be an intermediary. At least before you had to sit an agent's licence, had to get an agent's bond. Fifa basically gave up. There's less control and more people out there that could potentially have slightly different morals and values than you'd like. It's made it even harder to get the agents onside. Who are they? Where are they from?'

While keeping a wary eye on agents, Ashworth also wants to mobilize an army of grass-roots scouts. 'If we can educate volunteer mums and dads in what to look for in a player, that it's not just the biggest, strongest or quickest, it's the one who's the September or October birthday who should be in your team; spare a thought for late developers, for late birthdays, for different players. If we can improve them by 5 per cent that will improve the pool of players that the clubs are recruiting from by 5 per cent. That might improve England's pool by 5 per cent.' Parents: Your Country Needs You.

Deepening the pool is one thing, immersing such challengers in first teams is far, far harder. Pushing his plate to one side, Ashworth flips open his laptop to produce figures showing the number of league starts made by players involved in the European Under-21 Championship of 2015. Gareth Southgate's 23-strong squad manage only 188 league starts compared to the 324 of Germany, 345 of Italy, 349 of Sweden and 397 of Portugal. Italian players manage only 899 minutes in Europe followed by England's with 1,248. Portugal (3,298), Germany (3,682) and Sweden (4,786) boast far more experience of Champions League and Europa League football. (The figures are slightly skewed by England not taking Jack Wilshere, Alex Oxlade-Chamberlain, Phil Jones, Ross Barkley or Raheem Sterling, all eligible but deemed established in the seniors.)

Opportunity doesn't knock loudly. 'If they're not screaming talents that everyone can see, like Luke Shaw, Ross Barkley or Wayne Rooney at 17, and clearly ready for the first team, young players tend to get into the first team in adversity, because of injuries, the club in financial crisis, or on pre-season tour,' says Ashworth. 'One of the downsides of removing Financial Fair Play and the wealth of the Premier League is you fill your roster with the best twenty-five players you can possibly get for what you can afford. You're not bothered where they're from. It would be really hypocritical if I said I was because as technical director of West Brom we signed a lot of foreign players. You just get the best bang for your buck. It's something we can't control. We have to embrace the work of the Premier League. When young English players do get in, it's the best league in the world for them as it's a proper challenge every week.'

Surely, I ask Ashworth, the Premier League's not as tactically challenging as the Bundesliga, La Liga or Serie A? Ashworth shakes his head, believing it's a fallacy that the Bundesliga is more akin to international football than the Premier League is. 'You watch the German league and that's as near to the Premier League as you can get, with the intensity, speed, intensity of the supporters, the stadia. I watched a lot of the Bundesliga in my previous job and there's not a massive difference. There's a lot of German and Spanish players in the Premier League. If players are playing in a really stretching league, whether that's the Bundesliga, La Liga, Serie A or the Premier League, that's crucial to player development – mental resilience in a big environment, a lot of fan and media pressure. I don't think it's the tactical nature of any of the leagues, it's having to fight to win. That's a crucial part of a player's development.' Ashworth makes the England age-group fixture list more challenging, with tougher opponents, ensuring that 'the 88 touch points' – the maximum number of days' contact they have to influence players in their care from 15 to 21 – are used most effectively.

The debate keeps returning to that oft-quoted fear of Ashworth's chairman, Greg Dyke, about the Premier League 'being owned by foreigners, managed by foreigners and played by foreigners'. The Premier League counters that 93 per cent of Under-16s at Academies are English, 73 per cent of Under-17s and 61 per cent of Under-21s. Plans are in the pipeline to make the structure more competitive, boosting the Under-21s league, giving it more 'jeopardy' in Premier League parlance, possibly with entry in the Johnstone's Paint Trophy, more prize money and staging games at the club's home ground when the first team are away. Ashworth is more positive than his chairman, believing the production line is working. 'We've won the Under-17s Championship in Europe twice out of the last six,' he says. In 2010, England storm through the tournament in Liechtenstein, accounting for Paul Pogba's France in the semis and Gerard Deulofeu's Spain in the final. Ably organized by John Peacock, and buoyed by messages of support from the seniors, the Under-17s are indeed spiced with individual talent in Jack Butland, Ross Barkley and Saido Berahino. It's England's first age-group triumph in seventeen years, since Paul Scholes, Gary Neville, Nicky Butt, Sol Campbell and Robbie Fowler dominated the European Under-18 Championship; Julian Joachim stars too but does not follow those famous five into the seniors. In 2014, England keep their nerve to defeat Holland on penalties in the Under-17s final. They even convert all four kicks, through Ryan

Ledson, Taylor Moore, Callum Cooke and Jonjoe Kenny, indicating that when the seniors flatline it is not so much a failure of technique as the weight of pressure that accompanies senior life. Again well coached by Peacock, that Under-17s crop also includes the promising Lewis Cook, Patrick Roberts, Dom Solanke and Izzy Brown, who just need to find an open pathway to the top but frequently find it is a life on loan.

'We do have good players – as good as anyone in the world at 17, 18, 19,' Ashworth insists. 'I've not come away from a game and gone: "Oh my God, we're miles away." But it's not as good as it should be. We do have a feedback mechanism after every international to every club.' He liaises with the Premier League's director of youth, Ged Roddy, about accelerating the flow of information between clubs and national teams. 'One of the things Ged and I are talking about is that the national coaches are able to go into review meetings with the clubs. So Gareth can go in with Neil Bath at Chelsea and talk about the performance of Ruben Loftus-Cheek. It's a myth there's a conflict between the national association and the clubs. The clubs have been fully supportive. There have been very few player-release issues.'

At senior level, club versus country is less of an issue but it is still a problem with development teams. The Under-19s and Under-20s lose players. Some clubs don't want them to go. FA staff whisper about the time one kid gets ordered off an England age-group flight by his club manager. Agents tell clients they are too good for development teams, and so claim they are not fit to report. 'What happened at Under-21 level last summer wasn't acceptable,' says Sam Allardyce of England's lacklustre Euro 2015 show in the Czech Republic. 'It looks like, sadly, the players don't want to play for the country at Under-21 level when you look at the body language.' Harry Kane turns up in Olomouc and runs hard but is clearly shattered by a long season and then Spurs' ill-timed post-season tour to Kuala Lumpur and Sydney. Along with Roy Hodgson, Southgate and Ashworth spend time building bridges between clubs and country. 'We've worked hard at those relationships,' says Ashworth. 'We say to them: "Help us." We have six or seven events a year at St George's Park where the Academy managers come in. The national coach will come in and talk about his aims.'

Some clubs privately question the quality of FA coaching, arguing there are too many teachers at St George's Park. Ashworth is happy with the mix of coaches nurturing English prospects. 'There are three different sorts of coaches: educators like John Peacock, ex-player coaches with experience of playing for their country like Gareth Southgate and Gary Neville, and coaches with League experiences. Sean O'Driscoll and Aidy Boothroyd worked in youth, worked in the Premier League and lower leagues. They were dealing with first teams then. I felt those two had an understanding of what it took to push through. At 18s we had Neil Dewsnip who spent twenty years at Everton as Under-18 and 21s coach developing players; 17s was John Peacock, 16s was Steve Cooper.' Playing expertise is being used. 'Michael Owen has been in and talked to the players. Ugo Ehiogu came with us to a tournament [the Under-20s World Cup of 2013]. Rio Ferdinand has come up to St George's Park for the day. Tony Adams came in and worked with a group. You can't work with national players unless you've got an A Licence. Rio is at the start of his coaching pathway. Michael doesn't want to go down his coaching pathway because he wants to be an agent or whatever. Phil Neville has been involved quite a lot. They have to get some level of qualification. But we could use some in an ambassadorial or advisory capacity, more than we currently do. It's a fair point.' He works on bringing in experts to accentuate the talent of Hodgson's squad. 'If we can get a model where the players feel they're getting specialist coaching, specialist expertise, there won't be many players who won't want that. "Oh, blimey, somebody's paying me a bit of individual attention," whether that is one of the established coaches or an international superstar.'

Ashworth needs all his prodigious energy and desire to make a difference. At times, it feels the English youth-development structure is caught in the perfect storm of foreigners, ego, money, warped values and societal changes. Another issue presents itself, appropriately, over the pizzas: the tsunami of obesity rolling through a country seemingly addicted in parts to fast food and sugary drinks. Sport needs more muscle in Whitehall. It needs a stronger individual Cabinet presence, not simply being part of the monolithic Department of Culture, Media and Sport. When the current Health Minister, Jeremy Hunt, resides at DCMS in 2011, I get called in to his art-filled office next to Trafalgar Square to talk about football's ills and we end up discussing the 'obesity time-bomb', as the FA and Academy managers call it. More money needs to be invested in school sport not least to reduce the long-term pressure on the NHS. Some politicians won't adopt a long-term strategy because another party might be in power when the benefits finally arrive. Currently it's Hunt's job to defuse the bomb. 'Obesity is an issue,' warns Ashworth. 'It's something the whole Western world is looking at, not just us. America, Germany, Spain and Italy all have a similar sort of problem. Working closely with the government would be important. Do you know what? I haven't had the direct conversation with government.'

Ashworth attends a UK Sport working group consulting a range of people, including Olympic champions, to ascertain what a sporting athlete will look like in 2020, and he tells me of a startling revelation from another realm. 'The Marines have said the fundamentals of warfare haven't changed in fifty years: what it takes to defend, to stay alive, to win the battle,' continues Ashworth. 'The technology of the weaponry has changed. But the biggest thing that's changed for the Marines in fifty years is the raw material coming in. They've had to change their entry criteria – the distance they can run, pull-ups, press-ups – because physically we are so much more unfit as a nation [now].' Football recruits from the same area. That Sugar Tax is vital. One Academy manager confides that he looks at African kids because they are leaner, fitter, hungrier.

Another Academy manager divulges that his club scour independent schools for talent in the belief that their pupils enjoy a more balanced diet and access to better facilities. Ashworth nods. 'My wife's a primary school teacher, and the provision in primary schools for sport is poor. We could do that so much better. Most of the private schools play sports every afternoon. Football needs to use that as recruitment. The private system is definitely one that football hasn't tapped. We've got a couple of players in the system who've come through the private school system.' Will Hughes of Repton, Derby County and England Under-21s is one. Patrick Bamford of Nottingham High, Chelsea and England Under-21s is another. Will Huffer of St Peter's, York, reputedly the fourth oldest school in the world, represents Leeds United and England Under-18s. Offspring of former players like Gary Lineker and Martin Keown increasingly feature in the private system. The rather clichéd question raised about the sporting pedigree of independent schoolboys is whether they possess the hunger. 'I would have thought their success in numerous other sports would indicate they are hungry,' counters Ashworth. 'With rowing, there's no financial rewards in that, or very few, so I'd flip the argument on its head and say they are hungrier. There's no money in the Olympics. There's not the same money in rugby and cricket, and they've traditionally attracted kids from private schools.'

Ashworth has a train to catch. He leaves on a positive note, utterly convinced England will win a trophy by 2022. 'I am optimistic,' he says. 'Firstly, I know people say it's an impossible goal, but in 2016, '18, '20 and '22 we have four tournaments in the male game. Someone's got to win them. Why not England? We wouldn't be a rank outsider. Perhaps we would to our own media and supporters but I don't think anybody would be utterly surprised. It's not a Denmark [at Euro 92] or Greece [Euro 2004] where you'd think: "Blimey, where did *they* come from to win it?" Whenever we go to tournaments, we are always one of the teams who could win it.

'Secondly, I'm really confident because of some of the things that are happening with our own national team, with our own players, and also from EPPP [the Elite Player Performance Plan]. The type of player who is coming out of the Academy system now is very, very different to those five or six years ago. They are more tactically able. They are more technically able. Yes, we have a bit of work to do over physical and mental resilience in tournaments, which is not down to clubs because they don't experience tournaments.' Clubs face testing knock-out matches in the domestic cups and in the Champions

League and Europa League but the psychological pressures in those arenas simply do not match those that must be braved when travelling abroad with England for a tournament.

Ashworth has a final hope. 'We need a little bit of luck,' he says. 'You look at any of the nations who've won it and there's a defining moment in the tournament where things have gone for them. They've got a good refereeing decision, opposition have had a man sent off, it's penalties, whatever. You need a bit of luck before the tournament because you need to go with your best players. With the Under-21s last summer, losing John Stones [for two games], Luke Shaw and Saido Berahino on the eve of the tournament, that's tough. If the seniors in 2022 lost the equivalent of Hart, Rooney and Sterling all of a sudden that does really dampen your chances.'

Applying the premise that players ache with fatigue towards the summer, the winter World Cup in Qatar in 2022 could help England. 'I suppose that will ultimately test the theory,' continues Ashworth. 'We are saying our players are tired at the end of the season. If we do win it then it'll be an interesting debate afterwards, and let's hope we have it. We are going in the right direction. We will have a playing pool to win it, and if things go for us in one of those tournaments, why not? I can see us winning it.'

19

The Hunger Games 3: The Fear

'WE USED TO clean the kit and boots, make the tea, but you can't make a cup of tea these days – Health and Safety.' So says the ball-playing England defender Mark Wright of his Oxford United apprenticeship in the 1980s. The Academies that Dan Ashworth believes will end the years of hurt are viewed as luxury establishments by many old pros. Having heard from agents and administrators, I visit Manchester and London to consult three members of England's Italia 90 side – Chris Waddle and John Barnes as well as Wright – who have plenty to say about youth development and other predicaments bedevilling England.

Wright first. 'I may be a dinosaur but there's a happy medium,' he says. 'OK, you don't have to paint the stadium as we did at Oxford United, but just watching the first team train on that lovely grass pitch, saying "that's where I want to be", would give them that drive, toughen them up. We weren't allowed to drive a car into training. "Who do you think you are?" they'd say. "You're not in the first team yet. Get the bus or a lift in." That was at Oxford. I've never seen anything like it in the Liverpool car-park now when they come in. "What?" The cars! I went to Man City, an unbelievable set-up [at City Football Academy]. We used to take our butties in a carrier bag to training and they've got a five-star restaurant for the kids. This lad they paid £1m for turned up late for training at City, and they said: "You're late again. You've got to be here on time. Go and get changed."'

Visiting CFA at the time, Wright enquires of a friend who works for City: 'What's all that about?'

'He gets good money but we can't get him in on time.'

'Kick him up the backside then.'

'Wrighty, you can't.'

'The game's gone then. Do you send him home?'

'No.'

'They need to get him on the training field,' Wright adds, 'to get the money they've spent.'

Attitude is one issue. Aptitude another. Wright frets over the decline in the quality of England defending, a debate intensifying after the 2-1 loss to Holland at Wembley on 29 March. Wright argues that it needs urgent addressing in Academies, producing a new generation of Bobby Moores and Terry Butchers. 'When I was playing for England there were seven centre-halves,' he says. 'There was Butcher and [Des] Walker, me and Tony Adams, Dave Watson, [Steve] Bruce and [Gary] Pallister, all of us fighting to get two places in the England side. Not now. There are some good players but it's more about finding leaders, characters, and "stick your head in there". I was all about passion and drive, getting stuck in and trying my best. I gave everything, every single game, and that's why I'm looking as I am now with my nose all pulled to pieces, cuts everywhere, breaks in my legs, and my knees.

'I was on the phone to Brucey the other day. Brucey was a warrior but he didn't have his nose straightened, we had it clicked back in all the time. At Oxford United, there was a lad called Ken Fish [a legend of the club coaching staff]. I came off and he said: "Son, your nose has gone. Come over, let's have a look at it." He clicked it back in. I nearly keeled over. "Stop being a wuss and get back out there – go on, off you go." I was brought up by [Gary] Briggs and [Malcolm] Shotton, real men, proper centre-halves. I remember the first time I played, Briggs came up to me and said: "Son, you're too good to be at Oxford and you're not going to be here long. But while you're here you fucking do as you're told."

'"What do you mean?"

'"Well, if I jump first and I butt him, you have to butt him next."

'"What do you mean, 'butt him'?"

'"Exactly what we're saying."

'I laugh.

'"If you don't come off that pitch without a cut nose, or haven't hurt them, we'll hurt you."

'"Yeah, right."

'"Do we look as if we're joking?"

'"No."'

Wright pauses as he thinks back to a more physical era. 'That was my upbringing. By two real men in the game, who wouldn't be on the field long these days.' That toughness and mental resilience, though, is needed among some of the new generation.

For all the criticism following his slip against Holland, England's stylish young centre-back John Stones gives hope for the future. 'He has a good career ahead of him and there are not many British centre-halves you can say that about,' continues Wright. 'There are not many with that potential. Roberto Martínez is a friend of mine and has done very, very well to withstand the pressure of selling him. Stones can develop into a very good centre-half. I see him being able to come out with the ball. He's got that slender build, he sees the game, but he's still a kid. He's not going to get to be the best until he's 28. He's got a lot of learning and games first. Make defenders proper defenders, going in for tackles, putting your head in. You have to be brave, you have to be street kids, probably council estate kids more often than not. If I was going to coach John Stones, I'd say: "Be patient, son. Roberto's a good coach, good manager. If you're going to a Man City or Chelsea are you going to play as much football as at Everton?" Everything else will come. He's playing for England. Sit still, play for Everton. I'm glad Stones stayed as he'll get more games and that will benefit England in the long run. The more games you play, the more you learn, the better you become. It's no good sitting on the sidelines.' England still need a strong, left-footed centre-back, or someone comfortable on the left of the two. They need a new John Terry to emerge.

A recurring protest from ex-pros is that clubs and the FA are guilty of negligence in not tapping more into their expertise, getting them working with youngsters 'instead of taking in school teachers' in Wright's words. He craves the opportunity to pass on his enthusiasm and experience. So do many others. 'Some players can't pass their A Licences because of the written side of it,' says Wright. The FA confirms privately that one well-known player pulled out of a coaching course a few years back because he couldn't read. 'But those players have massive hearts,' Wright continues. 'They can teach kids and first-team players about heart. But clubs overlook them for people who can write reports. Clubs should have more specialized coaches. They have a goalkeeping coach so why not a defensive coach? I'd love to be a defensive coach for Liverpool, helping out the defenders, whether the kids or older. Liverpool have conceded a lot of goals from set-plays, corners and free-kicks over the past three seasons. They have a problem, and I know how to put that right. If Liverpool were to ask me to come and coach their defenders, as an ex-Liverpool player I'd be honoured, but they won't because I'm a strong character and managers get worried by strong characters. That's a shame. I know I could improve them.'

Wright also wants to confront the charlatans, reviving lost principles. 'It worries me how many people roll around, feigning injury as if they've been hurt when they haven't been touched. We'd have been embarrassed to roll around on the floor. I'd jump back up even if I'd got a bad injury. The game's become softer. If I'm brave enough of course I'm going to get a cut eye, bust nose. John Terry does that. The British people are about blood and thunder and guts – get after people, compete. It's becoming non-contact. The game has changed so much.'

Chris Waddle wants young talents liberated. Where are the real wingers, the modern Waddles, now? What's happened to the art of tricking a full-back and crossing? I find the former England winger at Wembley where he's sitting in a room overlooking the pitch he graced, slowly consuming a chilli con carne before enlightening BBC Radio 5 Live's listeners with his thoughts on the Euro 2016 qualifier with Switzerland. An hour-long private audience with Waddle, let alone then hearing his public utterances, leaves me even more bemused that he does not get summoned to give evidence to Greg Dyke's England Commission. Waddle brings additional experience and wisdom to the national debate from having played abroad at Marseille, from an

England career encompassing 62 appearances and two tours of World Cup duty, and from his clear-eyed analysing of his greatest skill, beating an opponent one-on-one. Waddle triumphs at the essence of the game, spiriting the ball past the enemy, gifts still remembered fondly at Newcastle United, Tottenham and Sheffield Wednesday, among others. Dyke's offices are scarcely two minutes away from where we talk, along a corridor, up in a lift, then along more corridors bearing the photographs of those Waddle played with and against.

'If I could change English football, I'd go back to three foreign players, make us work with what we've got,' says Waddle, recalling the old quota system. 'How much talent have we had? John Barnes, Peter Beardsley, Gary Lineker, myself, Tony Currie, Alan Hudson – we did produce a lot of skilful footballers which we don't produce any more because of the Academies.' Because of? How? Under-11s at a Category 1 Academy undergo eight hours' coaching a week for forty-six weeks a year. Surely that's a great education at a well-equipped institution that can cost £3m to run annually? Waddle explains: 'We've got all these Academies which are costing fortunes, but all we're doing is bringing in all these kids and saying "two-touch football".' Academies dispute this contention, claiming risk-taking dribbling is encouraged. 'The King of the Swaying Hips', as an adoring Marseille public called Waddle, disagrees. 'You're taking all that natural ability away. Academies work in other countries because of the way they coach, like at Ajax or in France. They find good wingers and don't say "two-touch football". They let them play as wingers and do what they're good at. Our coaching methods are completely different. What we're doing is throwing a net out, bringing everybody in, saying "you're a centre-half" or "a central midfielder", and playing two-touch football. Why? Because Spain do it. But Spain get the ball back, give it to someone and something happens. You still have to have those [truly creative] players.'

Waddle wishes the FA would adopt a different strategy, removing the straitjacket and reverting to a time when joyous technicians like him and John Barnes emerged naturally from the streets, from playgrounds, from kickabouts with their friends. Waddle craves football unplugged, not over-tutored. He feels the game is too structured too early for kids. He wants Academies to start at 14, not the current set-up where some clubs operate Under-6 teams with A Licensed coaches. 'Let the kids go and play with their mates,' pleads Waddle. 'Let them play for their schools, boys' teams, enjoy it, and then at 14 get a tap on the shoulder and somebody saying: "Do you want to come and play for our football club now? We like how you play. It's not been coached out of you. It's natural talent, raw." Take a few edges off that and we've got a player. Not working on them at 5 so when they come to 13 they're robots. If you go to an Academy you can't play with your boys' team on a Saturday, school team, county team. And when the club lets them go, they don't go to the boys' teams with their mates, and get stick off their mates saying "ahh, you're not good enough", they pack [it] in, hang their boots up on the pegs.

'We've got to get shot of the Academies. Go back to the old ways. One thing we were good at was producing gifted players. Every club had some great, tricky wingers, creative midfielders. People would say "he's a luxury" but they always had players the fans liked, a bit of magic, a bit of class. All we're producing now is athletes who can play two-touch football and are robotic. Raheem Sterling is the only one who runs with the ball with some end product. I was doing a phone-in and somebody said Alex Oxlade-Chamberlain runs with the ball, but I went "no end product". The difference with great players is end product. A cross that flies across! What a ball in! Goal!' Some hope emanates from the skilful, central thrusts of Dele Alli and Ross Barkley.

Waddle came late to the professional game, shifting in a sausage-seasoning factory (not a sausage factory as he wearily points out, tiring of the 'sizzling' headlines) until signing for Newcastle United aged 19. So he echoes all the 'too much too young' sentiments. 'There should be a cap on wages. Up to 21, if you're doing the business, you get a good drink. Bonuses. You can't give somebody a five-year contract on great money after three good games. Chairmen are frightened of kids leaving. They have to change the rules so from 18 to 21, if a club offers a player a contract with a certain wage, you should take it.' Waddle thinks of Sheffield Wednesday. He played so well for them in 1992/93, helping them to two cup finals, that us reporters voted him Footballer of the Year. Waddle cares for the club and doesn't want their Category 2 Academy raided. 'If Wednesday work with a player for five years, and he's coming along nicely, but when he's 16 one of the big boys comes in – bang, £100,000 it'll cost them. What's £100,000 for a Premier League club? Nothing. Who's getting stung? Wednesday. All the big clubs are doing now is nicking the ready-made ones – well, they think the players are ready-made. They collect them, £100,000. I'll have him. I'll have him. But they never get in the first team because the big clubs go all around the world buying all the best players. It's gone ridiculous. I'd love the Premier League to go bust because we'd go back to reality and work with players. We'd find a young player, give him a two-year contract on £300 a week and work with him. I'd let them go down the park.' Let them express them-selves. Let them learn to fight for the ball.

Waddle's weekend playing schedule as a teenager would turn current Academy managers into nervous wrecks. 'I used to play Saturday morning for my mate's works team, a printing company [HMH Printing]. Saturday afternoon I'd play for Pelaw Juniors. Sunday morning: pub team at 14, playing against grown men who'd had ten pints the night before. I got kicked from pillar to post. I learned how to take a tackle, to ride a tackle. Sunday afternoon: kickaround with the lads, twenty-eight-a-side, ages 10 to 20, no bibs, no shirts. If you didn't shout you didn't get a kick. You learned how to dribble.'

Skills acquired on a tricky surface, taking on player after player, serve him well throughout a fine career, scoring and creating so many goals for Kevin Keegan and Peter Beardsley at Newcastle, Clive Allen at Spurs, Jean-Pierre Papin at Marseille, and also Mark Bright and David Hirst at Wednesday. If one goal celebrates Waddle's flair it's an outrageous effort for Marseille against Paris St-Germain in 1989: ball taken on the chest, flicked over Joël Bats and then back-heeled over the line. It's not simply the technique and impudence, it's the way Waddle keeps his eyes trained on the ball all the time. It's a reminder of the skill-set and boldness fostered during those mass schoolboy gatherings in Gateshead. He loved it when the summer sun lit the early evenings.

'Do you fancy a game?' his mates would ask, knocking on his door. Of course he would. 'I'd play every night, competitive or fifteen-a-side on the back-field. Then I'd go under the street corner under the light. Then the parents came out: "Are you coming in or not?" "Yes, I'll be ten minutes." If there were only two of you, you'd end up playing "kerbs": control the ball on the chest, hit the ball at the kerb and it would bounce back. All the garages would be dented. Owners would come out and go mad. "What you doing?" We'd blast the ball at them. I don't see kids doing that now. I see it on Xbox. I never had a bloke ever tell me to pass the ball.' Travel broadens the mind and technical repertoire. 'Marseille always said they wanted me to dribble. It made me a better player going abroad. Too many people are in the comfort zone in England – got the money, the car, the house. They should go and embrace it. They may never come back.'

A kindred spirit on the wing, John Barnes, always regrets not following his friend abroad. Barnes believes young English players would benefit from experiencing life and football in another country. 'When I was 20 and scored that goal in Brazil [in 1984, after dribbling through the hosts' defence at Maracanã], when Luther Blissett went to AC Milan, I wanted to go,' recalls the former Watford attacker, talking in his quickfire manner in Manchester. 'But Graham Taylor would have said to me: "You're not ready to go. Only when you have another three years, and the experience necessary to handle that situation." I felt I was ready.'

Naturally confident, Barnes' many physical and technical assets are honed juggling the ball in Jamaica, before moving to England and taking on kids at Stowe Boys' Club in Paddington, west London, and then in the Middlesex League with Sudbury Court before Watford launch a stellar professional career. 'When I played for England, the pressure wasn't on me, even with the goal against Brazil. The pressure was on Ray Wilkins, Bryan Robson and the older players.' He worries about the footballing support structure around the likes of Raheem Sterling and Ross Barkley today. 'Now we are putting pressure on these young players. It's not necessarily the contracts we give them. It's the praise we give them and the importance we pay to them. No matter what Ian Rush did for Liverpool in his first year, he was in the reserves. He played and scored but he knew he had to have respect for Alan Hansen, who would protect him. Now the whole environment is putting pressure on Raheem Sterling and Ross Barkley because we don't really have enough experienced players around to protect them. Even the older players like Phil Jagielka don't have that much experience to alleviate the pressure on the young players because we had John Terry and Rio Ferdinand for such a long time. I wouldn't put pressure on England at these European Championships, but in the next World Cup with two years' more experience, I'll say: "You're under pressure to perform." If you put too much pressure on them now, and you criticize them, that could affect them and set them back.

'But I am confident for the future. If you look at our players now, they are technically proficient. While the time is right in terms of England changing its philosophy on the way football is played, the timing's wrong in that players are not getting the opportunities at their clubs. You saw Michael Owen coming in at France 98, become the main player for Liverpool, playing in Europe for the next five, seven years and then move on.' It's worth noting that Owen played 44 times for Liverpool in the season leading up to that World Cup. The pathway was clear. 'If these young players are playing with no fear for England but are still on the bench of their clubs for the next three, four or five years, or end up leaving to go to lesser clubs, not playing in the Champions League, how are they going to improve? That's the biggest problem we have.' Spurs give youth a chance. So do some others. More need to follow suit.

The English system largely fails many promising youngsters, giving them hope and money but little opportunity. These kids also have to take responsibility, straining every sinew, and working every hour, to ensure they have the dedication to demand managers include them. It's about hunger forcing opportunity. 'I think the young players still have that hunger,' says an England international of more recent vintage, Jermaine Jenas. 'The money is just part of the game. It was like when I went to Newcastle [from Nottingham Forest for £5m in 2002] and you were in that press room. You lot were chomping at the bit to say: "How are you going to deal with this pressure?" I was thinking: "The pressure is part of it, I didn't put the price on my head, let them put the price on my head, I just want to go out there and play." Raheem has just gone through a similar process where everybody is going: "£50m? Are you having a laugh?" This is just the way the game is going. You have TV companies pumping in loads of money. Everyone tries to put pressure on the player. But the players themselves, deep down in their core, want to get back to playing for their country. That's why you start playing football in the first place because you want to play for your country and want to win trophies.

'The pressure for me comes towards the latter stages of your career. Watch Wayne Rooney now to when he was a kid – two different players. Don't get me wrong, he's brilliant now. But he was fearless as a kid. He doesn't look fearless to me any more. He looks a lot more strategic, technically, and his experience is there, but the fearlessness of Wayne Rooney has completely gone. When people start to expect something from you, that's when the games start to become hard. There's a freshness in this England squad. It's a young squad. There are a lot of players in that squad who have nothing to lose. They have everything to gain. They came off the back of a bad World Cup. Hopefully that experience will hold everyone in good stead. You have a bunch of players who are fearless going into the [2016] Euros.' Jenas' old club, Spurs, have two of them in Alli and Kane.

The final word on the new breed goes to a former England captain. 'We're not producing them now,' Alan Shearer tells me when we discuss the game's lack of leaders. 'It's society, Academies and lack of apprenticeship. I'm reluctant to say "too much money too soon" but without doubt, if you put all that into a pot, and put all the foreign players in the game, that's why we're not very good – and haven't been for a while.'

Shearer's right. Yet still the fans believe; still they turn out in huge numbers to support England.

20

The Faithful

THE MOST SERENE Republic of San Marino is noted for having once been ruled by monks, for being the beautiful setting of a film starring Orson Welles, for its wealth, and for the fact that its population swells by 10 per cent whenever England visit. In expectation of Wayne Rooney and the lads celebrating qualification to Euro 2016, 2,500 members of the England Supporters' Club fly into assorted Italian airports and head for this tiny principality nestling in the hills near the Adriatic. The official party are joined by an estimated five hundred ticketless fans, vacating Rimini's beachside bars, flocking towards Serravalle. A few try to scam tickets off the FA, which has seen and heard all the 'dog ate my ticket' tricks before and now distributes them on the day of the game. Unofficial and official groups converge on the grandly named Stadio Olimpico. It's more municipal running track than five-ringed field of dreams but the locals are too pleasant to argue with. Some of the five hundred try to blag their way in. Others buy tickets off Sammarinese. The rest happily stand among the pines on the slopes behind the goals, enjoying a free view.

England's support continues to be a modern wonder of the foot-balling world, a mix of patriotism and masochism, adrenalin and alcohol. They launch into 'God Save The Queen' with usual gusto. As if singing a round, fans, band and players travel at different speeds through the twenty-nine words with the fans comfortably crossing the line first. Johnny Rotten wouldn't get through it quicker. Supporters laugh at the choral chaos, typically seizing any opportunity for merriment, as on-field pleasure is intermittent. Many of those present were at Wembley for the friendly with Hungary when England made their first public appearance after their dismal 2010 World Cup in South Africa. 'Never Was So Little Given By So Few For So Many' read one banner. Yet 72,024 turned up. They keep the faith despite being let down tournament after tournament, slagged off by Rooney in Cape Town, strong-armed by some police forces, ripped off by some of those offering accommodation, and occasionally pilloried by a media yet to be fully convinced that the dark days of hooliganism truly ended at Charleroi in 2000. They spend hard-earned cash chasing a distant dream. They resemble gamblers in Las Vegas, perching on a stool, feeding the slot machine for hour after hour, hoping for a pay-out, even though the odds are stacked against them and they continually run low on funds. The old romantics are granted occasional thrills – Holland in '96, Colombia in '98, the Munich 5-1, Denmark in 2002, Croatia at Euro 2004 – but these are rare shafts of sunshine in a storm. They still love it. Following England away denotes true diehard status, backing the team even though the returns are limited. It is about the crack, the beers and the sing-song. It is about the race to get their clubs' flags hung up in some distant stadium the quickest. These flags frequently denote affiliation to clubs outside the elite. Peterborough United, Wolves, Millwall and Exeter City are amongst the seventy-odd flags spotted in Berlin's Olympic Stadium when England visit in March 2016. England offer trips abroad. Nationalism plays a part for many. So does xenophobia for a few, although the mood is far removed from the thousands chanting 'I'd rather be a Paki than a Turk' at the Stadium of Light in 2003 or the skirmishing scarring countless trips from Rotterdam to Marseille, Dublin to Bratislava until a measure of calm is introduced through the holy trinity of CCTV, banning orders and self-policing by enlightened fans' groups like the Football Supporters' Federation. Trouble still lurks but mostly it is songs filling the air, not bottles or chairs.

Chants soon roll from side to side in San Marino. The England Supporters' Club occupy the South Stand running the length of the pitch. Peering into the setting sun, other fans congregate in Block C of the North Stand close to the away dug-out. 'Shit seats – and the sun's in your eyes,' jeer the South Standers. North, South and the hundreds of hillsiders cheer when Roy Hodgson controls a loose ball, a reaction that has him beaming with pride like a dad being unexpectedly complimented on his dancing. Fans sing about Scotland, deriding Gordon Strachan. They salute Rooney's penalty, equalling Sir Bobby Charlton's record of 49 England goals, and then go back to admiring the enthusiasm of the group of San Marino kids passionately supporting their team.

Those England fans online, their spell-check facility suspended, fill the Reddit game thread with a running, punning commentary on these third-form ultras:

'I am a massive fan of San Marino's firm of 10-year-olds.'

'Water balloons being chucked everywhere, disgraceful stuff.'

'Throwing lego pieces onto the field, someone's gunna get injured.'

'Them 10-year-olds have gone a bit quiet.'

'They will be waiting outside, though.'

'Fisher-Price pirate swords and all.'

'These high-pitched chants are really unsettling.'

'Green Street 4: San Marino primary school.'

'Have a safe trip home, boys. Stay out of the city centre and Toys R Us.'

'Got to be careful not to piss these 10-year-olds off, heard they pack Nerf guns.'

If San Marino's tyro *tifosi* impress the visitors, their players don't. England win comfortably 6-0, the Euros await, and it is time to return to Rimini. The bars are still open. Additional transport is laid on, even for the ticketless hillsiders. 'Will the England fans outside the ground please wait for coaches,' comes an announcement. It's been a good day, with an even better night in prospect.

Viewed from the outside as a homogeneous unit, England's support is formed of disparate elements: young farmers from Lincolnshire alongside squaddies from Teesside, husbands and a few wives, fathers and sons, stag parties and 21sts. A fan since childhood, I've attended

250 England games on the spin, including six as a supporter when placed on gardening leave by the *Telegraph*. The thought of missing a game induces palpitations. I walked out of a maternity unit in 1997 to race to England v. Mexico. England won. I've been spat at by a fan outside Wembley for daring to criticize the team I admire most. I've had players' parents vilifying me to my face, on the phone and via email for slating their offspring for underperforming for England. It's all worth it. It's a privilege to cover England, to travel the world from Sapporo to Rio and see them play, and to appreciate the passion they still inspire. I've had England fans kip on my floor, empty my mini-bar, and hitch lifts in hire-cars and cabs. Any sacrifice on my part is nothing compared to the commitment of those I meet on the road. I hear about the relationships and careers they put on hold, the employers, bank managers and credit-card companies they try to appease and the obstacles thrown in their way. When the game against Poland in Warsaw's National Stadium in 2012 is delayed twenty-four hours because of a sodden pitch (somebody forgot to flick a switch to close the retractable roof), many of the 2,500 England fans stay on. That's devotion. I invite a group of six out for a beer, and one spends twenty minutes on his phone explaining to his boss why he is still in Warsaw. He shrugs his shoulders at the thought of losing his job. England matter more.

In San Marino, I meet more of the devoted. 'I started going to World Cups in Italia 90,' says Martin Parkes, a member of England Supporters' Club. 'We recreated the game when Claudio Caniggia was being kicked by the Cameroonians in the first game. The best player among us was Caniggia and three of us had a go at him and one of us played Benjamin Massing.' A good kicking's administered elsewhere in Italy. English hooligans keep a twitchy Carabinieri on alert. Even the innocents are targeted. 'It was quite intimidating with the Italian police,' adds Parkes, a tiler, as we travel back from San Marino. 'When we played Belgium in Bologna, we got the train and were going to walk round the town but we got herded at gunpoint on to a coach, taken to a compound and locked in. We couldn't get a drink. We were in there for four hours, then herded back into coaches and taken at gunpoint to the stadium and then back to the station. We were sitting at the back of one coach and I looked back and behind us there was a police van. There was a 19-year-old on top of the van with a machine-gun pointing at us.

'There were some nasty people in the club at the time, a hooligan element in the old members' club. The press probably overplay it but that's the job of the media. The trouble in Charleroi in 2000 was over-played. A lot of it was down to policing in Belgium. A lot of England fans are "geezers" – not going to cause a lot of trouble on their own, but if pushed they will fight. The German police are very good, Dutch very good, but the Belgians were a complete contrast at Euro 2000. One morning at ten a.m. we were having a coffee in a café in Belgium. Then six riot police jumped out from a van in full gear. I thought they were coming for us but they wanted an England fan on the table next to us. He didn't have an England shirt on but they knew who they were looking for. They could have been even-handed and just walked up to him and said: "Can we have a word?" But they surrounded the table and grabbed hold of the bloke. Fair enough if guilty, but it was over the top.'

The mood has changed. Sitting in the Lansdowne Road press box in 1995, rapidly filing 'England's Night of Shame' copy after visiting thugs force the abandonment of the friendly with the Republic of Ireland, I'm accosted by an England fan, who charges over, insisting the trouble is the work of the Irish. His nonsensical claim is under-mined further when he tries to kick a Garda police dog as he runs off. Two years later, at Auschwitz-Birkenau, I see a laughing England supporter climb into an oven as another fan takes a picture. At Euro 2000, eight hundred fans are arrested after trouble in Brussels and Charleroi. I visit Vimy Ridge where a couple of raucous, drunk England fans are being asked to leave by Canadian Mounted Police. They should have been sobered by seeing the names and ages on the gravestones.

The turning point in England fan behaviour is widely seen as the 2002 World Cup in Japan and South Korea which is hailed as a huge success from a security perspective – all quiet on the Far Eastern front. Is the trend long-term? Cost deters many in 2002 so the focus turns with some trepidation to England's first away game after the World Cup, the 12 October trip to Slovakia for a Euro 2004 qualifier. Bratislava, where beer costs 55p a pint, is undoubtedly targeted by the violent wing of England's following. Slovakia seems an easy destination being bordered by Hungary, Austria, Czech Republic, Poland and Ukraine. The National Criminal Intelligence Service warns its Slovakian counterparts to be particularly vigilant. Some troublemakers slip quietly into Slovakia via Prague and Vienna. Some aren't that stealthy: ten fans are arrested in Prague after trashing a lap-dancing club. Eighteen known hooligans are stopped at UK airports, including three Carlisle United fans at Stansted.

Ensconced in his luxury Carlton Radisson hotel room in Bratislava, Sven-Göran Eriksson hears what he thinks are fireworks going off in the street outside. England's manager peers out of his bedroom window – which makes a change from people trying to peer in – to witness scenes he later describes to us as pure 'Wild West'. Private security staff shoot two England fans. Bleeding profusely, they take shelter in the porch of the Radisson until rushed to hospital and operated on. Along with the majority of the 4,500 travelling fans, the pair are blameless, just victims of local nerve-snapping. Some thugs are undoubtedly present, though. During the match, riot police wade into England fans. It's a deeply unpleasant evening, disfigured further by Slovak racist abuse of Emile Heskey, Sol Campbell and Ashley Cole.

Bratislava serves as a warning on many levels of the need to guard against complacency and all eyes are nervously on Marseille on 11 June. England followers have previous in the Vieux Port. Overall, though, most England fans have been giving peace a chance. At the 2006 World Cup in Germany, they fill the air with sirens, inflatable Spitfires and shouts of 'Don't tell him, Pike!' during the lengthy security checks going into grounds. At least they're just throwing barbs, not punches. The chants are frequently crude, such as the one directed at Sweden during Euro 2012 of 'you're shit but your birds are fit' – to which 10,000 Swedes instantly reply 'go home to your ugly wives'. The English laugh. Now when England's fans travel abroad they do so with more humour and respect than before, even taking wreaths to lay at war memorials and playing friendly games. Berlin still hears 'ten German bombers' and 'have you ever won a war?' Most fans are more enlightened.

'We went to Robben Island in 2010, did the museums in Ljubljana [in 2015] – we try to do the touristy bit,' Parkes tells me. 'I enjoyed South Africa. It cost over £4,000. But we are savvy in booking flights and accommodation in advance. We drove everywhere. Ukraine was under £3,000. Again we drove everywhere, Kiev to Donetsk. We got stopped four times for speeding but didn't pay anything. They just wanted a bribe. They'd say: "We've got you on camera. Do you want a ticket?" We'd say: "If it's too much trouble to write a ticket." Eventually the copper said: "Just go." For San Marino the flight was £100, €45 per night including breakfast and £30 for the ticket.

'I've got slight concerns over younger fans who'll go to tournaments. There's the possibility of trouble. We saw [that] in Tallinn [Estonia] with some of the younger ones who'd not been to the game. Tallinn is a stag place and many came without tickets. We'd been in a bar earlier and were the first ones back there after the game. The barman said: "Thank you very much for smashing up our toilets." It wasn't us. It was a group of England fans who didn't have tickets, who watched the game in that bar and then pulled pipes off the wall in the toilets and flooded the place. The England fans who came in afterwards tried to sort the mess out. One guy who was a plumber was working on the pipes. We do see new groups around town, bringing club issues into it.

'But there's not the organized trouble like before. There's still a racist element but that reflects society. It does make a difference when the FA talk about it and say not to sing certain songs, more so when Hodgson and Rooney are saying it.' In advance of England's return to Dublin in 2015, the FA pleads with supporters to desist from singing 'No Surrender' and 'Fuck the IRA'. It calls on fans to chant 'Follow England away' instead of 'Fuck the IRA'. Same tune. Fans resent being lectured and come up with their own version. 'There is a chant of "fuck the English FA" but that's over the caps,' explains

Parkes. The 'caps' controversy is a classic FA cock-up stained with greed. 'Caps' are a points system based on games attended with the reward of greater access to tournament tickets. Keen to fill Wembley during a boring qualifying campaign, the FA awards double caps for attending home games rather than away. Eventually sanity prevails and this is changed after creating an unnecessary grievance among the most loyal of England fans. They show a mischievous streak in Dublin, noting how the Football Association of Ireland accepted money from Fifa to keep quiet about the Thierry Henry hand-ball against the Republic in the 2010 World Cup play-off in Paris. 'Sepp Blatter – he paid for your ground,' they sing.

Supporters regularly debate whether players love England as much as they do. 'I think players care,' insists Parkes. 'There's a lot of stuff about players being paid so much money, but that's immaterial. I was a fan of Raheem Sterling until all the transfer business. But you can see they love the game. They want to play for England but it seems their club managers say "don't". The Premier League works against the national team. We've not invested in young players like Germany. When they had their problems fifteen years ago they invested. I don't like it when a number of players don't go to Under-21 competitions. Other countries send all their players and some come through and go on to the senior team. Rooney certainly cares. A lot of the players care.'

Yet it's Rooney who lambasts fans during the World Cup in 2010 after the goalless draw with Algeria, sneering into a camera, 'Nice to see your own fans booing you, you football "supporters".' Parkes shakes his head at the memory. 'Cape Town was awful, probably the worst performance, along with Northern Ireland away,' says Parkes, remembering the 1-0 Windsor Park loss in 2005. 'I wasn't booing [in South Africa] but a lot of fans were. Rooney had a go at us with his comment into the camera but he was terrible. It was like he'd turned into Carlton Palmer with his ball control in that game. I don't understand Rooney sometimes – the ball bounces off him.' Cape Town is particularly disappointing as the pitiful football contrasts with a glorious day. The England band, a brass ensemble not entirely appreciated by supporters, boards a boat called the *Nautilus* and sees off a ferry of loud Algerians with 'Britannia Rules the Waves'. Green Point Stadium shakes with boisterous expectation before kick-off. One flag reveals: 'Serena & Dave. Just Married. World Cup Honeymoon 2010'. Through thick and thin with England. More than 150 England banners and flags add to the occasion. Then the horror show begins. Eventually the booing by England fans is so loud it even drowns out the vuvuzelas. In the ensuing game against Slovenia, supporters hold up the protest banner reading '6,000 miles for what?' They're soon chanting 'we're not going home' and 'Rooney' when England win. All's forgiven. Hope's back in town. England descend in huge force on Bloemfontein for the Germany game with around 25,000 present. One hotel requires a code to access the door; England fans immediately choose 'Dambusters'. Hope is soon run out of town. England are knocked out, but many fans stay on. At the final between Holland and Spain at Soccer City I count forty-two St George flags. Maybe they just dreamed England would be there. Many keep the faith and are in San Marino, and many flock to the Euros in France.

If anyone deserves an end to the years of hurt, and England escaping the lengthening shadow of Premier League clubs, they do.

21

In the Shadow of the Show

IT'S TOUCHING 5.30 A.M. and I'm waiting impatiently outside Ye Olde King's Head on Santa Monica Boulevard. A few yards away in Palisades Park the homeless are asleep or lifting themselves slowly from makeshift beds. Early-bird runners power past along Ocean Avenue before dropping down to the boardwalk, disappearing off towards Venice Beach. Late-night revellers saunter by. I peer again through the pub window for signs of life when suddenly the door swings open and Raul Dourado ushers me in. He's a Dubliner: loquacious, knowledgeable about the game, and his love of conversation is rivalled only by his infatuation with Manchester United. He's diplomacy personified when that Liverpool legend Steven Gerrard walks in a few days earlier.

Raul unlocks right on time. It's 13.30 UK time. West Brom and Chelsea are kicking off in the first of the Premier League's Sunday televised games. California streamin'. Fans arrive fast, timing their run for the opening door, taking up favoured vantage points in a pub lit by low lights and fifteen screens all showing events at The Hawthorns. West Midlands invades the West Coast. Walls are covered with photos of famous visitors, David Beckham and Liam Gallagher, and old advertisements for Newcastle Brown Ale and Boddington's Pub Ale ('the sign of a pub with character'). Raul wanders around, saluting familiar faces, greeting newcomers and sorting drinks. The cocktail list oozes a patriotic flavour: Her Majesty's Spiced Tea and Penny Lane Elixir. 'You can have a beer at six,' confides Raul when I tell him I'm an English journalist.

Sticking to coffee, I settle down to watch the match and examine the clientele. This is nirvana for Richard Scudamore, the executive chairman of the Premier League. This is a freeway to revenue heaven, a gathering of football junkies by the Pacific wearing official merchandising and worshipping at the altar of the Premier League – a scene repeated across the world. Under Scudamore's astute, ambitious leadership, the Premier League explodes from English drama into the most-followed sporting soap opera on the planet. It's screened to 212 'territories' (Premier League-speak for broadcasting countries). It rivals the reach of a brand like Coca-Cola. From LA to Laos, viewers love the glitzy packaging and ever-changing script, including today's new cast members like Pedro and compelling older characters like José Mourinho. Absorbed like rubberneckers, international onlookers love the relentless carnage, the flawed entertainment, the spills-mean-thrills content, enacted in raucous arenas. It's honest too. There's no fear of a game being rigged or a referee being fixed. Few notice or worry that the England national team, the intended beneficiaries when the FA Premier League is formed in 1992, labour increasingly in the shadow of the Show, elbowed from centre-stage by this intoxicating universal passion-play with its tsunami of foreign talent. The lure is strong. 'Gerrard's been in with his family,' says Raul. I check with the LA Galaxy midfielder later and he smiles, admitting he's been to the King's Head for a shandy and to check the games. After joining New York City FC, Frank Lampard finds an Irish pub in Manhattan showing Premier League matches, noting how the abuse he used to endure at away grounds simply enhances the atmosphere and adds to the viewers' entertainment. Lampard also attends packed Chelsea fans' forums in New York. MLS grows in popularity but Uncle Sam, and especially his younger offspring seeking new ventures, are intrigued with the Premier League.

A mix of American and English accents debate Chelsea. 'Why is Courtois playing?' asks one after the Belgian's penalty save from James Morrison. 'Isn't he banned for three games?'

'No, it wasn't dangerous play,' explains another of Courtois missing the last match for bringing down Swansea City's Bafétimbi Gomis.

'But I thought Chelsea appealed and lost. Isn't that an extra game?'

Here we are at dawn in Tinsel Town and a disparate group, many of them strangers, are earnestly discussing the footballing parameters of the word 'frivolous'. That's the power of the Premier League. In the background can be heard the Chelsea contingent in the FCL Global Smethwick End taunting their hosts with 'champions of England, you'll never sing that'. Given that West Brom provide visiting fans with details of the club including their pride in being champions in 1919/20, Chelsea's sniping is as ill-informed as it is arrogant. The watching billions around the world probably won't know the history. It's the Premier League, the modern mania, that counts.

'We get mobbed in here for big Premier League games,' says Raul, who fell in love with Ye Olde King's Head within hours of landing in LA a decade ago. 'I got drunk here straight off the plane. Arsenal were playing Real Madrid. Nil-nil. Arsenal had loads of possession but couldn't score. Typical Arsenal. During the week, people organize their lunch around games. It's about a fifty-fifty split between ex-pats/tourists and Americans who've become obsessed with the Premier League. We'll get tourists out here on holiday, walking in and saying "are you showing the Leicester game this week?" or "the Norwich game?" Hell yes! We show *all* the games! We've got all the screens. Random lads come in like an Aston Villa fan needing his fix on holiday. You can watch more live football here than you can in England. It gets rammed when you get a big game like United against City. There's a great atmosphere. There's never any trouble, although I get emotional when United are involved.' Raul opens up his phone to show me his car sporting a 16KEANE licence-plate. 'I couldn't believe it when a friend got KEANE16,' he adds, slightly grumpily. He scrolls through pictures of Paul Scholes signing a shirt for his son, Ronin. 'My wife wouldn't let me call him Ryan.'

Raul breaks off to serve another customer in a Chelsea top. Chatter is ceaseless about the game. Forget rolling news. What the Premier League really generates is rolling views. Ye Olde King's Head's debating society has so much to digest and dispute, taking in Pedro's influence, Nemanja Matić's foul on Callum McManaman and the reasons for booing James McClean. A discussion about McClean's refusal to wear a poppy peters out. Too nuanced. They've come to enjoy a game, not discuss politics. Anyway, the plot-line changes by the minute. When Chelsea's new match-day medics run on, the King's Head screens almost shake from their fittings at the response of West Brom supporters highlighting the absence of Eva Carneiro following the good doctor's fall-out with Mourinho. 'You're getting sacked in the morning!' and a plaintive 'Eva, Eva!' reverberate from the TV, prompting a further confab among the dawn chorus. What's Mourinho up to? Is the Special One cracking up? Should he go? Surely that thought's heresy? In an age when everyone has a view, a compulsion to express it and the digital equipment to launch it, the Premier League offers excitement and connection. It's Tinder for the terraces. Can't get to the match? Want to hook up with those who are? No problem. Engage via social media. Join the debate. Tweet the stars too. Be gushing, belittle, be part of the Show.

I recall a recent visit to Premier League Productions at Stockley Park to contribute to Andy Townsend's discussion programme transmitted to all rights-holders. In a neat industrial estate near Heathrow, Stockley Park is Bletchley Park in reverse, broadcasting to the world, not eavesdropping on it. It's a hive of activity, spreading the Premier League gospel via TV, web and social media, working particularly hard at bringing China onside. Before the show goes live, one of the guests, Michael Owen, reads some welcome messages to new Chinese broadcasters. It's the Foreign and Commonwealth Office with balls. It's certainly powerful: my Twitter following leaps almost a thousand within a few hours of appearing on PLP. World Cup finals and England internationals generate significant spikes in social media traffic but it is the daily drama of the Premier League, the sackings and signings, controversies and matches, that captivates more.

'It's also about the characters in the Premier League,' adds Raul. 'There's Mourinho. There was Fergie. People love all that. It really is a soap opera. There's controversy.' Endless. Controversy creates more talking points, more fuel for the raging bonfire warming the world. Club rules. 'We had some Liverpool fans here in 2007 for the Champions League final, the one they lost to AC Milan,' continues Raul. 'Some Americans in here said to the Liverpool fans "it's only a game" at the end. It got a bit feisty.' People care. 'There's an American lad who comes in here, a Liverpool fan called Doug, who goes to all their games, Europe too. I tell him I won't serve him in that shirt!'

The Show goes on. Always. It's intoxicating. 'The biggest problem for England is the Premier League – it's bigger than the international stage,' says Sam Allardyce, who warns the FA about the shadow when interviewed for the England job in 2006. 'The Premier League's almighty, and growing even greater. And of course the greater it grows the more it diminishes the player availability for England level. Fewer around. How many has Roy Hodgson got in total? Not more than seventy. This country is probably the hardest to get the international team to its peak because of the Premier League. I had a discussion with the FA over the fact that I would have to spend a lot of time with the managers of every club to encourage letting the player go and that they would be in safe hands, that I wouldn't do anything ridiculous to upset them as a manager and not get the player injured.' Injury on England duty is expensive financially as well as distressing physically and emotionally for the player. Everyone counts the cost when Michael Owen suffers a bad knee ligament injury just four minutes in against Sweden in Cologne at the 2006 World Cup finals. The figures of compensation are indicated at the time when Newcastle's then chairman, Freddy Shepherd, intimates the club receives £10m from the FA and Fifa on 25 June 2007. Injuries understandably infuriate clubs, alienating them from the FA.

English football needs a strong FA. England's protectors risk being consumed by the monster it helped spawn. The FA struggles to drag England out from the shadow of the Show. The organization can rely on few public advocates, although that is true of most governing bodies. It administers discipline which invariably aggravates those in the tribal club world. The FA is an easy punch-bag for those railing against the game's numerous ills. It gets slated for problems in grass-roots football when government is more culpable. It even receives phone-calls blaming it for the weather when games are cancelled. It gets panned when a multi-millionaire star misses a penalty. The timeline of FA mistakes is certainly long – being too scared of Brian Clough's charisma to damaging FA Cup tradition by playing semi-finals at Wembley and moving the kick-off for the final, among many other miscalculations. The FA has many faults; but those who work for a non-profit-making organization, often for modest remuneration, strive over time to provide the ideal environment for England to succeed. Everyone at the FA is obsessed with England. Down the years, those occupying the FA offices, whether at Lancaster Gate, Soho Square or Wembley, feels pride in seeing the Three Lions, receiving letters with the crest on, wearing the England badge. They're England fans. New staff head down to Simpson's-in-the-Strand in London for an hour-long fitting for FA blazer or England suit, standing there proudly as tailors busy around with measuring tapes and French chalk. Even staff who leave FA employ have the suit or blazer hanging up at home, a cherished souvenir of time in the frontline of sports administration. One confides he looks nostalgically at the gold buttons. Others keep the '5-1' cufflinks forged after that epic win in Munich in 2001. Others preserve the Paul Smith suit for France 98 and the tie with the FA crest woven through it. Those who wear the FA uniform describe it as 'magical' and a 'privilege' for all the travails, grim headlines and critical reviews that accompany working for the organization. When the FA announces extensive redundancies in 2015, a sense of bereavement pervades the building. Many people deem it an honour working for the FA and severance hits hard. All this devotion gets overlooked as the public perception of the FA is shaped by occasional scandal, disciplinary machinations, the years of hurt and frequently weak leadership, condemning England to shiver in the Premier League's shadow.

It could have been different. As the game goes on at The Hawthorns I think back to 26 June 1999, to an FA Council meeting at the Carden Park spa-and-golf estate near Chester. The Blazers are voting in a new chairman and Geoff Thompson, the ultimate FA committee man, deeply religious and committed to the line of least resistance, is up against David Sheepshanks, the enthusiastic and forward-thinking chairman of Ipswich Town. Thompson wins 53-31 and the FA loses a vital opportunity for change. Sheepshanks plans to recruit Scudamore as chief executive, which would give the FA a proper cutting edge. But Thompson prevails and Scudamore remains at the Premier League. The man perceived by some as a Bond villain could have been Bond.

Scudamore, the impresario of the Show, is the most accomplished administrator in the country, in any sport, a leader who surrounds himself with loyal, hard-working colleagues who occasionally feel their boss's wrath when things do not go to meticulous plan. Those who experience a Scudamore dressing-down talk of its galvanizing effect. He has mastered the art of constructing, marketing and sustaining a lucrative commercial product, predicting trends, bewitching broadcasters and running rings round government. He takes a problem, analyses it, strips it down to its component parts and rebuilds it like a Rubik's Cube. Few in football rival Scudamore's work ethic, rising early and using his time efficiently, assiduously maintaining relations with key 'stakeholders', attending games, visiting clubs and pressing the flesh. Nobody works the owners better. Even recent furores do not really damage Scudamore. He survives the PR disaster of the '39th game', a move to play a match abroad which would harm the sporting integrity and balance of the Premier League, let alone rip a club away from its local community, pandering to global demand. He emerges largely unscathed from unpleasant headlines that follow a temp's discovery of sexist emails. Female employees rally to his support. By all accounts, Scudamore's a good boss if you accede to the primacy of the Premier League.

Hope for the FA is at hand. Its personable new chief executive, Martin Glenn, a respected marketing man from his days running Walkers Snack Foods and United Biscuits, builds a decent working relationship with Scudamore, trying to find common ground. Some hope is also offered by Raul at Ye Olde King's Head. 'It's not just about the clubs,' he says, returning to the conversation. 'England certainly get a good crowd. When the [2014] World Cup was on, for an hour before England games I put on CDs with "Three Lions" and "World in Motion". The musical prelude may have been more entertaining than some of England's football in Brazil. The fleeting visit confirms that the physical and emotional intensity of the ten-month Show drains its stars, leaving some running on empty by June. The case for a winter break is unanswerable. After Brazil 2014, Fifa's Technical Studies Group picks out certain players as particularly excelling: 'Messi, Robben, Müller, Rodriguez, Neymar, Sánchez in attack, Mascherano, Hummels or Sneijder in midfield and defence, and Neuer, Bravo, Romero and Navas in goal'. None had just endured a Premier League season. Most enjoy the winter break available in Italy, Germany, France and Spain, nations that think more deeply about the game.

In all the tests taken at England training before the 2002 World Cup finals, the fittest member of the squad proves to be Owen Hargreaves, a Bayern Munich player at the time. The FA has long pleaded with clubs to grant a winter break. In August 2002, one of Glenn's predecessors, Adam Crozier, and Sven-Göran Eriksson lobby the clubs, receiving the backing of leading managers like Sir Alex Ferguson, Arsène Wenger, Gérard Houllier and Terry Venables. Sensible, experienced football men know it will relieve pressure on players close to collapse on the English treadmill set to high speed. Eriksson addresses chairmen armed with research from Linköping University in his native Sweden that reveals the Premier League suffers four times as many stress injuries as those countries which enjoy a healing hibernation mid-season. He reminds his audience of Michel Platini's observation that 'English players are lions in the autumn and lambs in the spring'. He could also provide X-rays of the metatarsal plague afflicting England. In February 2004, nineteen Premier League chairmen, barring Richard Murray of Charlton Athletic, vote for a January shutdown. This preserves the beloved Christmas and New Year festive programme, and also offers a weekend showcase for the Football League. Just imagine many of that 400,000-strong weekend Premier League audience feeding their footballing addiction by heading to welcoming Championship, League One, League Two and non-League venues. Just think of the cash injection for the have-nots. The

FA senses a breakthrough. Officials turn to Scudamore and Sky. Will the broadcasters agree to a two-week hiatus? They won't. They can't find other dates available. Scudamore and Sky have a point. The FA needs to return to the negotiating table prepared to sacrifice FA Cup replays, having ties settled on the night with extra time and penalties. It needs to persuade the Football League to make the League Cup semi-final a one-off rather than two-legged affair. Compromise can surely be reached for the benefit of England in tournaments, and also giving elite clubs some physical respite, and precious coaching time, before the Champions League knock-out stages. Smaller Premier League clubs fear they'll suffer cash flow problems with gate receipts delayed, an argument now voided in the age of £8 billion TV deals.

Broadcast revenue streams are so swollen because Scudamore can sell a league that never sleeps. Bundesliga, La Liga and Serie A close down. Not the nutty English. Not the land without a winter break. Scudamore can offer exclusive product for broadcasters around the world desperate to fill schedules, to pack Ye Olde King's Head here in LA. 'The Americans love the Premier League,' Raul resumes. 'The queue to get in here can go round the block. They sit outside on their beach chairs. It's all about the Premier League. I never tune in to Spanish football. I just don't find it entertaining or competitive. Barcelona and Real Madrid are great teams, but Spanish football is really just about them. In the Premier League, anybody can beat anybody on any given day.' Ask Chelsea, the champions who endure such a challenging season in 2015/16, during which Mourinho is sacked. On the screens, Chelsea progress to victory over West Brom but it's hard work. Albion push them all the way. Twenty sets of players never yielding lightly is one of the League's many popular selling points. Clientele in Ye Olde King's Head approve.

Raul darts back to the bar. It's six a.m. Miller time. Actually, it's Fuller's time. Raul pours pints of London Pride, loosening tongues and lubricating debate further. A carousing couple tumble through the door. They're locals looking to continue drinking and happily take in events from The Hawthorns. 'I hate Chelsea from deep down in my heart,' says the LA woman suddenly. The door swings open again, introducing a pair of fans in Manchester City shirts, looking for breakfast and stools at the bar to catch the eight a.m. kick-off at Goodison. The conveyor belt of Premier League action continues. Southampton supporters enter, followed by a Watford fan, taking up position in front of one screen now switching to the live feed from Vicarage Road. 'I can't believe Targett's starting; what's wrong with Bertrand?' complains a Saints fan. On the main screen, the final whistle blows on a 3-2 Chelsea win.

Soon the main blue in the bar belongs to Evertonians. Two sport Bešić shirts, others demonstrate loyalty to Leighton Baines and John Stones. The emotional rollercoaster sets off on its 90-minute ride again. They dissolve in screams of frustration when Romelu Lukaku's effort is ruled out for offside. They laugh when Raheem Sterling slips, prompting another discussion of one of the issues of the day: young players and loyalty, or lack of it. Sterling's manufactured escape from Anfield outrages many present. Another topic of conversation to engage the watching world.

At the bar a City fan with a strong Manchester accent patiently explains to his American girlfriend exactly what Fernandinho does. 'He sits in front of the back-four, and protects them,' he says over a pint, bacon and eggs. Nearby is a sign celebrating Manchester United's '19 times', and models of Winston Churchill and a London bobby. Short of getting Barbara Windsor behind the bar and Jamie Oliver in the kitchen, it couldn't be more English. Raul's super-busy now, taking orders for full Englishes from an Everton fan with his two young children, all in club garb. As they watch 'sixty grand, sixty grand, Seamus Coleman' trying to deal with Sterling, the father explains why and when full-backs show wingers 'outside' or 'inside'. The understanding, the passion, the club loyalty gets passed on to another receptive generation. When the camera pans to Tim Howard, all the Americans gathered in Ye Olde King's Head applaud.

The entertainment continues, the audience now assessing the potential of Stones as he tries to deal with Sergio Agüero. The Watford fan proudly educates a local about Elton John's involvement with the club, the 1984 FA Cup final and the merits of Graham Taylor. It's always uplifting, though never surprising, to hear this sort of fervour for a club. Talk to any stranger in England and club affiliation will quickly be established, and lengthily expounded. It's in our blood. Back in LA, the widespread perception of English football as still possessing a sporting culture is confirmed with applause when City return the ball after Brendan Galloway goes down injured.

I return to England with renewed love for Santa Monica and a request from Raul for a United programme. So I head to the English *Clásico*, United's historic tussle with Liverpool dating back to 1894. On Sir Matt Busby Way, hawkers do decent business selling half-and-half United v. Liverpool scarves. 'Eight pounds – two for fifteen,' they recite. I tweet a picture, and a wave of digital disgust rolls back within seconds. The half-and-half concept is alien to true supporters, an abomination, especially items knitting together ancient adversaries. Ventured tentatively, the argument in the scarves' favour is they are souvenirs of an occasion. Rubbish. Programmes are a more legitimate keep-sake at half the price and with none of the tradition-shredding tourist nature of the scarf of shame. Programmes should be promoted and preserved, especially those of the quality of West Brom's that mix in-depth interviews, homages to club greats, touches of whimsy and innovative covers. Half-and-half scarves are commercialism writ large, an item for day-trippers, not for those who see Premier League rivalry as more visceral than viscose. Encouragingly, the Old Trafford experience submits evidence of a reverence for the past. Mickey Thomas, smartly suited, gets mobbed by thirty fans from the Far East as he marches past the megastore. Still ultra-fit in his fifties, the former United winger could drop a shoulder and outrun them but he happily pauses and signs autograph after autograph. As I wait for the gates to open, I flick through Twitter and see United's neighbours, City, retweeting photographs of their fans tuning in for their game with Crystal Palace from all over the world, from Philadelphia, Egypt, Lake Garda, Bali, Dallas, Buenos Aires and 'sunny, sweaty Singapore'. The Show truly is the League of Nations.

Inside Old Trafford, the Show again delivers. Even with a number of tourists, the atmosphere is good, masking the lack of quality in the game. Two tribes go to war. 'You'll never get a job' follows 'Walk On' follows 'United, United' follows 'Steve Gerrard, Gerrard, he slipped on his fucking arse'. With Leeds United and Manchester City on his CV, Liverpool's James Milner is the lightning rod for Stretford End invective. Milner is one of only seven Englishmen amongst the starting XIs on the team-sheet, a piece of paper resembling an alarming prognosis on the state of England's health. There's Chris Smalling, Michael Carrick and Luke Shaw for United and Nathaniel Clyne, Joe Gomez, Danny Ings and Milner for Liverpool. Watching Shaw shine down the left, certainly in the first half, Smalling continue to mature and Ashley Young and Jordon Ibe coming on is uplifting for those who want Englishmen involved but none of these nine is in a match-changing position and Shaw is soon to suffer cruel injury in Europe. The goals come from a Dutchman, Daley Blind, Spain's Ander Herrera, Belgium's Christian Benteke and the £50m French teenager Anthony Martial – another reminder of Dyke's warnings about the foreign invasion and the dark side of the Show.

An hour after the final whistle, the former England captain Bryan Robson strides out of the tunnel towards the car-park, eliciting loud cheers from a five hundred-strong throng. Such a group will never properly reflect the make-up of United's match-day crowd, as most locals have gone home, but it does highlight global interest. The chant of 'Robbo, Robbo' reveals accents from Spain, Scandinavia and Germany. Filming anything that moves is a Japanese woman in a Newton Heath scarf. And now the players come. Hundreds of iPhones record the passage of modern icons towards their gleaming motors. Bastian Schweinsteiger stops to sign autographs, delighting one Dutch fan by scribbling on his hand. Soon heard is, 'Five pounds – your souvenir scarves.' The hawkers are back around the honey-pot. 'Get your winners' scarves – Martial,' says one, proffering a scarf with the goalscoring, debut-making teenager's image on it. All those associated with the Show have their names sung, even Coleen Rooney as she wanders from the tunnel. TV men like Lee Dixon and Graeme Le Saux are name-checked, remarkably politely given their playing loyalties at Arsenal and Chelsea respectively. The popular Sky Sports reporter Geoff Shreeves is serenaded. 'Give us a selfie, Geoff!' comes one shout. Even the news-bringers are the news in the Show. Even the suits are applauded. Popular after recruiting Martial and getting David de Gea to sign that new deal, United's executive vice-chairman Ed Woodward responds to cheers with a clenched-fist salute. 'Sign Ronaldo now!' shouts a fan. Ambition rules in the Show.

So does enmity. The vanquished manager, Brendan Rodgers, strides to the Liverpool coach to catcalls and cries of 'getting sacked in the morning', and it won't be too long. Jordan Henderson, smartly suited, his back ramrod straight, ignores the boos and chants of 'scum'. Emre Can is greeted with '*Auf wiedersehen*'. Tribalism reigns. From Santa Monica to Manchester, the Show rules.

22

Pathways

To walk into the Nou Camp, Barcelona's ancient fortress, on the night of 2 November 1994 is to encounter a selection of surprises. First shock registering on the Richter scale is the sight of Manchester United's mighty goalkeeper, Peter Schmeichel, standing at the press-room bar, sipping a coffee. I ask him whether I've entered the wrong area, but Schmeichel's almost speechless. The Great Dane, as English newspapers love to call him, looks bemused and unimpressed. He's not playing. The next revelation is supplied by the team-sheet for Barcelona's Champions League game with United. Alex Ferguson has had to juggle his team to accommodate the quota system, which permits three foreigners and two 'assimilated' foreigners, essentially those playing in England for five years or since the youth team. So Ferguson controversially omits Schmeichel, starting Gary Walsh, to ensure he has the right balance in a side including Denis Irwin, Ryan Giggs, Roy Keane, Andrei Kanchelskis and Mark Hughes. The door opens for United youngsters. Nicky Butt starts and Paul Scholes comes on for Giggs. On the bench are David Beckham, Simon Davies, Kevin Pilkington and Gary Neville. They have ringside seats to a mauling, Barcelona running out 4-0 winners as the inexperienced Walsh is exposed. Seven of Ferguson's squad, including the English likes of Butt, Beckham and Neville, return five years later to triumph in the Champions League final over Bayern Munich. Their education works. The 3+2 quota system helps.

Neville looks back on those Nou Camp nights and can see the

link. The celebrated Class of '92 is given a chance to shine. 'When we came through in the nineties, people said, "Oh, it's a special gener-ation," but actually with the foreigner rule we were forced to travel from an age of 16, 17, 18 to meet the criteria,' says Neville. 'I'll never forget the experience of seeing Hristo Stoichkov and Ronald Koeman that night.' Romário, the quicksilver Brazilian, is particularly elusive that evening, scoring twice. 'Sitting on the bench watching Barcelona was the experience of a lifetime,' Neville continues. 'The manager was bringing us in anyway but maybe it was accelerated in the Champions League. It was restricted on quotas, and that meant that we were given experience.'

For Neville, it adds to a learning process already including the cultural splendour and match-day mayhem of Istanbul. 'I came on for twelve minutes in the game against Galatasaray [in November 1993] where Eric Cantona was sent off, and that atmosphere was the greatest atmosphere I've ever seen in a football ground.' United receive the full 'Welcome to Hell' treatment of toxic banners, slit-throat gestures, smashed windows on the coach and police goading Cantona. 'If it wasn't for that rule on quotas, I wouldn't have been in that great ground, in that atmosphere, having that experience. When you talk about pathways, quotas would definitely assist pathways, and I do support quotas.'

As a coach assisting Roy Hodgson with England, Neville knows all about the ramifications of the Premier League clubs' pursuit of foreign players, blocking entry for the home-grown. He's generous with his time, agreeing to meet at England's hotel at the Grove after the Estonia qualifier for Euro 2016 and then talking from his base in Spain during his four months as head coach of Valencia. As typified during his acclaimed time analysing games on Sky Sports, Neville is eloquent and forthright, brimming with ideas for ending the years of hurt as well as exuding a positive spirit about the current England set-up.

'There are two schools of thought: one, we are not producing the players any more, and the other is the pathway is blocked. I can't believe all of a sudden that English football has just stopped producing players. To me there might be a problem with the Academies, but certainly the pathways are blocked. I'm over in Spain now and in a club regarded as one of the top clubs over the past hundred years, and they think they are crazy in English football in respect to prices [for English players]. When you come over here and see the quality of players available for the money you understand why clubs do invest in players from this league, from the French league, because you are getting a higher level of player for a lot less money.'

He sees how quotas help in Spain. 'Over here, you're only allowed to have three non-EU players so we have Danilo [Brazil], [Aderlan] Santos [Brazil] and Enzo Pérez [Argentina].' Valencia have more non-EU but only three are allowed on the field at any one point under Spanish Federation rules. 'There is a level of quota in place. Even here in Spain, where 60 per cent of the league is Spanish, they are complaining. I do feel in England it cannot continue to keep going, these decreasing levels of English players. It cannot be healthy. Chelsea and Man City have been prolific in winning Youth Cups in the last few years but still don't produce first-team players, which for their own clubs is a crying shame. There's always this feeling [at] United that a Youth Cup-winning team will produce two or three players for the first team.

'If I thought we were getting the highest levels winning the Champions League every year, you'd say: "OK, maybe there's a price to pay for English football promoting itself all around the world, it's a fantastic product." But the fact that the League is decreasing in quality in the last five years, and teams are suffering in the Champions League, and the four Champions League places are under threat, it's almost like a lose-lose. The England team is not getting stronger and the League isn't getting stronger. Look at Bayern Munich, the likes of Thomas Müller, Philipp Lahm and Bastian Schweinsteiger. Look at Barcelona and all those players they've produced. That proves you can develop players and have success at club and international level.

'I don't believe the English football fan going to a stadium is any happier than ten to fifteen years ago. You could argue with the increase in prices and that it's getting more difficult to get tickets for the man on the street; potentially the fan is becoming more cynical about the Premier League at a local level. Maybe not at international level.'

The Premier League is a hit around a world uninterested in English disquiet over player development. Back in Spain, rules are more stringent. 'The B team in Valencia is called Mestalla and they play with very strict regulations,' continues Neville. 'It's a very competitive league.' The part-owner of non-League Salford City understands concerns about the state of the Under-21 league in England. 'People do complain about reserve team football, about Academy football, the competitiveness of it, to the extent where even at Salford there have been one or two examples this season where League clubs have sent us players to toughen them up and show them the harsh side of football. They don't believe they get those harsh experiences in Academies where everything is done for them. That tells you that they're not getting the grounding some clubs believe is required to bring them through.

'We were so fortunate, so privileged. Maybe it was timing, maybe it was the manager, maybe it was the quota system, but we could be travelling to Russia on a Tuesday night just to carry the boots for Norman the kit-man, and having an unbelievable experience in Moscow, watching us go out on penalties in the Uefa Cup.' Neville makes his debut in the home leg against Torpedo Moscow and is taken to the Torpedo Stadium for the return on 29 September 1992. Variety is the spice of development life. 'Then on the Thursday night we could be playing Wolves away in front of 10,000 people with Dion Dublin, Mike Phelan, Neil Webb, Clayton Blackmore, Danny Wallace, playing at the age of 17 or 18 against five or six 27-year-olds for Wolves who were hardened professionals. On the Saturday morning we might play in the A team away at Marine or at Morecambe in a non-League ground. We were getting this vast experience of different atmospheres, different types of games, different life experiences, really. You could be staying in a five-star hotel on the Tuesday, travelling on a bus three hours on the Thursday, and playing at Marine on a Saturday for Eric Harrison, who was shouting and bawling at you, and ten aggressive Marine players wanting to kick hell out of you. We really did experience all types of football. We travelled to three or four tournaments a year in Europe.

'I still think there are fantastic experiences to be had for young players but I wonder whether players who come through at 18 have the experience we had. Nowadays it is Academy football, Under-21 football, and does it replace reserve football? Things move on. Facilities move on. Sports science moves on. But I wonder whether it has moved on in the right direction.' He notes Greg Dyke's England Commission into youth development. 'I suppose what the Commission has tried to look at over the past eighteen months is, is there that competitive level of football? Is that pathway there? Does there need to be quotas? Something's not right. Ultimately there does need to be some level of change. Because we have a lot of strengths in English football, but there needs to be some adaptation.'

Neville is passionate about England. He hates imperfections, injustices, the blocked arteries affecting St George's health. He's an England great, thirteenth in the all-time appearance list with 85 caps, having competed with sustained urgency in five tournaments, and now helping empower the current generation of players through his admired work for Hodgson. He's a perfectionist, driven, cramming his calendar with his 'attack the day' credo. He speaks sense at length. That bruising spell at Mestalla at least provides experience that will merely make Neville a better manager in the long-term. He also has much to deliver with his country.

As ever with England, history is all around us. In the Grove's well-tended gardens behind Neville stands a black walnut tree, a gift to the owner, the Earl of Clarendon, from Captain Cook. George Stubbs painted here. Queen Victoria took tea here. Neville takes coffee and looks back on his career with undiminished vigour, recalling the buzz of his first England call. 'It was incredible. I was over in Zurich for the Blue Stars Fifa Youth tournament with Manchester United's Under-20s, a wonderful tournament, playing against Bayern Munich, Barcelona and all the best teams.' It's June 1995. A highly competitive full-back building a hugely productive right-sided understanding with David Beckham, Neville's beginning to establish himself at

United, starting the FA Cup final against Everton a fortnight earlier, but Ferguson clearly feels Neville needs more experience. So he finds himself at this annual post-season youth event in Switzerland. All part of the learning curve. It's hard to imagine a member of the current English generation tipped for international recognition starting the Cup final and then being dispatched to a youth tournament.

Over in Zurich, Neville's phone goes. It's his father.

'You've been selected in the England squad.'

'No, I haven't, I'm over here with the Under-20s.'

Neville smiles at the memory. 'I wasn't even a full-time United player in my own mind. I was so excited but so nervous going to meet up, thinking "I won't play". Warren Barton was in the squad. I thought Terry Venables was just bringing me in for experience.' After reporting to Burnham Beeches, the 20-year-old is soon training at Bisham Abbey with the likes of Alan Shearer, Stuart Pearce, Paul Gascoigne, Teddy Sheringham and David Platt in preparation for the Umbro Cup. Venables, Don Howe and Bryan Robson take training. 'The attention to detail was incredible. We always think other nations have innovative people who can give you information on styles of play and snippets of tactics that are ahead of us, but I always got the feeling with Don, Terry and Bryan that there was a real high understanding of international football, of tactics, of how to play, of interaction with the players. I always remember Terry involving me – a 20-year-old! – and asking me: "What system should we play?" Terry really integrated me into feeling it was a collaboration. I learned so much.' Neville looks the part as England beat Japan 2-1 at Wembley. 'It was a complete privilege and honour,' he says of his early England days. 'I couldn't believe I was exposed to playing with Gascoigne, Shearer, Adams. My feeling was of excitement and nerves, and feeling: "I'm playing for England at Wembley!" That feeling never left me to the moment I actually played my last game for England [twelve years later].'

All the time, Neville looks and learns. 'There was an influx of foreign players in the mid-nineties – Cantona [to Leeds in '92], Dennis Bergkamp [to Arsenal] in '95 and Gianfranco Zola [to Chelsea in '96] – and they weren't just fantastic players, they were fantastic professionals. I saw Mark Hughes, Paul Ince, Roy Keane, Steve Bruce, Denis Irwin, Peter Schmeichel and the intensity in their training, their will to win. We were exposed to that at 17, 18. You have no excuse as a young kid not to have that intensity. The big question as a kid was: "Have you made it?" "You've made it now, you're in the first team." You never felt with those players that they ever felt they'd made it. With the generation at United, the lads at Liverpool – Steven Gerrard and Jamie Carragher – or Chelsea – John Terry and Frank Lampard – and the lads with England – Beckham and Scholes – I never got the feeling with any of those lads that they felt they'd made it. They all went on until they were 36 or so, giving their absolute all. That's the trick. Never believe you've done it. Never believe you've achieved. Never believe you've done well. Have that mentality of keeping going. There are players with England who are not affected by their achievements, the expensive contracts they've received. Look at Michael Carrick with England or James Milner, the experienced players, Phil Jagielka and Leighton Baines. Scott Parker [with Fulham] and Ashley Cole [LA Galaxy] are still going, every single week, still giving their all, still good professionals.' Dedication helps clear pathways.

Some youngsters need guidance. At 23, Ravel Morrison should have 30 caps for England by now such is his talent, a gift sadly overshadowed by off-field issues and distractions. 'I've got a very good relationship with Ravel,' says Neville of a midfielder raised in the Manchester United Academy. 'Even now I still speak to him. I had some messages with him last week. I still hold the hope that he will achieve what he wants to achieve. I saw him just before Christmas in Manchester and had a five-minute chat with him, and he's a different person than he was five, six years ago. He will mature. I hope Ravel does. I like him as a person. I hope he can achieve with the talent he's got. Oh, he's got huge talent, and has got huge belief in himself. He needs to achieve that consistency in his life, on and off the pitch, to be the player that he can be.'

Some players are simply not used intelligently. Frustration still exists that England did not deploy Paul Scholes in his optimum, central position. He eventually retires from international football on the flight back from Euro 2004 where he is used tucked in on the left to accommodate Gerrard and Lampard in the centre and Beckham on the right. 'You can look back now and cry yourself to sleep at night over the use of Paul Scholes for England,' says his old United and England team-mate. 'He should have been dictating the game for England. The team should have been built around him. In the end he was almost shoehorned into a very talented group of players.

'Paul Scholes was a unique player; he could control and dictate the tempo of a match on his own because of his ability. There weren't many who could do it, not like how Andrea Pirlo was running the Italian team, Xavi running the Spanish team or, in the same way, Toni Kroos or Bastian Schweinsteiger running the Germany team. We should have used Scholes the same way because in a tournament you need possession, you need somebody to control and dictate the tempo, but he was stuck out on the left. I look at what Roy's done now with Jack Wilshere. I'm not putting him on the same level but Jack's an extremely talented player and Roy's put him in the very fulcrum of the team, and put him in a position where he can dictate control and get on the ball and have the most influence. Paul Scholes in that role ten years ago would have been perfect.'

Neville's thoughts return to the pathway. He particularly respects managers who give English players a chance. When Dele Alli makes his England bow against Estonia in October 2015, newspapers trumpet the fact that nine of the fifteen most recent debut-makers have been nurtured by Mauricio Pochettino at Southampton or Tottenham Hotspur. 'Honestly, when I look at what Mauricio Pochettino has done in the last three years I have the utmost admiration for him. Before I came away to Valencia, I felt he was my favourite coach in the Premier League, along with José Mourinho, when Spurs played Chelsea pre-Christmas. I went to visit him for a game at the end of last season. I was so impressed with his manner, his work, his attitude. When I came over here to Valencia, some of his words stuck in my mind, like he believed it was so important to have a core of players, important to adapt to local lifestyle, get to understand the Academy coach, understand who the young players were. I thought it was admirable the way he was operating.' Neville's was in the Sky Studio analysing events at St Mary's when Everton visit on 21 January 2013. 'I always remember doing Pochettino's first game in English football, with Southampton, Monday Night Football, and me being slightly sceptical in terms of Nigel Adkins just having been sacked. He'd done a very good job, got promotion, and they weren't in trouble of relegation, and I'm thinking: "Where has this come from?" But three years later you stand corrected.

'Pochettino's a fantastic coach. I love the way his teams play, and he seems to be able to extract the maximum amount [out] of the players there. I love the way he is able to turn Eric Dier from a central defender into a very good central midfielder who is now playing for his country. Dele Alli has been found at a lower level of football and he's turned him into what he is. He's got Harry Kane, although the process started before Pochettino got there. He's done a fantastic job. What he's done at Tottenham and Southampton is definitely a method to follow for all coaches who travel abroad, including myself, immersing themselves in local culture. Don't have this feeling that "my players from my country, or from where I know, are better". "I respect players from this country," – that's what he's always said, and I admire him for that.'

Pochettino has turned the Lane into a pathway. Youngsters hungry for first-team chances, like Alli, are more likely to be tempted there. 'What did I want as a youngster?' says Neville. 'I wanted opportunity. If you're the parent of a talented child, you would look at the club, and go: "Hold on, am I going to get the opportunity here? What do I have to do to be a first-team player?" You look at certain clubs in the Premier League and say: "To be honest, my chances, unless something changes dramatically, will be very slim." If you go to certain clubs, like Manchester United, Southampton, even Liverpool – and you could look at Tottenham now, and Everton, and I've not named every one – you know full well that if you're talented they'll give you a chance, they'll put you in the team. That must count for a lot.'

Neville urges the next generation, and those who guide their careers, to pick clubs on opportunity not salary. 'If a parent's going to Manchester United, Manchester City and, say, Liverpool, I suppose they could look at where the child is most happy when they go for a week's trial. Some parents would look at who they support. They also look at what's the biggest contract, what's the best money. But that's natural in life that you would look at it that way. The question we should be asking is not should parents have a responsibility but should agents be allowed to play a part in children's careers at 14, 15, 16. I don't think so. Agents are all over these kids, hoarding them like sticklebacks in a net out of a pond, knowing full well that clubs are now paying good money for talented youngsters. The money that's getting thrown at parents of children at 13, 14, 15 is incredible. I always remember when eight of us got given contracts on the same day in 1993. We all got given exactly the same contract by Sir Alex Ferguson: me, Butt, Scholes, Beckham, [Ben] Thornley, [Keith] Gillespie, [Chris] Casper and John O'Kane. Because the strength of the group was in the group, it wasn't the individuals. It was actually dangerous to start separating us. Kids talk; they're sensitive, vulnerable. All the other 15-year-olds: "They must think more of him because they've offered him a better deal."'

One solution to the softening impact of large salaries is Colin Gordon's idea of the introduction of trust funds. 'It would be actually very clever of clubs that money was held for them pre-21, even pre-23, and a player lives off decent money for an 18- to 21-year-old,' Neville says. 'How can money not impact you? But you get into EU challenges. The idea of restricting people having money they have earned is probably something that is not allowed. Somebody will challenge it and win. We have to concentrate on the education of youngsters in how they cope with the money, and support systems around them, rather than thinking we need to put a trust fund in place. We're not going to change the system.'

The 'too much too young' verdict is only one critique of the Academy system, of course. Another is that the process fails to nurture leaders. Neville believes good coaching can maximize leadership potential. 'You can develop leaders. Look at Chris Smalling at Manchester

United in terms of his developing over the last couple of years. I look even at Jack Wilshere with England or Jordan Henderson, who display leadership qualities. Henderson is a different person to when he came to the European Championship in 2012. If you look at Iniesta for Barcelona, a leader is somebody who has the courage to take the ball all the way through the match, not necessarily someone shouting, bawling, organizing. In the modern game there's an increasing lack of players who communicate on the pitch, compared to what there was. Maybe society's changed. People are less comfortable to speak out in the group. But under Roy in this last three years, in all our meetings, the players are encouraged to speak, and do speak. In the unit meetings we have, the players really engage. It is an enjoyable place to be when Roy is having a meeting, or me and Ray [Lewington] are doing a meeting, whether post-match or pre-, or reviewing principles of play. We do it in small rooms, and the players interact. It's been encouraged by Roy.'

Hodgson offered Neville a pathway into the England team. 'I'd never met or spoken to Roy before he rang me up and said: "We'd like to have a chat with you." I went over to his house. His reputation was one of caution, "He'll always play 4-4-2." I've seen diamonds, I've seen 4-3-3, 4-2-3-1. I've seen Alex Oxlade-Chamberlain playing his first competitive game in 2012.' With the 18-year-old Arsenal attacker starting, Hodgson's side draw 1-1 with France in the Euro 2012 Group D opener on 11 June in Donetsk. 'In Roy's biggest ever game, Montenegro, he gave Andros Townsend his debut, and then [his second cap] against Poland [to seal qualification for the 2014 World Cup]. I've seen the [2014] World Cup first game against Italy with Sturridge, Sterling, Rooney and Welbeck in the same team. I've seen Dele Alli, Eric Dier and other young players [like John Stones and Ross Barkley] playing against France [at Wembley in November 2015]. I've seen young players continually promoted over a three-year period. I've seen Luke Shaw taken to a World Cup over Ashley Cole. I've seen Ross Barkley taken to a World Cup over Michael Carrick. What Roy's been over the last four years is bold. He's taken the average age down from 28/29 to 23/24 from Euro 2012 to Euro 2016.'

And they're hungry. 'Last June was a big, big moment for me. We had the games in the summer [of 2015] against Ireland and Slovenia. Roy picked a squad of twenty-four players and none pulled out. Not one player. It was easy to pull out and say "I've got a slight hamstring" or "I want a full summer off" but that never happened. You might say it's ridiculous that players pull out, but you go through every European squad, or every England squad named for summer games in a non-tournament year, and how many times can you say that players have not pulled out? It's a myth that players don't want to play for England. It's absolutely untrue. They love wearing the shirt, the pride in the shirt.'

But the 2014 World Cup is poor. Getting knocked out in two games is unforgivable. Still, as England's World Cup dream swiftly dissolves, Hodgson, Neville and the team are saluted by supporters in Belo Horizonte. 'We owe those fans something. The way in which they treated us at the end of that game against Costa Rica, when we walked over to them, I've never seen that before. I hope people recognize there was an 18-year-old on the pitch against Costa Rica in Luke Shaw, there was Ross Barkley [20], Phil Jones [22], all youngish lads apart from Frank [Lampard, at 36].' Jack Wilshere was 22, and the 19-year-old Raheem Sterling came on. 'Yes, people would argue that the 2014 tournament in Brazil was a major disappointment. I'd agree with that, but this summer is a big moment in terms of how the four years will be viewed in terms of the four-year contract we were all given. People will judge it based upon tournaments. I think Roy can be proud of an excellent piece of work. It needs a good finish in the summer. My view would be that he would go on beyond the summer because at this moment in time he's doing the right things and making the right decisions, not just for himself, but for the team long-term. I think of 2010 in South Africa and old players called back out of retirement and panic calls on the last day to players to come and play. Roy went the other way. He went with Barkley, Sterling, Welbeck, Jones and Smalling. [Jon] Flanagan and Stones were brought in pre-tournament [the Miami warm-up for the 2014 World Cup]. Post-tournament, Alli and Dier were brought in among others. He's made a series of really good decisions for the English team but also for future tournaments for the next two to four years and hopefully he, we, can see that through. Roy's brought calmness. Players respect him. They say: "Yes, I like him." There's nobody looking at Roy and thinking: "He's a bad man, he's arrogant." Actually they say: "I've got a lot of time for him."'

And he's English. Neville believes the England manager should be English – a shift in his original thinking. 'I've been on record on the importance of Sven[-Göran Eriksson], of removing the emotion from the job [after the Kevin Keegan era]. However, it would now be very dangerous of the FA to appoint a non-Englishman with what's happened. With St George's Park, with what's happening to the Premier League [the foreign invasion], with the FA Commission that's been set up to improve English coaching, English football and Academies, it's very difficult to think the FA couldn't have an English coach. If the English team can't appoint an English coach then you can have no complaints whatsoever when a Premier League team doesn't appoint an English coach or buy English players. That's not to say it will never happen. Wherever possible it should always be an English coach. That's not just me saying it because I'm an English coach and I want the job, but actually we have to start thinking about looking after ourselves and promoting from within. I complain about the pathway for English players and coaches. If you then don't have an English national team coach it would send the wrong message.'

Pathways involve English coaches as well as players. Neville steps from the comfort zone of television punditry to La Liga, stretching himself, taking a risk. He wants others to follow. 'It has to be a concern that some of the really good brains in English football are being lost to television. You could blame the attitude of the player. "Oh, he's made so much money he won't want to do coaching." In TV now there is a huge amount of money on offer to become a pundit and you are only expected to work forty-six days a year. It's an easy life, and yes, there is something in that. But what's football doing? Look at pathways of coaches in English football. Look at Ajax, who put someone in at 14 to 15 level with some understanding there's a pathway to becoming a first-team coach.' Frank de Boer worked his way up at Ajax; Dennis Bergkamp has followed. Phillip Cocu coached youth sides at PSV Eindhoven before graduating to running the first team. 'What clubs in England are actually giving the opportunity that if you perform well as a coach in our youth team we will push you up towards the first team in the next few years? I can't think of any club in England who'd do that. There isn't that level of promise any more. Football has to look at itself as well as the individual player, and say: "Is the environment right for players at the end of their careers to go into coaching?"'

Time spent analysing from the couch or standing in front of a touch screen going through slow-motion clips is still beneficial. Neville's reputation for perfectionism would see him arrive at the Sky studios at 9.30 a.m. for a show starting at seven p.m. He hungrily absorbed information and studied angles before dissecting moves and enlightening the viewer. 'I believe going into television helped me at the end of my career. It improved my knowledge of football, it enabled me to watch lots of different teams. I do believe that with the technology now in television, with the video angles available, pundits are actually expected to be like coaches, giving tactical information. The tactical cameras can now see all the pitch, the speeds, the average positions, the pass maps, the stats – all the stuff that is available is arguably [at] a higher level than [ever] in the professional game.'

When Valencia's owner, Peter Lim, who also co-owns Salford City, presents Neville with an early opportunity to manage, he leaps at it, leaving the safety of the studio for the insecurity of the Mestalla dugout, a place so insecure he lasts only four months. 'I felt I needed to experience it at the coalface of coaching – the head coach, not just coaching, because I'm obviously a coach for England,' Neville says, talking to me from Spain. 'I turned down coaching roles at differing levels including a couple of Premier League jobs. I just didn't feel it was right. But when I got offered the Valencia job, I thought: "This is an incredible opportunity. This is a challenge that is enormous, something that I would lose credibility if I turned down." The timing was right – I'd done three years in television.

'It is a worry that Carragher, who I worked with for two years, is lost to the game momentarily. He has a fantastic brain, he's got knowledge, a lot of determination, and he's a thinker who could hand a lot of information down to young players, any players. That's where the game needs to say: "Well, OK, how do we get a Jamie Carragher back in, or do we say he's lost to television, they pay him too much money and that's where he wants to be?" Some of the most knowledgeable minds that I've spoken to about the game analytically are in TV.' Old team-mates, players Neville spent hours discussing the game with at tournaments around the world, are now on Sky, BT and the BBC. The Golden Generation has become the Chattering Class. 'Look at Gerrard, Lampard, Carragher, Ferdinand, Owen, Beckham, Terry, Ashley Cole, Sol [Campbell] – how many of them have gone into coaching? You're talking about a whole England team, the best players, and probably only me coaching, and I'm in television as well. David James has done a bit of both. Every one of them has gone into the media. I do know that Rio Ferdinand has been down to St George's Park, Jamie has been down to a 17s game. Dan Ashworth is trying to integrate ex-players into the system to get them involved, within the FA, within the young teams, to try and give them that bug to make them think, "OK, I want a team under my control."' A team leading one day, perhaps, to the top job.

23

Mr Hopeful

THE MAN STRIVING to find the possible in the 'Impossible Job' strolls into a genteel hotel on the banks of the Thames near Twickenham, declines some exotic nectar from the Rugby World Cup cocktail menu and launches into a long discourse on how to end the fifty years of hurt. Under Roy Hodgson, England qualify serenely for Euro 2016 and the clamour, scrutiny and multiple hazards of another tense tournament. Hodgson is in particularly expansive mood, having spent an agreeable morning catching up with old friends like Alan Curbishley at Motspur Park, the training ground where Hodgson himself shaped Fulham's run to the 2010 Europa League final. Equally relaxed in this riverside haven near his home, the England manager appreciates the calm before the storm. These are the good moments. Serenity rules for now.

Born in Croydon, Hodgson feels real pride in his south London roots but occasionally sighs with a hint of disdain at becoming public property. He enjoys travelling by Tube, beating the bumper-to-bumper gridlock on journeys into town or Wembley – another blocked pathway to negotiate – but admits to frequent frustration at passengers' seizing of a photo-opportunity with an alacrity straying into the intrusive. Sitting on the Tube, Hodgson sometimes cannot read a paper without each turning of the page being accompanied by the click of a cameraphone. He briefly contemplates retreating permanently to the roads, and dicing with the London traffic, when comments to a fellow passenger on the Jubilee Line about Rio

Ferdinand's international future in October 2012 lead to an 'End of the Line, Rio' headline on the back of the *Mirror* and an apology to one of England's few seriously accomplished defenders of recent years. The episode reveals much about the England manager. He's more bemused than embarrassed, a civilized man caught out by an old-school naivety that a private chat could end up in large print splashed across a red-top. Manners matter to Hodgson.

On his decision to accept the role in 2012 after Fabio Capello's sudden departure, Hodgson admits to one initial apprehension. Not the media pressure, over-inflated expectation, or club-versus-country strains; no, his concern is whether the players truly crave success with England. They're so well rewarded by their clubs, so wrapped in their Premier League comfort blanket, that surely some lack total commitment to the national cause. For somebody brought up in post-war London, and a friend of patriots like the late Sir Bobby Robson, Hodgson is maddened, as he takes the job, by the thought of individuals not being inspired by representing their country. He knows some of the players, the likes of Steven Gerrard and Glen Johnson, from his brief time at Liverpool, but most are unknown to him.

So he drives into the Lowry, England's hotel in Manchester, on 23 May 2012 with a certain uneasiness, as he recalls over lunch. 'I did wonder: "How many egos am I going to encounter here? How desperate are they going to be to share my desperation to do well? How am I going to be able to persuade them of the importance of England?" I asked myself that.' During the unravelling of the Capello era at the 2010 World Cup in South Africa and afterwards, such questions are asked by the country. 'Yet right from the very first minute, walking into that group of players, I had the feeling that it was not as I feared,' Hodgson continues. 'It was their welcome to me, their reception. It's not a bunch of highly paid egotists doing England a favour.' Hodgson tells his new players that, 'First of all you've got to prepare well, then really believe in yourself, then trust each other. Then you might have to deal with some unbelievable injustices on the field and in relation to how people look at you.'

Before heading off for training at the Etihad the following morning in preparation for a friendly with Norway and then the Euros, Hodgson exchanges views with his trusted assistant Ray Lewington about their first impressions.

'What do you think?' Lewington asks Hodgson.

'This will be easier than doing a club, because we're getting the best,' replies Hodgson. 'We're not getting the wannabes, who are the ones usually giving you problems. These are the best.'

He admires their attitude. 'It's a bunch of blokes who want to do very, very well for England and who are grappling with what people have been grappling with for many, many years. They're grappling with the expectations and the system we have in England which means people play an enormous amount of games in such a compromised period. They're grappling with the fatigue factor and the pressure that comes with England, all those things that no one can change.' Sounds depressing, I venture. 'There's no feeling that they don't want to grapple with these problems, that they don't want to find a solution,' Hodgson responds. 'They do. Whether we can do well enough to battle all these obstacles thrown at us is another matter. The most important thing is we've got a group of people who want to do it. Wayne Rooney embodies that. Steven Gerrard did too.' Captains present and past honour a pledge to their country. 'You don't get 100 caps without having that commitment. I've been very lucky. I've had Ashley Cole, then Frank Lampard, then Steven and now Wayne reach 100 caps during my time as England manager. Even if you're playing for a successful international team, and get to the major tournaments, it's going to take you ten years, without injury, to get to 100 caps. We need to put to bed the thought that the players lack commitment. That thought comes from people with no inside knowledge, who are so far on the outside. If the commitment of the players comes out in your book that will be good. It's difficult to get it across in press conferences.'

That commitment definitely comes across in a fraught phone-call Hodgson makes to the Norwich City goalkeeper, John Ruddy, before the World Cup in Brazil. Hodgson informs Ruddy it's a 'toss-up' between him and Fraser Forster for the final goalkeeping position behind Joe Hart and Ben Foster and he's decided on Forster. Unable to hide his hurt, Ruddy tells Hodgson he's made a 'bad call' and that being such a 'patriotic' person he finds this omission particularly cruel. Wearing 'that Three Lions on the chest is the pinnacle', Ruddy says to Hodgson. After ending the call, Ruddy immediately sends Forster a text saying 'well done', then packs for a holiday, relishing the prospect of spending time with his family but also hoping to get over his heartache. England matter.

Men like Ruddy want to follow in famous footsteps. So does Hodgson – with a chunky caveat. 'Whenever I walk past busts like Sir Alf's at Wembley or the Bobby Moore statue, I'm made more and more aware that I'm part of a very privileged society. There are people within that society that I've been fortunate enough to get to meet and know. I do hope that one day I might match their achievements, but it is too romantic a notion to suggest it. The reason I never read books by football people is that's the sort of thing they write: "I walked past the statue of Bobby Moore and dreamed one day I'd be holding the World Cup." It's comic-book stuff. I've come too far, been in the game too long, to have those comic-book feelings. I'm very pragmatic about my career.' This is not the answer I'm expecting. He surely feels emotional about the honour of being England manager? 'I suppose I do. I'll get more emotional when the day comes when it's finished. I am an emotional person, but any emotional feelings of "how wonderful it is to be here" and "what a fantastic privilege" aren't particularly helpful to the day-to-day job. I have to keep emotion well harnessed. The only thing that would really make me happy is to have some sort of success in this job.' So what is success? 'I don't think anyone who is really honest in football should ever ask for more than at the end of his work to say he did an honest job, he did the best job he could possibly do, given the circumstances. Given the cards he was dealt, he played them as well as he possibly could. Because there's so much fortune involved, so much fate involved.'

He's very aware of the golden achievement of Ramsey, and also the runs to the semi-finals orchestrated by Bobby Robson at Italia 90 and Terry Venables at Euro 96. 'I met Sir Alf only once. I was working abroad at the time and Reg Drury [the widely respected chief football correspondent of the *News of the World* who passed away in 2003] invited me to a football writers' dinner. Reg knew Alf well.' During the '66 World Cup, Ramsey used to walk from Hendon Hall Hotel to Drury's nearby home for a cup of tea. 'There were eight or nine of us at the table at the dinner with Sir Alf,' continues Hodgson. 'It was just general chitchat but I can still boast I met him.

'I knew Bobby well. Bobby was a fantastic human being with such an incredible energy, enthusiasm and passion for the game which rubbed off on people. He was fiercely protective of his players. I never forget meeting him several times when I was working in Sweden, and he was over. He was always raving about some young player he had at Ipswich, a young player he thought was going to be something special. Bobby always had that real interest in players; the players felt it, responded to it, and someone like a young Paul Gascoigne was really responsive to the type of management skills that Bobby had.'

Hodgson respects how Robson drew on the knowledge of wise coaches like Dave Sexton and Don Howe. 'Bobby had the confidence to not be afraid of using people of that quality around him. They all worked for him. Don was his permanent number two. He had Dave Sexton with the Under-21s and scouting. He had Terry Venables there as a younger coach. He embraced them all. He wanted to use their experience and expertise. Bob didn't want to be: "Well, I'm the big man, you're just the number twos and threes." That's a strength in itself, to have that humility, to realize there are other people with brains worth tapping into. I got to know Don, Dave and Terry. They were more about coaching and tactics than even Bob was. You won't find better coaching sessions, tactical sessions, advice and instructions to players than those Don, Dave and Terry gave.'

Robson would stir players by calling on their pride, challenging them, even resorting to tub-thumping. 'Sometimes I do that, but I have to weigh that up very, very carefully,' says Hodgson. 'Players are different now. Managers of Bobby's generation – Bob Paisley, Bill Shankly and later Alex [Ferguson] – were dealing with a certain type of player. I'm dealing with a very, very different bunch now, different from a Paul Gascoigne or Paul Ince.' That duo responded to emotional exhortations. 'Emotional cards can be useful played from time to time but they can also be damaging, they can daunt people. I can tell lots of anecdotes from my career to keep the players amused or enthused but I'm always aware that sometimes they can't relate to it. It's a different world.' Hodgson is reminded of that when telling that unfortunate joke about a 'space monkey' at NASA to make a tactical point to Andros Townsend at half-time during England's 2-0 win over Poland at Wembley in October 2013. After a brief furore, Hodgson issues an apology to Townsend, who tweets: 'I don't know what all this fuss is about. No offence was meant and none was taken! It's not even newsworthy!' However innocent the intent, it's an inappropriate story open to being misconstrued, and also time-consuming given the frantic nature of half-time dressing-rooms.

For all the generational differences, Hodgson is popular among England players. He's considered a solid manager and a likeable uncle figure occasionally prone to odd remarks. He's no Ramsey but he does have many admirers, more on the Continent than in his homeland, following his work particularly in Sweden, Switzerland, Denmark and Italy. Well-travelled and multi-lingual, Hodgson teaches French at school while playing for Berea Park in South Africa in 1973, becomes fluent in Swedish within three months of arriving at Halmstads in 1976 and quickly finds German and Italian tripping off the tongue. He frequently appears on Uefa technical groups. In September 1998, during his brief tenure at Blackburn Rovers, Hodgson is even approached by the Deutsche Fussball-Bund about the possibility of succeeding Berti Vogts as Germany coach. Franz Beckenbauer scuppers the plan, arguing that the role should belong to a German. The Kaiser wants a home-grown chief, reflecting the country's heavy-weight footballing status.

Parachuted in by a grateful FA after Capello's welcome depar-ture from a dressing-room simmering with dissent, Hodgson brings instant calm to the squad. He has a free hit at Euro 2012 where England reach the quarter-finals before fading against Italy, being given a master-class in the art of possession by Andrea Pirlo, and bowing out meekly on penalties, notably to a Panenka from Pirlo. Mistakes are undoubtedly made, Hodgson maintaining the England tradition of deploying unfit players and unwise tactics. He errs in taking Scott Parker, still restricted by an Achilles problem. His 4-4-2 tactics are too static. A quick visit to Casa Azzurri, home of England's nemesis, finds Pirlo chiding England for 'being too cautious' in a game when they have only 38 per cent possession. 'We do need to do better at keeping the ball,' sighs Gerrard as England beat a familiar retreat from a tournament, the stats mocking them.

Hodgson finds himself judged more closely and acerbically two years later in Brazil. His ill-judged, if slightly media-spun, comments at the draw in 2013 about Manaus being 'the place ideally to avoid' (for climatic reasons) guarantees a spiky reaction when England are duly sent up the Amazon. It's another reminder of the need for diplomacy, especially in the age when everyone has a social media platform on which to debate and disparage. Hodgson does have a point, though. Exercising in Manaus feels like doing star-jumps in a sauna. The day before England's opening game with Italy, I join some fans from Huddersfield outside Arena Amazônia marvelling at the newly laid tarmac melting in the ferocious heat.

A flurry of boos greets England's arrival in the steamy stadium on 14 June, the locals having neither forgotten nor forgiven Hodgson's remarks. Conditions, touching 31°C but with humidity falling to 60 per cent, demand an appreciation of possession – never England's forte. Stretching back many decades, English inability to keep the ball is a malady both infuriating and costly. It's a disease latent in playgrounds where manic forward momentum is the order of the school break. It's a sickness triggered by games on cold nights, by the convention of the physical before the cerebral. Grapple, turnover. It's an affliction spreading through the Premier League where supporters demand 'attack, attack, attack', where teams don't worry about risking possession knowing it'll be gifted back soon enough. Fans smile at the end-to-end domestic drama and seethe during international tournaments as the ball is given away cheaply. England look decent in the boxes in the warm-up, guiding the ball first-time around, but then pass-the-ball turns into pass-the-parcel. Get rid. Get up. Get beat. Tournament after tournament, the English are given a lesson in the art of possession. In Manaus, it's Andrea Pirlo who once again runs the game, at the age of 35. England show some zest in the movement of Raheem Sterling in a 2-1 defeat otherwise scarred by lax defending, especially from Gary Cahill, who loses Mario Balotelli for Italy's winner. Hodgson is targeted for some criticism but it's not his fault that the talent pool, particularly defensively, is shallow.

At Hodgson's post-match debriefing, the first waves of censure begin to roll. I wander into the press conference at the Arena Amazônia, musing out loud whether 'we could be out before we finish our malaria tablets'. A weak joke is picked up by Jere Longman, the *New York Times* reporter present in the crammed, slightly sticky press room, and incorporated in a clear-eyed dissection of English travails. 'As the inventor of modern soccer, world champion in 1966 and mostly an underachiever since, England always seems to enter the Cup with a sense of entitlement and insecurity,' Longman writes. 'Hopes are high, but something is sure to go wrong. It always does – often in a penalty-kick shoot-out.' If only. England do not even reach the knock-out stage. Five days later they lose to Luis Suárez's Uruguay in São Paulo. Hodgson hardly helps the mood going into the match in the Arena Corinthians by stating that Suárez cannot yet be considered world-class. As often with Hodgson, his sentiments are correct – Suárez has yet to deliver consistently at a World Cup – but it's still a hostage-to-fortune remark about somebody just voted Footballer of the Year after scoring 31 times in the Premier League for Liverpool. Headlines operate in black and white, ignoring the shades and nuances of an argument, the world Hodgson inhabits. Suárez certainly responds. Hodgson's judgement doubtless feeds into his conviction that the English establishment, whether FA or media, is fuelled by a desire for him to fail. The Uruguayan strikes me as a competitor driven by a desire to prove himself, to keep running from an impoverished childhood, and to provide for his adored wife Sofia Balbi, the rock in his life.

Suárez is undoubtedly fired up in São Paulo, remarkably so given his recovery from injury. During Uruguay training on 21 May, Suárez damages the meniscus in his left knee, undergoes keyhole surgery and is pictured in a wheelchair, yet five weeks later puts England in casualty. The signs are ominous the moment he sprints out for training in the Arena Corinthians the night before and spanks a ball into the roof of the net. The following evening, he scores twice. Watching the tape back reinforces the reality of England continuing to wrestle with old and new woes. For Suárez's first, Gerrard loses the ball (that England staple), and Johnson fails to get tight to Edinson Cavani, who crosses towards the far-post. Phil Jagielka misses Suárez's run and a header duly flies past Joe Hart. Rooney equalizes but England are then undone by, of all things, a Route One goal. Gerrard misjudges a long ball from the Uruguayan keeper, Fernando Muslera, and Suárez pounces. Poor concentration when fleet-footed opponents go for the jugular again costs England dear. Gerrard looks drained. Hodgson and the FA made a mistake in not giving the ageing England captain a break in November 2013, instead insisting he's at the FA's 150th birthday celebrations against Chile and Germany. The FA puts pomp before circumstance and Gerrard is exhausted seven months later. The doomed fate of Gerrard and his team is confirmed when Italy fail to vanquish Costa Rica in the other group game in Recife that day. England are out.

Even now, two years on, the experience rankles. 'In the game against Italy we were really unlucky,' argues Hodgson. 'We were the better team, we had the better of the game, but they scored two and we scored one. Uruguay's goals were offside if the truth be known. Had we gone on to win 2-1, nobody could have really questioned it.' Those neutrals present would contend that, certainly against Uruguay, England got what they deserved for a mistake-strewn display.

In the long, painful inquest on a sweltering day at their Urca training centre after returning from São Paulo, Rooney finds some positives, arguing that 'if you look over the previous two or three tournaments, we've not attacked teams, we've been cautious, but here we've had a go', and agrees that England need to be more 'streetwise'. Uruguay's captain Diego Godín, already booked for hand-ball, forces his right arm into the neck of Daniel Sturridge, clearly impeding the striker as he chases a pass from Rooney. It looks a routine yellow, a second one bringing red, but England do not rush around the referee Carlos Velasco Carballo, pressuring him to make a decision, as Gabriel Batistuta does with David Beckham in 1998 and Cristiano Ronaldo with Rooney in 2004. 'Maybe we're too honest,' is Rooney's conclusion at Urca. He's not advocating cheating, merely acknowledging that many of the successful sides contain 'nastiness' in their make-up.

On hearing mention of the 'streetwise' debate, Hodgson shakes his head. 'What is streetwise? Where is the dividing line between streetwise and cheating? Streetwise . . . words are so dangerous. It's gamesmanship. I don't know how you go about doing it, unless you happen to be that sort of person. I don't know how you go about teaching it. I don't know, if you're a player, how you go about encouraging others to do it if it's not in their nature. Does it mean you start leaving out certain people because they have different qualities? I wouldn't call someone like James Milner "streetwise" but does that mean we don't take James Milner and we go for Joey Barton because he might grab a guy's bollocks and get him sent off? Streetwise? I don't see too many of those Germans doing it. Is Bastian Schweinsteiger streetwise? Is Philipp Lahm streetwise? Is Thomas Müller streetwise? Is Manuel Neuer streetwise? They just happen to be good footballers, knowing what's required of them, doing their job and playing well.' Even those of us long-time admirers of the dynamic, prolific Müller will concede he occasionally crosses the line, responding theatrically to Pepe's flailing arm as they contest possession with Germany leading Portugal 2-0 in Salvador at the World Cup, for example. Enraged, Pepe leans over the writhing, face-holding German and applies an admonitory headbutt. Pepe deserves his ensuing red but the Serbian referee, Milorad Mažić, should really caution Müller. Hodgson's overall point on the Germans carries undeniable substance, however; they receive only six yellows in seven games at the World Cup. They get on with the game, largely eschewing gamesmanship, certainly compared to others.

Germany famously triumph over Argentina in the Maracanã final with a goal from a substitute, Mario Götze, reflecting a theme of the World Cup: almost a fifth of the goals, 32 of the 171, come from subs, eclipsing the previous mark of 23 in 2006. The importance of strength in depth is underlined, as is the acumen of coaches like Germany's Joachim Löw and Holland's Louis van Gaal, a particular master of altering a game's destiny in Brazil. Four of Holland's 15 goals come from those rising from the bench, some of them important interventions. Memphis Depay scores 23 minutes after coming on against Australia to make it 3-2. Leroy Fer strikes within a couple of minutes of running on and Depay within 21 minutes against Chile to give Holland a 2-0 win. Klaas-Jan Huntelaar finds the mark within 14 minutes against Mexico to make it 2-1.

Use the cavalry astutely. This is a salutary lesson for the English as they try to end the years of hurt. Hodgson is far less successful in Manaus and São Paulo at trying to turn the tide with substitutions. Against Italy, he sends on Ross Barkley for Danny Welbeck, Jack Wilshere for Jordan Henderson and Adam Lallana for Daniel Sturridge. Against Uruguay, Hodgson introduces Barkley for Sterling, Lallana for Welbeck and Rickie Lambert for Henderson. Barring occasional moments of promise from Barkley, the changes don't pay off, although their attacking intent needs acknowledging. Hodgson's failure to influence proceedings with his reserves needs addressing, although a shortage of high-class, experienced understudies is also to blame.

More changes are inevitable for the final group game, a dead rubber. On travelling to Belo Horizonte, England have only pride to play for against the surprise group winners Costa Rica (population 4.79m) on 24 June. The Brazilians present in Estádio Mineirão enjoy England's distress, chanting one word over and over again. Almost over-eager to translate, a steward takes my notepad and writes down 'ELIMINADOS = ELIMINATED'. Obrigado. In the face of such local crowing and total ignominy, England's fans are superbly stoic. Back in the bad days, a decade or so ago, they might have responded by running amok; here, they form congas and sing 'Always Look On The Bright Side Of Life' and 'England's going home'. They chant 'super

Frankie Lampard' and cheer every stride of Gerrard's warm-up as a sub. The stock of England's players falls in Brazil but their fans make many friends. England, chastened, draw with Costa Rica, only Ben Foster earning much praise, before returning to Rio and vacating their Royal Tulip Hotel in São Conrado. The French Wags immediately move in, the smell of cologne replacing the stench of defeat. It's a humiliating, early retreat for England. 'It hurt everybody,' recollects Hodgson, especially those like Gerrard and Lampard retiring internationally. 'The ones who stayed on have done well to galvanize themselves, and not get their heads down too much, Wayne being a good example of that.'

Shrill calls for Hodgson's dismissal are briefly heard yet it's swiftly clear that he enjoys the FA's continued loyalty. Having learned from its painful hesitation over Capello in South Africa, the FA moves quickly in the wake of the Uruguay defeat (and subsequent confirmation of England's elimination) to quell any suggestion of prevarication. On the flight back from São Paulo to Rio, the FA chairman Greg Dyke meets with members of his board and Club England officials and agrees to back Hodgson. Gary Neville is keen for the FA to voice its support for the manager. They all know that if they waver, delaying any declaration, it will be perceived as the FA hedging its bets on Hodgson, and the feeding frenzy will be instant and ferocious. Shortly after landing, Dyke announces: 'We're supportive of Roy Hodgson, we've asked him to stay as manager. We think he's done a good job, it's an approach over four years, and we hope to do better in the European Championships.' The FA privately rejects the suggestion that it might have reconsidered its support of Hodgson had England's long-suffering following subsequently turned on him in Belo Horizonte after the Costa Rica game. Rather than catcalls, Hodgson is greeted with cheers when joining his players in saluting the 4,000-strong conga-ing throng. Such a show of commitment to Hodgson and his players undoubtedly influences the press. Had the fans barracked Hodgson in Estádio Mineirão, more newspapers would undoubtedly have followed the *Daily Mail* in campaigning for the manager's sacking.

It's still pretty abject that England are out of the World Cup before Germany have even played two games. Yet a comment from Löw resonates with many of those sympathizing with Hodgson. One of the most well-attended and instructive press conferences during the World Cup occurs on 3 July in Rio when the Germany coach observes: 'In England there are many foreigners and perhaps that is not always beneficial . . . it becomes difficult for the national coach to get things moving.'

As Hodgson finds. English players contribute roughly a third of playing time in the Premier League, down from two-thirds twenty years ago. 'Most of the star players in our club teams are foreigners,' laments Hodgson. 'Just take the past eight years here – look at the change. Once upon a time to play for England you had to be the first name on your club team-sheet. It would have been unthinkable for Terry Venables, Glenn Hoddle, even Steve McClaren to put someone in the team as a regular starting player who didn't play for his club team. That's 30 per cent of our players. That's the change.'

Gary Neville bemoans that his celebrated Manchester United 'Class of '92' would struggle to break through en masse nowadays. You'll win nothing with kids? Hodgson harks back to that famous generation at United, the boys who became men who became champions of Europe. 'Ferguson in '92 didn't go out and buy,' says Hodgson. 'When players like Denis Irwin disappeared, in came Neville.' Both Gary and Phil seize their chances. 'Gary says quite often to me that he doesn't think that today he and his brother and Nicky Butt would have got anything like the same chance. With Scholes and Beckham, who knows? They got their chance. It's about pathways. We've flooded so much money into the Premier League that they don't need to trust in the youngsters any more. Before, you were given the chance when a vacancy arose. Now they go out and buy any foreign player that takes their fancy for quite huge sums of money.'

United invest £38m basic in Anthony Martial after 70 games and 15 goals for Monaco, rising to £58m if certain caps, goals, Champions League and Ballon d'Or targets are achieved. 'Let's be fair,' insists Hodgson, 'Martial is a very talented 19-year-old Frenchman, but everybody knows he's a very talented 19-year-old Frenchman because he's been playing for a year or two in a top team. Monaco played him.' Hodgson's inference is clear: Martial is given a chance by Monaco, who spot his burgeoning class at Lyon, recruit him for around £4m, back him and allow him to learn in the most advanced classroom of all – on the pitch. France reap the benefits.

The idea of imposing quotas on the Premier League, a route pursued by Greg Dyke, brings a shake of the head from Hodgson. 'You're not going to get round EU law for a start,' he says. Let alone Premier League intransigence. Ambitiously, Hodgson dreams of an age of enlightenment among owners appreciating the talent within their Academies and, even more ambitiously, encouraging their results-driven managers to promote youth. 'It's got to be self-regulatory. I've got to hope more and more owners will tell their managers to do it. I've proved it at Fulham and West Brom.'

Hodgson is also a pragmatist. On succeeding Lawrie Sanchez at Fulham in December 2007, he drafts six players in during the January transfer window: a Canadian (Paul Stalteri), a Dane (Leon Andreasen), a Norwegian (Brede Hangeland), an American (Eddie Johnson) and two Finns (Toni Kallio and the 36-year-old Jari Litmanen, who never plays a first-team game for the club). He does give British players a chance, building around Danny Murphy, Bobby Zamora, Simon Davies, Aaron Hughes, Chris Baird and Paul Konchesky. But there are still only four Englishmen – Murphy, Zamora, Konchesky and Jonathan Greening – in his match-day 18 for the 2010 Europa League final loss to Atlético Madrid in Hamburg.

Hodgson's ill-received labours at Liverpool, where he signs Konchesky and Joe Cole but also the expensive Dane Christian Poulsen amid a growing backdrop of dissent from the Kop, are swiftly curtailed in January 2011. Six months later, in his first transfer window at West Brom, where he's head coach operating in more of a Continental recruiting structure with Ashworth, Hodgson oversees the arrival of a £5m Irishman (Shane Long), a Northern Irishman (Gareth McAuley), two Hungarians (Zoltán Gera and Márton Fülöp) and three Englishmen (Billy Jones, Jamie Edge and

Ben Foster on loan from Birmingham City). He sends the 18-year-old Saido Berahino out on loan.

The demands of the game, namely staying aboard the gravy train of the Premier League, preclude major gambling with youth, yet Hodgson emphasizes he has form for evolving teams. 'I'm entitled to speak about it as I've done it throughout my career. At Malmö we won five championships [in the 1980s] with three teams and replaced players from within.' Home-grown starlets like Martin Dahlin flourish under Hodgson at Malmö where the Swedbank Stadion boasts a 'Roys Hörna' – 'Roy's Corner', a part of a foreign field that will for ever be indebted to an Englishman.

Hodgson articulates a message he would love Premier League owners to tell their managers. 'I'd like the owners to say: "Yes, you'll be able to buy players, but because I'm spending bundles on this Academy and we're producing one or two very good players, I want you to not necessarily go racing out to buy the latest Dutchman every time someone goes down injured."' Affront creases Hodgson's face. 'How many more Dutchmen are we going to get who've scored 20 goals in Holland, come over here and can't deal with the pace of the game? There are very, very talented young players at Chelsea who wouldn't be far off our national team like Ruben Loftus-Cheek, Lewis Baker and Dominic Solanke, but what's the point in them coming through when there's nowhere for them to go?' As our conversation occurs before José Mourinho's dismissal, I ask Hodgson whether he consults the Special One on Loftus-Cheek, Baker and Solanke. 'No! Because what José Mourinho has to do is win matches for Chelsea. If Nemanja Matić goes down injured just before the window, José will go and find the best central midfielder for £30m, £40m or £50m.' This is where Hodgson wants Roman Abramovich to step in. 'The owner should say: "Hold on, we're not spending any more money. We've got a boy here, Ruben Loftus-Cheek, that you tell me is going to be a good player. I accept as owner that we won't win as many games as with Matić and we might not win the championship this year but I'm not giving you £30m, £40m, £50m to go and buy a Dutchman, Frenchman, Italian or South American. I want you to give

Loftus-Cheek a go." There's no doubt we're going to miss a lot of players if we're not careful because they're going to reach a certain level and then not play. The worse thing is they become too good to sell and not good enough to play.'

One of his most significant players, Andros Townsend, has faced such a conundrum. The winger excels for Hodgson, even providing the momentum that sweeps England towards Brazil, but is not always trusted by Mauricio Pochettino at Tottenham Hotspur (and the smart Argentinian is actually one of the better overseas coaches at backing local contenders). 'Townsend is a great example. He can get selected over other people to play for England but he can't get in the Tottenham side,' rues Hodgson. The main alternatives out wide, Érik Lamela and Nacer Chadli, cost substantial sums, £25.7m and £7m respectively, while Townsend is home-grown, developing in nine loan spells, but now 24. 'It needs to be brought to people's attention more that the next time we win something, there's a good chance that the player who scores the winning goal will not play for his club team, he'll only be a sub. It doesn't mean to say that the player who starts for us but not for his club is a bad player. It just means he's in an environment where he's surrounded by lots of foreign players who may be chosen over him for experience, or may be chosen over him because the manager thinks Lamela and Chadli are better than Townsend.' When the January 2016 window opens, Townsend speeds off to Newcastle United.

Sensitive to their plight in what can be a cruel system, Hodgson still wants other bit-part club players to be stronger, shaping their own future by pushing for a move rather than sitting on the bench, however plumped up the financial cushion is to make the position bearable. 'Players have to take responsibility. We need more players with a bit of ambition to say: "Look, you don't want me, you're not making me number one and I think I'm good enough. I want to go and play elsewhere. I'm not prepared to spend the next two years as your number-one sub."' But will they say that? Their agents tend to stick to the path offering most riches. 'In an ideal world I'd like to think their agent would have the common sense to be saying to them: "You need to play, you need to leave this club, accept less money. Give up your £50,000 a week, go and play for £30,000 a week and kick-start your career and play." '

As a mild inquest starts after Brazil, Hodgson has to live with the reality that he does not have a James Rodríguez, Lionel Messi, Alexis Sánchez, Neymar or Müller, going for it, using quick transition to exploit defenders out of position and raid into the final third. At least Dele Alli's bold approach stirs the adrenalin. 'Major tournaments are won by individuals and individual moments of talent,' Hodgson continues. 'What you really need is that individual in your ranks. Have we got it? Have we had it? That's the question. Traditionally, we are stronger as a team than having an individual talent who can totally change a game and win a game on his own. There's a good chance that the team who wins the Euros isn't necessarily the best but does have an outstanding individual. Germany have proved that the team can do it too with a number of very good players, without being one where you say, "If we put him out of the game, they're finished." The individual – the "marquee" player as the Americans call him – is always going to be very important and his importance will increase the higher the level of competition. He will be important in the quali-fiers but where he will really stand out is in the finals, making the difference for a team that's not special by scoring a fantastic goal or creating a chance. That Argentina team of '86 had players who weren't necessarily a lot better than England's but Diego Maradona was. He picked up the ball, ran through the whole team and scored [in the Azteca].'

It comes back to the relative paucity of English talent, or failure to use it properly, as occurred when Glenn Hoddle and Paul Scholes were playing. 'I don't think there's a suspicion of flair players,' counters Hodgson. 'Maybe in the past, I don't know. Scholes wasn't a flair player. Hoddle was. He was a very special talent. Scholes was unfortunate. Building a team around him would have meant jettisoning one of Gerrard and Lampard, so he was unlucky. You're saying the coaches at that time chose the wrong one? Jettison Gerrard or Lampard? Jettison Scholes or push Scholes out to the wing where he was never going to be as good? More and more there's an awareness that if you've got an outstanding player you have to use him in his best position. The big question is, do we have those outstanding individuals? I'm not certain. If we had one – a Scholes, Messi, Ronaldo or Maradona – I think we'd use him. I don't think there's any fault in our psyche which would have us not using him. Are we actually producing him at the moment? Looking at the current team, if he exists, he's still an embryonic version. Don't forget, Maradona's first World Cup in '82 wasn't a great individual success for him: he got kicked to death [by cynical markers like Italy's Claudio Gentile], got sent off [for retaliating against Brazil's João Batista da Silva], and he was only 21. I think we've been a bit unlucky with them. Michael Owen – injuries. Wayne Rooney – couple of injuries. With any player, however we label him, "Steady Eddie" or "Flair", he's got to produce. There's no good having a flair player for England who doesn't do what you think his flair is going to do.'

Such is the frequency with which England footballers mention needing to perform in a tournament that 'time to deliver' is number one in the Lingo Bingo played by the England press when players are interviewed. Unfortunately, penalty shoot-outs scupper that. 'We make too much of penalties,' says Hodgson. 'But it'll always be chucked at us because we've lost in shoot-outs. Historically, it's there: quarter-finals with me, semi-finals during Terry and Bobby's time.' Not forgetting the round of 16 under Hoddle and two quarter-finals with Sven-Göran Eriksson. 'I can't deny it. If somebody says to me: "I tell you what – you're no good at penalties," what can I say? I can't say, "Yes we are. We're terrific at penalties." "No you're not, you fucking lost." "OK, get the stick out, yeah, we lost." It's an easy stick to wield against us but I have to keep divorced from that and concentrate on the main aspects of the job. There's no doubt when we come to the tournament [in 2016] penalties will once again be a factor for us. We will practise them. We will try to make sure we're ready. But there's only a 4 per cent chance of that [a shoot-out] happening, so 96 per cent of the work is going to help us win the game and put the shoot-out out of the question in the first place. An awful lot of things go on in 90 minutes, 120 minutes.

'Every now and again in a tournament a game can't be decided over 120 minutes and it comes down to the hazard of a penalty shoot-out, and how many mentally strong, confident players you have in your team. It's certainly not to do with technique. In a park, under no pressure, ten Argentinians against ten Englishmen, the result would be 10-10. I remember doing penalty shoot-outs in training in Brazil on a regular basis and if one was missed that would be surprising. Ashley Cole, who was one of the players who missed in Ukraine [at Euro 2012, against Italy], did not miss a penalty in training. Not one.' It's that old Hoddle critique of not being able to replicate the tension. 'It's the history, the occasion; can you keep your emotions in control, can you focus?' adds Hodgson. 'Focus, mental strength and confidence will hopefully be improved by all the work we're doing with players.' Dr Steve Peters, the sports psychiatrist, has earned many disciples among the England congregation. Hodgson approves. 'Can people be helped to be mentally stronger and retain their confidence? Yes they can. Can penalties be practised? Yes they can.'

Alerted to the contention voiced by Gerrard in LA that England need to rely on regular club penalty-takers, Hodgson shrugs. 'We're in the hands of the clubs. I don't know if I can persuade José Mourinho [or his successor, interim coach Guus Hiddink] to take Eden Hazard off penalties and give them to Gary Cahill. I don't know there's a certainty that Louis van Gaal would give the penalty to Wayne Rooney; he might not, he might decide Juan Mata's a better penalty-taker.'

Pausing briefly, Hodgson then makes a statement arrowing straight to the heart of the England job: 'A lot of our work these days is on the mental side.' He warns against players believing the hype emanating from gushing headlines after a bravura exhibition or two. 'You have to be very, very aware of anything that will soften you and make you complacent,' Hodgson tells them. He's also aware that putting on the England shirt has become a daunting test of character, partly because of the intense scrutiny. I relate the story of the ex-England international whose last thought on leaving the Wembley tunnel is what match rating he'll get in the papers. 'Well, that's sad,' replies Hodgson. 'I've tried to encourage players not to look at that. I tell them no journalist has ever scored a goal or prevented a goal. People can get into your head. It's unacceptable that a player's not fully focused on what we want him to do because someone's written an article he doesn't like.

'We try to cocoon ourselves so we don't leak performance-enhancing qualities because we're getting battered with people saying "you're no fucking good". If we're no good, then that's got to come from within us. We've got to look at each other and say: "Hold on, we're not any good. What's wrong? Can we not defend? No?" If we agree that we're no good because we can't defend, can't score and crumble when we face a little bit of pressure, what are we going to do about it? What's the solution? Forget what journalists are writing about you. Forget what your mum and dad are telling you. Forget what your agent's telling you. Look in the mirror. Tell *us* what you think's wrong. We'll tell you what *we* think's wrong. Can you handle it?'

Hodgson's speeches to players can be delivered with more conviction than critics believe. 'One thing we definitely preach is that "it's in our hands, we control it". We don't accept excuses like we're put under too much pressure by the English media, we aren't getting enough time together, we don't have a winter break, we're not giving ourselves the best possible chance. If we fail, then the debate about things like a winter break will go on and, who knows, maybe one day there will be a slight improvement, but at the moment we have to work with the situation we find ourselves in.'

The thought of a restorative time-out brings a sigh from Hodgson. Like all of his predecessors, the England manager craves a period of January hibernation for his players but knows full well that the broadcasters, especially overseas rights-holders, will demand the Show goes on. 'Our voice isn't powerful enough to override commercial interests,' says Hodgson, who wants a radical re-think of the calendar, stretching the club game into the summer. 'It's common sense. No one can justify to me dismissing two and a half months and then fitting in fifty to seventy games in the remaining nine and a half months. Why do we have to stop? I'd play League matches in the summer.

I don't want five weeks doing nothing. I'm a footballer. The most enthusiastic you'll ever see footballers play and train is when they come back after the long summer break. You have to be very careful: they're so pleased to be back they run their bollocks off and get injured.

'That's where the winter break makes sense: to give them a physical and mental break in January to recover from an intensive period – the early League games, the Champions League and international matches – to let them get their breath back, lift their head up, take their eyes from the floor, out of the mire, and see there is a world out there. Dubai, Vegas, Indonesia, wherever you want, take a couple of weeks. You'd find when they come back they'll be refreshed. Like the Italians do, over Christmas and New Year because they're religious. We like our Christmas and New Year games, so let's push it back to January, even early February. Let the players have something to look forward to when they're thinking "it's getting tough now".'

Hodgson shivers slightly in frustration at discussion of a winter break, knowing how significant it would be to England's aspirations but also not wanting to give players any more reasons for self-doubt. 'There's a no-excuses culture. I'm trying to make players more and more aware of what's really important and what's peripheral – your agent, commercial appearances – when at times they can be led to believe it's important but really it gets away from the nitty-gritty of the game, and you're going to suffer for it. I think they do understand it. We're trying so hard to develop an England mentality, an England philosophy, but we don't have an "England Way", really. They are the clubs' players, paid by the clubs, belonging to the clubs. We get the benefit of them ten, twelve times a year for a short period of time. We just work with the players as we feel they should work. We're not going to go [with] that DNA business,' he concludes, referring to the 'England DNA' document published in 2014 by Ashworth, scripting how 'the future England player' should be technically and tactically accomplished, and possess physical, psychological and social strengths.

Hodgson is not a huge fan of documents. PowerPoint presentations and new-fangled coaching-speak don't float his boat. He's not a big admirer of players' advisers either. 'I have nothing to do with agents. I never speak with agents. I never work with agents. People say Leon [Angel, a chartered accountant at Hazlems Fenton] is my agent. He isn't, really. Leon's never got me any jobs. What Leon did when I got contacted by Liverpool [in 2010] is I got him to speak about my contract. But it wasn't him who got me the Liverpool job, far from it. Christian Purslow [Liverpool's managing director at the time] decided to put me up [for the job].' Hodgson is well connected, and when his time with England expires he will doubtless be approached by clubs and, probably, Scandinavian countries seeking his services. Uefa also seems an obvious port of call.

He's respected as a hard-working systems man, spending most training-ground time on team shape, religiously drilling the players, stopping training frequently to make them understand fully his plan. Such methods are simpler at club level, with time to mould a mentality. With England, Hodgson tries to keep things simple, building on a back-four because he feels it best covers the width of the field defensively and provides cover when a full-back pushes on. He preaches the importance of pairs all over the pitch, from the centre-halves to full-backs dovetailing with wide midfielders, to central midfielders (and he occasionally namechecks Italy's World Cup-winning blend of Pirlo and Gennaro Gattuso), to centre-forwards, increasingly with one up, one off (noting Francesco Totti dropping off Luca Toni in 2006). Hodgson loosens up tactically during his time as England manager, moving from 4-4-2 at Euro 2012 to 4-2-3-1 in Brazil, then qualifying for Euro 2016 with a mixture of diamond, 4-3-3 and 4-2-3-1. Has he changed? 'I work with England as I worked with Halmstads in 1976 in some way, hopefully a damn sight better. If you're talking about the actual core of the work, and what I believe in, and what I think will lead to success, that hasn't changed radically, just as I'm sure Sir Alex Ferguson hadn't changed radically from Aberdeen or St Mirren. You get wiser.'

As our meal draws towards coffee and a close, Hodgson checks his phone to see whether his son Chris has reached Heathrow en route back to his US home. England's manager then gets up to drive the short distance back to his riverside residence. Three hours in his company provides a welcome response to those who feel the England camp don't care, as well as a sad reminder of the myriad impediments to success. England matter massively, even in the changing landscape of modern football. 'Sometimes we are encouraged to believe that it's the Champions League that counts, and people don't want international football, but that isn't true,' says Hodgson. 'Not everyone can watch Arsenal, Chelsea, Liverpool, Man City and Man United. This is a big country, sixty million people, and many haven't got a top-class team within fifty miles, and even if they did they wouldn't be able to afford to buy a ticket to go and watch them play, so internationals are important. England are important.'

With that statement of intent, Hodgson heads off to continue the fight to end fifty years of hurt, knowing full well that this nation yearns for the chance to dream again, to watch a team with the guts to rival the Boys of '66. To feel proud again. It's taking so long it's more than anyone can bear. As Hodgson walks off to his car, I shout after him: 'Good luck.'

24

A Blueprint for Change

A FOOTBALLING NATION as historic, wealthy and obsessed as England must target more than heroic failure in quarter-finals. England's Dele Alli generation will mature, hitting its peak at the 2022 World Cup. They'll enjoy that tournament's winter timing, when English players are less knackered. To facilitate their journey towards Qatar, and confronting the fifty years of hurt, five areas need tackling.

No. 1: England's dressing-room. Banish the fear factor. Lighten up. Stage more open training sessions for fans. Hold informal gatherings with media. Worry less, think more. All age-groups to contribute to team-talks and tactical reviews. Analyse the art of penalty-taking. Invite Alan Shearer to training. Stage penalty shoot-outs after every friendly. Pause on the walk to the penalty spot. Take more responsibility.

No. 2: St George's Park. Attach ex-internationals to age-group teams, inspiring kids, even mentoring them, and educating aspiring coaches. Train up more English coaches, more inventive ones, to deepen the pool of England managerial contenders. Fast-track ex-pros. Develop more skills coaches and send them into schools and estates. Invite Glenn Hoddle in to foster flair, complementing Dan Ashworth. Appoint former internationals to the FA board, advising on mind-sets and future managers. Campaign on childhood obesity, a ticking time bomb for the NHS and England. Lobby the government to grant the Sports Minister full Cabinet status. Compile that President's Book of advice from outgoing England managers and players, and include the thoughts of fans' representatives.

No. 3: Academies. Encourage responsibility-taking on and off the pitch. Secondments abroad from the age of 13. Complete further education. Introduce performance-related pay and trust funds for Under-21s. Coach man-to-man marking. Scrap the Under-21s league and reintroduce a reserve league contested at main stadia – televised, free entry, with substantial prize money. Outside Academies, revolutionize the school season to stretch into summer with indoor, small-sided leagues, possibly futsal, in winter. Teach parents to stay quiet in schoolboy matches. Silence is golden. Compile a list of agents approved for representing youngsters, focusing on pathways not pay-outs.

No. 4: Premier League. Reward Academies financially for England debut-makers. Invite the Premier League to have a base alongside the FA, Football League, Professional Footballers' Association and League Managers' Association at St George's Park. Fight the Premier League to have club fixtures moved before major England games. End the season earlier in a tournament year. Ban England players from end-of-season club tours. Place a surtax on overseas signings to go into grass-roots. Spend more time training. Reduce Premier League to eighteen clubs, scrap FA Cup replays, and introduce a winter break between the FA Cup third and fourth rounds.

No. 5: Wembley. Improve the supine atmosphere. Make Wembley more intimidating, more of a home for England, rather than a featureless, multi-purpose stadium. Get the decorators in. More England banners and flags. More drums. More incentive to arrive earlier with subsidized catering vouchers with tickets. Make teams enter from a tunnel in the corner, building up expectation. Move at least one home game a year away from Wembley to the north-west or north-east, re-engaging England with fans who live far from London.

Change the anthem to one more suited to England than Great Britain. Consult players and supporters. Anyone for 'Jerusalem' in England's green and pleasant land?

Try it. Try it all. Be bold. England expects better. The years of hurt have to end.

Acknowledgements

My immense gratitude to all those who gave generously of their time and thoughts: Jack Charlton, Alan Mullery, Peter Shilton, Duncan Revie, Glenn Hoddle, Lady Elsie Robson, Gordon Hill, John Barnes, Peter Reid, Chris Waddle, Mark Wright, Gary Lineker, Ian Wright, Alan Shearer, Michael Owen, Gary Neville, Steven Gerrard, Frank Lampard, Colin Gordon, Martin Parkes, Gareth Ainsworth, Jermaine Jenas, Raul Dourado, Roy Hodgson, Dan Ashworth and Howard Webb. Also my thanks to those who helped on a non-attributable basis. In appreciation of all of their contributions, donations have been made to the Sir Bobby Robson Foundation and the Bobby Moore Fund.

My thanks, also, to those who helped in setting up interviews: Mark Whittle at the FA, Helen and Will Logan of Northumberland Tea, Liz Luff at the Sir Bobby Robson Foundation, Mel Chappell at I Will Know Someone, Simon Marsh at Michael Owen Management, Paul Mace, Sam Cooke at New York City FC, Brendan Hannan at LA Galaxy, Simon Felstein and Jonny Davies at Tottenham Hotspur.

My thanks, also, to Paul Gascoigne, Stuart Pearce and Pete Davics for the Q&A at the Ritzy for the launch of the *Gascoigne* film, to Joel Kennedy and Alex Hamilton of Entertainment One, to Ian Dennis, Cat Elliott Winter, Phil Shaw and Craig Mann. Thanks, too, to the National Memorial Arboretum, Premier League, FA, Football League, MLS, FIFA for its World Cup technical reports, the *New York Times*, *The Times*, the *Daily Telegraph* and the *Sun*. I drew particular inspiration from Mark Pougatch's *Three Lions Versus The World* and Clive Leatherdale's *England's Quest for the World Cup*.

And, finally, thanks to my literary agent David Luxton, my editor Giles Elliott, copy-editor Dan Balado, Ben Willis, Alice Murphy-Pyle, Vivien Thompson and everyone else at Transworld Publishers who helped make this book happen.

Picture Acknowledgements

All photographs supplied by Press Association Images, with credits as follows:

Cricket match; exhausted players; Jan Tomaszewski; Ron Greenwood; Hoddle debut; Waddle and Barnes all © PA Photos/PA Archive/Press Association Images

Taylor, Eriksson and Capello; Gerrard dejection 2004 all © Owen Humphreys/PA Archive/Press Association Images

Shearer and Lady Elsie © Anna Gowthorpe/PA Archive/Press Association Images

Euro '96 fans; Sheringham celebration; Ince and Wright all © Adam Butler/PA Archive/Press Association Images

Terry Venables © Neil Munns/PA Archive/Press Association Images

Hoddle and Wright © Fiona Hanson/PA Archive/Press Association Images

Gerrard dejection 2006 © Martin Rickett/PA Archive/Press Association Images

St George's Park © Rui Vieira/PA Archive/Press Association Images

Moore statue; Moore plinth both © Cathal McNaughton/PA Archive/Press Association Images

Index

Bell, Colin 45, 55
Bell, Donald 256
Bellamy, Craig 95, 221
Bennaceur, Ali 84, 85, 86, 88
Berahino, Saido 278, 280, 293
Bergkamp, Dennis 159, 336, 344
Best, George 67, 84, 121
Blake, Noel 245
Blatter, Sepp 86
blueprint for change 369–71
boardrooms 287
Boer, Frank de 343
Bonetti, Peter 43, 44
Boothroyd, Aidy 295
Bowles, Stan 4, 64
Brazil
　v England in World Cup (1970) 36,
　　38–41
　v England in World Cup (2002) 200–1
Briggs, Gary 300
Brighton
　Academy 42
Brooking, Sir Trevor 221
Brown, Izzy 282, 287, 294
Bruce, Steve 300
Brynner, Yul 15–16
Bundesliga 292–3
Butcher, Terry 83, 138, 141
Butland, Jack 174, 269, 293
Butt, Nicky 293, 331, 358

Cahill, Gary 353
Cameroon 82, 107, 119, 145
　v England in World Cup (1990) 8, 133
Campbell, Sol 69, 293, 314
Caniggia, Claudio 312
Cantley, Sir Joseph 59
Capello, Fabio 3, 4, 156, 163–4, 209, 210,
　212–14, 244, 264, 351
'caps' controversy 315–16
card-schools 253–5
Carragher, Jamie 238, 344–5
Carrick, Michael 209, 337
Carvalho, Ricardo 207–8
Chalobah, Nathaniel 288
Chambers, Calum 139

Champions League 189–90, 191
Channon, Mick 55
Charlton, Bobby 67, 76
　and FA 218
　and World Cup (1966) 13, 17, 18, 19,
　　21, 25, 26–7
　and World Cup (1970) 44–5
Charlton, Jack 13–30
　treatment of by FA 28–9
　and World Cup (1966) 11, 13–14, 16,
　　17, 18–19, 20–3, 24–7
　and World Cup (1970) 27
cheating 134–6, 355
Chelsea 34, 286–8, 321, 326, 360
Chile
　v England (1998) 174–5
Chivers, Martin 31
Christmas Truce memorial 243, 255,
　259
Clarke, Allan 47, 56
Clemence, Ray 31, 55, 221
Clough, Brian 64, 157, 223, 288
club-versus-country issue 48, 57, 250,
　294–5, 316, 322
Clyne, Nathaniel 139
coaches/coaching 50, 284, 343–5
　courses 301–2
　home-grown 168
　qualifications 9
　specialized 302
Cocker, Les 15
Cocu, Phillip 344
Cohen, George 1, 18, 218
Colchester, Max 238
Cole, Ashley 83, 241, 271–2, 337, 348, 364
Cole, Joe 212
Collina, Pierluigi 180
Collinge, Danny 290
Colombia
　v England in World Cup (1998) 177–8
Connery, Sean 15
consultancy 74–5
Cook, Lewis 294
Coppell, Steve 67, 152
Crooks, Garth 193
Cross, John 270

ABOUT THE AUTHOR

Henry Winter is Chief Football Writer of *The Times* and a five-time winner at the Sports Journalists' Association awards.

He loves the England national team with a passion that borders on masoschism and has covered every one of their games from Wembley to Beijing, Chicago to Rio over the past twenty-two years, as well as seven World Cups. Along with Wayne Rooney and Roy Hodgson, he also has the third English vote for the Ballon d'Or award for the world's best player.